The Irish in the Victorian City

Edited by

ROGER SWIFT and SHERIDAN GILLEY

CROOM HELM
London • Sydney • Dover, New Hampshire

Croom Helm Ltd, Provident House, Burrell Row,
Beckenham, Kent BR3 1AT

Croom Helm Australia Pty Ltd, Suite 4, 6th Floor,
64-76 Kippax Street, Surry Hills, NSW 2010, Australia

British Library Cataloguing in Publication Data

The Irish in the Victorian city.
1. Irish – Great Britain – History – 19th century 2. Cities and towns – Great Britain – History – 19th century
I. Swift, Roger II. Gilley, Sheridan
305.8'9162'041 DA125.17

ISBN 0-7099-3333-9

Croom Helm, 51 Washington Street, Dover,
New Hampshire 03820, USA

Library of Congress Cataloging in Publication Data
Main entry under title:

The Irish in the Victorian City.

Bibliography: p.
Includes index.
1. Irish–Great Britain–history–addresses, essays, lectures. 2. Great Britain–ethnic relations–addresses, essays, lectures. 3. City and town life–Great Britain–history–addresses, essays, lectures.
I. Swift, Roger. II. Gilley, Sheridan.
DA125.17175 1985 941'.0049162 85-19484

ISBN 0-7099-3333-9

Printed and bound in Great Britain by Mackays of Chatham Ltd, Kent

Contents

The Irish in the Victorian City

Notes on Contributors

Bernard Aspinwall is Lecturer in Modern History in the University of Glasgow, the author of numerous articles on Scottish and Roman Catholic history, and of *Portable Utopia: Glasgow and the United States 1820–1920* (1984).

John Belchem is Lecturer in History in the University of Liverpool, the author of articles on British working–class history, and of the forthcoming *Orator Hunt: Henry Hunt and English Working–Class Radicalism*, to be published by the Oxford University Press.

Gerard Connolly, a former Leverhulme Fellow now teaching at Heythrop College, London, is the author of numerous articles on Roman Catholic and Mancunian history, and of the forthcoming *A Missionary Church in England: Catholics and English Society 1791–1918* to be published by Croom Helm.

Owen Dudley Edwards, Reader in Commonwealth and American History in the University of Edinburgh, is the author, in a distinguished body of historical writing, of four works directly concerned with the Irish in Britain, two on James Connolly, and *Burke & Hare* (1980) and *The Quest for Sherlock Holmes* (1983).

Frances Finnegan is Lecturer in Social and Economic History at the Waterford Regional College, Eire, and is author of *Poverty and Prostitution: A Study of Victorian Prostitutes in York* (1979), and *Poverty and Prejudice: Irish Immigrants in York, 1840–1875* (1982).

Tom Gallagher is Lecturer in Peace Studies in the University of Bradford, and is author of articles on Scottish working class history and of *Portugal: a Twentieth Century Interpretation* (Manchester, 1983).

Sheridan Gilley is Senior Lecturer in Theology in the University of Durham, and author of numerous articles on modern Irish and Roman Catholic history.

David Large is Senior Lecturer in History in the University of Bristol, and recently edited *The Port of Bristol 1848–1884* for the Bristol Record Society.

John McCaffrey is Lecturer in Scottish History in the University of

Glasgow and is author of numerous articles on modern Scottish history.

Pauline Millward's research on the Stockport riots stems from her interest in local history and her recent project in a now awarded Open University degree.

Alan O'Day is Senior Lecturer in History in the Polytechnic of North London, and author of *The English Face of Irish Nationalism: Parnellite Involvement in British Politics 1880–86* (1977) and of the forthcoming *Parnell and the First Home Rule Episode* to be published by Gill and Macmillan.

Gearóid Ó Tuathaigh is Lecturer in History in the University of Galway. His numerous publications include *Ireland before the Famine 1798–1848* (1972).

Raphael Samuel is Tutor in Social History at Ruskin College, Oxford, a founder–editor of the *History Workshop Journal* and co–editor of the forthcoming Workshop volume, *Religion and Society* to be published by Routledge and Kegan Paul.

Patricia Storey is Secretary of the Department of Archaeology in the University of Edinburgh and the author of articles on modern social history.

Roger Swift is Senior Lecturer in History at Chester College and the author of numerous articles on nineteenth–century social history.

Dedicated

to the Irish in Britain

as a small contribution

to a better British understanding

of their common history

INTRODUCTION

Sheridan Gilley and Roger Swift

The crowds who packed the exhibition in the Tate in 1984 on Pre-Raphaelite painting saw Walter Howell Deverell's picture of 1853–4, 'The Irish Vagrants', showing a pauper family beside an English road. One man is asleep, a second is sunk in dejection, a sleeping infant clasps a woman impressive and impassive in despair, while two half-naked children stand, one of them pleading for alms from an unheeding lady riding by. The painting is a Christian Socialist comment on a great natural calamity, the Irish pauper influx into Britain in 1845–51 in the wake of the Irish Famine. Yet that flight from starvation only hastened an existing trend: Irish immigration was a trickle in the 1790s, a stream in the 1820s, a river in the 1840s, and a flood from the late '40s, as the Irish-born population of England and Wales rose from 291,000 in 1841 to 520,000 in 1851, reached its peak of 602,000 in 1861, when it constituted about 3% in a population of sixteen million, falling to 427,000 at the end of the century.

These figures do not, however, include the children of immigrants born in Britain, while as a proportion of the population, the statistics for the Irish in Scotland are still more striking: 128,000 in 1841 and 207,000 in 1851, or 6.7% of the Scottish population, remaining roughly at this level for fifty years: the figure in 1901 was 205,000. Most of these immigrants settled in the industrial towns of Lancashire and Western Scotland, especially in Liverpool and Glasgow, and in London, with smaller concentrations in the midlands, the north and Yorkshire. In London they were a little under five per cent of the population, though this rose to nearly a quarter in Liverpool, and eighteen percent in the non-metropolitan centre of Dundee, and through this concentration in towns and cities, they stood out from the host population by their poverty, nationality, race and religion. This apartness – or 'outcastness' – has discouraged British historians from bothering much about them, but there is now a growing body of local studies by a generation of young historians, some of which are contained in this volume. The best brief attempt to synthesize this new material stands as the first paper in this collection, a magisterial survey of the whole subject by Gearóid Ó Tuathaigh, whose merits are sufficiently attested by the fact that most of the contributors refer to him. A number of his themes run through these essays, which have been assembled as a modest contribution towards a fresh critical study of the Irish immigration, in its social, political, cultural and religious dimensions, as a new generation of scholars descend upon the hapless family by a Victorian roadside.

Poverty was the most unambiguous of the immigrants, disadvantages. It was the driving force of emigration into Britain, which at least at first received the emigrants least able to move on to North America or Australasia. A majority of the new–arrivals crowded into slum tenements, lodging houses and cellar dwellings in the long–established and already over–populated districts of Irish settlement in Lancashire and London, and even in smaller centres their destitution tended to consign them to the filthiest and foulest of neighbourhoods, as David Large shows for Bristol, Roger Swift for Wolverhampton and Frances Finnegan for York. Though the early emigrants often came as harvesters, they had no capital to become other than casual workers on the land; even the York field labourers lived in the city slum, tramping long distances to work each day in the surrounding countryside. So like more recent refugees from pauper rural economies, the great majority entered the lowliest and least healthy of urban occupations, unless they enlisted in the army, which was thirty per cent Irish in the mid–Victorian era, though this had fallen by 1900. Indeed among the country immigrants to British towns the Irish were the least well–prepared to succeed in their new environment, a minority of skilled workmen entering sweated industries like tailoring, the great majority with no skills being concentrated in unskilled occupations, casual labour at the docks and street–selling. These were occupations for which a highly sophisticated city like London, with a highly specialized labour force, had very few rewards, and the Irish could only get into the metropolitan economy with difficulty.

It is difficult to strike a proper mean between the lighter and darker sides of Irish poverty, which differed from one settlement to another. The Famine influx often made matters dramatically worse; sometimes resulting in a socially immobile and unintegrated ghetto, isolated in particular streets and courts from the surrounding population and contributing to the crime rate in disproportionate numbers in the categories for petty theft and casual violence. Dr. Finnegan describes for York a classic slum, with a high turnover of population and a reputation for dirt and disorder which lasted until the clearance programmes in the 1920s and '30s. Yet as Dr. Finnegan also shows for York and Dr. Swift for Wolverhampton, this crime rate, while remaining disproportionate, fell in the decades from 1860. Dr. Swift interprets the criminal statistics in terms of a developing police force with a military background, exercising a new rigour in policing illegal drinking and overcrowded lodging houses, which brought them into conflict with the local working class population, especially the Irish, even though as David Large notes for Bristol, some of the new policemen were Irish themselves.

The Famine also casts a long shadow in Tom Gallagher's account of Liverpool, where work opportunities, housing and sanitation were overwhelmed by the sheer volume of the '40s immigration. The city was a trading and a commercial rather than an industrial centre, and the employment available was largely in unskilled occupations for which Catholics and Protestants were in active competition. Dr. Gallagher makes a contrast with Glasgow, where the Irish were able to find jobs in mills and mines, though excluded from engineering, the shipyards dominated by the Orange Order, and skilled trades controlled by craft unions. Bernard Aspinwall and John McCaffrey point another contrast, with Edinburgh, the home of a rentier class and of legal, literary and ecclesiastical establishments, in which the Irish were largely confined to such dependent menial occupations as general labouring in building, domestic service, portering, street–cleaning and street–lighting. There is, however, a range to even this experience which suggests a complex answer to the controversial and much debated question, as to whether Irish immigrants lowered English wages. Part of the Irish employment pattern is shown in the most detailed of these occupational analyses, David Large's study of the census returns for the Irish settlement in Bristol, which most usefully explains its own method. Large also points out the presence of Irish Protestants, and of a small Irish middle class, and indicates a paradox also discussed by Dr. Finnegan, that at least before 1860 and the relaxation of the settlement provisions of the Poor Law, the Irish made a much smaller call on public and private charity than their poverty and English prejudice might lead one to suppose.

A second criterion of Irish outcastness is Irish nationalism. Here, again, there were grounds for British conservative prejudice, in the tradition of Irish agrarian outrage and of the 'physical force' resort to street violence and armed rebellion, or more impressively, the recourse to passive mass defiance. This defiance was an attraction rather than a deterrent to some English political radicals, and all radical historians are aware of such distinctively Irish gifts to English Chartism as Feargus O'Connor and Bronterre O'Brien. Yet the Irish provided more than these well–known Chartist leaders, and despite Daniel O'Connell's opposition to the movement, ordinary Irish Catholics before 1848 were often an integral part of a popular British proletarian culture, in which English radicals actively championed the Irish cause and sought, and gained, Irish Catholic support. John Belchem describes both this cooperation before 1848 and the distinctive Irish contribution to the last phase of Chartism, and he argues that its failure had a decided effect on the increasing social and political isolation of the Irish in Britain in mid–century. There was, therefore, an Irish Chartist echo in England to the rising of the Young Irelanders of 1848, and in the 1860s the revolutionary tradition returned to England with the Irish Republican Brotherhood, and most spectacularly, with the Clerkenwell prison explosion of 1867. Indeed after the abortive Fenian rising of the same year, every young Irishman of spirit was a sentimental Fenian, and the agrarian violence of the Land War from 1879 points to the survival of a popular view of the right to rebel unique in its intensity and continuity in British political life, surviving underground to erupt in Dublin in 1916.

Yet the whole conception of the Irish as offering the 'outcast' alternative in English radical politics needs the most sensitive statement. It is true that the Irish nationalist M.P.s after 1829 formed an often discordant element in English political life, and different aspects of the Irish question helped to destroy a conservative administration in 1846 and did destroy the Liberal party in 1886. Again, the Irish campaigns for Repeal of the Union in the 1840s and for Home Rule after 1880 did seem to many Englishmen to threaten the destruction of the Empire at its heart. But the actual Irish threat to the Empire was much exaggerated. Dr. Belchem argues that the Irish element in Chartism lent itself to the conservative exploitation which was one cause of its defeat. Dr. Gallagher shows how uniquely in a major British city, the very strength of Irish nationalism and Catholicism in Liverpool gave a populist Orange Toryism a century of almost uninterrupted ascendency in local politics. Pauline Millward depicts the No Popery Toryism of Stockport, while Drs. Finnegan, Aspinwall and McCaffrey describe largely politically apathetic communities in York and Edinburgh, though the last was the nursery of James Connolly, this apoliticism being a reflection of the marginal position of the Irish in the economies of these cities, and the leadership of a conservative Catholic Church. The greatest successes of Irish political activity came only in the 1880s, when the Irish parliamentary party created a mass organization harnessed to constitutional nationalism, which as Dr. Ó Tuathaigh describes it, gained a measure of respectability through Gladstone's conversion to Home Rule. Though the pauper Irish were difficult to register as voters, and were only numerous enough to return a nationalist M.P., T.P. O'Connor, in one British constituency, in Liverpool, the late Victorian Irish communities and M.P.s were, as Alan O'Day has demonstrated, an increasingly well-integrated element in British political democracy, the symbols of a degree of acquiescence in British rule which post-1916 perspectives have obscured.[1] Yet as Dr. O'Day also shows, registration was not the chief cause of their ineffectiveness: the Irish, in east and south London, were concentrated in safe Liberal seats and therefore made little difference to the political landscape, nor did they have much real influence on the Liberals whom they helped to elect. On the other hand, the Irish alliance with the Liberals was fairly solid and lasted until 1916, despite the division created by Liberal attacks on Catholic education and the Liberal inability to deliver on Home Rule. There was, then, a considerable complexity to Irish political experience, a complexity masked by the revolutionary activities of the Irish Republican Brotherhood. The great majority of Irish Catholics were not in fact revolutionaries but behaved as loyal if not always enthusiastic subjects of the Crown, in England and Scotland, as in Canada, Australasia and in Ireland itself.

The whole history of this pattern of increasing Irish political integration is as yet a subject largely unexplored for mainland

Britain. Yet it is highly relevant to a third criterion of apartness, the hostility towards the Irish as a separate 'race', through the pseudo–scientific mid–Victorian rationalisation of an older English national prejudice. The difficulty with anti–Irish racism is partly one of terminology, partly a matter again of defining the position from which the Irish were 'cast out'. The Irish were defined as a separate racial group as 'Celts' to be distinguished from the English 'Anglo–Saxons'; and Anglo–Saxons were alleged to be at least racially superior as rulers or governors to the racially anarchic Celts. Victorian racial theory, however, was in the form of the claim that the English were racially superior as a 'mixed race', not as a pure one, as a product of mingling of the aboriginal British Celts with the Norse and Danish invaders, as well as with the Anglo–Saxons. Thus the best mongrel English had the good 'Celtic' qualities as well as the good Anglo–Saxon ones. It is as if a member of the National Front were to claim a superiority based on his double descent from a Norman and a black Jamaican. Much of the evidence for anti–Celtic racism comes in *Punch* cartoons depicting the Celt as a gorilla, as if he stood on a lower rung on the evolutionary ladder. Yet the Irish so depicted are also under attack on political or religious grounds, while loyal Celts, no less Celtic for their loyalism, *Punch* shows with a Grecian purity of feature like the figure of Hibernia herself.

In any case Anglo–Saxon racism was not identical to hatred of the Irish, and some of the exponents of Celtic racial theory also supported Home Rule. The anti–Celtic stereotype was a complex one, as Celts were generally acknowlegded in the manner of Matthew Arnold, to be as superior as poets to the Saxon Philistine as they were inferior as politicians, and to be as chaste, hospitable, witty, kindly and generous as they were feckless, stupid, violent, unreliable and drunken. Indeed this view of the Irish is arguably partly of Irish origin: its completest expression being the analysis of the Irish character by an Irish Catholic bishop with which Dr. S.J. Connolly opens his recent study of the Church in pre–Famine Ireland,[2] though some parts of it are also to be found in the street ballads sung by the Irish themselves. There is a further paradox about the Anglo–Saxon attitude which treats the Irish character as racially Celtic. As a highly sophisticated intellectual prejudice developed by ethnologists, historians and poets, Anglo–Saxonism was restricted by its very nature to literate members of the Victorian middle class, and cannot therefore be invoked to explain the attitudes of the anti–Irish mobs ignorant of the intricacies of ethnological theory. On the other hand, as a middle–class prejudice, anti–Celticism seems to have been wholly inoperative against the advancement of the small Irish Catholic middle class, suggesting that the prejudice was one essentially against Irish paupers, as a parallel with the more negative attitudes to the English poor. The careers of the Irish Catholic journalists so wittily and memorably described in the essay by Owen Dudley Edwards and Patricia Storey were not impeded by a racist anti–Irishness.

Yet as Dr. Ó Tuathaigh, echoed by Dr. Belchem, stresses, the negative aspects of the *working class* Irish stereotype tended to be dominant in the '50s and '60s, for example, in the *Punch* cartoons. Those guilty arguably include Marx and Engels, and an 'anti-Celticism' did exist, but most frequently in mongrel form, especially towards pauper Irishmen, in association with national and religious prejudice. It is, therefore, difficult to isolate it from other aspects of anti-Irishness and anti-Catholicism, as a phenomenon standing on its own.

Last, there is the claim that the Irish were outcast because they were Catholics. The English, Scots and Welsh were overwhelmingly Protestant by tradition, and after 1790, the strength of popular Protestantism was vastly reinforced by the Evangelical revival. Protestant 'No Popery' also gained an increasing ascendency over the Established Church of Ireland and the once-liberal Ulster Prebyterians, and Ulster immigrants of the Orange order introduced their fratricidal strife with Irish Catholics into a number of British towns, chiefly Liverpool, where as Dr. Gallagher shows, sectarian competition for jobs in a weakly unionized economy polarised politics between the Orange and the Green, the followers of a dead Dutchman and a live Italian. Yet where Dr. Gallagher contrasts the endemic street warfare and sectarian conflict of Liverpool with the comparative calm of Liberal-controlled Glasgow, Drs. Aspinwall and McCaffrey describe the Glaswegian host community as 'repulsive', obsessed 'with superficial appearance, with conspicuous consumption and superior social station', and with the great gulf between Irish Catholic *mores* and the respectable Scottish Presbyterian values which made it impossible for Irish Catholics to become Scots. Yet Dr. Gallagher points out that there was a rationalism and egalitarianism in Scottish Liberalism and Presbyterianism which were wholly lacking in bigoted Tory Liverpudlian Orange Anglicanism, despite the Scottish No Popery excitements of the 1850s and John Cormack's anti-Irish Protestant Action Party in Edinburgh in the 1930s. On the other hand, one must point to the strand of anti-Irish racism deriving from the Scottish Enlightenment, described by Owen Dudley Edwards in *Burke & Hare*.[3] Here there are obvious difficulties of emphasis and interpretation, and Drs. Aspinwall and McCaffrey also offer different explanations of the two periods of anti-Catholicism, that mid-Victorian No Popery reflected Scottish self-confidence, while the 1930s outbreak arose from an anxiety that Scottish values were in decline and under threat from a growing Catholic population.

Some of the difficulties of interpreting the new sectarian violence of the 1850s are carefully set out by Pauline Millward in her paper on the Stockport riots of 1852. The riots may have arisen from the underlying antagonism between the masses of new immigrants and hard-pressed English cotton workers who resented the incursion of cheap Irish labour into the mills, but this evidence is difficult to interpret, and the antagonism was insufficient to cause the riots by itself, the actual occasion being the restoration of the Catholic hierarchy in 1850, fanned to a flame by the 'respectable' anti-Catholicism of local Anglican clergymen and electorally vulnerable Tory politicians playing the Irish card in a bid for power. Some of these themes recur in Dr. Swift's account of the different kinds of unrest involving the Irish in Wolverhampton, with the additional dimension, already noted, of a more provocative kind of policing, and Dr. Swift also argues that the anti–Catholic disturbances of the 1850s and '60s, in which Irish Catholics stood firm against the advent of anti–Catholic lecturers, may reflect, in contrast to the sporadic Irish protests of the 1840s, a new self–confidence in the Irish Catholic community and its organization, which evoked a new and bitter Protestant response.

Yet whatever its place in popular prejudice, the No Popery influence was, after 1850, arguably a declining one in the mainstream English Churches outside Lancashire. These were themselves divided between mostly Tory Anglicans and mostly Liberal Nonconformists, so that though Nonconformity was predominantly Evangelical and anti–Catholic, the Irish Catholic crusades for an end to the laws against Catholics could count on the support of Protestant Dissenters also opposed to the privileges of the Church of England. Catholics and Dissenters were often united in their campaigns against the Church as by law established, and appealed to the rising forces of political Liberalism, in demanding the redress of their disabilities within the Anglican confessional state. Catholics and Nonconformists were, therefore, often on the same political side, from the repeal of the Test and Corporation Acts in 1828 and the abolition of church tithe and church rate through to the disestablishment of the Protestant Church of Ireland in 1869. Catholicism was at war with political liberals on much of the continent, but the most conservative British Catholics instinctively appealed to liberal principles in their claim to legal equality with their fellow countrymen. Thus on the religious level, the Irish were outcasts in kind if not in degree with their non–Anglican Dissenting brethren, who were also, as Valentine Cunningham recently reminds us, 'everywhere spoken against'. Catholics and Nonconformists shared in a common exclusion from the world of Anglican wealth and privilege, and in the same sense of being borne upwards to freedom by the triumphing Liberalism of the age.

Yet was there an effective church establishment against which an outcast Catholicism was defined? As the Church of England recovered its religious momentum, it became an ill–assorted umbrella–network of feuding 'church parties' all claiming to be 'outcast' themselves. The Liberals endured the denunciations and heresy trials of their Low and High Church enemies. The Evangelicals nourished their Puritan estrangement from the fashionable world, within the Church and outside it, and they never felt respected or accepted, in spite of the bishops appointed from their ranks by their great philanderer–patron Palmerston. The old High Church party of country parsons preserved something of their local status and power, yet also felt that these were slipping from their hands. Witness the heroic efforts by incumbents to protect their village schools from government inspection, and their churchyards from intrusion by dead Dissenters. The new High Churchmen, the Anglo–Catholics, endured public vilification and mob violence, and even saw some of their best priests imprisoned for conducting illegal rituals. This was not a fate suffered by any Irish Catholic, or indeed by any Roman Catholic priest, though a few of these, and even a bishop, were gaoled for debts owing on their missions. Indeed it was the Anglo–Catholics, who by introducing Popery into the very heart of the Establishment, did far more than the Irish to inflame the passions of Victorian anti–Catholicism.

Yet the Anglo–Catholic movement began in a High Church revival intended to preserve the power and privileges of the Church establishment; its irony was that when some of these Anglo–Catholics apostasized to Rome, they found themselves like John Henry Newman, given over to 'hearing the general confessions of dirty Paddies'. It was a former High Church Archdeacon, Henry Edward Manning, resolver of the Dock Strike of 1889, who described his life as it neared its end as one of labour for the Irish immigration in England. In short, the very soul of Anglicanism gave the Irish Catholic mission a number of its most devoted pastors, some of whose names occur in this volume, with those of native English Catholic priests, a score of whom died while ministering to the victims of cholera, even though by background they were in everything except their religion quite as much a part of the English nation as anyone.

Were then, the Irish 'outcast' as Catholics? They were not more 'outcast' *as* Catholics than English or foreign Catholics on the ground of their Catholicism alone. Catholicism was unpopular as a living ideological force, being regarded with the same suspicion as modern Communism. Indeed conversion to Catholicism was, as W.H. Auden puts it, a disaster that could happen in the best of families. There can hardly have been a wealthy Victorian household which was not divided by at least one conversion to Rome, and the full force of anti–Catholic prejudice in such cases did not fall on the Irish. Some Protestant polemicists regarded Irish immigrants with more indulgence than either converts or nuns, as the Irish were a least in possibility converts to Protestantism; it was the nuns, rather than the Irish who were, if Professor Arnstein's recent book is to be believed,[4] the most unpopular single group in Victorian England. Nuns, though less numerous than prostitutes, have at least as good a claim as prostitutes to be considered Victorian 'outcasts', even if unlike the prostitutes they were predominantly women of good family. Thus Victorian No Popery was much more than anti–Irishness. Catholicism was regarded even by good Victorian liberals as foreign, exotic, dangerous, the religion of England's traditional enemies, France and Spain, the ally of reactionary governments and the creed of superstitious peasants everywhere. The more Protestant–minded hated Rome as unscriptural and anti–Christian. But though the Irish were disliked as Catholics, so was the Duke of Norfolk, the head of the English peerage, the Queen of Spain and the local Italian organ–grinder; and if we are to look to the roots of the outcastness of the Irish, we must look at other things beside Catholicism.

Thus in summary. The Irish Catholic immigrants look like the outcasts of Victorian society, outcast from British capitalism as the poorest of the poor, from mainstream British politics as separatist nationalists and republicans, from the 'Anglo–Saxon' race as 'Celts', and as Catholics from the dominant forms of British Protestantism. The Irish were the outcasts of Victorian Britain on the basis of class, nationality, race and religion, with an accumulated body of disadvantages possessed by no other group of similar size until the Jewish immigration. It was on all these grounds taken together that they were the largest unassimilated section of their society, as a people set apart and everywhere rejected and despised.

Yet these antagonisms were not simple, they were ambiguous. An English radical or Liberal repelled by an Irishman's Catholicism might well rejoice in his radicalism or Liberalism; a High Churchman repelled by an Irishman's Liberalism might well respect his Catholicism. It is perhaps no accident that the greatest of nineteenth–century Englishmen, the English politician most wounded by the wrongs of Ireland, was both a Liberal and a High Churchman, William Ewart Gladstone. Gladstone was not quite the typical 'Victorian', because there is no such thing as a typical 'Victorian', yet he usefully reminds us that the Irish could not be considered wholly beyond the pale of British life either as nationalists or Catholics or Celts.

Even here, however, there is more to say. The various aspects of the apartness of the pauper Irish Catholic Celt tended to reinforce one another, as in the effect of the church–related Irish culture on Irish poverty, as the resulting social segregation inhibited the development of closer personal contacts with, and therefore of wider economic opportunity in, the English Protestant–owned and run economy. A different argument stresses the role of Catholic education and charity, in encouraging social mobility by providing schooling and communal self–help in poverty–stricken neighbourhoods, but the full measure of this revolution only occurred in this century. There is a most impressive record of social work by priests and sisters, though this was less important than self–help among the poor and took years to catch up with the much more considerable achievements by Protestants and then the state. Even humane Catholic ecclesiastics often opposed the work of non–Catholic philanthropists like Dr. Barnado as proselytising in aim, as indeed it often was.

The degree of survival of the loyalties to Faith and Fatherland is also still a matter for academic enquiry. At least half the pre–Famine and Famine emigrants from Ireland were not regular churchgoers in their homeland, and in a remarkable argument from the growing if disputed body of scholarship on the point, Dr. Gerard Connolly queries the simple identification of 'Irish' with 'Catholic'. Immigration into England was largely from eastern Ireland, where formal religious practice was higher before 1850 than in the west, yet London, with its immigrants first from Leinster and then Munster, never had rates of churchgoing much above 30% of its nominally Catholic Irish population. The immigrants in northern England came from Ulster and then Leinster, but again, only a third of the Catholic population was given to regular religious practice before 1840, though through missionary effort this may have risen as high as 60% by 1860. Thus Irish Catholic rates of Sunday church attendance were often below those of English Protestants, if higher than those for the English working class. Certainly Irish Catholics were less inclined to formal worship than English Catholics, and could be regarded as an embarrassment to the English Catholic Mission rather than a reinforcement of it. Dr. Connolly argues that the challenge of the unchurched Irish to clerical idealism and corporate self-interest played a vital part in bringing the English Catholic Church, with its lay traditions, under clerical control, and in reinvigorating the priesthood as a profession; he also describes the difficulties of defining the non-churchgoing Irish Catholicism which was outside this clerical influence, and which was rooted in an ancient Gaelic-speaking tradition of native Irish spirituality and in a pre-Tridentine popular peasant culture of the home and pilgrimage, rather than in Mass-going in a new shrine church. Even here, however, the traditional sources of priestly authority were reinforced by the Rome-inspired Ultramontane revival, which introduced warmer, more colourful Baroque and romantic devotions, to the Blessed Sacrament, the Virgin and Saints. These devotions recalled many Irishmen to the practice of their religion, and Sheridan Gilley's paper shows on a local pastoral level how the new religion was defined for the immigrant community, in an Ultramontane movement of popular piety pioneered by Fr. Frederick Faber paralleling (albeit on a small scale), what Emmet Larkin has described as a 'Devotional Revolution' after 1850 in Ireland. Something of the continuities and discontinuities of Irish Catholic culture are also pointed up by Dr. Connolly, while the popular foundations of priestly authority are shown by Raphael Samuel in his beautifully written and magnificently researched paper on popular Catholicism, which has circulated in *samizdat* typescript among the *cognoscenti* for nearly twenty years. This demonstrates, by lavish quotation and example, the *ethos* and atmosphere which lay at the heart of the Irish Catholic community, in the special relationship between the Catholic priest and the Irish people.

Indeed insofar as it was successful, the creation of this church-related culture was also the creation of a low profile community founded in family relationships and in many ways invisible to outsiders; occasionally resulting in an hereditary Irish closed-shop, as in the case of the Greenock sugar workers and the stevedores' union in the East End, and often, as when in the 1920s the Irish moved from their traditional Liberal allegiance to Labour, exercising a pervasive Christian Socialist influence in the Labour Party, on local councils and the local M.P.. The fact that the clergy were often the only professional people resident in working class areas also gave them a political role, which not a few of them were very willing to play, especially on the education issue, and they were often formidable allies or enemies. The end result was as Dr. Ó Tuathaigh brilliantly describes it, a curious combination of achieved Irish integration and acceptance with a surviving Irish apartness. Catholics of Irish ancestry could maintain a separate culture and identity in their own 'Little Ireland', yet move easily among the surrounding population, with little obvious sense of difference from them, while yet still retaining their own traditional hidden life.

For the Irish that was a kind of success: not the individualistic success of the self-made man, though there were Irish Catholics of that kind, fewer perhaps in Britain than in America. Rather, granted their generally low economic possibilities and aspirations, the Irish in the long term had the kind of success possible only to people who know who and what they are. The reader will find much in this volume to show just what this meant, and two stories at least which touch on the *lacrimae rerum*, both in Raphael Samuel's paper, of the priest who went to prison rather than betray a poor penitent, and of John Denvir's mother, who thrice implored Fr. Mathew for a miraculous cure for her sick child and on the third occasion was rewarded. All the essays are based on original research. Yet the editors are only too conscious of what is missing from this book, in the way of the valuable papers and monographs by Cormac Ó Gráda, J.A. Jackson, Neville Kirk, Lynn Lees, W.J. Lowe, Dorothy Thompson, James Treble and William Walker, though even their achievement is but a part of what there still remains to do. We need a major study of Irish women, though readers will note that Gerard Connolly and Raphael Samuel comment on their religious culture and David Large and Frances Finnegan on their patterns and levels of employment. We also need more lives of community leaders, though the two O'Connors, Feargus and 'T.P.', have recently found good biographers. The sparkling paper on the ambiguities of perception in Irish journalism in Britain by Edwards and Storey must stand as our principal contribution to the study of the small but influential Irish Catholic middle class. We need to know more about Irish Protestants, who appear chiefly in the light in which Catholics saw them, and have few historians, and about the Irish in Wales. A few of these papers touch indirectly on Irish sport, but none draw on oral history, and there is no central library, archive and museum for the preservation of tapes, books, papers and artefacts relating to the experience of the Irish in Britain. Even the richest of archival resources, the Roman Catholic Church, has, through her recent vandalistic treatment of her own buildings and traditions of worship, destroyed much of the continuity and setting of the old popular culture, and secularization and new patterns of affluence and leisure seem bound to sweep much of what still survives away.

What is possible, however, for Irish studies is suggested by the great growth of the subject in America,[5] which is the more important because the average Irishman's loyalty was not merely a local communal one to the Catholic Church and nationalist society, but to these entities in their widest manifestations. Religious, national and ethnic identity came together in the *international consciousness* of the Irish Catholic emigrant, who was aware through his newspaper, parochial organizations and political parties of what was happening in Ireland and throughout the Irish diaspora, and was therefore part of an *international community* pervaded by the nationalist movements and by the Roman Catholic Church. For that double success, by priests and politicians, in the creation of Irish Catholic communities, in Britain and abroad, one is tempted to search for social explanations. One explanation goes, however, beyond social history, to a perennial fact about mankind. Whatever the Irish Catholics' faults, theirs was not a poverty of the spirit, for their pride in their religion, nationality and race, the differences which sharpened their sense of separation, also gave them the assurance that even in their poverty they stood higher in the providence of God and in the light of history than the prosperous heretical Anglo–Saxon stranger. Possibly Raphael Samuel's paper comes nearest to defining it, through the individual evidences he cites of piety, aspiration and struggle. Moreover underpinning this pride was even a pride in poverty itself, in that holy poverty in which they were one with Christ and with his saints before them. The Irish created in their nationalist organizations and in the Roman Catholic Church a spiritual Empire both in Ireland and across the seas. In one sense their Empire was an answer to that British Empire whose existence had made their Empire possible: just as Christianity had been the answer of slaves and outcasts to the Empire of ancient Rome. For there is always a spiritual dignity possible to those who do not achieve in the eyes of the world the best things which the world thinks that it has to offer them, the dignity which a beaten nation, be it Poland or Ireland, can sometimes achieve upon its knees. There is no need here for idealisation. Church and party could be oppressive and exploitive, even the journalist had a living to make from his fellow–countrymen and there were also the more or less exploitive parasites and middle–men, of a kind known in Ireland, produced by the community itself. Yet the Irish spirit was more than a matter of false consciousness, it was a source of dignity and strength, offering them hope in this world and for another. In this they did no more than draw on the innermost resources of their nationality and religion, for the Catholic Christian sees mankind in some sense as outcast, and all in need of a dignity and strength, which the spirit gives, and which the world can never know. There was tragedy here but also pride. The Irish may have been exiles in Britain, but most were not exiles in spirit from their Faith, their Fatherland and their God.

Notes

1. Alan O'Day, *The English Face of Irish Nationalism: Parnellite Involvement in English Politics* (Dublin, 1977).
2. S.J. Connolly, *Priests and People in Pre–Famine Ireland 1780–1845* (New York, 1982), p.1.
3. Owen Dudley Edwards, *Burke & Hare* (Edinburgh, 1980).
4. Walter L. Arnstein, *Protestant versus Catholic in Mid–Victorian England: Mr. Newdegate and the Nuns* (Columbia and London, 1982).
5. Seamus P. Metress, *The Irish–American Experience: A Guide to the Literature* (Washington, D.C., 1981); R.A. Burchell, 'The Historiography of the American Irish', *Immigrants and Minorities*, vol.1, no.3 (November 1982), pp.281–305; D.N. Doyle, 'The regional bibliography of Irish America: a review and addendum', *Irish Historical Studies*, vol.xxiii (1982–83), no.91, pp.254–83.

THE IRISH IN NINETEENTH–CENTURY BRITAIN: PROBLEMS OF INTEGRATION

M. A. G. Ó Tuathaigh

Unlike their American cousins, the Irish immigrants in nineteenth–century Britain have, until recently, received comparatively little scholarly attention from historians. This is not to say that their presence in Victorian Britain has gone unnoticed; far from it. Throughout the nineteenth century the doings and, much more often, the misdoings of the immigrant Irish were logged in massive detail by an army of social investigators, philanthropists, clergymen, royal commissions and parliamentary committees. But, with very few exceptions,[1] the scholarly analysis of the data has only begun in earnest during the last two decades, and especially during the past few years. In a growing body of local and regional studies, and in studies of particular aspects of the Irish presence, the literature on the Irish immigrants is becoming not only more plentiful but also conceptually more sophisticated. Two recent collections[2] concentrate on providing a comparative framework for discussing the presence and problems of various groups of immigrants and minorities in British society during the past two centuries. This growing body of scholarly writing is to be welcomed, and it is especially to be hoped that further local studies will follow, to enable us to test more rigorously our assumptions and generalizations about the Irish in nineteenth–century Britain.

Perhaps it is not altogether surprising that there should have been for so long this relative neglect of the immigrant Irish in nineteenth–century Britain. For one thing, the Irish in Britain constituted a somewhat peculiar minority. Indeed, E. P. Thompson asserts with some force that 'the Irish were never pressed back into ghettoes. It would have been difficult to have made a people who spoke the same language and were British citizens under the Act of Union into a subject minority.'[3] A 'subject' minority they may not have been; but, in their own perception of themselves and in the way the natives of the host society perceived them, the immigrant Irish were undoubtedly a minority of some kind. Yet it is difficult to fit them into the more conventional or accepted typology of minorities. Without becoming enmeshed in unhelpful semantics about what constitutes a minority, we may (as A. C. Hepburn has done recently)[4] identify two main types of minority. The first kind is that minority, usually immigrant, which seeks the maximum degree of assimilation and integration into the majority society, but which regards itself as the object of collective discrimination by the majority. In short, a minority whose urge to integrate is resisted. Secondly there is the European–type minority (based on religious, ethnic or linguistic grounds) which finds itself (through the accident of war or geography) in a minority status and which seeks to retain its distinctiveness and to resist assimilation into the majority community. The Irish in nineteenth–century Britain, as we shall see, shared certain characteristics of both of these types, while fitting snugly into neither mould.

A second explanation for the relative lack of scholarly interest in the immigrant Irish may be the fact that within the context of Irish emigration in general in the past two centuries, the emigration to Britain was very much the smaller part of the story. Throughout the nineteenth century the volume of Irish emigration to Britain was small in relation to the total volume of Irish emigration.[5] Nevertheless, in absolute numbers it was quite significant. Of course, Irish emigration to Britain did not begin with the nineteenth century. For centuries previously the Irish had been travelling and settling in Britain – and it is worth pointing out that from the outset they were officially 'visible' as a problem group, cropping up in enquiries into vagrancy and the like. By the late eighteenth century there were already sizeable Irish settlements in some British towns and cities, particularly London and Lancashire, and their presence had already produced varieties of social tension and occasional violence.[6]

However, the really heavy influx of immigrant Irish only intensified in the early decades of the nineteenth century, and at an accelerating rate from 1815 to 1845, by which time it had firmly established its predominantly urban character.[7] The influx reached its climax during and immediately after the great famine of 1845–51 in Ireland. Already in 1841 there were some 419,256 Irish–born residents in Britain, and a decade later (as a consequence of the famine influx) the figure had climbed to 727,326. These settlers reached their maximum figure in 1861, when the total number stood at 806,000. Thereafter, the decennial figure for Irish emigration to Britain declined continuously from the 1870s to 1939 (with the exception of the early 1900s which saw a sharp rise in Irish emigration from the north–east to Britain). By 1901 the total figure for the Irish–born immigrants was down to 632,000.[8]

As a proportion of the total population of Britain these figures were quite modest – the Irish constituting under 3.5% of the total population in 1861, at its maximum, and as low as 1.7% in 1901.[9] These national averages, however, conceal the wide regional variations in the density of Irish settlement.

The 1851 census revealed the following figures for select British towns and cities.[10]

	% Irish-born
Liverpool	22.3
Dundee	18.9
Glasgow	18.2
Manchester and Salford	13.1
Paisley	12.7
Bradford	8.9
London	4.6

A few towns (e.g. Greenock) reached their maximum percentage of Irish-born later in the century.[11] Of course, these figures relate only to the Irish-born; and as such represent the minimum volume or density of Irish immigrant settlement. The inclusion of at least the second-generation Irish would give a more realistic picture of the actual size of the Irish immigrant minority in nineteenth-century Britain.

The overwhelming majority of these immigrants came from rural Ireland, though there was also an artisan and small middle-class urban element. The three main emigrant routes were (1) the northern route, from Ulster and North Connacht to Scotland; (2) the midland route, from Connacht and most of Leinster via Dublin to the north of England and the midlands; and (3) the southern route, from South Leinster and the Munster counties to London, often via Bristol. In addition to the young, single, adult emigrant (i.e. in the age-group 15-40) Irish emigration to Britain in the first half of the nineteenth century featured a substantial amount of family migration, particularly to the textile towns where prospects were most favourable for the employment of women and children as well as the household head. Again, in the pre-famine decades at least, the Irish emigration to Britain comprised the least well-off elements of the Irish emigrant stream, the more comfortable elements going to North America. From the 1860s onwards, however, these differences began to disappear; the young and single came to dominate the Irish migration flow to Britain as well as to the United States, and there was a general levelling in the condition and circumstances of the Irish emigrants irrespective of their destination.[12] Finally, in terms of sex-ratio, while there were some regional variations (reflecting differences in economic and occupational structure between different British towns and cities), generally there was a preponderance of males in the total Irish immigrant stream up to the 1890s, after which the female element achieved a slight majority.[13]

With few exceptions (such as the few settlements of Irish agricultural labourers in Scotland), the immigrant Irish concentrated in the main cities and towns of industrial Britain – in London, Liverpool (a quarter of whose population was Irish-born in 1861), Glasgow, Tyneside, Cardiff, Bradford and other industrial areas of Lancashire, Yorkshire, and the English midlands, and the east and west of Scotland. The three main clusters of concentrated Irish settlement were in Lancashire, the west of Scotland and London. By 1851 more than 80% of the Irish-born in Britain were resident in towns with a population of more than 10,000. Of course, in talking of 'settlement' it is worth remembering that for certain categories of Irish immigrants in Britain permanent settlement in any real sense was often a very late development; these categories would include not only the seasonal labourers (ranging from c. 60,000 to 100,000 per annum in the decades 1840–1860, after which their numbers declined drastically),[14] but also certain categories of labourers with an exceptionally high mobility rate – in construction and railway navvying.[15]

Within their new habitat, the Irish were heavily concentrated in what one commentator, speaking of more recent immigrants, has described as 'the most disadvantaged parts of the social structure of British cities'.[16] Rent levels, proximity to work-place, transport costs (where, as in London, these were relevant) were all important determinants of the settlement habits of the immigrant Irish. As it happened, they were heavily concentrated in city-centre areas, or in dockside settlements, 'where residential competition was least intense'.[17] Their living conditions were generally the very worst which the Victorian industrial slum could offer. Some of these inner-city Irish settlements became bywords for industrial slum living. The 'Little Ireland' ghetto in Manchester, the London courts and rookeries, the Glasgow tenements, the Liverpool cellars and similar quarters in Cardiff, Bradford and other centres of British industry, displayed the full spectrum of social evils – appalling over-crowding, little or no sanitation, open sewers and cesspools, unhealthy diet, inadequate clothing, vagrancy, disease, alcoholism and general squalor; a high quota of unemployed paupers, or of underemployed casual labourers; and a high incidence of casual violence (very often provoked by drink). These were the conditions which appalled Engels, terrified Carlyle, and absorbed the attention of a generation of social investigators and commentators from the 1830s to the 1860s. What is remarkable is that they survived in many cities not only into the last years of Victoria's century, but indeed well into the present century. Booth's description of the rat-infested Irish ghetto of dockside London at the close of the nineteenth century is as chilling as anything penned in the worst years of the famine influx.[18]

Turning from habitat to occupational structure, the immigrant Irish were disproportionately concentrated in the ranks of the semi-skilled and unskilled casual labour force – in construction, transportation, dockside labour (as stevedores and casual labourers), in food distribution and in railway construction. Again, in certain industries such as sugar refining, textiles (especially where the Irish acted as sweated labour in declining trades), in gasworks and paper-making, as sawyers, coal-heavers and porters – in all of these categories the Irish were disproportionately numerous. John Denvir (an invaluable contemporary chronicler of his fellow immigrants in nineteenth-century Lancashire and, indeed, in Britain in general) asserted that in the mid-nineteenth century, and for long afterwards, it was unusual to find a stonemason's labourer who was not an Irishman.[19] There was also an Irish labour element in the coal-fields of South Wales, the west of Scotland and, to a lesser extent, in the

English north-east and the midlands, and in the unskilled labour sectors of the heavy industries.

The occupations most common among female Irish immigrants were in textile factories, laundry work and domestic service (though here the supply always ran ahead of demand, and in certain areas, such as in certain towns in Scotland and the north of England, Irish girls faced strong local competition in domestic service).[20] Many Irish women survived, or contributed to the family income, through earnings from piece-work (such as needlework, sewing or rag-picking) in their own homes. Both male and female Irish immigrants were heavily involved in hawking and street-trading in the larger centres of population, while the keeping of lodgers was an important source of income for the enterprising immigrant family, both because of the rent and the laundry services often rendered for cash by the woman of the house.

The army and navy were an important source of employment among Irish immigrants. It has been calculated that in 1830 the Irish accounted for 42.2% of the non-commissioned ranks of the British army, and while this proportion gradually declined in succeeding decades, it was 14.0% as late as 1891. In round figures, the Irish presence in the army ranged from 55,000 in 1868 (the maximum figure) to around 25,000 as late as 1896.[21]

Not all Irish immigrants belonged to the ranks of the unskilled labouring classes. There was a sizeable Irish artisan or tradesman element in most of the larger British towns, especially during the first half of the nineteenth century, with tailors, masons and shoemakers being particularly numerous.[22] Moreover, though not very numerous, there was a middle-class element among the immigrant Irish – doctors and lawyers, writers and journalists, with a sprinkling in the world of business and finance.[23] But the Irish presence in these higher reaches of the occupational structure was disproportionately small, whether this disproportion is measured in terms of the occupational structure of the Irish immigrants themselves, or in terms of the occupational structure of the communities in which they settled. For example, Lawton found in Liverpool in 1851 that some 6.5% of merchants, bankers and business men in the sample areas of Liverpool were Irish-born – whereas the Irish-born in Liverpool at this time were of the order of 23%; similarly in Greenock, whilst the Irish-born comprised 16.1% of the population as late as 1881, the percentage of Irish-born among the higher white-collar category jobs was only 5.3%.[24] Even within general categories, there were marked variations. Thus, for example, among settled traders with premises, Irish publicans were numerous, but Irish shopkeepers were not as plentiful as one might expect.

It would be wrong to suggest that this was a static picture throughout the nineteenth century. Undoubtedly in the second half of the century, and at a moderately accelerating pace from the 1880s, there was some demonstrable improvement in the general status of the immigrant Irish – in terms of both jobs and living conditions. Some mobility did take place – outward from the inner-city ghetto and upward from the chronically congested ranks of the unskilled labour force. Some of the changes in occupational structure were forced changes – forced by structural changes in the economy. The completion of a railway line or of a major construction job obliged some immigrants to seek new jobs – very often as maintenance men on railways or in some other 'settled' job in the manual labourer category. Though the evidence is unsatisfactory, it seems likely that there was only a very limited penetration of the white collar jobs by second–generation Irish.[25]

The commercial directories of some British towns in the 1890s show a modest increase in the number of Irish names when compared to the names listed in the 1850s. Irish penetration of the skilled trades, especially the highly unionized trades, appears to have been much slower. Indeed, it seems most likely that it was easier for the modestly educated son of an unskilled labourer to move into the white–collar ranks of the clerks and book–keepers than to join the ranks of the skilled tradesmen in the occupational category most closely related to his father's job. Nevertheless, there was unquestionably some degree of upward social mobility, and at the turn of the century John Denvir perceptively noted that it was 'a sure sign that our people are rising on the social scale', when the local Irish in Lancashire no longer monopolized the job of bricklayer's labourer.[26] Indeed some of this improvement in status occurred even among the first–generation Irish immigrants – an ambitious and prudent labourer might, with the assistance of the earnings of his wife, or other kin, be able in his mature years to set himself up in business – as a lodging–house keeper, a publican or, more rarely, as a shopkeeper. The accumulation of a modest amount of capital was all that was required.

In the same way, in social and particularly residential circumstances no less than in occupational structure, the Irish as a group improved their position during the final third of the nineteenth century. Improvements in public health provisions, municipal activity in housing, the impact of railways, roads and other major construction works on slum clearance and on city–centre settlement generally – these were some of the important developments which led to some dispersal of the Irish from the inner–city slums during the closing decades of the nineteenth century. However, it would be unwise to exaggerate the pace of this dispersal and consequent improvement in housing and social conditions. Depending on structural changes in the economy, slum clearance and general urban renewal could be, and was in fact, a rather protracted business – coming as early as the 1860s and 1870s in some places (London and Birmingham), but as late as the 1930s in others (Greenock).[27] Nor should it be imagined that dispersal from inner–city slums and resettlement in more peripheral areas automatically meant accelerated assimilation for the immigrant Irish. The evidence for London, for example, suggests that in short–distance migration or dispersal within the city, the immigrant Irish succeeded to a remarkable degree in reproducing in their new neighbourhoods the cohesion and self–segregation of their original slum. As Lynn Lees concludes in this context, 'Mobility did not produce geographic assimilation'.[28] For all that, however, it may be conceded that during the closing decades of the nineteenth century some improvements did take place in the living conditions of sections of the immigrant Irish.

While this evidence of increasing Irish mobility, of immigrant adaptability to changing conditions of employment and accommodation, is of considerable interest (especially for the purposes of comparisons with experiences in other countries, such as the United States),[29] what is far more remarkable is the fact that such a relatively large proportion of the immigrant Irish remained tied for so long to the old pattern of jobs and localities. This remarkably conservative pattern of occupational and social structure among the immigrants is worth examining more closely.

There are, of course, many obvious and common–sense explanations for this conservatism among the immigrants. It is reasonable to accept the view that 'kinship relations between emigrant and would–be emigrant in many cases probably determined both the place he went to and his choice of work'.[30] In more general terms, effective Irish control of recruitment in certain occupations soon established a tradition for immigrants' sons, or eased the initiation of the newly arrived immigrant into his new situation. A ganger on a building site or on the dockside might easily establish a recruitment pattern from among his fellow countrymen, or indeed his fellow county–men. There is abundant evidence, for example, that among stevedores on dockside London, or in the sugar–refining factories in Greenock, the establishment of a dominant Irish influence soon led to the operation of something approaching an 'Hibernian closed shop' in subsequent recruitment of workers.[31]

Again, familiar faces and accents, a general ease of social intercourse, familiar landmarks (such as pubs and shops), all these undoubtedly helped in creating a sense of cohesion among the immigrant community and in reinforcing their social and occupational conservatism.

Finally, it is likely that the very high illiteracy rate of successive waves of Irish immigrants (the available data suggest an illiteracy rate among Irish immigrants about twice as high as the average for their social equivalents among the indigenous population in the 1860s) further retarded the mobility, social and otherwise, of the Irish immigrants as a whole.[32]

However, while acknowledging these conservative patterns of settlement and occupation, it seems that there were certain fundamental factors inhibiting the early and successful integration of the immigrant Irish into their host society. Some of these factors relate to the attitudes of the immigrant: to the strength or weakness of his desire to integrate. Others relate to the willingness or otherwise of the host community to accept and absorb him. In the case of the Irish immigrant, there were strong currents running against the desire to integrate. These currents were in the first instance psychological. The very proximity to home, the disappointment of those whose original aspirations had centred on a passage to America, the high mobility of a section of the Irish labour force; all these factors combined to encourage among many immigrants an attitude of refusal to accept the permanency of their exile. Furthermore, the Irish immigrant communities had, deriving from their historical sense, an unusually ambivalent attitude towards their host society. While acknowledging that Britain was providing them with the means to live, and while always ready to acknowledge the better wages and hopes of improvement which prompted emigration in the first place, among the immigrant Irish the sense of obligation or of gratitude for these benefits was nullified, to a considerable extent, by their belief that it was Britain's misgovernment of Ireland which had caused them to be uprooted in the first instance. These attitudes contributed to a situation where the primary loyalty of the immigrant Irish was to their homeland or to the immigrant community itself, and only lastly, if at all, to their new society.

While granting the Irish tendency towards self-segregation – the understandable clannishness of immigrants and the manner in which this was facilitated and reinforced by social and economic structures in industrial Britain – there can nevertheless be no doubt that the Irish in nineteenth-century Britain encountered very strong opposition from many elements in the host society in their efforts to gain acceptance, not to speak of integration. David Steele is surely correct in asserting that 'nowhere else, save in Orange Canada, did the Irish abroad meet with such sustained antagonism' as in nineteenth-century Britain.[33]

There were many reasons for this antagonism. Anti-Irish prejudice (or, more correctly, attitudes) in British society had a long and complicated history, and its sources are a matter of some controversy.[34] That this antagonism was an odd compound of religious, social and political elements, of the rational and the irrational, is not in dispute. However, some recent American writing has described this set of attitudes and antagonisms, which sections of British opinion showed towards the Irish at home and abroad, as evidence of a clear example of racial prejudice.[35] In the case of Professor Curtis, his examination of these attitudes has concentrated on sections of the mid- and late-Victorian intelligentsia, chiefly literary men and cartoonists, among whom he detects the emergence, c. 1860–80, of a firm set of anti-Irish prejudices based on 'the assumption or conviction that the "native Irish" were alien in race and inferior in culture to the Anglo-Saxons'.[36] In essence, this was a set of racist assumptions.

Professor Curtis's analysis has been strongly disputed by, among others, Dr. Sheridan Gilley.[37] Gilley very properly insists on the adjective 'racial' being used with some precision and consistency, and he takes Curtis to task not merely for imprecision, but for clear contradictions in his use of the racial stereotype to describe English 'prejudices'. More positively, Gilley sees the British stereotype of 'Paddy' as having a benign as well as a menacing face, and as being every bit as much an Irish as a British creation (with Irish elements of self–image contributing heavily to the making of the stereotype). Finally, Gilley argues that it was only on specific politico–religious issues that anti–Irish attitudes became dominant among the British and, furthermore, that there were very understandable social and economic reasons for much of the popular hostility shown to the immigrant Irish, reasons which do not deserve to be described as prejudices.[38]

There is much sense in many of Gilley's arguments and, certainly, the attitudes of the Victorian intelligentsia towards Irish political demands are too complex for the procrustean frame of simple anti–Celticism. However, it may be that Dr. Gilley underestimates the extent, the pervasiveness and the endurance of this antagonism towards the Irish immigrants. And, while he acknowledges that 'anti–Celtic racism became a partial, and temporary component of English nationalism as a fleeting mood in the euphoria of the hey–day of the Anglo–Saxon "lords of human kind"',[39] this does not go far enough in conveying the extent to which the vocabulary of race was resorted to in popular discussions of the 'Irish problem' – in the press and the journals – from at least the 1840s. While 'national' rather than racial may be a more accurate description, as Gilley would have it, of anti–Irish attitudes, there was an almost universal tendency from the 1840s onwards to describe the immigrant Irish and their problems in distinctly racial terms. The balance of emphasis here is crucial. The idealized Ireland – the suffering but beautifully melancholy lady of *Punch* cartoons, or good–natured 'Pat'; these are idealized types so far as the cartoonists were concerned. They are somewhat unreal, and are certainly not the stereotype likely to be related to the bulk of the immigrant Irish. In short, it seems that, on balance, from the 1840s the immigrant Irish benefited much less from the idealized and benign elements of the 'Paddy' stereotype in cartoons and elsewhere than they suffered from its malign elements.

Whatever may have been the balance between the 'good' and 'bad' images of the Irish before 1800, the antagonisms against the Irish intensified and became more widespread from the early decades of the nineteenth century, as the social and economic problems of pre–famine Ireland and the transformation of the British labour market, under the impact of the industrial revolution, combined to send an increasing volume of the unemployed Irish to Britain. Anti–Irish feeling had its rational side; to a certain extent it did rest on an indisputable 'body of social fact'. The Irish did indeed represent a major social problem. British rate-payers resented the heavy burden of Irish paupers on their poor–rates, and further feared them as disease–carriers. The British working man had reason to resent the Irish immigrant labourer, who was prepared to work harder and longer and for lower pay, and to live in more brutalizing conditions than his British counterpart. Again the use of the Irish as strike–breakers, though its incidence was probably exaggerated, left a long and bitter legacy, dividing the native labouring classes from the Irish.[40] Some other aspects of the Irish immigrant impact on the British labour market are less clear. For example, E.H. Hunt's study of inter–regional wage variations in early nineteenth–century Britain suggests that the Irish influx may have increased or widened these variations,[41] a view at variance with what historians have until now accepted to be the case.[42] It has also been argued that by flooding the casual labour market the Irish, even if unintentionally, were responsible for the native British labourer's becoming more skilled or otherwise moving up a rung on the ladder of the labour hierarchy. Finally, in this context of the British labour market, the point was made as early as the 1830s by George Cornewall Lewis that the Irish were concentrated heavily in employment which required exceptionally high mobility, and were an indispensable part of a dynamic economy.[43] But in the case of attitudes and prejudices, what is demonstrable is very often of less consequence than what is feared; and the Irish were generally perceived as a threat, a nuisance, a contagion. Indeed, writing as late as the 1930s the late J.H. Clapham wrote of 'the decisive and degrading influence of the early nineteenth–century Irish immigration on housing habits and housing conditions', and further stated that those areas where the Irish had not settled 'had been spared a social disease'.[44]

The huge famine influx of Irish brought native fear and resentment to fever pitch. The flooding of ghetto areas by impoverished and disease–ridden Irish, and the violence and social misery which was a by–product of such a brutalizing environment, together with a ready acceptance of the notion that Irish peasant society was inherently violent, formed for sizable sections of the British public an explanation for all Irish troubles and misfortunes which rested on 'the fundamental weaknesses of the Irish national character'. A stereotype of the brutalized 'Paddy' was formed, in greater detail and enjoying wider currency than ever before; intemperate, improvident, violent, totally innocent of any notions of hygiene, mendacious and undependable – not so much a lovable rogue as a menacing savage. The popular imagination had, in general, little time for reflection on the environmental factors which dictated the over–representation of the immigrant Irish on the poor–law and crime lists, and in the alcoholic gutters.[45] Weakness of national character was an easily accepted explanation. During the middle decades of the nineteenth century these prejudices were systemized within a somewhat crude anthropological typology.

The *Punch* cartoons of the late nineteenth century illustrate very well that caricature of what a Glasgow newspaper referred to as 'the ape–faced, small–headed Irishman', who showed 'the unmistakable width of mouth, immense expanse of chin, and "forehead villainous low", so characteristic of the lowest Irish'.[46] And, of course, the vast majority of the Irish in nineteenth–century Britain belonged to 'the lowest Irish'. While the ineluctable fact of colour is missing here, it is still difficult to describe this kind of language as other than racial.

The intensity of these prejudices and this hostility towards the Irish immigrant community varied from time to time, from place to place, and between different classes. In south–west Scotland, anti–

Irish prejudice was especially bitter, with large areas of urban Lancashire not far behind.[47] Not surprisingly, the prejudices were almost everywhere directed against 'the lowest Irish', the Irish immigrant working class. Irish birth or extraction does not seem to have hindered in any significant way the prospects of the Irish professional man in Britain. British journalism presented plenty of opportunity for talented Irish pens; in the late Victorian era some of the most respected names in Fleet Street, Justin McCarthy, William O'Malley and the legendary T.P. O'Connor ('Tay Pay') were Irish.[48] Likewise, Irish entertainers and music–hall artistes added a welcome dash of provincial colour to the Victorian and Edwardian stage.[49] Even among certain 'blue collar' communities (such as in some industrial areas of Tyneside) the local work–situation, and the dominant modes of political and religious behaviour, seem to have been adequate defence against discord, even where the Irish immigrant influx was substantial.[50] Nevertheless, it remains true that, whether dormant or roused by accidental circumstances, a deep–rooted set of anti–Irish attitudes was widespread in British society throughout the nineteenth century.

Both the Irish reluctance to integrate and the host society's reluctance to accept can be seen as functions of a more fundamental and more complex problem underlying the relations between the two communities. This was the 'cultural distance' separating the Irish immigrant community from the native population. This cultural distance proved, in the event, very difficult to bridge. Despite being white and, for the most part, English–speaking,[51] the sense of identity of the Irish immigrant, his consciousness of himself and of his history, was sufficiently acute to present considerable difficulties in the way of early or successful integration.

To the social and economic forces making for self–segregation we must also add some other cultural features which increased internal cohesion within the immigrant community while simultaneously working against its assimilation.

It is easy to enumerate some of the ways in which this determination of the immigrant community to retain its identity manifested itself. The full spectrum of immigrant associations dedicated to the cultivation of Irish music and song, Irish debating and literary clubs, Gaelic League branches, G.A.A. clubs in the 1880s and 1890s, and the growth of informal and formal countrymen's associations – all these constituted a mosaic of ties binding the immigrant community to the homeland. The ultimate celebration of this distinct group identity was the annual St. Patrick's Day celebration in British towns. In Sheffield, for example, at the St. Patrick's Day concert in 1891, there was a large and representative gathering of well–to–do Irish; distinguished guests from the local community were there to be impressed by the good representation of professional and white collar Irish. The hall was decorated with shamrocks and other recognizably Irish bunting, and the rendering of Moore's melodies and especially T.D. Sullivan's *God Save Ireland* (a kind of immigrant anthem) was especially enjoyed.[52] This, of course, was the high point of the nostalgic graph. But the Irish pubs on Saturday nights regularly saw the collective nostalgia of the labouring 'Paddies' indulged to the full, albeit with a more earthy flavour.

These activities, however, are but the simple manifestations of group identity not uncommon among many immigrant groups in many lands. There would seem to be no particular reason why they could not have been accommodated without any great difficulty by the host community, as indeed they are at the present time. However, the two main cultural props of the immigrant community conflicted directly with the norms of behaviour acceptable to wide sectors of British society. These were the religion and the political allegiance of the Irish immigrants.

The fidelity, or at least the emotional loyalty, of the Catholic Irish to their religion has been attested by historians and social commentators alike. But it is not enough simply to say that the Catholic Church was a central institution in the lives of the immigrant Irish in Britain.[53] The extent of its influence, and the ways in which this influence manifested itself, call for some elaboration. While it is true that, unlike their spiritual brothers in America, the Irish never succeeded in capturing the commanding heights of the Catholic Church in Britain,[54] nevertheless, through sheer weight of numbers, the Catholic Church in Britain in the nineteenth century became, at a popular level, very much the church of the immigrant Irish. By a permeation, or rather saturation, of its structures, the Catholic Irish succeeded in moulding the shape of an institution which, although it differed in crucial respects from the Catholic Church they had known in rural Ireland,[55] was nevertheless an institution much closer to being an Irish Catholic Church than the majority of the native hierarchy, or the vast majority of indigenous British Catholics, would have desired. As Lynn Lees has put it, 'support for an ultramontane Church and for moderate brands of Irish nationalism permeated Roman Catholic rhetoric, rituals and social life'.[56] Some of the attempts made by English priests to marry Irish nationalist-type popular religious practices to more universally 'Roman' habits of Catholic worship produced an amusing litany of incongruities. Such, for example, was the spectacle of a well-drilled religious procession of Catholic children after Sunday school briskly stepping it out to the strains of *The Wearing of the Green* or, more incongruously still, *God Save Ireland* (the hymn to the Manchester Martyrs).[57] Attempts to infuse Irish Catholic habits and pieties with a Smilesian dose of sobriety and self-help, and indeed a more general drive to 'raise the tone' of the Catholic Irish, did not always meet with the success which its idealistic sponsors hoped for.[58]

The Catholic Church in Britain encountered considerable problems in ministering to the immigrant Irish. Human, physical and financial resources were intolerably over-strained during the famine influx, and in the post-famine decades there was a chronic and constant shortage both of priests (particularly of Irish priests, though their numbers undoubtedly increased in the final third of the nineteenth century)[59] and of money, shortages which severely hampered the English Catholic mission to the immigrant Irish from the 1840s onwards. Failure in any aspect of this mission added further to what gradually emerged as the central problem for the Catholic Church in nineteenth–century Britain, the problem of 'leakage' of baptized Catholics out of the Church. Leakage in this sense did not mean a repudiation of Catholic teaching, or conversion to an alternative faith, or an explicit profession of atheism. It simply meant ceasing to practise regularly.

The precise extent of this 'leakage' among Irish Catholic immigrants in nineteenth–century Britain is difficult to calculate, though by the third quarter of the century it was deemed to be considerable enough to cause great anxiety to the hierarchies of Britain and Ireland, and indeed Rome itself. Catholic commentators, like Edward Lucas of *The Tablet*, and bishops , such as Bishop Vaughan of Salford (who collected statistical data on the 'leakage' problem), were unanimous in their view that 'leakage' was the major challenge facing the Catholic Church in Britain, and that it was increasing as the century got older.[60] What they meant, of course, was that the regular attendance at Mass and the sacraments, and particularly the performance of Easter duties, was not satisfactory when related to the total number of nominal Catholics resident in Britain.

But even the alarmists acknowledged that in the case of many immigrant Irish, relative 'indifference to Catholic ritual' should not be confused 'with indifference to Catholicism'.[61] And even if we accept that there was a relatively low level of regular attendance at Mass among working–class Catholics in particular, two points are none the less worth keeping in mind. First, that, low as it was, religious observance among the labouring Irish Catholics was considerably higher, as K.S. Inglis has shown, than religious observance among other sectors of the native British working–classes.[62] Secondly, even those whose attention to the repeated exhortations of the Catholic hierarchy to attend Mass and the sacraments regularly was, to say the least, indifferent, seldom lost their emotional loyalty to the Catholic Church. This is well attested both by the rueful testimony of disappointed evangelical Protestant missionaries and by the fact that even for those Catholics who were not regular attenders, the key dates in the life–cycle (birth, marriage, death) were seldom celebrated without the Church's benediction.[63]

In talking of 'leakage' historians generally accept the contemporary view that the main problem was in the second and subsequent generations of immigrants. E.D. Steele's comment that 'whenever the Irish settled, the first generation rarely lost all contact with their religion, but the second and third generations did so' is not untypical of the late–Victorian period and of later historians.[64] Sheridan Gilley, for example, sees two contradictory forces as contributing to this 'leakage'; the one, upward social mobility, rendering old values irrelevant or obsolete, the other, 'a total submersion in the common culture of poverty'.[65]

However, even in the face of such a consensus there is need for caution. The evidence on marriage behaviour is of relevance here. The view that 'mixed' marriages were on the increase, at least in the

1880s and 1890s, was voiced by contemporary Catholic leaders, and has been accepted by historians.[66] Such dense smoke makes it highly unlikely that there was no fire. Yet there is independent evidence of an extraordinary incidence of intra-group marriages among the immigrant Irish. Lynn Lees, for example, basing her findings on data from 1851 to 1861, concludes that 'the London Irish generally married within their own ethnic group; there was little inter-marriage with people of English ancestry or with continental Catholics . . . First and second generation Irish . . . would seem to have intermarried freely.'[67] Similarly, in analysing data for Greenock, R.B. Lobban found a high degree of intra-group marriages among the immigrant Irish in 1851 and again in 1891. And while there was a weakening in the intra-group pattern in the years between 1851 and 1891 (from 86% of Irish men and women finding partners within their own group in 1851, to 72.4% in 1891), the weakening was not dramatic, and the group solidarity was still remarkably strong by 1891.[68]

While the evidence is patchy, and clearly requires further local studies on this particular aspect of the problem, nevertheless these figures for intra-group marriage patterns are a further warning to us not to take at face value all the dire forecasts of Catholic observers during the late-Victorian era. As with attendance figures, so also with marriage patterns, the evidence suggests that there was a much stronger emotional loyalty to the Catholic Church than many commentators suspected; and, furthermore, that nominal, occasional or symbolic membership of the Catholic Church was a psychological necessity for a much greater number of immigrant Irish Catholics than were prepared to attend regularly at Mass and the sacraments.

While group solidarity in marriage patterns was, perhaps, the most crucial way in which the Catholic Church sought to preserve its congregations intact, there were also many other ways in which a self-contained, almost self-segregated community was encouraged by the Church and its activities. The system of Catholic schools, the litany of social, recreational and educational societies sponsored by the Church for its Catholic children, all of these were part of a general strategy whose purpose was the creation, as far as possible, of a self-contained Catholic community of sobriety and solid good behaviour. In short, the Catholic Church was a crucial force inhibiting, indeed actively discouraging, the assimilation of the Irish immigrants in the working-class culture of the native majority.

In another sense, too, a negative sense, the Catholic Church, whatever spiritual or social comfort membership of it may have given to the immigrant, raised a barrier between the immigrant Irish and his host society. This was because Catholicism in itself, without any exertions on the part of its leaders, was suspect in the eyes of major sections of British public opinion. It is not necessary here to analyse in detail the sources of anti-Catholicism in Britain, particularly in the Victorian era.[69] Papal interference and Jesuitical intrigues in international politics, sacerdotalism and excessive priestly influence in private and public matters, vestigial elements of medieval superstition and idolatry in Catholic rites, authoritarianism in Catholic teaching and organization – these were some of the main planks in the anti–Catholic platform. Moreover, anti–Catholicism was, in a sense, an integral part of the national myth of both the English and the Scots since the sixteenth century. Loyalty to Rome was seen as compromising loyalty to the national state, involving, as it did, the acknowledgement of a jurisdiction, albeit a spiritual one, outside the state.

While the violent 'No Popery' campaigns of earlier times found relatively faint echoes in late–Victorian Britain, there was, nevertheless, a strong anti–Catholic prejudice present in many levels of British society for most of the nineteenth century. As the *Salford Weekly News* wrote in 1868:

> Nobody who has not the sublime audacity of Mr. Disraeli dare now raise the old anti–social 'No Popery' cry; but there are a great many left who have a lingering instinctive dread of Roman Catholicism gaining ground. It is not easy work combating a feeling of this kind.[70]

This was in 1868, and far from being a 'lingering instinctive dread', anti–Catholicism had, if anything, been experiencing something of a temporary revival during the previous twenty years. The Irish influx in these crucial decades probably helped to heighten fears of Roman Catholicism gaining ground, at least numerically, in Britain, and in this suspicious and fearful mood the violence of the denunciation of Catholic pretensions which followed the reconstitution of the Catholic hierarchy in Britain in 1850 was hardly surprising.[71] It has been noted that on relatively few occasions did this anti–Catholic mood result in overt violence, in attacks on Catholics, especially when compared to the story in America.[72] Notwithstanding such notorious exceptions as the Stockport riots of 1852 or the Murphy riots of the late 1860s, this contention is substantially true.[73] Nevertheless, the long list of public agitations which accompanied every airing of the Catholic question, from Brunswick Club opposition to Catholic Emancipation in the 1820s to the political storm over Peel's Maynooth grant in 1845, to the Durham letter of 1850, and finally to the outrage of papal claims as asserted in the Syllabus of Errors and the infallibility decree – all these represent a continuous, enduring and deep–seated popular British suspicion of Rome, its influence and intentions.

However, anti–Irish attitudes were not simple varieties of anti–Catholicism, though religious prejudice undoubtedly entered into it. It was not only the non–Catholic British who had misgivings, or worse, about the Catholic Irish. Many of the native British Catholics found their Irish co–religionists a decidedly uncomfortable presence among them. There were class and cultural factors involved here. British Catholics, were, by historical circumstances, an ultra–loyal minority, with (at least in England) a leadership drawn from aristocratic and intellectually patrician circles. In their long struggle to win acceptance as full political members of their state, loyalty and discretion (and, of course, tenacity) had been their invaluable weapons.[74] Many of them found it extremely difficult to come to terms with the hordes of Irish Catholics who came among them during the nineteenth century. They found some of the transplanted forms of peasant piety embarrassing. Their intellectual no less than their social snobbery was, in turn, deeply resented by the Irish. True, Henry Edward Manning managed to reach across this cultural divide; but Mannings were in relatively short supply.[75] It is also true, of course, that many English Catholics found in the mission to the Irish poor the ideal, and idealized, outlet for their Christian witness.[76] But there remained a number of major issues which soured relations between the leaders of the Catholic Irish immigrants and the British Catholic establishment. The most serious of these issues was the political role of the immigrant Irish. In fact, it was the peculiarly strong political connotations of Irish Catholicism which caused the tensions and divisions within the Catholic ranks in Britain. Where Irish experience encompassed an easy, indeed natural, fusion of religion and politics, the English Catholic required that they be kept separate. Or, more correctly, since political exertions in the interests of Catholic education were quite legitimate, he did not want his Catholicism compromised through association with Irish nationalist politics. And yet, as the immigrant Irish permeated 'the rhetoric, rituals and social habits' of the Catholic Church in Britain, there was a constant danger of just such an association. It remains for us to offer an explanation for this problem of Irish political demands and their implications for the immigrants in Britain.

For most of the nineteenth century the majority of Irish immigrants had a political objective – the broad nationalist one of redefining in some way Ireland's constitutional relations with Britain – which lay outside the range of objectives accepted as legitimate by British public opinion. The Irish deviance was resented. When it intruded violently on the British domestic scene (as, for example, in the Fenian escapades in Manchester and Clerkenwell) native indignation and anger were widespread and deep. Furthermore, not only in objectives, but also in political organization, the Irish were to a considerable extent a self–contained political entity, at least up to the 1880s. There was no Irish–based political organization, clandestine or constitutional, from at least the Repeal movement of the 1840s, which did not have affiliated, if not always fully obedient, branches from all centres of Irish settlement in Britain.[77] Neither was there any shortage of local leadership among the immigrant Irish, chiefly 'professional men', as Denvir noted.[78]

In electoral terms, at local and parliamentary level, the immigrant Irish 'fifth column' was an interesting element in late–Victorian and Edwardian politics. Yet it is important not to exaggerate the electoral strength of the Irish in late Victorian Britain.[79] True, the Irish gained from the extension of the franchise in 1867 and again in 1884. Indeed, after the creation of largely single–seat constituencies in 1884, the Irish vote was probably crucial in a small number of constituencies.[80] But against that, it ought to be remembered that the Irish working classes, partly because of their relatively high rate of mobility, partly because of the general inadequacy of their accommodation and education, were especially prone to disqualification from voting owing to their failure to satisfy some of the difficult qualifications laid down in the franchise acts.[81] The dominance of the 'national question' in Irish immigrant political behaviour severely retarded, indeed almost entirely precluded, significant Irish participation in domestic British politics for the greater part of the nineteenth century. True, it is possible to identify a thin green line of Irish participation in the various streams making up the British radical tradition during the nineteenth century – from the correspondence societies of the 1790s to the early advocacy of general unionization by John Doherty and the more significant, if short lived, attempt at fusing Irish nationalist and British democratic demands in the Chartist campaign of the 1840s.[82] But the religious and cultural modes of Irish nationalism could not be made to fit easily into the mould of British radical politics. Indeed, even where opportunities were most favourable for Irish participation in domestic British politics (such as within elective school boards in the 1870s), there was remarkably little Irish participation in such domestic politics up to the 1880s.[83]

But, as in other areas, the political obstacles to the more successful integration of the immigrant Irish into British society began to weaken during the last two decades of the nineteenth century. In this context, Gladstone's 'conversion' to Home Rule in 1886 was the decisive turning point, and its significance has not been sufficiently appreciated by historians writing on the immigrant Irish, since it effectively legitimized their political aspirations and objectives. They could not advocate moderate nationalist demands (anything short of separation) without incurring the charge of treason or subversion of the empire. In the short term, the Liberal–Irish alliance of 1886–92 broke down many psychological barriers in British constituencies, as Liberal and Irish nationalist leaders shared the same election platforms, advocating the 'union of hearts'. Admittedly, not all Liberals (even the most loyal) could share in the Pauline conversion of 1886, and in the aftermath of Parnell's downfall and death, with the Liberal imperialist firmly in the party saddle, there were times when the thread of Liberal commitment to 'Ireland' was very thin indeed. But the decisive break–through had been made. After Gladstone's conversion there could be no going back to the pre–1886 consensus. The Irish nationalist case was no longer automatically damned as heretical in British politics.[84]

Gladstone's 'conversion' had further political repercussions. By stitching Home Rule into the Liberal party banner he ensured the continued support of the majority of the Irish in Britain for the Liberal party up to the outbreak of the Great War. This loyalty to the Liberals was, on the whole, strong enough to withstand both the enticing carrot of Conservative education policies, and the more natural political claims of a nascent Labour party on a largely working–class community.[85] It was not until the third decade of this century, after the war, the Liberal collapse and the drastic reconstruction of Anglo–Irish relations had transformed the political landscape, that mass Irish support for Labour became a feature of British politics.

In the industrial context, however, Irish involvement in the Labour movement was already increasing in the closing years of the nineteenth century. With the growth of the 'New Unionism' among the unskilled, the Irish for the first time *en masse* began to play a major part in the general struggles of the British working classes. This was well attested by the strong Irish participation (right up to leadership level) in the London Dock Strike of 1889.[86]

Finally, with the arrival in the late nineteenth century of a wave of new immigrants from central and eastern Europe, the Irish were eclipsed as the most visible and problematic minority group in British society.[87]

These developments in industrial and political life, together with the blunting of the edge of religious prejudice consequent upon the spread of religious indifference, meant that by the early twentieth century the Irish immigrant working man had gradually, if at times grudgingly, won a wide measure of acceptance in British society. But the process had been a slow one. Many anti–Irish attitudes were very slowly abandoned, and were likely to surface at times of public excitement, as, for example, in the reaction to Irish republican bombings in Britain during the Second World War. Moreover, the 'no Irish need apply' notice in advertisements for jobs and accommodation served constant notice, long after 1922, that old prejudices die hard.[88]

One last point. For the Irish immigrants in nineteenth–century Britain, as for their American cousins,[89] expatriate nationalism may have served an important and complex psychological function, giving, as it did, an exalted sense of purpose to lives which were otherwise spent in adverse social circumstances and, by demanding freedom for the homeland, allowing immigrants to engage in a kind of revolt by proxy against their own depressed condition. On this reasoning, the achievement of national independence, the creation of a national state in the homeland, might be expected to act as a kind of liberation, a collective rise in self–esteem for the expatriates. The establishment of an Irish national state (whatever its shortcomings) in 1922 signalled the end of an era in Irish immigrant history. Thereafter, the Irish immigrant in Britain could devote his entire energy and his full attention to making his way and making the best of his chances in his new society.

Notes

1. The exceptions include A. Redford, *Labour Migration in England, 1800–1850* (London, 1926; revised edn., Manchester, 1964); J.E. Handley, *The Irish in Scotland* (Cork, 1943), and *The Irish in Modern Scotland* (Cork, 1947); J.A. Jackson, *The Irish in Britain* (London, 1963); R. Lawton, 'Irish Immigration to England and Wales in the Mid–Nineteenth Century', *Irish Geography*, vol.iv (1959–63), pp.35–54. It

would be absurd to exclude from this list the far from scholarly, sadly dated, but splendidly informative J. Denvir, *The Irish in Britain* (London, 1892). See also the bibliography.

2. C. Holmes (ed.), *Immigrants and Minorities* (London, 1978); K. Lunn, (ed.),*Hosts, Immigrants and Minorities* (London, 1980). For the process of migration itself, see A. Jackson (ed.), *Migration*, (Cambridge, 1969).

3. E.P. Thompson, *The Making of the English Working Class* (1976 edn.), p.480.

4. A.C. Hepburn, (ed.), *Minorities in History* (London, 1978), pp.1–2.

5. Though the figures for Irish emigration to Britain have, it seems, hitherto been underestimated, see C. Ó Gráda, 'A Note on Nineteenth–Century Emigration Statistics', *Population Studies*, vol. 29 (1975), pp.145–8; 'Some Aspects of Nineteenth–Century Irish Emigration', in L.M. Cullen and T.C. Smout (eds.), *Comparative Aspects of Scottish and Irish Economic and Social History, 1600–1900 (Edinburgh, 1977), pp.65–73.*

6. *See, for example,* Dorothy George, *London Life in the Eighteenth Century* (London, 1930), pp.125–30.

7. See Redford, *Labour Migration*, pp.150–64. The most detailed source of opinions on the pre–famine Irish immigrants is G. Cornewall Lewis's report on the state of the Irish poor in Britain in the early 1830s (*Parliamentary Papers*, 1836 (40), vol.xxxiv, app. G).

8. Derived from statistical tables in Jackson, *Irish in Britain*, p.11.

9. *Ibid*. See also B.R. Mitchell and P. Deane, *Abstract of British Historical Statistics* (Cambridge, 1962), p.6.

10. Cited as percentages by Brenda Collins, *Aspects of Irish Immigration* (unpublished M.Phil. Thesis, University of Edinburgh, 1978), p.22.

11. R.D. Lobban, 'The Irish Community in Greenock in the Nineteenth Century', *Irish Geography*, vol.vi (1971), pp.270–1.

12. Lynn H. Lees, *Exiles of Erin: Irish Migrants in Victorian London* (Manchester, 1979), pp.39–40, 42–4; Ó Gráda, 'Aspects of Irish Emigration', pp.66–7.

13. *Reports of the Commission on Emigration and Other Population Problems (1948–54)*, P.R. 2541 (Dublin, 1965), Table 90, p.120.

14. For seasonal migrants and their impact, see B.M. Kerr, 'Irish Seasonal Migration to Great Britain, 1800–38', *Irish Historical Studies*, vol.iii (1942–3), pp.365–80; C. Ó Gráda, 'Seasonal Migration and Post–Famine Adjustment in the West of Ireland', *Studia Hibernica*, vol.13 (1973), pp.48–76; E.J.T. Collins, 'Migrant Labour in British Agriculture in the Nineteenth Century', *Economic History Review*, 2nd. ser., vol.xxix (1976), pp.38–59.

15. For Irish railway navvying see, for example, T. Coleman, *The Railway Navvies* (London, 1965); J.E. Handley, *The Navvy in Scotland* (Cork, 1970); J.H. Treble, 'Irish Navvies in the North of England, 1830–50', *Transport History*, vol.6 (1973), pp.227–47; D. Brooke, 'Railway Navvies on the Pennines, 1841–71', *Journal of Transport History*, new ser., vol.3 (1975–6), pp.41–53.

16. K. Boyle, 'The Irish Immigrant in Britain', *Northern Ireland Legal Quarterly*, vol.19 (1968), p.422.
17. Lees, *Exiles*, p.55.
18. F. Engels, *The Condition of the Working Classes in England* [1845], ed. W.O. Henderson and W.H. Chaloner (Oxford, 1958), esp. pp.30–87, 104–7; T. Carlyle, *Chartism* (London, 1839), esp. pp.28–33; H. Mayhew, *London Labour and the London Poor* (4 vols., London 1861–2: reprinted New York, 1968); C. Booth, *Life and Labour of the People in London* (London, 1902–3), esp. Series 3, 'Religious Influences'. It should be noted that the Irish did not bulk as large as a social problem in Booth's work as they had done for Mayhew a generation before.
19. J. Denvir, *The Life Story of an Old Rebel* (Dublin, 1910), p.5.
20. Lobban, 'Irish Community in Greenock', p.272.
21. See the excellent paper by H.J. Hanham, 'Religion and Nationality in the Mid–Victorian Army', in M.R.D. Foot (ed.), *War and Society: Essays in Honour and Memory of J.R. Western* (London, 1973), pp.162, 176–7.
22. Some of these are noted in passing in *Parliamentary Papers*, 1836 (40), vol.xxxiv, app. G.
23. It is difficult to quantify this element. They emerge from Denvir's survey of the immigrant Irish (*Irish in Britain*), and particularly in the study of the political leadership of the immigrant Irish. See also C. Richardson, 'The Irish in Victorian Bradford', *The Bradford Antiquary*, vol.9 (1976), pp.303–4.
24. Lawton, 'Irish Immigration', pp.48–54; Lobban, 'Irish Community in Greenock', pp.274–7.
25. See Lees, *Exiles*, pp.88–122, for the general discussion of mobility.
26. Denvir, *Life Story*, p.50.
27. Lobban, 'Irish Community in Greenock', pp.277–8. J. Hickey, *Urban Catholics* (London, 1967), pp.99–113, discusses dispersal in Cardiff, for which see also M.J. Daunton, *Coal Metroplis: Cardiff 1870–1914* (Leicester, 1977), pp.89–105, 125–46. See also Richardson, 'Irish in Victorian Bradford', pp.301–2, and, for the impact of railways and other construction on cities, H.J. Dyos and M. Wolff (eds.), *The Victorian City*, esp. chs. 10–15.
28. Lees, *Exiles*, p.63.
29. See particularly the work of S. Thernstrom, *Poverty and Progress: Social Mobility in a Nineteenth–Century City* (Cambridge, Mass., 1964); *The Other Bostonians* (Cambridge, Mass., 1973), pp.45–75, 111–44, 145–75, 220–6, which highlights the disappointingly limited mobility of second–generation Irish–Americans relative to certain other immigrant groups.
30. Boyle, 'Irish Immigrant', p.429.
31. Lobban, 'Irish Community in Greenock', pp.273–4; J. Lovell, 'The Irish and the London Dockers', *Society for the Study of Labour History: Bulletin*, vol.35 (1977), pp.16–18; *Stevedores and Dockers: a Study of Trade Unionism in the Port of London, 1870–1914* (London, 1969).

32. The estimate is from E.D. Steele, 'The Irish Presence in the North of England, 1850–1914', *Northern History* (1976), p.224. See also Lobban ('Irish Community in Greenock', p.279), who suggests that the percentage may have been higher.
33. Steele, 'Irish Presence in the North of England', p.226.
34. A reasonably scrupulous backward glance would go at least as far as Geraldus Cambrensis, in A.B. Scott and F.X. Martin (eds.), *Expugnatio Hibernica* (Dublin, 1978). For Elizabethan attitudes, see D.B. Quinn, *The Elizabethans and the Irish* (Ithaca, N.Y., 1966).
35. L.P. Curtis, Jr., *Anglo–Saxons and Celts* (Bridgeport, Connecticut, 1968); *Apes, Angels and Victorians* (Newton Abbot, 1971); R.W. Lebow, *White Britain and Black Ireland* (Philadelphia, 1976).
36. Curtis, *Anglo–Saxons and Celts*, p.5.
37. Gilley, 'English Attitudes to the Irish', pp.81–110. See also W.L. Arnstein, 'Victorian Prejudice Re–examined', *Victorian Studies*, vol.xii (1969), pp.452–7.
38. This bald summary does scant justice to Gilley's carefully argued case.
39. Gilley, 'English Attitudes to the Irish', p.94.
40. For examples see Redford, *Labour Migration*, pp.161–2, and E.H. Hunt, *Regional Wage Variations in Great Britain, 1850–1914* (Oxford, 1973), p.296.
41. Hunt, *Wage Variations*, pp.286–323.
42. But for doubts on Hunt's thesis, see Ó Gráda, 'Aspects of Irish Emigration', pp.65–6, 71, note 6.
43. See *Parliamentary Papers*, 1836 (40), vol.xxxiv, app. G, especially pp.xxx–xxxviii.
44. J.H. Clapham, *An Economic History of Modern Britain*, 3 vols., (Cambridge, 1926–38), vol.ii, p.494.
45. Richardson ('Irish in Victorian Bradford', pp.310–12), shows that the Irish received special notice in the Chief Constable's annual reports.
46. Cited in Handley, *Irish in Modern Scotland*, p.105.
47. These were the areas of heaviest Irish settlement and also the areas with a substantial Orange immigrant element from Ulster, two factors which increased the likelihood of communal tension and violence. See Denvir, *Irish in Britain*, pp.406–9, 429–38, 446–58.
48. T.P. O'Connor, *Memoirs of an Old Parliamentarian* 2 vols. (London, 1929); W. O'Malley, *Glancing Back* (London, 1933).
49. For contrasting views on the 'stage Irishman', see G.C. Duggan, *The Stage Irishman* (New York, 1969), and J.M. Nelson, 'From Rory and Paddy to Boucicault's Myles, Shaun and Conn: The Irishman on the London Stage, 1830–60', *Eire–Ireland*, vol.13 (1978), pp.79–105.
50. See J. Keating, 'History of the Tyneside Irish Brigade',in F.R. Lavery (ed.), *Irish Heroes in the Great War* (London, 1917), which is useful but written with wartime recruitment in mind; R.J. Cooter, 'Lady Londonderry and the Irish Catholics of Seaham Harbour: "No Popery" out of Context', *Recusant History*, vol.13 (1975–6), pp.288–98; T.P. MacDermott, 'Irish Workers on Tyneside in the Nineteenth Century', N. McCord (ed.), *Essays in Tyneside Labour History*,

(Newcastle–upon–Tyne, 1977); R. Moore, *Pit–Men, Preachers and Politics* (Cambridge, 1974), pp.64–77, 179–80.
51. From Ó Gráda's revised figures for Irish immigrants to Britain (above, note 5) and their provenance, it may be inferred that the number of Irish speakers in the immigrant stream to Britain was higher than has been allowed for. This, of course, has implications for literacy, social isolation and religious life among the immigrants.
52. Programme of St. Patrick's Day concert in the Albert Hall, Sheffield, 1890 (Sheffield Central Library: H.J. Wilson Papers).
53. The most thorough attempt to investigate this subject is the work of Gilley, cited bibliography.
54. A point noted, self–consciously and defensively, by D. Gwynn, 'The Irish Immigration', in G.A. Beck (ed.), *The English Catholics, 1850–1950* (London, 1950), pp.265–90.
55. For which see E. Larkin, 'The Devotional Revolution in Ireland, 1850–75', *American Historical Review*, vol.lxxvii (1972), pp.625–52; D. Miller, 'Irish Catholicism and the Great Famine', *Journal of Social History*, vol.ix (1975–6), pp.81–98.
56. Lees, *Exiles*, p.194.
57. See Steele, 'Irish Presence in the North of England', p.231.
58. For amusing examples, see Lees, *Exiles*, p.196.
59. On the crucial role of Irish–speaking priests in administering the sacraments (especially confession), see the letter sent in November 1865 to Mgr. Kirby, Rector of the Irish College in Rome, by the Rev. George Montgomery of the parish of Wednesbury in South Staffordshire, where 'nineteen twentieths of my flock' came from Connacht (Irish College, Rome, Kirby Papers, Kirby/65/269). See also C. Richardson, 'Irish Settlement in Mid–Nineteenth Century Bradford', *Yorkshire Bulletin of Economic and Social Research*, vol.20, p.56.
60. K.S. Inglis, *Churches and the Working Classes in Victorian England* (London, 1963), esp. pp.119–30.
61. Lees, *Exiles*, p.184.
62. Inglis, *Churches and the Working Classes*, pp.16–18, 119–30.
63. Lees, *Exiles*, pp.180–2.
64. Steele, 'Irish Presence in the North of England', p.220.
65. Gilley, 'English Attitudes to the Irish', pp.92–3.
66. In theory, of course, a 'mixed' marriage was as likely to lead to the 'gain' of the non–Catholic partner as to the 'loss' of the Catholic.
67. Lees, *Exiles*, p.153.
68. Lobban, 'Irish Community in Greenock', pp.278–9.
69. E.R. Norman, *Anti–Catholicism in Victorian England* (London, 1968); G.A. Cahill, 'Irish Catholicism and English Toryism', *Review of Politics*, vol.19 (1957), pp.62–76; G.F.A. Best, 'Popular Protestantism in Victorian Britain', in R. Robson (ed.), *Ideas and Institutions of Victorian Britain* (London, 1967), pp.115–42.
70. *Salford Weekly News*, 18 April 1868, cited in R.L. Greenall, 'Popular Conservatism in Salford, 1868–1886', *Northern History*, vol.ix (1974), p.131.
71. The materials for popular anti–Catholicism were plentiful enough

without taking the immigrant Irish into account at all. See Sheridan Gilley, 'Protestant London, No Popery, and the Irish Poor, 1830–1860', *Recusant History*, vol.10 (1969–70), pp.210–30.
72. Steele, 'Irish Presence in the North of England', p.226.
73. For Murphy, see W.L. Arnstein, 'The Murphy Riots: a Victorian Dilemma', *Victorian Studies*, vol.xix (1975), pp.51–71. For a good example of the combustible materials of religious and national antagonism at work in Wales in 1882, see Denvir, *Irish in Britain*, pp.296–314.
74. See Beck (ed.), *The English Catholics*, and, for a sympathetic portrait over a longer period, D. Mathew, *Catholicism in England, 1535–1935* (London, 1936). The outstanding recent account is J. Bossy, *The English Catholic Community, 1570–1850* (London, 1975).
75. For Manning, see V.A. McClelland, *Cardinal Manning: His Public Life and Influence, 1865–92* (London, 1962).
76. Sheridan Gilley, 'Heretic London, Holy Poverty and the Irish Poor, 1830–1870', *Downside Review*, vol.89 (1971), pp.64–89.
77. See Denvir, *Irish in Britain*. Also H.W. Benjamin, *The London Irish: a Study in Political Activism, 1870–1910* (unpublished Ph.D. Thesis, Princeton, 1976), and E.P.M. Woollaston, *The Irish Nationalist Movement in Great Britain, 1886–1908* (unpublished M.A. Thesis, University of London, 1958).
78. Denvir, *Life Story*, p.177.
79. There is a useful discussion of this in Alan O'Day, *The English Face of Irish Nationalism: Parnellite Involvement in British Politics, 1880–86* (Dublin, 1977), pp.108–25. See also H. Pelling, *The Social Geography of British Elections, 1885–1910* (London, 1967).
80. Nor should it be forgotten that T.P. O'Connor sat as an Irish Nationalist M.P. for the Scotland Division of Liverpool from 1885 to 1929.
81. N. Blewett, 'The Franchise in the United Kingdom, 1885–1918', *Past & Present*, no. 32 (1965), pp.27–56.
82. Thompson, *Making of the English Working Class*, pp.82, 146, 179, 183–8, 483–4, 523–6, 557–8, 632, 650, 653–5, 707, 771; R.G. Kirby and A.E. Musson, *The Voice of the People: a Biography of John Doherty, 1798–1854* (Manchester, 1975); Rachel O'Higgins, 'The Irish Influence in the Chartist Movement', *Past & Present*, no. 20 (1961), pp.83–96.
83. But for an early breakthrough, See Denvir, *Life Story*, pp.155–6, 172.
84. The writer hopes to explore some of these aspects of the subject in greater detail in a forthcoming work on British public opinion and Irish Home Rule in the Gladstonian era.
85. For a perceptive view of this dilemma, see T.W. Moody, 'Michael Davitt and the British Labour Movement, 1882–1906', *T.R.Hist.S.*, 5th. series, vol.iii (1953), pp.53–76.
86. B. Tillett, *Memories and Reflections* (London, 1931). See also H.A. Clegg, A. Fox and A.F. Thompson, *A History of British Trade Unions since 1889* (Oxford, 1964), vol.i, pp.55–96.
87. For which see the essays in C. Holmes (ed.), *Immigrants and Minorities*, and K. Lunn (ed.) *Hosts, Immigrants and Minorities*.

88. See Jackson, *Irish in Britain*, pp.97–8, 124.
89. L.J. McCaffrey, *Irish Nationalism and the American Contribution* (New York, 1976), and, particularly, T.N. Brown, *Irish–American Nationalism, 1870–1890* (Philadelphia, New York, 1966), pp.17–34, 178–81.

THE IRISH IN BRISTOL IN 1851: A CENSUS ENUMERATION

David Large

The Irish-born inhabitants of nineteenth-century Bristol have received no attention from historians, and the history of its nineteenth-century Catholicism has yet to be written. Nor did the Irish attract more than passing mention from contemporary observers. Andrew Carrick and John Addington Symonds (father of the well-known Victorian man of letters of the same name), two leading Bristol doctors, who compiled a medical topography of the city in 1833, referred to 'hordes of Irish adventurers' living among Bristol's poor and displaying a supremacy in the art of packing themselves into extremely exiguous accommodation. 'On one occasion', they wrote, 'it happened to us to discover that thirty individuals, on one night, slept in a room the measurements of which did not exceed 20ft. by 16. The people thus congregated were Irish; they chanced to be on their way from London to their native country. At that period cholera was hovering over us, and on the night to which we refer, it swooped down on nine out of the thirty, and seven became corpses in the course of a few hours.'[1] The well-known *Report on the State of the Irish Poor in Great Britain* of 1836 did not deign to mention the Bristol Irish, nor did Sir Henry de la Beche in his report on Bristol to the Health of Towns Commission in 1845.[2] George Clark, in his much more detailed inquiry of 1850 into the sanitary conditions of the city for the General Board of Health, made just a few casual references to the Irish living in very overcrowded cottages in Cannon's Court off Lewin's Mead in the parish of St. James and to the 'low Irish' as being particularly numerous in certain insalubrious houses in Marsh Street in the parish of St. Stephen.[3] But the Irish received not a mention in the 1,500 manuscript pages which record the proceedings of Bristol's Local Board of Health (1851-1872)[4], or in the lengthy *Report on the condition of the Bristol poor* of 1884 initiated by the Bristol press.[5]

Nonetheless, as Table i shows, the Irish-born were a sizeable minority throughout the nineteenth century:

Table i

Irish-born in Bristol[6]

Census year	Irish born	Total Population	% of Irish born
1841	4,039	122,296	3.3
1851	4,645	137,328	3.4
1861	4,363	154,093	2.8
1871	3,876	182,552	2.1
1881	3,204	206,874	1.5
1891	2,511	221,578	1.1

In the early Victorian age, the Bristol Irish were the largest Irish group throughout the south-west, south Wales and much of the midlands. When the first enumeration of the Irish-born was made in 1841 there were almost as many (4,039) as in Birmingham (4,683) or in the whole of Devon (4,084) and many more than in other ports in south-western and southern England such as Portsmouth (937), Southampton (420), Plymouth (1,000) and Devonport (1,302). Likewise in 1851, Bristol's 4,645 Irish-born outnumbered those in Newport (2,069), Merthyr Tydvil (3,051) and Swansea (1,333).[7]

The raw figures of Table i indicate that before the great hunger of the late forties in Ireland there was a sizeable Irish-born population in Bristol. Communication between Ireland and Bristol substantially improved in the 1820s: regular steam packet services were instituted between Bristol and Cork, Dublin and Waterford in 1821, 1822 and 1826 respectively.[8] Fares were low, and there was no great travelling obstacle to Irish migration. However the incentive to migrate, so forcibly posed by the Great Famine, which was particulary severe in Co. Cork from which so many of the Bristol Irish hailed, did *not* swell their numbers significantly. This was not surprising: Bristol's economy scarcely flourished in the first half of the nineteenth century. Nor did the city exert any great magnetic attraction as a source of employment in the latter half of the century, so that it is not surprising that its Irish-born population gradually declined both absolutely and as a proportion of the growing total population of the city.[9]

Since the Bristol Irish were relatively inconspicuous, it is far from easy to discover them. This essay is a sighting shot, and further investigation is needed if a full picture is to emerge. As the peak in numbers of the Irish-born in the city was recorded in the 1851 census, it seemed best to begin defining their characteristics from the returns of the census enumerators of that year. An attempt has therefore been made to collect the information in the surviving manuscript enumerator's books for *all* individuals whose birthplace was returned as Ireland. In all , information for 4,299 individuals was assembled. This falls a little short of the published figure of 4,645 in the printed volumes of the 1851 census, and one can only speculate why this is so. One possible explanation is that the notes in these volumes on the Bristol registration district refer to 770 persons on board vessels in the Floating Harbour and the river Avon being counted as living in the parish of St. Stephen. Enumerator's books for these do not appear to have survived. There may well have been numbers of Irish–born among them. Nevertheless 4,299 returns provided reasonably firm data for analysis.

Why was a sampling technique not adopted to lighten the labour? This was because it became apparent that there was no concentration of Irish in a limited district in Bristol among whom sampling could usefully be conducted. There was no Irish ghetto. While the Irish were concentrated in particular streets and courts, they were also widely scattered throughout the city, and spanned the whole range of class difference, from the two ladies who returned their occupations as 'earl's daughters' to the four individuals who said they were beggars. Morover, 'Irish–born' cannot be equated with 'Catholic'. The role of the smarter parts of Clifton as a holiday or retirement resort for the leisured classes complicates any examination of the Bristol Irish, since it housed a significant if indeterminate minority who were Protestants. There were more Irish–born Anglican clergy than Irish–born Roman Catholic priests among Bristol's Irish, and among the Irish–born were the headmaster of the city's 'blue coat' school, Queen Elizabeth's Hospital, the Principal of the Western Institution for the Deaf and Dumb and the proprietor of one of its leading newspapers,[10] all of whom were almost certainly Protestant.

If there was no 'little Ireland' in Bristol, where did the Irish live? The 'Bristol' of this essay is the municipal and parliamentary borough whose boundaries since 1835 were coterminous. Population growth outside these boundaries in 1851 was still small except in the Gloucestershire parishes of St. George with 8,905 inhabitants[11] and Stapleton with 4,840, of whom 1,387 were inmates of two large workhouses, so that it is realistic to regard the parliamentary and municipal borough in 1851 as 'Bristol'. In subsequent years this becomes less and less realistic, as the city's population increasingly spilled over its political boundaries, which were not extended significantly to take account of this until 1897.[12] For census purposes the municipal and parliamentary borough was covered by three registration districts: Bristol, no.329, Clifton, no.330, Bedminster, no.328.

Registration district [329] Bristol comprised the ancient city with its 18 parishes and one extra–parochial district (Castle Precincts). Almost two–thirds of the Irish–born (3,284) lived in the ancient city in 1851. Scarcely any lived in the small and well–to–do parishes in the commercial centre – none in St. Ewin or St. Mary–le–Port, only one each in St. Werburgh and All Saints, six in St. Leonard, twelve in St. Peter (excluding inmates of the Corporation of the Poor's hospital) and fourteen in St. Thomas, just south of Bristol bridge. Altogether, however, these seven parishes only numbered 3,636 inhabitants and the first five only mustered 658. If the remaining eleven parishes and one extra–parochial district are ranked in order of the greatest number of Irish among their inhabitants, it becomes clear that they had a distinct tendency to settle close to the waterfront of the Floating Harbour, particularly on its northern side, and to be more thinly scattered in the districts south of the harbour or east of the castle. Of the three parishes of about ten thousand inhabitants, the Irish were considerably more numerous in St. James (1,109) and St. Augustine the Less (475), which were closer to the harbour than St. Paul, which had only 177 Irish-born residents. Likewise the parishes of St. Michael and St. Stephen, the first with rather over 4,000 inhabitants and the second with rather less than 3,000, but both near the Floating Harbour, had 225 and 332 Irish respectively, while St. Philip and Jacob (within), east of the castle and comparable in population with St. Michael, had only 82. Temple (93) and St. Mary Redcliffe (79), both south of the harbour and with populations more than twice as great as St. Stephen, had fewer than one-third Irish.

Table ii summarizes the distribution by parish of the Irish in the ancient city:

Table ii

Parish	Population	Irish-born
All Saints	154	1
Augustine, St., the Less	9,891	475
Castle Precincts	1,825	48
Christchurch	1,079	102
Ewin, St.	52	nil
James, St. (within)	10,658	1,109
John, St.	1,190	51
Leonard, St.	123	6
Mary, St., le-Port	230	nil
Mary, St., Redcliffe	6,812	79
Michael, St.	4,431	226
Nicholas, St.	2,076	108
Paul, St. (within)	10,750	177
Peter, St.	1,000	12
Philip, St. and Jacob (within)	4,522	82
Stephen, St.	2,778	332
Temple	6.060	93
Thomas, St.	1,508	14
Werburgh, St.	99	1

Excluding 14 in St. Peter's Hospital

A glance at the very mixed registration district [no.330] of Clifton shows that it is easy to exaggerate the tendency of the Irish to live close to the harbour. The registration district stretched outside the boundaries of the municipal and parliamentary borough to Gloucestershire villages like Shirehampton, Westbury-on-Trym and Henbury, though the great bulk of its population in 1851 lived within the boundaries of the city and county of Bristol. This population included the wealthy parish of Clifton with 17,634 inhabitants, and, in dire contrast, what Mr. Chick, who had been its assistant overseer of the poor for twenty–three years, described in 1854 as 'the very poor parish'[13] of St. Philip and Jacob without, in east Bristol, with 24,961 residents. The Irish in the parish of Clifton numbered 580, while those in St. Philip and Jacob without totalled 419, to which should be added another 96 dwelling in the united out parish of St. James and St. Paul, which had a population of one–third of that of St. Philip and Jacob without. In short, there were appreciable numbers of Irish in the outer eastern and western parts of the city away from the harbour.

Finally part of the Somerset registration district of Bedminster, lying south of the New Cut in which the river Avon had flowed since the making of the Floating Harbour in the first decade of the nineteenth century, fell within the boundaries of the municipal and parliamentary borough of Bristol. In this very neglected district, there were 157 Irish–born.

There was, therefore, no single well–defined Irish ghetto in mid–nineteenth–century Bristol. Further analysis does show that in three parishes the Irish were heavily concentrated in particular streets and courts. In St. Stephen, Little Tower court with 65 Irish and Marsh Street, Marsh Street Court and Fountains Entry where 147 Irish dwelt contained two–thirds of the Irish in this parish (332). In St. Michael, Host Street sheltered 62 Irish, Narrow Lewins Mead 32 and Steep Street 41, that is over half the Irish in the parish (225). Likewise in St. James nearly half (511) of the 1,109 Irish lived in Lewins Mead (202) and six courts, Cannon (23), Greyfriars (30), Greyhound (51), Fox (147), King's Head (32) and Providence (26). But such a degree of concentration did not exist elsewhere in the city. The 419 Irish–born in the parish of St. Philip and Jacob without were spread over 106 streets, lanes and courts and the 580 in the parish of Clifton were to be found in 149 different locations.

But as might be expected from the occupational structure of the Irish, there was considerable correlation between the locations picked out by George Clark in his *Report to the General Board of Health on a preliminary inquiry into . . . the sanitary condition . . . of Bristol* in 1850 as being particularly filthy and insanitary, and many of the dwelling places of the Irish. When Clark inspected the parish of St. Augustine the Less he listed Lamb Street, Warren's Court, Anchor Lane, Stephen's Court and Limekiln Lane for adverse comment – as well as other streets and courts.[14] Lamb Street contained 25 Irish; Warren's Court 14; Anchor Lane 18; Stephen's Court 8; and Limekiln Lane 31. Clark's report and the census enumerator's returns together show that many Irish lived in streets and courts which had experienced the ravages of the cholera epidemic in Bristol in 1849. Nevertheless because the Irish were spread widely throughout the city as well as in a small number of miniature 'little Irelands', there was an appreciable number not dwelling in the most unhealthy parts of a city which in 1845, by the general mortality rate, had an unenviable record as the third most unhealthy provincial city in England next to Liverpool and Manchester.

Where did they hail from in Ireland? The only quantitative evidence arises from the practice of a considerable number of enumerators of recording not simply that an individual was born in Ireland but also in what county and in a few cases in what parish or town, although this last was too infrequently recorded to provide any statistically valid information. This was not the case with the naming of counties. 45% (1,936) of the Irish–born can be ascribed to their counties of origin. Table iii shows that just over half originated in Co. Cork and almost a quarter from Dublin and Waterford, demonstrating that the steam packet connections of Bristol with these three ports played a major role in Irish migration to Bristol. Clearly, too, there was an understandably heavy bias of migration from the south–west of Ireland: men from Connaught and Ulster were comparatively rare among the Bristol Irish.

Table iii

Counties of origin of Irish–born in Bristol in 1851

Cork	987	Kerry	43
Dublin	238	Belfast	38
Waterford	186	Wexford	29
Limerick	115	Down	26
Tipperary	79		

Counties with fewer than 25 entries have been omitted in the above
Total including counties with fewer than 25 entries 1,936
Total Irish born .4,299

The census enumerators' books show that 2,237 males of all ages born in Ireland returned themselves as following 392 separate occupations, on the principle that *any* difference in wording in the occupational column is counted as differentiating one occupation from another, however slight or non–existent the difference may seem today. The total also includes entries which should more properly be called status rather than job description, such as eleven who called themselves 'landholders', four who said they were 'gentlemen' and one each whose occupation was listed as 'fundholder' and 'railway shareholder'. It is difficult to devise a simple classification of these 392 occupations as a guide to Irish occupations, particularly since the classification used by the census takers of 1851 has many limitations and later recastings of it have not always been satisfactory either. What is presented in Table iv is an attempt to preserve the mid–Victorian flavour without resorting to the artificial devices of the 1851 census takers, as in classifying occupations by the materials such as wood, iron, wool etc. used by practitioners.

Table iv

Occupations of male Irish (all ages)

Occupations	number	of total (2,237)
Labouring and portering (all types)	813	36%
Tradesmen	363	16%
Domestic Servants (including errand boys, gardeners and wheel–chairmen)	87	4%
Hawking, dealing, selling, travelling, scavenging and begging	75	3%
Commercial pursuits excluding hawking, etc.	48	2%
Professional men	42	2%
Armed services, including pensioners	39	2%
Seamen (all types)	33	1%
Government and local officials including retired	28	1%
Others	745	33%

Another way of describing the occupations most commonly followed by Irishmen is to list them in rank order beginning with the commonest and excluding any occupation followed by less than ten of them, as indicated by Table v.

Table v

Rank order of occupations of the male Irish (all ages)

Occupation	Number of Irish	Occupation	Number of Irish
Labourer	397	Mariner	17
Mason's Labourer	155	Quay porter	17
Tailor	101	Errand boy	16
General Labourer	54	Hawker	14
Shoemaker	32	Cattle dealer	12
Quarry Labourer	31	Porter	12
Gardener	24	Plasterer	12
Farm Labourer	22	Accountant	11
Mason	24	Sawyer	11
Carpenter	20	Landholder	11
Chelsea Pensioner	20	Hatter	10
Journeyman Tailor	19	Clerk	10
Servant (general)	18	Ship's labourer	10

Labouring and portering were predictably the chief occupations of Irishmen in Bristol, even though only three of them described themselves as 'navigators'. Indeed, in addition to the labouring and portering occupations pursued by more than ten Irishmen in Table v there were another 115 labourers and porters distributed in packets of fewer than ten who added their place of work or their employer's occupation to the designation 'labourer' or 'porter'. Some of these men can be ascribed a niche, however, humble, in Bristol's industries and enterprises, such as the nine Irishmen who were labourers at sugar refineries, seven at the Gas Works, three at a timber yard, two at a soap factory and one each at a vinegar works, a fruit warehouse, a vitriol works and a steam packet yard. Only small numbers of Irishmen found employment in the characteristically 'modern' enterprises of mid–Victorian industry – eight in engineering, seven with the railways, five in cotton, two in coal and one as an iron founder. On the other hand, few were involved in declining activities: there were just two Irish male handloom weavers and five nailmakers in Bristol.

If an Irishman was not a labourer or porter he was likely to be a tradesman, working at the cheap end of the trade where rewards were likely to be low. 121 Irishmen stated their occupation as tailoring. They formed one in ten of Bristol's male tailors, and it was by far the most popular trade among Irishmen. Only one of the 121 tailors called himself a master tailor and only 19 said they were journeymen. Irish shoemakers (32), masons (24), carpenters (20), plasterers (12), sawyers (11), hatters (11), cordwainers (8), were to be found in smaller numbers, but masters and journeymen were few and far between among them. No Irishman described himself as a master carpenter, joiner, cordwainer, painter or plasterer and of the 363 tradesmen only six were masters, thirty–four journeymen (nineteen of these were tailors) and six apprentices. In short, even in the clothing and building trades in which the Irish chiefly figured, they seem to have occupied a fairly humble position. There were also important trades in the city, often followed by several hundreds of people, in which the Irish were not numbered, or only to a very small extent, as Table vi illustrates:

Table vi

Number of Irishmen in selected trades[15]

Trades	Males employed (all ages)	Number of Irish
Bakers and confectioners	832	2
Blacksmiths	687	4
Brassfounders	168	nil
Butchers	529	9
Cabinet Makers and upholsterers	506	7
Coachmakers	315	3
Coal miners	321	1

Coopers	369	3
Grocers	639	3
Hairdressers	150	nil
Printers	273	1
Ropemakers	188	nil
Shipwrights and ship-builders	482	1
Watchmakers	155	1
Wheelwrights	116	1

Some features of male occupations deserve brief comment. First, the considerable part played by the Irish-born in the British army is certainly reflected in the numbers of Bristol Irish Chelsea pensioners (20), and to these should be added a couple of Greenwich pensioners and one from Woolwich, not to mention five half-pay army officers, a staff sergeant and three soldiers. Secondly, as some evidence that Irish birth was not such a barrier, as has sometimes been suggested, to acceptance in English society, seven Bristol Irish had become policemen in the recently formed borough police, and one had gained admission to the new railway police. Thirdly, and no doubt largely and probably exclusively drawn from the Protestant Irish, there were men of some social standing among the Bristol Irish – eleven who described them as landholders, four who said they were 'gentlemen', a Vice-Admiral R.N., a banker, four East India Company pensioners and perhaps most unusual of all, Samuel Lover, painter, song-writer, novelist, author of *Handy Andy*, living with his daughter at 29 Royal York Crescent, Clifton.

The range of occupations pursued by Irish women was much smaller than for Irish men, and proportionately fewer of them had occupations other than 'domestic duties', to use the term sometimes listed in the enumerator's books in the occupation column, usually in reference to married women. 871 Irish-born women of all ages returned themselves as having 131 separate occupations, using the same definition of a separate occupation as was used for the men. Table vii seeks to classify the 131 occupations and to indicate the proportions of women engaged in each category:

Table vii

Occupations of female Irish (all ages)

Occupation	Number	% of total (871)
Servants (all types)	305	35
Charwomen, laundress, washer-women Ironer and mangler	161	18
Dressmaker, tailoress, seamstress, milliner and allied occupations	126	15
Annuitants, fundholders, gentlewomen, landed		

proprietors and others subsisting on unearned income	89	10
Hawking, dealing, selling, travelling, scavenging and begging	52	6
Trades	36	4
Nurses and midwives	19	2
Others	85	10

Another way of indicating the occupational structure of the female Irish is to list their occupation in rank order beginning with the commonest and excluding any occupation followed by fewer than ten Irish women. Table viii sets out the result.

Table viii

Rank order of the occupations of the female Irish (all ages)

Occupation	Number of Irish	Occupation	Number of Irish
Servant	136	Seamstress	19
House Servant	93	Nurse	17
Charwoman	63	Lodginghouse Keeper	16
Laundress	59	Fruit Seller	13
Annuitant	45	Gentlewoman	13
Dressmaker	39	Housekeeper	12
Washerwoman	33	Fundholder	12
General Servant	30	Hawker	11
Tailoress	26	Landed Proprietor	11

Domestic service was predictably the chief occupation of Irish women, dividing approximately one third as house servants living–in with their employers and two thirds at their own homes or in lodging houses, thus bearing out a recent observation of Dr. Higgs that many domestic servants, contrary to the popular image, did not live in the homes of paying employers.[16] Nearly every species of domestic servant was represented among Irish women, but it was only a small minority who described themselves by the terms in general use among the middle and upper classes such as 'parlour maid' or 'lady's maid', the great majority being content to call themselves 'servant', 'house servant' or 'general servant', which suggests that the one Irish woman who called herself 'a maid of all work' was probably describing accurately what most Irish domestics in fact did.

In some respects the occupational pattern of Irish women resembled that of women in general in Bristol. Domestic service employed far and away the largest number of women in the city, followed by the business of washing clothes and cleaning houses, as was the case with Irish women. There was also a considerable workforce employed in the Bristol rag trade, particularly millinery, which occupied 3,378 women, but in this trade Irish women were scarcely noticeable – only nine described themselves as milliners. Indeed, the paucity of Irish women practising a trade is noteworthy. Shoemaking employed 1,508 women in the city and among them there were only eleven Irish, yet this was the trade with the largest number of Irish women. There was virtually no evidence that Irish women entered the professions. There were 687 schoolmistresses and governesses in Bristol in 1851: only one was Irish–born. The great majority of Irish women who declared an occupation probably occupied the lowest range of the employment ladder, the one exception being most of those living off rents, dividends and annuities, the majority of whom had Clifton addresses and were most probably Anglo–Irish Protestants.

It is misleading, however, to consider Irish women solely in terms of their occupation, for though so many of them were married to men of low earning power, particularly labourers and porters, they were rarely able to supplement the family income by work outside the home. No fewer than 792 Irish–born wives had no occupation other than 'domestic duties', while 21 of the 871 who stated an occupation did so by a status statement such as 'labourer's wife', 'sailor's wife', 'clockseller's wife', 'valet's wife', 'gentleman's wife' and so forth. The number of Irish women who returned no occupation was also swelled by a considerable number of elderly women usually living with grown–up children supporting them, and by an appreciable number of daughters of working age who seem to have been absorbed in domestic duties or, in some Clifton families, in the social round pending marriage. It was a minority rather than a majority of Irish women who had a job , however humble.

Finally, children should also be taken into account in any consideration of Irish occupations. Did Irish children work, or go to school, or neither? A preliminary problem is how to define a child. The age at which attendance at school might be expected has to be decided and also the age at which a child ceases to be one. Should just those children who were born in Ireland be considered or in addition those born in Britain but of Irish parentage? It seemed reasonable in the light of contemporary assumptions to fix the years 5–12 inclusive as constituting childhood, and to include children of this age–range born in Britain as well as those born in Ireland, provided one or both parents were Irish–born. Table ix sets out the proportion of children so defined who were at work, in the sense of having an occupation in the relevant column in the enumerator's book, those who were designated scholars, those called 'scholars at home', those who were pupils at a boarding school, and those who had no occupation and were not designated either scholars or pupils, it being assumed that such children were not on the rolls of any school.

Table ix

Educational and work experience of Irish children aged 5–12

Category	Number	% of total (1,171)
At work	43	4
Scholars	567	48
Scholars at home	27	2
Pupils at boarding school	20	2
No occupation and neither scholar nor pupil	514	44

Remarkably few Irish children were reported to the census takers as having a job, and of the 43 who were so returned, fifteen were errand boys, ten were servants (eight of them girls), nine were labourers and four were beggars, hawkers or scavengers. The remaining five included an apprentice, a match seller, a charwoman and just two girls who probably worked in Bristol's cotton mill and were described as cotton weavers. Evidently opportunities for employment for Irish children were very limited. Nor can it be said that they were all dutifully attending school. Table ix shows a substantial number were returned to the census–takers as 'at home' rather than as scholars, that is on a school roll. Furthermore, if we are to believe Mary Carpenter, a highly prejudiced witness who resented the way in which the Catholic school in Trenchard Street drew Irish children away from the Ragged Schools and the reformatory institution with which she was associated, there were many Irish children on the school roll who did not attend school. Her evidence to the parliamentary Select Committee on the Education of Destitute Children in 1861 painted a fearsome picture of these children. They were, she said 'the very lowest class of population which can be found anywhere', containing 'some of the lowest and most active class of juvenile offenders', according to a Bristol police investigator. The master at the Trenchard Street school told Mary Carpenter that he could do little with the younger children who lived with their parents in clans in Host and Marsh streets which were 'no go' areas for the police. The children often deserted school, sometimes to go hop–picking in the surrounding countryside, and when the priest provided clothes for the children to come to school their parents promptly pawned them. Mary Carpenter believed that what the children needed was not instruction in the 3Rs but 'moral and religious instruction to teach them to labour and feel a pleasure in labouring'.[17]

In fact it would appear that the opportunities for labouring were not great, as analysis of the work pattern of young people (13–18 years old) from Irish households suggests. Almost a half of the girls of this age group either had no occupations or remained at school and the same was true of a third of the boys. As Table x shows, for those who had work there is no sign among the girls that the jobs they did differed in any way from those of adult women. The most popular was domestic service. The same was broadly true of the boys, labouring being the most usual occupation.

Table x

Occupations of young people (13–18 yrs.) in Irish households

Occupation	Male Number	Male % of whole (308)	Female Occupation	Female Number	Female % of Whole (292)
None	50	16	None	113	39
Scholar	48	16	Scholar	30	10
Labourer	60	19	Servant	50	17
Errand boy	16	5	Tailoress	11	4
Mason's labourer	10	3	Dressmaker	11	4
Porter	8		Laundress	7	2
Others	101	33	Others	70	24

The census not only provides much basic information on Irish occupations but also on the structure of the Irish household. Thus it enables us to be precise about intermarriage. Did Irish men or women frequently or only rarely marry natives of Britain or were the overwhelming bulk of marriages between Irish folk? If there was much intermarriage it was more likely that the 'Irish' characteristics of the Irish in Bristol would be considerably diluted, at least in time. To investigate this, the number of marriages made by the Irishborn has to be ascertained in order to obtain an index of the popularity of marriage among the Irish. Were there many single Irish men or women? And what about the frequent allegations that the Irish produced large families? Did they generally live as a nuclear or as an extended family or was the characteristic unit a nuclear family with a lodger or two? To what extent was 'home' for many Irish, a place in some wretched, insanitary and overcrowded lodging house? The census can at least provide hard if limited information on these matters.

In investigating the marital state of the Irish, it has been assumed that the marriageable population among them consisted of the 2,778 of the total of 4,299 who returned their ages as 18 or over, since no example has been found of anyone marrying below that age although there are instances of individuals marrying at 18. Table xi summarizes the various categories into which the 2,878 naturally fall.

Table xi

Marital condition of the Irish in Bristol in 1851

Category	Number		% of total existing marriages (1,420)	% of total 18 years and over (2,778)
Irish-born married to Irish-born	707		50	25
Irish-born men married to non-Irish born wives	290			
Irish-born women married to non-Irish born husbands	199	489	49	18
Irish-born men on whom there is no data on the birthplace of their wives	95		7	3
Irish-born women on whom there is no data on the birthplace of their husbands	129		9	5
Total of existing marriages	1,420			
Irish-born widows	321			
Irish-born widowers	122	433		16
Unmarried Irish-born men of 18 and over	408			
Unmarried Irish-born women of 18 and over	517	925		33

Total number of single and previously married . . .1,358
Total number of all Irish-born of 18 years and over . . .2,778

As the table shows, two–thirds (67%) of the Irish in Bristol married,[18] although 16% had suffered a dissolution of marriage by death, an experience three times as likely to be experienced by women as men, so that there was an appreciable population of Irish widows. A break–down by age of these 321 widows – almost one in twelve of the whole Irish population – shows that a high proportion (62%) were 50 or over. In mid–Victorian conditions this meant that they were elderly, and were often unable to earn a living. The most aged, Catherine McGrath, claimed to be 91. These elderly Irish women were often dependent for support and lived with their children. How some of the children managed to support an elderly widow, given that the children were often low–earning labourers or porters, beggars the imagination, but somehow they did, for only a small percentage of the Irish were in receipt of poor relief and, as Table xii shows, many Irish widows lived to a considerable age:

Table xii

Irish–born widows by age cohort

Age	Number	% of total number of widows (321)
20–29	17	5
30–39	14	13
40–49	63	20
50–59	75	23
60–69	83	26
70–79	34	11
80–89	6	2
90 and over	2	–

A striking feature of the marital pattern of the Irish in Bristol was the high degree of intermarriage between the Irish and the non–Irish. For those marriages in which the birthplace of both partners is known and the marriage had not yet been broken by death – 1,196 in all – 707 were between Irishmen and Irish women but no fewer than 489 were matches in which only one partner was Irish. Irish males showed a greater disposition to find non–Irish partners than Irish women. In many cases it was a matter of an Irishman marrying a Bristol girl or one born in one of Bristol's neighbouring counties. The extent of this intermarriage must cast doubt on notions that English hostility to the Irish was so great that they were beyond the pale. Yet some qualification is necessary. There were particular parishes in which marriages between Irish–born men and women were a good deal commoner than elsewhere. Nearly two–thirds (61%) of these 707 matches were to be found among the Irish in the four parishes close to the Floating Harbour of St. Augustine, St. Michael, St. James and St. Stephen, while there were relatively few in Clifton, St. Mary Redcliffe and St. Paul . Intermarriage with the natives, as might be expected, was more common in parishes where the Irish were less concentrated in particular streets or courts.

The Census therefore throws light on the household structure of the Irish as it was in 1851, although to report the result succinctly is far from easy since the variety of living patterns was substantial. At one extreme, a single person household was that of Anna O'Lochlan, a 57 year–old widow who was born in Loughrea, Co. Galway, gave her occupation as laundress and lived at 6 Marlborough Hill, St. James. At the furthest extreme, in Pithay, St. James, there lived Bartholomew Murphy of Irish birth, head of a household with no fewer than 41 persons on the census schedule which was not treated as an institution. These 41 included Bartholomew's wife and mother, two servants, a cousin and thirty–five lodgers, a dozen of whom were Irish; the rest were a party of German musicians visiting Bristol. Thus, the number of categories into which households can be grouped is considerable.

First, an Irish household has to be defined: it is taken to be one in which the head for census purposes is Irish–born and includes in it all the individuals who are named on the census schedule, whether born in Ireland or not. By this definition there is left on one side a considerable number of Irish (698) who did not live in an Irish household. They can be categorised, as Table xiii indicates.

Table xiii

Irish dwelling in non–Irish households

Category	Number
Irish lodgers in non–Irish households	268
Irish wives of non–Irish heads of house–holds	199
Irish servants living in non–Irish households	154
Irish visitors in non–Irish house–holds	81
Irish relatives living in non–Irish households	96
Total	798

The Irish not living in Irish households represented 16% of the whole Irish population in Bristol (4,299) and it is particularly note–worthy how many of them were to be found lodging in non–Irish households. Fewer than twice as many (451 as against 268) lodged in Irish households, thus providing further evidence that there was not such a rigid separation between the Irish and the local inhabitants as has often been claimed.

The Irish households themselves totalled 1,292. Table xiv sets out the basic facts about the types of household which existed and their proportions to the total.

Table xiv

Types of Irish households

Type	Number	% of the whole (1,292)
Single persons	83	6
Irish husbands and their wives only	162	13
Irish one–parent families	166	13
Irish husbands and their wives and children	477	37
Irish households with co–resident kin	151	12
Irish households with lodgers	169	13
Irish households with visitors	90	7
Irish households with lodgers and visitors	15	1
Irish households with co–resident kin and lodgers	33	3
Irish households with co–resident kin and visitors	24	2
Irish households with co–resident kin, lodgers and visitors	5	–
Total households		1,292

It is immediately striking to find the conventional nuclear family making up only a minority (37%) of all households. On the one hand there were substantial numbers of households lacking either children (162) or one parent (166) or consisting of single persons (83), making up 32% of the whole and, on the other, complex households containing various combinations of lodgers, visitors and co–resident kin as well as an Irish head of household, which represented 38% of the whole. Quite clearly there was no typical Irish household but a great variety of patterns, for reasons which it is easy to propose but which are difficult to pin down with precise evidence.

Certainly between 20 and 30 of the larger more complex households represent enterprises in the form of lodging houses run and patronised by the Irish, particularly by single male labourers. It is also probable that some of the households swelled by lodgers were temporary extensions of the nuclear family providing shelter for couples, sometimes with a young child, who had yet to find a home of their own. In other cases it seems likely that the presence of lodgers indicated a need by the host family to supplement its income. The total number of Irish households with lodgers is 222, 17% of the total, a percentage much in line with Professor Lees's finding for her London sample (18.5%) which, as she remarked, was much higher than that for the native population in the metropolis yet lower than that found by Professor Anderson's investigation of the industrial town of Preston.[19] As for the presence of co-resident kin in the Irish households – so often the result of the destruction of a nuclear family by the death of the wage earner – the proportion containing kin was almost the same as those with lodgers (213 or 16%). This was a little higher than the proportion in the London Irish sample (13%) but much below figures for Preston (23%), York (22%) or the native population of London (19%).[20] About twice as many co-resident kin were in the 15–45 age bracket, with almost equal numbers of under 15s and over 45s. Certainly it was more likely that additional members of Irish households would be lodgers or co-resident kin than servants. Only 10% (124) of Irish households could afford to keep servants, a figure which was, however, almost twice as high as among the London Irish.[21]

Just under three-quarters (915 or 71%) of the Bristol Irish households were headed by a married man and just under a quarter (281 or 22%) by a woman, the remaining 96 (7%) by a single man, figures which compare fairly closely with the London Irish sample, although the percentage of women heading households in Bristol was significantly higher at 22% than the figure of 17% in the capital.[22] Two-thirds of the females heading households were widows (186 or 66%) the rest being nearly equally divided between single women (40 or 14%) and married women (55 or 20%), some of whom indicated that their husbands were sailors and away from home on census day. Most of the widows dwelt with their unmarried children, either young or adult, and it was rare to find a widow living alone without kin, lodgers or visitors.

What of the size of the Irish household? Taking first the nuclear family – parents and children only – it would be wrong to imagine a typical Irish family as large. If a nuclear family of 6 and over (including the parents) deserves this description, a mere 194 or 15% fell into this category. 85% consisted of 5 persons or less. It would, of course, be incorrect to suggest that this tells us much about fertility among the Irish in Bristol. Plainly the hazards of child-rearing in such an unhealthy place as mid-Victorian Bristol must have led to the truncating of Irish families by premature death, but on what scale it is impossible to say, such is the difficulty of obtaining satisfactory vital statistics for the Bristol Irish.

Household size, swelled by co-resident kin, lodgers and visitors, was on average significantly greater than for the nuclear family. But, the proportion of large households of 6 persons or more was not very great (385 or 30%), still leaving 70% of households consisting of 5 persons or fewer, and if we take 8 or more as a very large household, then this percentage falls to 12%.

Having examined where the Irish in Bristol lived, where they came from in Ireland, what jobs they had and the structure of their households, it is possible to consult the census returns for further clues to the Irish impact on Bristol. It is apparent that the Irish made no serious inroads into either rate–financed poor relief or privately funded charity. In the census year 1851 there were four workhouses which catered for the destitute of Bristol. The Bedminster Union, which included that part of Bedminster within the municipal and parliamentary boundaries of Bristol, had its workhouse at Farleigh in Long Ashton parish immediately to the west of the city; Clifton Union had established a large house at Stapleton some three miles from the city centre, and so had the Bristol Corporation of the Poor which had administered poor relief in the ancient city since 1696, where it also had St. Peter's Hospital which was used for the destitute sick, the mentally ill and the able–bodied destitute.[23] The Irish were not conspicuous for their number in any of these institutions in 1851, as Table xv indicates.

Table xv

Irish on indoor relief, 1851

Workhouse	Number of paupers	Number of paupers who were Irish
Bedminster (Farleigh)	311	3 (1%)
Clifton (Stapleton)	641	10 (2%)
Bristol (St. Peter's Hospital)	246	14 (6%)
	1,916	49 (2.5%)
Subtract paupers with unrecorded birth places	224	
	1,692	49 (3%)

The number of Irish returned to the census enumerators as paupers on outdoor relief was also small, only 53 of 4,299 or just over 1% of all the Irish, and if one adds to these those on indoor relief enumerated above (49), we have a total of 102 (2% of all the Irish) in receipt of aid from the poor rates. Such figures, if reliable, scarcely justify any accusation that poverty–stricken Irish folk were eating ratepayers out of house and home.[24]

Nor, with one significant exception, were they making inroads into the resources of philanthropy. None of the residents in Bristol's almshouses was Irish. The same was true of the 299 'orphan scholars' in Muller's famous orphanage, and the 40 inmates of the Ashley Hill orphan asylum, while among the 299 residents of the New Orphange, Ashley Down, there were just two Irish girls. There was just one Irish charity boy at Pennywell Road Industrial School, none among the 27 residents of the Western Institution for the Deaf and Dumb in Park Row and only two out of 30 patients at the city's General Hospital. At the other older and larger voluntary hospital, the

Bristol Royal Infirmary, however, 19 of the 231 patients were Irish and, most strikingly, of the 52 inmates of the Refuge for the Homeless Poor, in St. John's parish, 14 were Irish. No doubt this was a sign of extreme poverty among the Bristol Irish, as was the fact that of the 1,819 clients for whom the Bristol and Clifton Mendicity Society provided meals during 1851, 721 were Irish–born.[25]

While the Irish in Victorian Britain often had an unenviable reputation as law–breakers, there is not much evidence to substantiate this from the census returns of the inhabitants of Bristol's gaols. Of the 184 prisoners in Bristol gaol (situated in the Bedminster registration district), only eight were Irish–born, five women and three men; two of the 24 prisoners at Lawfords Gate prison were Irish and four out of the 52 held at the city's Bridewell. Such evidence is insufficient as a measure of the degree to which the Irish broke the law and reflects the limitations of the whole investigation of the 4,299 Bristol Irish through the census returns.

A little more information can be gleaned from the separate religious and education census of 1851, though it has to be noted that the manuscript versions of the religious returns for Bristol have not been preserved at the P.R.O., leaving only the bare facts of the printed return.[26] This shows that the Catholic Church in Bristol could provide chapel accommodation. In the coterminous municipal and parliamentary borough there were seven Catholic chapels, three in the ancient city and four in the Clifton registration district, which were returned as having 2,254 sittings. That this was insufficient to accommodate all the Catholics in the city is clear from the morning attendance figure of 2,782. Nevertheless, the shortfall was by no means substantial, and it is probably a fair inference that a considerable proportion of the Bristol Irish were provided with the means of worship if they so desired, and the attendance figures suggest that many did so, though it needs to be remembered that there was certainly an English Catholic body in the city of long standing and of by no means negligible if indeterminate size.[27] There were also Catholic visitors to Clifton: indeed, one of them, Mrs. Charlton, a Northumbrian gentlewoman, in the late 1850s commented most disparagingly on her fellow worshippers: 'I never knew', she wrote, 'to what degree of perfection Irish filth could be raised until I visited the Hibernian colony in Bristol, and duplicity went hand in hand with dirt'.[28] As for schools, the provision according to the census appears not very satisfactory.[29] There were only five Catholic schools, four in the ancient city and one in the Clifton registration district, and scholars on the books numbered 564, a figure which corresponds very closely with the number of 5–12 year olds returned as 'scholars' in the enumerators' books (567) which, as we have seen, leaves almost as many in this age group (514) who were neither scholars nor had a specific occupation.

In essence, this examination of the 1851 census provides a snapshot of the Bristol Irish at a particular time. The census returns of 1861, 1871 and 1881 need to be analysed to explore the changes they underwent as time passed on. Was there any change in their geographical location? Was there any evidence of upward social mobility? Did they become better educated? Were there fewer general labourers and domestic servants among them? These are but a few of the questions which further research might illuminate. Needless to say there is much scope for extending this survey by investigating the records of the Catholic Church in Bristol.[30] Similarly, no firm conclusions can be reached about the relations of the Irish with the law without considering the evidence from the police and the courts. Finally, there remains the enormous task of combing the extensive Bristol press for evidence of the role of the Irish within the city[31] and of how others saw them.

Notes

1. A. Carrick and J.A. Symonds, 'Medical Topography of Bristol', *Transactions of the Provincial Medical and Surgical Association*, vol.2, no.2 (1833), p.168.
2. Sir Henry T. de la Beche, *Report on the state of Bristol and other large towns* (London,1845).
3. G.T. Clark, *Report to the General Board of Health . . . on Bristol* (London,1845), pp.22, 67.
4. Extracts from these will appear in a forthcoming volume of the Bristol Records Society.
5. *Report of the Committee to inquire into the condition of the Bristol Poor presented to the Bishop of the Diocese* (London,1885).
6. The 1841 figure is to be found in the *Census of Ireland*, 1841, Appendix to the Report of the Commissioners, p.lxxxciii and the remaining figures in the Census of Great Britain.
7. *Census of Ireland* (1841), Appendix, p.lxxxviii.
8. G. Farr, *West country passenger steamers*, 3nd edn. (Prescot, Lancs., 1967), Ch.2.
9. For a review of the economic development of Bristol see B.W.E. Alford, 'The economic development of Bristol in the nineteenth century: an enigma?' in P. McGrath and J. Cannon (eds.), *Essays in Bristol and Gloucestershire History* (Bristol,1976), pp.252–283.
10. This was Joseph Leech, owner of the *Bristol Times* for whom see A. Sutton, (ed.), *Rural rides of the Bristol Churchgoer* (Gloucester 1982), pp.ix–xiii.
11. There were only 19 Irish–born in this parish in 1851.
12. For an analysis of this process see F. Hewitt, *Population and Urban Growth in East Bristol, 1800–1914* (unpublished Ph.D. thesis, University of Bristol, 1965).
13. *Select Committee on Medical Relief*, *P.P.* (1854), vol.xii, p.78. Mr. Chick said that average wages in the parish were 10/– to 15/– a week and the 10/– a week man would pay 1s 9d to 2/– a week rent.
14. G.T. Clark, *Report*, pp.58–60.
15. Figures from Census of Great Britain (1851).
16. E. Higgs, 'Domestic servants and households in Victorian England', *Social History*, vol.8, no.2, p.205.

17. *Select Committee on the education of destitute children, P.P.* (1861), vol.vii, pp.96–103.
18. This figure corresponded closely with the marital condition of the inhabitants of Bristol and Clifton registration districts as a whole. 70% of those of 20 years and upwards were either married or had been married.
19. Lynn Hollen Lees, *Exiles of Erin* (Manchester 1979), p.135.
20. *Ibid.*, p.134.
21. *Ibid.*
22. *Ibid.*, p.130.
23. One of the barriers to further investigation of poor relief in Bristol is that the records of the Poor Law Unions covering the city were eventually centralized at St. Peter's Hospital which was totally destroyed in the blitz.
24. Of course the impact of the Irish on poor relief is not exhausted by the above observations e.g. Thomas Rankin, Governor of St. Peter's Hospital, reported in 1834, that the Corporation of the Poor had the burden of either returning back to Ireland destitute Irish emigrants who wound up in Bristol or at times, because it was cheaper, giving them temporary relief. (See *Report of The Poor Law Commissioners, P.P.* (1834), vol.xxxviii(i), p.61.
25. *Bristol Mirror*, 21 February 1852, quoting the Annual Report of the Society for 1851.
26. Census of Great Britain (1851), Religious Worship, England and Wales.
27. Some evidence of this is provided by the *Registers of St. Joseph's Chapel, Trenchard Lane (now Street), Bristol 1777–1808* published by the Catholic Record Society, vol.iii (1806), pp.181–329.
28. L.E.O. Charlton, *The Recollections of a Northumbrian Lady* (London,1949), p.228.
29. *Census of Great Britain* (1851), Education, England and Wales.
30. Recently these have been listed by Miss Judith Close, formerly of the Bristol Record Office. She has been engaged on their study for some years.
31. Not to mention newspaper sources outside the city, e.g. *Northern Star*, 10 January 1848, tells us that there was an Irish Confederate Club in Bristol called the *Erin–go–Bragh* Club which met at Rebbeck's Coffee and Reading Rooms, 1 Tower Hill, Old Market.

THE IRISH IN YORK

Frances Finnegan

This study of the Irish in Victorian York, in common with other recent works on post–Famine Irish communities in Britain and America, examines aspects of immigrant life which have been neglected by historians who have accepted the nineteenth–century view of the anti–social behaviour of the Celt. It attempts, by measuring the real extent of Irish contribution to crime and Poor Law expenditure in the city, by examining the total Irish community at each census over a thirty year period and by looking at all the evidence available, to achieve a more balanced insight into the lives of this particular sub–section of the poor, who, apart from the enumerators' notebooks (the only source in which they appear in their entirety) are on record largely as paupers or delinquents. This evidence is examined against the background of prejudice which the immigrants undoubtedly encountered in their new surroundings, and their continuing poverty.

I

Immigration

Before 1846, there was little to distinguish York's small pre–Famine Irish community from the rest of the population. At the 1841 census out of 28,842 inhabitants, 430 were born in Ireland, and a further 351 individuals, married to or children of the latter, formed part of the immigrant community, which was 2.7 percent of the population. In this year the Irish were distributed throughout all but one of York's thirty–four parishes, yet there were already noticeable concentrations of immigrants in the poorest, most unhealthy and most notorious areas, including Walmgate, Hungate and the Water Lanes. Thus 21.5 percent lived in St. Margaret's parish and 15.6 percent in the neighbouring parishes of St. George and St. Dennis. All three were in the Walmgate district. At the same time, more than 15 percent lived close by in the adjacent Hungate parishes of St. Saviour, St. Crux, All Saints Peaseholme and St. Cuthbert. Other areas which were subsequently to show marked degrees of Irish settlement such as the Bedern, parts of Aldwark and the fringes of St.

Maurice and St. Lawrence, were merely extensions of this group of congested parishes in the south–eastern quarter of the city, most of which bordered, at least in part, the unwholesome river Foss, and contained some of the worst slums in York. This Irish concentration was even more apparent in individual streets and courts, which after the arrival of the Famine victims, were to be taken over by the immigrants. Until the late 1840s, however, the Irish formed only a small percentage of York's poor, so that even in St. Margaret's, where they were most numerous, they were less than 14 percent of the total parish population.

The pre–Famine Irish were employed in a wide variety of occupations, 77 different types of employment being listed for males and 19 for females. The only single occupation accounting for a significant proportion of their number, however, was that of labourer, 60 individuals being labourers (21.8 percent of occupied males). These represented only 7.6 percent of the 787 unspecified labourers in the city. Fewer than 18 percent of Irish females were employed, and of the 2,175 women in domestic service in York, only 13 were Irish, the next most numerous occupation being nuns (7), labourers (6) and hawkers (6).

At this time there was a far greater degree of inter–marriage between the two communities than was afterwards the case. Of the 280 married persons listed on the census, 40 marriages (28.6 percent) were between partners who were both Irish–born; 59 marriages (43.1 percent) were between Irish males and non–Irish females and 29 marriages (20.7 percent) were between Irish females and non–Irish males. The remainder had no birthplace listed or the spouse was absent.

The immigrants were represented in every social class, with 2.6 percent belonging to Class I, 6.1 percent to Class II, 48.5 percent to Class III, 12.2 percent to Class IV and 26.4 percent to Class V. Although the Irish in the city were living largely in overcrowded conditions (31 percent of the total were crammed into cottages containing 15 or more persons), out of a total of 198 houses occupied by Irish people, almost 60 percent were shared with non–Irish residents – a proportion which was to decline drastically with the successive waves of post–Famine immigration. A significant difference between the two communities was family size, with the Irish having a higher proportion of larger families – 16.9 percent containing more than six individuals, compared with only 7.7 percent for the population as a whole.

Analysis of the Guardians' Application and Report Books for 1840/41 shows that out of a total of 1,674 applications, only 46 (2.7 percent) were identified as Irish – the same proportion as was the immigrant community of the total population of the city. Applications were made for a variety of reasons such as funeral expenses, destitution through disability, absence of husband, sickness and infirmity, and as such were similar to non–Irish applications. The vast majority stemmed from poor parishes, and the greater part of these were concentrated, whatever the birthplace of the applicant, around what were soon to be the main areas of Irish settlement – most notably from Walmgate itself. As for crime, of the 206 offenders brought before the magistrates and reported in the weekly newspapers, only seven were identified from the enumerators' notebooks as Irish (3.4 percent), indicating that, though these figures were small, the early immigrants' recorded criminality was already slightly disproportionate.

Thus in the immediate pre–Famine period, the small Irish community in the city differed little from the rest of York's population. The immigrants, though scattered, were mainly to be found in the slums in overcrowded, unhealthy conditions, similar to those of the non–Irish poor. They were employed in a variety of occupations, were represented in all social classes and the extent to which they married and lived with non–Irish persons indicates a fair degree of assimilation. Though Irish beggars were often brought before the magistrates, this community posed no more of a problem for the Poor Law Guardians than did the non–Irish poor. Most of these characteristics were to alter within the next decade.

By 1847 the increasing numbers of sick and destitute Irish passing through York began to alarm the authorities, who complained that about 45 persons daily were now being given assistance. Many of these were suffering from fever, smallpox or measles, and in March an outbreak of 'Irish' or typhus fever occurred in one of the lodging houses in Butcher Yard, Walmgate, where the Irish were reported to be swarming together in conditions of wretchedness and filth. A derelict house in Jubbergate about to be demolished was used as a temporary shelter, but as the influx of Irish grew the conditions there 'baffled all attempts to describe. Parties hungering, exposed night and day to all weather, almost naked and engendering pestilence as they proceeded, were to be seen literally crawling not able to support themselves erect, by the mingled effect of sickness and starvation'.[1] Wooden sheds (the temporary fever hospital) were hurriedly put up in a field in Heslington Lane, and by the end of the year 632 cases had been admitted, the vast majority from the Walmgate parishes of St. George, St. Dennis and St. Margaret.[2] According to Richard Thomas, the Union Surgeon, this increase in fever was due to 'its gradual extension from the destitute Irish to our own inhabitants in . . . Walmgate, Water Lanes, Long Close Lane, Bedern.'[3] The Guardians' temporary measures contained and eventually stamped out the epidemic of typhus, though other problems associated with the immigrants' arrival remained. Reports of begging, petty theft and disturbances increased with the continuous flow of immigrants into the city; and their threatening presence – alien, destitute and diseased – increased alarm and hostility. By flocking to the poorest and most unhealthy parts of the city they aggravated and became identified with already appalling sanitary conditions, and increased pressure on both housing and employment to such an extent that many overlooked the fact that the very poor, with their consequent living standards and unsociable behaviour, were very much in evidence both before and during the period of Irish settlement in the city. Laycock had described the effects of such poverty as early as 1844,[4] and Rowntree was to do so at the turn of the century, reporting that the majority of the occupants of the Hungate slums (by then largely non-Irish) were dirty and careless, some being 'people of filthy habits', and others with children 'pale, starved-looking and only half-clothed.'[5] It was his opinion that even London slums were not so filthy and degrading as some of those visited in York.

Why, as refugees from the Great Famine, did the Irish seek shelter, however briefly, in such an unlikely place as York?

In the mid-nineteenth century, York was still a largely pre-industrial Cathedral city – an important, though declining, social centre with a high proportion of gentry, clergy, professional classes and small craftsmen, many catering to the needs of the large surrounding agricultural area. Apart from the new Railway Carriage Works, which by 1855 employed about 1,200 men, the largest manufacturing concerns in the city were the glassworks and a group of small industries such as iron, chemical and linen manufacturies, leather trades and comb-making, none of which employed more than 200 workers. York's largest single occupation, accounting for over 70 percent of women workers in 1841, was domestic service. Given the almost complete absence of factory conditions, the relatively high proportion of Irish immigrants who were continuously drawn to the city in the first decades immediately following the Famine is surprising. However, an expansion of the local building industry, the continued prosperity of York's markets and Fairs, and York's extensive agricultural hinterland together provided opportunities for casual labouring, cattle driving, hawking, begging and, above all, employment as field labourers hired on a daily basis, and these occupations undoubtedly attracted many of the immigrants. The popular myth that the Irish came in connection with local railway development can be dismissed, since the York line was opened in May 1839, several years before the Irish arrived in large numbers, and the 1841 census lists no Irish railway employees. In 1851, only 11 of the immigrants were engaged in any category of railway work, in 1861 the figure was still only 13, and by 1871 it had increased to only 33. Yet by 1851 the number of York's Irish-born residents had increased to 1,963 or 5.3 percent of the total population – a figure higher even than most industrial towns in central and north-eastern England. The enumerators' notebooks reveal that of the Irish community of 2,618 (a figure including non-Irish partners and children), 443 or 16.9 percent were employed as agricultural labourers, representing 31.7 percent of the total Irish labour force in the city.

The majority of the remainder were labourers, indicating that the appearance of the immigrants was due both to the possibility of unskilled casual labour in the city itself, and agricultural employment in the surrounding countryside – a role which Irish harvesters and reapers had already undertaken seasonally in the locality for many years.

A particular form of agricultural employment – that of chicory cultivation – seems to have been especially associated with the Irish, but since less than a third of their labour force was engaged in agriculture of any kind, this work can hardly account for the surprisingly high numbers settling, however briefly, in the city. The chicory workers were gangs of men, women and children who tramped considerable distances each day to tend the crop in villages as far off as Clifton, Dunnington and Middlethorpe. It is likely that their alien presence in the quiet villages and suburbs of York attracted increasing attention, and since the fairly recent emergence of chicory as a large-scale industry in the area roughly coincided with the arrival of the immigrants, no doubt an exaggerated importance was placed on their unpopular association with the crop.

Other Irish farm labourers worked as far afield as Tollerton, Barmby Moor, Stockton-on-Forest and Wheldrake, villages which would have imposed a daily tramp of up to twenty miles. The Irish were unable to find cottage accommodation in the countryside, the chronic shortage being apparently the deliberate policy of many rural landlords who were reluctant to let any workers acquire settlement and a claim to Poor Relief in the parish – but particularly so in the case of the immigrants. Many Irish field labourers, therefore, were compelled to live in the city, and their choice of accommodation was limited by poverty.

II

Settlement

Between 1841 and 1851 the York Irish community increased from 781 to 2,618, or 7.2 percent of the city's total population. This rose to 3,248 (8 percent) in 1861 and 3,380 (7.7 percent) in 1871. Throughout the period the immigrants continued to concentrate in the early areas of settlement – most notably the four Walmgate parishes of St. Dennis, St. George, St. Margaret and St. Peter-le-Willows, which together accounted for 40.1 percent of their population in 1841, 42.7 percent in 1851, 53.1 percent in 1861 and 49.4 percent in 1871. Additional smaller settlements included the Bedern, a small overcrowded court near the Minster, which in 1851 housed more than 14 percent of the immigrants; the notorious Water Lanes – three narrow streets running between Castlegate and the River Ouse containing low lodging houses to which the Irish flocked in the early part of the period; and the Hungate district, a congested slum area which contained a few scattered pockets of early Irish concentration.[6]

With the Castlegate Improvement Scheme and the building of Clifford Street at the end of the period, however, many of the worst rookeries and lodging houses in that district were demolished; and similarly, by 1871 the whole of the Hungate area contained only 217 Irish. In contrast, the four Walmgate parishes in that year housed 1,669 Irish people, half of the Irish community in the city.

A brief description of the Walmgate district, referred to by Rowntree together with the adjacent Hungate neighbourhood as the poorest section of the city, indicates the conditions in which the bulk of the immigrants lived.

The four Walmgate parishes formed a roughly square area on the south–eastern side of the city, two sides of which were enclosed by the curving river Foss and the other two by the city walls, the extent of the parishes conforming exactly to these boundaries. The whole area was completely intersected by the main thoroughfare of the district, Walmgate, a broad street running from Walmgate Bar – the eastern gate of the city – to Foss Bridge, where the river skirted the outer edge of the parish of St. Dennis. Here the street became Fossgate and continued through the neighbouring Hungate district towards the centre of the city.

Walmgate had once contained fine Georgian houses and shops, which, by the mid–nineteenth century, had mostly been abandoned by the well–to–do and converted into multi–occupied tenements. Branching off the street were numerous courts and alleys, often placed behind the many public houses and inns such as the Old Malt Shovel, the Bay Horse, the Barley Corn and the Duke of York, whose yards had been infilled with clusters of one–up, one–down, usually single back cottages. These inn yards, though containing few dwellings, were chronically overcrowded, and many of them were colonized by the Irish. Barley Corn Passage, for example, contained five houses in 1851, which were occupied by 49 Irish individuals; and Malt Shovel Yard, with seven houses, sheltered 36 immigrants. Other yards off Walmgate, though hardly more spacious, were even more congested. Thus Britannia yard, containing 16 two–roomed cottages was occupied by 171 persons in 1851, 154 of them Irish, and in 1861 the 13 tiny houses in Clancy's Yard accommodated 104 individuals, 76 of whom were Irish. Many of the yards in the area contained slaughter–houses, pigsties, stables and small manufactories haphazardly mixed with the houses of the poor. In Butcher Yard, a notorious court halfway up the street, where the 1847 outbreak of typhus first occurred, the Poor Law Guardians complained of overcrowded lodging houses, thickly inhabited cottages and a slaughter house all packed into a narrow and confined space.[7]

In addition to these overcrowded and insanitary yards off the main street, the Walmgate area included a second type of working–class housing development – rows of small, through or back–to–back dwellings containing two or at most four rooms. These streets included Long Close Lane, with about 60 cottages in the late 1840s, many sheltering 25 to 30 Irish individuals, Hope Street, housing 322 Irish in 1861, Albert Street and Charles Street to the south side of Walmgate, and Navigation Road, Rosemary Place, St. Margaret's Terrace and Speculation Street to the north.

As well as this densely–packed working–class housing, the district contained smithies, breweries, flour mills, stone masons' and coach works, piggeries, stables and offensive trading premises belonging to skin and bone merchants and gut scrapers. A further nuisance was the immense dung heap situated just behind St. Margaret's Church, off the main street, which according to Laycock in 1844 'quite pollutes the atmosphere round it'.[8]

The Foss, bounding so much of the Walmgate district, was

described by John Smith in his Report on the Sanitary Condition of York in 1850 as 'a great open cesspool, into the stagnating waters of which the sewers of near half the city sluggishly pass', and it was to this river, which periodically flooded and polluted nearby streets, that the exceptionally high death rate of the inhabitants of the area was attributed. Further nuisances arose from the pig market next to Foss Bridge, the cattle market and pens outside Walmgate Bar, the numerous slaughterhouses in the district and the heavier industries in the area such as the glass works, the gas works and the iron foundries off Walmgate.

One of the district's most intensive areas of immigrant concentration, Britannia Yard, was typical of the cottage–type property occupied by most of the immigrants in the city.

Britannia Yard, built about 1810, was the second of the 33 yards branching off the right hand of Walmgate proceeding from Walmgate Bar to Foss Bridge. The Irish began to monopolize the court in about 1847, though even in 1841 one of the houses sheltered nine of their number. By 1851, 15 of the 16 cottages, which stretched in a single row the entire length of the yard, were Irish–occupied. These contained 154 Irish persons, together with 10 non–Irish lodgers, a further seven non–Irish people living in the remaining house. In all, therefore, the yard was occupied by no fewer than 171 individuals. The pressure for accommodation for the poor in the city – and particularly the Irish – was so great that several of these one–up, one–down dwellings were actually common lodging houses, Irish heads of household occasionally being charged with receiving too many lodgers. At this census, the occupants averaged 11 per house, with only four dwellings containing fewer than eight individuals, and two housing 18 persons. The residents of the yard were almost all labourers, only one joiner, one dressmaker and one agricultural labourer being otherwise employed.

By the following census the population of Britannia Yard had fallen to 132, 120 of whom were Irish, none of whom now lived with non–Irish persons. Their occupations were again almost entirely limited to labouring. By 1871, the Yard's inhabitants numbered 91, all of whom, except for two lodgers, were Irish. There was considerably less overcrowding than in previous censuses (the average number of occupants per house now being only five), and a greater variety of employment, though labouring was still overwhelmingly the major occupation.

The immigrants in Britannia Yard displayed a high level of geographic instability. Of the 154 Irish individuals recorded there in 1851, not one was still living in the Yard at the next census, and only five were enumerated elsewhere in the city. Similarly, of the 120 Irish persons listed in the entirely new population of the court in 1861, none remained ten years later and only eight were still present in other parts of York. Significantly, of the 13 who stayed in the city for more than a decade, not one, by a change of address or even parish, detached himself from the main Irish ghetto. In subsequent censuses all were to be found within a few hundred yards of their original place of settlement.

Britannia Yard, dubbed 'Hibernian Yard' by the press, was recognised as one of the most intensive areas of Irish settlement and was the scene of occasional disturbances and outbreaks of fighting and disorder. In spite of the undoubted poverty of its inhabitants, however, and its situation in one of the main brothel areas in the city, at no time throughout the period were there any references either to prostitutes living there or to any of its residents being associated with the activity. Yet the destitution of the occupants and their vulnerability to disease are indicated by the frequency of and reasons given for their applications for Poor Relief, most of these stemming either from sickness, or being requests for funeral expenses, particularly for young children.

The fact that all the houses in the yard eventually became Irish-occupied, and that the number of non-Irish residents decreased from 17 to 2 over the period, indicates that there was a very low level of assimilation in what was virtually a ghetto within a ghetto. This is even more apparent from the almost complete absence of mixed marriages in this community. Over the whole period only two Irish individuals were married to non-Irish partners, both appearing on the 1871 census.

The cottages in Britannia Yard were condemned by Laycock in 1844, but continued to house the poor for nearly another century. The Clearance Schedules and photographs of 1933, when the place was eventually demolished, indicate that its unfortunate inhabitants were still living in appalling conditions, with the houses 'infested with bugs, cockroaches and fleas', there was still no water supply or pantries inside the houses and the walls were dilapidated and damp.[9] But the records establish a precise picture of overcrowding, with the two rooms in the houses each measuring only 12 ft. square. Nor were these cottages the worst, though they continued to be occupied longer than most. Smith's Buildings, a block of 20 back-to-back cottages of even smaller proportions formed part of Long Close Lane. Having complained of the two filthy privvies being shared by 140 persons, the overseers reported in 1849 that:

> The insides of the houses were nearly as bad as the privvies. From 25 to 30 of the Irish lived in each house, which contained only two rooms, and by their dirty habits, the health of the neighbourhood was in jeopardy.[10]

Worse still, and regarded as even more of a threat to public health, were some of the one-roomed tenements in the Bedern, a place which was the subject of many outraged editorials and reports, and was described by the Inspector of Nuisances as 'The Modern Black Hole of Calcutta'.

The limited number of occupations in which most immigrants were employed, and the fact that the Irish often formed a high proportion of those engaged in such activities, is an indication of, and to some extent accounts for, their low level of assimilation. Of the 994 occupied Irish males on the 1851 census, almost 70 percent were concentrated in only eight occupations; and more than half of the overall total (52 percent) were either agricultural or general labourers. Similarly of the 382 employed Irish females, 75 percent took part in only six activities, with almost half of these being field or general labourers. Irish women accounted for all female field labourers listed in the city, and for almost 80 percent of the general labourers. The 65 who were domestic servants, on the other hand, represented only 3.5 percent of all female domestic servants in York. Detailed analysis of the distribution of the Irish labour force in York shows that certain occupations tended to be concentrated in particular parishes or even courts, the majority of farm workers, being recorded in the most 'Irish' of these – Minster Yard with Bedern, St. George and to a lesser extent St. Dennis; and almost 90 percent of unspecified labourers being found in St. Margaret, St. Peter le Willows and St. Mary Castlegate.

By 1861 little change had taken place. Agricultural and general labourers still accounted for 49 percent of all occupied Irish males, with only bricklayers' labourers, army personnel and hawkers each accounting for more than 2 percent of those at work. The same was true of women, who remained concentrated in their previous occupations, still dominating field and general labouring, and with even fewer of their number (60) being employed as domestic servants. By 1871 a slight decrease in occupational concentration had occurred. Of the 1,062 employed males, only 38 percent were now recorded as agricultural or general labourers, but again, only four other occupations (bricklayers' labourers, 8.9 percent; army, 7.8 percent; foundry labourers, 3.5 percent, and glassblowers, 2.4 percent) accounted for more than 2 percent of the total. For the 393 occupied women at this census a similar pattern emerged, but in spite of a slight diversification, Irish women were still largely confined to four or five activities, still dominated field labouring and had even fewer of their number (54) engaged as domestic servants. The most significant change was the sharp fall in the number of labourers – 65 in 1851, 30 in 1861 and only 4 in 1871.

The greatest changes in the social structure of the Irish in the city took place between 1841 and 1851, when, with the arrival of the post-Famine immigrants, the percentage of persons in Classes II and III was more than halved, and in Class IV (with the inclusion of the agricultural labourers) was more than trebled. In the two subsequent censuses little fundamental change occurred, with less than 2 percent of the immigrants at each census belonging to Social Class I, between 2.8 and 3 percent belonging to Class II, between 23 and 28 percent to Class III, between 40 and 37 percent to Class IV and 30 and 28 percent to Class V. Obviously, for the majority of immigrants, little occupational mobility took place, and as was the case with mixed marriages, that which did, took place mainly among those living furthest from the ghettoes.

III

Poverty and Crime

The degree of Irish reliance on Poor Relief in the period can be estimated by comparing details of the 8,034 applications made to the York Guardians in the four censual years with information relating to the computerized alphabetical print–out of the Irish community in the city. In 1841, the number of applicants identified as being Irish was 2.7 percent of the whole. By 1851, Irish applicants in the January to March quarter numbered 53 or 6.4 percent of the total. By 1861 this figure had risen to 690 (34.7) and by 1871, though the number of Irish applicants had dropped to 551, they now represented 43.7 percent of the whole. Yet for the three post–Famine decades the Irish formed only between 7 and 8 percent of the city's total population.

It might have been expected that the number of Irish applicants for Poor Relief in 1851 would have been higher than at any other time in the period. Admittedly the immigrants in York were constantly being replaced by new arrivals from Ireland, who no doubt contributed to the continuing poverty of their community. Nevertheless, the greatest degree of distress among the immigrants occurred in the late 1840s, when emergency measures such as soup kitchens and temporary fever hospitals were hastily introduced and immigrants were reported as collapsing and dying in the streets. Yet the figures show that the chief increase in Irish applications took place not between 1841 and 1851 but in the two subsequent decades, and it seems likely that this was primarily the result of the changes that took place in the Laws of Settlement.

By 1851 it was still the case that applicants for Relief, together with their families, could be removed to their place of origin if they had not been resident for at least five years in the parish to which they applied. Bearing in mind the reasons why they left Ireland in the first place, the continuing state of distress in that country, and allegations that such people were dumped at the nearest Irish port and left to find their own way back to their native parishes as best they could, it is hardly surprising that the immigrants, however great their need, were deterred from applying for relief. In 1861, the residential qualification for settlement was reduced to three years, by which time, no doubt, in spite of the high turn–over among the Irish in the city, some would have lived there long enough to qualify for relief. Since such a high proportion of applications were for temporary relief only, because of sickness or confinement, the York Guardians probably preferred to give limited financial aid rather than incur the expense, trouble and odium of transporting removable paupers to their place of legal settlement in Ireland. In 1865, the period of settlement was further reduced to one year, so that whatever the policy, many more of the immigrants were by that time eligible for relief.

The offence which more than any other gave the Irish community in the city its reputation for lawlessness was that of disorderly behaviour, often coupled with drunkenness and fighting, and occasionally developing into small–scale riots. In the four censual years, however, the only ones for which a reasonably accurate estimate of the actual numbers of Irish offenders can be made, it is clear that even in this their most common crime, they were outnumbered by non-Irish offenders, and that such outbreaks occurred with less frequency than the weekly Guildhall reports, listed in the *Herald* and *Gazette*, would suggest. Evidence on all offenders described as Irish in the inter-censual years indicates that the numbers of such cases are exaggerated by the use of remarks such as 'another Irish disturbance' or 'more Irish riots'. But such outbreaks certainly occurred more frequently and on a large-scale among the immigrants than the non-Irish population, and it was this type of behaviour, presenting as it did a real threat to law and order, which was most often complained of by York magistrates.

In all, between 1840 and 1875, there were 40 Irish disturbances involving between 20 and 400 people, with most of these occurring in the first decade of post-Famine settlement in the city. The majority involved about 30–50 people, among a few of whom drunken brawling often broke out. Typical of these smaller disturbances were 'Another Irish Riot' in the Bedern in 1852, 'A great muster of the Irish in Walmgate' in 1853, and an 'Irish riot' in Walmgate in 1849, though in each case most of the 'rioters' seem to have been onlookers rather than participants.[11] The fact that certain Irish individuals were constantly brought before the magistrates in the period also contributed to the enduring notoriety of the immigrants – a reputation which was, on the whole, undeserved by the majority of the York Irish. Characters like the Battle family, first appearing in court in 1851 and still being charged in 1874, Michael Brannan, making his 43rd. appearance before the magistrates in February 1873 and Michael Morgan, drunk and disorderly for the 24th. time in York as early as September 1852,[12] must have confirmed in the public mind the image of the lawless Irish community which was continuously conveyed in the press.

By checking the names and, where possible, addresses of all offenders recorded in the weekly newspaper reports of the Magistrates' Court proceedings against the details of all Irish individuals recorded in the city at each census, an attempt has been made to measure the extent of Irish criminality in each of the censual years. To minimise the risk of Irish offenders escaping identification, the analysis was based on all offences committed for six months on either side of the taking of the census. The accuracy of this method was indicated by the fact that few offenders actually described as Irish by the newspapers (who were generally anxious to present this information) were missing from the computerized alphabetical print-out of the total Irish population in the city. Of the crimes committed in York between October 1850 and September 1851, 23.6 percent were found to be Irish, though the immigrant community at that time represented only 7.2 percent of the city's total population. For the same period in 1861, by which time the immigrants formed 8 percent of the community, their contribution to crime was 21.1 percent and for 1871, with a total population of 7.7 percent, Irish offences were 16.5 percent of the whole. Thus, though diminishing throughout the post-Famine period, the Irish contribution to crime was greatly disproportionate to the community's size.

Apart from drunk and disorderly behaviour and disturbances, which often involved assault, the most common crime committed by the immigrants was theft, usually of a very trivial kind and obviously associated with their poverty. This was particularly the case in the late 1840s, as in April 1848, for example, when two Irishmen, John McDonald and John Smith, were charged with stealing bread. One of them entered a shop in Coppergate, asked for a loaf and, when refused, 'sprang to the counter with an oath, saying he would have some'. For this offence both were committed to the House of Correction for two months with hard labour.[13] An even more severe sentence was passed on Irishmen Thomas Joyce and John Delaney. Brought before the Bench on a charge of 'wandering about the streets with the intention of stealing', they were each given hard labour for three months.[14] Another petty crime, apparently confined to Irish offenders and indicative of their poverty, was the fairly frequent occurrence of women with hungry children 'milking cows without leave' – for which they were either imprisoned for seven days or dismissed with a reprimand. Some were desperate enough to commit crimes merely to gain admittance to the Vagrant Office or even the House of Correction for the sake of food and shelter or more adequate clothing. In December 1849, on being discharged from jail for the second time for breaking gaslamps, Irishman James Cornwall immediately repeated the offence; and on the same day his countryman Thomas Burn was committed to 14 days on an identical charge. In the same month, Dennis Donovan, hoping to obtain 'another night's lodging' at the Vagrant Office, was arrested for smashing gaslamps with oyster shells, and a few weeks later James Donolly, 'another seeker after comfortable lodgings and something to eat' and 'one of Erin's unfortunate sons', was charged with breaking gaslamps in Jubbergate. A year previously 'two strolling vagabonds', both Irish, were sentenced to seven days hard labour for destroying their clothes at the Vagrant Office, and in April 1849 Irishman William Clark, confined in the House of Correction for begging, was sentenced to extra imprisonment for a similar offence. Only a month previously 'an incorrigible character James Smith, a native of the Emerald Isle', had been found on the streets by the police and taken into custody for begging – after which he too, apparently, tore up his clothes during the night in an attempt to obtain a new suit. 'In this idea, however, he was mistaken for instead . . . he was covered with a horse rug, and in that habiliment was taken to the Guildhall'.[15]

Such incidents could hardly have made a favourable impression on the citizens of York; ragged and half-starved, congregating in threatening numbers in the Bedern or Walmgate, begging, snatching loaves, stealing milk and collapsing in the streets from hunger and disease, the gaunt presence of the Irish must have been an alarming, if not horrifying, spectacle. Yet it must be remembered that, in spite of continuing waves of immigration to the city, it was largely in the early years that this behaviour occurred.

It has been shown that the Irish contribution to crime in the city had dropped by 1871 to 16.5 percent of the whole. Yet stories persist to this day of police, even in the 1930s, patrolling the Irish districts in pairs, of priests being summoned to break up fights and of a virtual monopoly by the Irish of crime, disorder and drunkenness in the areas in which they lived. The main district referred to in such accounts, and the one which was apparently avoided by all respectable and prudent individuals, was the Walmgate area which contained 1,699 Irish individuals by 1871, or half the Irish community in the city. Yet even at that time they formed only 30 percent of the total population of the four Walmgate parishes combined, and were thus considerably outnumbered by the neighbourhood's non–Irish poor.

The area had traditionally been associated with drunkenness, violence and prostitution, a result both of the poverty of the residents and the unusually high concentration of public houses and beershops in the district. Well before the Irish began to arrive, most offences taking place in York, especially those associated with prostitution or drink, were already occurring either there or in the Water Lanes.

At the turn of the century, Rowntree noted that there were 39 public houses in the Walmgate/Hungate district (one for every 174 of the population) and additional beer shops and other licensed premises clustered around the cattle market just outside Walmgate Bar. Most of the inns dated from York's pre–railway eminence as a major coaching centre, and being concentrated along the main streets of Walmgate and Fossgate, were largely responsible for the reputation of the area. It is evident from Police Reports that these premises attracted low–class custom not only from the rest of York and the nearby Barracks, but from the surrounding towns and villages; and that in consequence they were also responsible for the high numbers of prostitutes resident and operating in the district. Statistics of addresses of York prostitutes reveal that, even before the Irish settled there, almost a third of the city's street–walkers lived in Walmgate alone, and following the partial demolition of the Water Lanes many more flocked there later in the period. Prostitution in York has been the subject of a separate study,[16] in which it was found that the Irish, though poor and congregated in the city's main brothel area, rarely engaged in the activity, and judging by the silence in this respect of an otherwise hostile local press, this appears to have been recognised. Over the years, however, the immigrant community has, in popular tradition and memory, become vaguely associated even with this type of behaviour.

The small pre–Famine Irish population of York posed few problems for those concerned with the city's law and order. After the Famine, few took into account, with Samuel Tuke, the prominent York Quaker, the destitution of the numerous immigrants, their physical incapacity for sustained labour and the psychologically demoralising effects of being whirled into urban slum communities – hostile and alien in culture, race and religion. Few were prepared to acknowledge with him that 'they are in as good a moral state as that class of labourers in this country', or that 'in times of distress the proportion of criminal commitments to the population [even] in England, increase(s) very greatly.'[17]

Considering the extreme distress of the early post–Famine immigrants and the continuing poverty of their successors, their disproportionate, though diminishing contribution to crime is hardly surprising.

IV

Assimilation

It has been suggested that Catholic immigrants in this period, both in America and Britain, displayed a marked indifference to 'getting on' and were considerably less interested in occupational and educational achievement than their Protestant and Jewish counterparts. This was particularly true of the Irish who, conforming to codes of conduct endorsed by the priests, remained distinctively 'Irish' wherever they congregated and were thus virtually 'cut off from the mainstream of working–class aspiration.'[18] Thernstrom, comparing mobility rates among first and second generation immigrants in Boston, observed a 'handicap' attaching to Catholics, not explicable in terms of prejudice, illiteracy and lack of familiarity with urban life. Even residential segregation was not, in his opinion, of fundamental importance as an obstacle to mobility and assimilation, because of the rapid turnover of the population of the slums, and the fact that, unlike the Irish, other ethnic groups who concentrated in ghettoes were often highly successful.

In York, however, where the Irish were the only discernible immigrant group and where, in the absence of other newcomers, they remained at the bottom of the social ladder, the ghetto as a mobility barrier may have been of greater significance. Though, as in Thernstrom's study, inter–censual comparisons reveal that the ghetto itself, rather than its inhabitants, was permanent, the immigrants nevertheless seem to have been trapped within its confines for the extent of their stay in the city. The majority remaining long enough to be recorded on more than one census (and these are the only ones whose occupational mobility can be measured) continued to live in Irish neighbourhoods regardless of frequent changes of address, so that a move from Long Close Lane to Bedern or one of the Walmgate Yards, would be unlikely to increase an immigrant's contact with the outside community or to affect his attitudes and patterns of behaviour. Distinct cultural differences, consciously clung to and reinforced by new arrivals from Ireland, were obviously important factors, as were the disastrous circumstances in which many of the immigrants had been forced to leave their homes.

It may be true, as Thernstrom suggests, that Catholic schools 'muted, rather than heightened aspirations and fostered a sense of alienation from the larger society', but in a strongly Protestant city like York, where there was openly expressed anti–Catholic feeling at the time, this sense of alienation would in any case, have been imposed from outside.

The enumerators' notebooks show that between 1851 and 1871 the total numbers of Irish scholars in the city rose from 294 (53.9 percent of all immigrant children aged between 5 and 15 years) to 695 (78.4 percent). Information from Catholic education statistics, however, indicates that though officially 'on the books', fewer than 60 percent regularly attended school. Further, of the 814 Catholic children on school registers in 1868 (a few of these, of course, being non–Irish), only 41 attended non–Catholic schools. Of the remainder, the vast majority (594) were registered at St. Georges Catholic Poor Boys' and Girls' Day Schools, built in 1850 in the heart of the Walmgate district, and catering almost exclusively for the recent influx of the Irish poor.[19]

These children, regardless of whether or not they were listed as scholars on the census, mixed very little with the non–Irish population in the city. Those actually recorded as working (between 8 and 15 percent over the three censuses) were largely field, general or agricultural labourers, hawkers or beggars, presumably hoeing, harvesting and tramping the countryside with other members of their group. Others were required to stay at home to care for younger brothers and sisters while their parents worked, and even those with no occupation listed probably spent most of their time at home or playing in the streets of the Irish neighbourhoods, none of which activities would have helped towards integration with the non–Irish in the city. At the same time, many, even of those listed as scholars, attended St. Georges so irregularly as to imperil the future of the school, with seasonal employment, York's Fairs and Markets (which provided opportunities for occasional hawking and begging) pitifully poor health and even lack of clothing being the causes of large–scale absenteeism. Such circumstances not only inevitably cut off immigrant children from those of the host population, but hindered their integration even with their non–Irish co–religionists, as well as with the more 'respectable' class of Irish in the city.

Until 1852 'respectable' Catholic children attended the Day School of the Bar Convent, Blossom Street, at a charge of 2d. or 3d. per week. In that year it was decided to transfer these children (who, however, continued to pay fees and were taught separately from the 'free' children) to St. Georges. So great was the stigma of association with the children of the Walmgate slums, however, that the venture was a complete failure, and within two years the number of paying scholars had so dwindled that the Day School had to be moved back to Blossom Street. The withdrawal of these superior children resulted in acute financial, examination and attendance problems for the school, which was in a district described in 1869 by Sister Christiana, the nun from the Bar Convent in charge of the Girls' premises, as consisting:

> exclusively of the poorest of the poor . . . In the winter months the congregation is reduced to the lowest ebb of misery and starvation with their consequent fevers. Deaths from want of food have occurred daily during the past few months.[20]

Thirty years later Rowntree, selecting the inhabitants of precisely this area to illustrate the conditions of an urban population living in poverty, noted that 69.3 percent of the inhabitants lived in primary or secondary poverty, as opposed to only 27.8 percent for the city as a whole. Further entries in the Headmistress's Log Book reveal that clothing was distributed, hungry children were fed in the school cellars, treats were awarded for good attendance and a creche was opened nearby to enable older children, kept at home to look after younger brothers and sisters, to go to their own school. But even these measures met with little success, and it is clear that the immigrants' educational provision – barely made use of on the one hand, and limited to exclusively Catholic tuition and predominantly Irish neighbourhoods on the other – could have contributed little to their assimilation.

It has been noted that even in the Walmgate district, which by 1871 contained half the Irish community in the city, the immigrants formed only 30 percent of the total population of the area. Though they continued to monopolize various courts, yards and streets in the neighbourhoods, they were surrounded and out-numbered by non-Irish individuals living in conditions of equal poverty and filth, which had been condemned as early as 1844. Yet in this period there was little integration, even between the Irish and their social equals of the neighbouring Walmgate slums. Taking the city as a whole, the proportion of mixed marriages between the two communities fell from around 31 percent of all married persons in the Irish community in 1841, to about 14 percent in 1851, 11 percent in 1861 and 15 percent in 1871. Most of these mixed marriages involved immigrants living outside the Irish ghettoes, indicating either that the individuals forming such unions were already detached from the main Irish community, or became so, after their marriage. Conversely, where a street or yard was wholly or almost entirely colonised by the Irish, mixed marriages occurred hardly at all. In Gill's Yard, Aldwark, for example, settled by the Irish in the late 1850s, there were 64 Irish residents in 1861 and 83 in 1871 – with a complete absence of mixed marriages. In Cross Alley, Water Lanes, only enumerated properly in 1851, all 55 occupants were Irish, and none had married partners other than those of Irish birth. The Bedern, housing 372 Irish residents in 1851, 368 in 1861 and 244 in 1871, accounted for only three, two and three Irish persons in mixed marriages at each respective census, while in Britannia Yard, Walmgate, almost wholly Irish-occupied throughout the period, of the 154 Irish individuals in 1851, 120 in 1861 and 89 in 1871, only two had non-Irish partners.

A further indication of this lack of assimilation is the fact that there was little change in the pattern of Irish settlement. By 1871 the traditional major Irish parishes still contained the bulk of the immigrants, and any movements away had been largely to the fringes of neighbouring parishes. They continued to monopolize particular streets and courts, some of which they took over completely, until the areas themselves were finally demolished in the 1920s and '30s. Only then were these and similar Irish communities eventually dispersed. Further, whereas in 1841 there had been a significant amount of mixed rish/non–Irish occupation of individual houses, this had been reduced onsiderably by the end of the period.

Similarly there was little diversification of employment, and fter the arrival of the post–Famine immigrants, little change ccurred in the distribution of the community's social classes. Had he immigrants' employment involved them in factory or workshop onditions, increasing their degree of contact with those outside heir own community, then a greater and more immediate degree of ssimilation might have occurred. As it was, however, the city ffered few opportunities in this respect, particularly for the Irish, bout a third of whose workforce was forced to seek employment as gricultural labourers elsewhere. As such they worked the countryside n gangs, rarely mixing with the rural population or with that of ork, from which they were often absent from dawn until dusk. The ther main occupations – casual labouring – whenever work was to be ound – and hawking, were scarcely favourable to assimilation. inally, the increasingly low proportion of Irish women employed as omestic servants in the city suggests a further lack of assimilation, ndicating either a reluctance on the part of employers to engage the mmigrants in their households, or an unwillingness on the part of the omen to take part in the largest single source of female employment n the city.

The religion of the immigrants, whether or not it muted their spirations, created barriers which isolated them further, and was articularly prejudicial to their acceptance in one of the principal entres of Protestantism in the country, where anti–Catholic feeling as openly, though not violently, expressed. It is clear, however, hat the major reason for their lack of assimilation was their eographical mobility – the fact that few of the Irish remained in the ity long enough to become integrated, whatever the circumstances of heir stay.

Analysis of all individuals in the Irish community remaining in ork for more than one census shows a continuous turnover throughout he period. Among the remaining few, 'Irishness' was reinforced by uccessive waves of newcomers, while the hostility of the host ommunity was sustained by fresh and often resentful arrivals from reland, many of whom, like their predecessors, were destitute and nskilled. Predictably perhaps, of the 1851 Irish community, 97 ercent had arrived in York since the previous census. More urprising however, is the fact that in 1861 the figure was 94 percent nd in 1871 it was 74 percent – demonstrating that the immigrant opulation was practically replaced within each ten year period.

Only 27 occupied males remained in York from 1851 to 1871, and f these only two improved their status – one having moved from abourer to publican and the other from labourer to general dealer. oth, though living in Walmgate, were married to non–Irish wives. Two thers changed their occupations but not their social class, and the emaining 23, of whom 17 were labourers or agricultural labourers, nade no change whatsoever. Evidence of inter–generational mobility is xtremely limited since of the 36 employed sons of the above occupied males, all but two had either left York after being recorded, or were too young to have been recorded more than once. One, the son of a shoemaker improved his status from railway cleaner in 1861 to engine driver in 1871. The other, whose father was a recruiting sergeant, changed from plumber to painter in the ten year period. The majority of sons, however, whatever they may have subsequently become, began their working lives in the same occupation as their fathers.

Thus in 1851, 39 year–old Michael Roun, labourer, his wife Mary, 29, labourer, his son Hugh aged two, born in York, and his father Patrick aged 77, also a labourer, lived with their 13 lodgers at 16 Britannia Yard. The lodgers were split into at least six families. Most, including the women, were labourers and all had been born in Ireland. The overcrowding in the two–roomed house must have continued, as in 1852 and 1854 Michael Roun was charged with keeping too many lodgers. By 1861 the family had moved to a small terrace house in the neighbouring parish of St. Lawrence, the enumerator recording that the adults had all been born in County Mayo. They now had an additional son, and had reduced their lodgers to two. These, like Michael and his 84 year old father, were both labourers, though Mary was now listed simply as 'wife'. By 1871 the family was still living in Lawrence Row, the grandfather was no longer present, Michael was still a labourer and had been joined in the occupation by both his sons. No occupational mobility had taken place in a family, three generations of whom, including the wife, were general labourers.[21]

An indication of slight social mobility is the fact that between 1851 and 1871 the proportion of individuals recorded as lodgers fell from 25.6 percent to 4.5 percent. Given the high rate of turnover of the Irish population already discussed, however, the figures demonstrate not so much improvements in the circumstances of individuals, but rather that successive waves of newcomers were taking up residence as householders rather than lodgers. Yet overcrowding, though less severe than in earlier years, had by no means diminished, since many families still found it necessary to occupy houses jointly.

Thus the vast majority of immigrants did not stay long enough to settle and even those who did, were not integrated, and did not significantly improve their situation in the period. It is apparent that throughout, they remained largely distinct from the non–Irish population, the very lowest ranks of whom were encouraged to think themselves superior to the new arrivals. Isolated from other classes by their poverty, the Irish congregated in the worst, most squalid and overcrowded slums in the city, intensifying already appalling conditions for which they received much of the blame. Any integration must inevitably have been with others among the poor from whom they could hardly have acquired the social graces dear to respectable society. Their religion, catered for in St. George's, the new Catholic church off Walmgate, was a cause for complaint rather than satisfaction; their only recorded amusement – pitch and toss – seems to have been confined exclusively to their community, and even their drinking took place largely in Irish pubs and beerhouses. A final indication of limited assimilation in the period is the Irish community's almost complete absence of political involvement, the only exceptions being isolated instances of Ribbonism and suspected Fenian intimidation,[22] activities unlikely to endear them to the citizens of York.

V

Prejudice

The extent of prejudice towards a particular section of society cannot be measured, and the attitude of the non-Irish poor towards the immigrants – having like the Irish themselves, left little or no record of their opinion – is even more difficult to establish. There are occasional newspaper accounts of Irishmen being attacked or outbreaks of fighting between the two communities, but these are unusual incidents, very different from the anti-Catholic riots elsewhere, where Catholic chapels were attacked and threats made to drive the immigrants away.[23]

Nevertheless, there was a marked degree of anti-Irish prejudice in the city, stemming mainly from the middle classes and apparent in the attitudes and utterances of the Poor Law Guardians, Sanitary Inspectors and magistrates, and particularly evident in newspaper editorials and the coverage of local news. If these attitudes were not merely reflections of the public's views, but were also instrumental in forming them, then their influence could have been considerable. Those in authority, English, middle-class, respectable Protestants, were prejudiced against the immigrants, and prejudice led them to make stereotyped, misleading judgements about the Irish, leaving a legacy of official reports, containing evidence apparently but not always in reality based on fact, a matter which has been too rarely considered.

Proposals to increase the grant to Maynooth College, the opening of St. George's Church in 1850 and the enthronement there of Dr. John Briggs as the Bishop of Beverley, provoked outraged anti-Catholic editorials in the *Gazette*, widely attended protest meetings and a York City Council petition to the Queen.[24] Even before the arrival of the first Famine victims to the city, the Irish were stereotyped as violent, lazy and dirty by the local press.[25] After 1847 individual immigrants were repeatedly presented to the public in a hostile way. Irish offenders brought before the magistrates were frequently 'ugly', 'miserable looking', 'incorrigible pests' or 'wretched sons of the Emerald Isle' and their hard-drinking, hard-fighting image was evoked on the slightest pretext. In 1860, for example, an unoffending Irishman, fetching the police to stop a fight (and mistakenly being arrested himself in the confusion that followed) was referred to by the *Gazette* as 'possessing that remarkable (in an Irishman) idiosyncracy of character – a peaceful disposition.'[26] And in the case of meat seized as unfit for human consumption, a butcher giving evidence declared, to the amusement of the court: 'Some part of the meat was not fit for human food; other parts perhaps an Irishman would eat – (laughter) – and it might not do him any harm.'[27]

Anti-Irish magisterial outbursts were not uncommon and both the court and the newspapers frequently treated the bewilderment and ignorance of the immigrants with undisguised contempt, as the following three incidents demonstrate.

In 1849 three immigrants, charged with stealing potatoes, had called another Irishman as witness on their behalf. He stated that he had met one of the prisoners about ten miles from York at five o'clock and walked home with him, reaching his house in Long Close Lane (Walmgate) at about midnight .

> Lord Mayor: 'About midnight. What time is midnight?'.
> Witness: 'Midnight. About six o'clock.' (Laughter)
> Lord Mayor: 'Was it daylight?'.
> Witness: 'It was daylight'.
> Lord Mayor: 'Then you were ten miles off York at five o'clock and here at six. Did you fly or how did you come? (renewed laughter) What do you call midday if six o'clock be midnight? Is it before breakfast or after?'
> Witness: 'It is before breakfast.' (Renewed laughter)
> Lord Mayor: 'I don't believe a word you say . . . hold your tongue . . . as to what you Irish say we can't pay any attention to it scarcely . . . to bring forward such a man as witness who has just been before us is a burlesque of evidence and we English people can't do with such things.'[28]

The court was similarly entertained in 1850 when following 'Another Irish row' on Christmas night in Britannia Yard, 'a host of witnesses' appeared – among them the Kilmartin brothers, who charged their neighbours with throwing cobblestones through their windows. As proof of the attack they brought the stones in a basket, one brother declaring (to the amusement of the court and *Gazette* readers) that he saw a neighbour digging up the paving stones, one of which he swore 'hit and kilt me'.[29]

Sixteen months later a 52 year-old widower and father of eight children was killed trying to defend his married daughter involved in a fight with neighbours. All those involved lived in Smith's Buildings, Long Close Lane, Walmgate, all were chicory workers and all were from Sligo. The man's name was James Flannery, or as the *Gazette* commented:

> Flannely, for as we may here observe, such is the depth of ignorance of these people that the members of the family were not able to speak at the inquest with any degree of certainty as to the spelling of their own name.[30]

The fact that the recently arrived Irish family, shocked by the death of their father only that morning, were unable to spell their name is reported by the *Gazette* with obvious malice.

The living conditions of the Irish were also repeatedly condemned, without regard to the poverty which caused them, and rarely 'ere the owners of the slum properties in which they lived (and for hich they were charging highly inflated rents) apportioned any blame. he fact that these miserable conditions had existed in the city for ıany years before the arrival of the Irish, was largely ignored, as 'as the presence of other slum communities whose members lived in a tate of overcrowding, filth and squalor hardly distinguishable from ıat of the immigrant poor. Instead, the dirty and unsociable habits f the Irish were smugly contrasted with those of the native opulation of York, as in 1850 when the latter were described in mith's Report on the Sanitary Condition of York as 'a cleanly eople', so different from 'the unfortunate sons and daughters of rin, whose national habits are less orderly', and who lived in ıouses which are totally unfit for human habitations . . . not fit ven for pigsties.'[31]

This contrast between the housing conditions of the two ɔmmunities is curiously similar to one applied to London's East End t the turn of the century. In this case, however, the disgusting abits and filthy abodes of the newly–arrived Jewish immigrants are eing condemned – in idealised contrast to their scrupulously clean nd well–behaved Irish predecessors.[32]

Notable exceptions to these attitudes to the Irish in the city ere those of the York Quakers, and in particular the Tukes. For many ears Samuel Tuke had been actively concerned with the Irish question nd in 1846, together with another prominent York Friend, Joseph owntree, he visited Ireland and took part in Quaker Relief Work ere. A year later, addressing a meeting of Friends at Devonshire ouse in London he protested against the 'wholesale condemnations of e Irish people' who, though weakened by want and disease, labouring the heaviest of employments and sending remittances to their milies at home, were, nevertheless stigmatized as lazy, reckless and gardless of human life.[33]

As a Guardian of the Poor he had been one of the four Inspectors the Walmgate Court in which typhus first occurred in 1847, and he ad quickly allowed a field of his to be used as the site for the ver sheds – no–one else in York being willing to provide land for e purpose.[34] His concern for the sick immigrants met with little ıpport from the other Guardians, one of whom, objecting to Mr. Tuke's oposals for their relief, described the immigrants as 'the most eastly set of men on the face of the earth', and another suggesting at those who were ill should be 'carried away in river essels.'[35] Tuke's subsequent attempts to improve the diets of the ver patients in the hospital, who were confined naked to their beds ecause of the Guardians' refusal to supply them with nightshirts, ere opposed on the grounds that items such as cocoa were unnecessary xuries 'such as the Irish were not accustomed to at home, it being eir habit to live on the coarsest kind of food.' Tuke reminded the ommittee that 'turnip tops, etc., was not what they lived, but what ey died upon.'[36]

His descriptions of the early immigrants directly contradict the aims made by others in authority, such as the Managers of York's

Ragged Schools, who reported quite incorrectly in 1851 that 'three-fourths of those brought before the magistrates in the city ar Irish.'[37] In a letter to Jonathan Pim, one of the Quaker Relie Committee working in the West of Ireland, in autumn 1847, Tuke state that the York Irish 'are in as good a moral state as the class o labourers in this country.'[38] A contrasting but more typical attitud is that displayed by the York Postmaster Mr. Oldfield, who only thre weeks earlier had written to the Poor Law Guardians complaining of:

> The great nuisance caused during the week and particularly o Fridays by great numbers of Irish and other paupers, many o whom were afflicted with contagious and other diseases, lyin about the door of the money order office, to the great annoyanc of ladies and gentlemen.[39]

Tuke's son, James Hack Tuke, gave further evidence on thi subject in his letter (subsequently a pamphlet) *A Visit to Connaugh in the Autumn of 1847*, addressed to the Central Relief Committee o the Society of Friends in Dublin, which drew attention to th 'honourable traits of character which the conduct of Irishmen i England strikingly exhibits.'[40]

The younger Tuke became a leading authority on the economic an social conditions of the poorest districts of the West of Irelanc Like his father he worked tirelessly during the Famine Years organising the distribution of Friends' Relief, particularly i Connaught and Donegal, investigating the extent of distress there writing pamphlets and raising subscriptions. He was equally active o behalf of immigrants arriving in York, contracting typhus in the feve hospital in 1848 from which he never fully recovered. Yet th evidence of these undoubted authorities on the subject, who, fror their unique experience of Famine conditions in Ireland were certain better informed than anyone in York – and probably in England – ha been strangely neglected, even though they were intimately involve with the arrival of the Irish in the city and the problems of thei settlement. Their evidence has been ignored in favour of that fror sources both biased and inaccurate, which has exaggerated the exter of the anti–social behaviour of the Irish in York and in the countr as a whole. It is only when such attitudes are balanced by th perception, humanity and sympathetic understanding of the Tukes tha the extent of anti–Irish prejudice in the country can be recognised and some allowance made for its misleading impressions an uncharitable distortion of the facts.

For many of the immigrants, the enumerators in each of the thre post–Famine censuses omitted to record County of Birth. From th number for whom such information is available, however, it woul appear that there is a probable link between the Tukes investigations, relief work and distribution of Friends' funds in th West of Ireland, and the surprisingly high proportion of Connaugh immigrants arriving in York. In 1851 almost 40 percent of the tota for whom County of Birth was listed were from Mayo, with a further 2 percent from Sligo, Roscommon and Galway. Thus about 70 percent wer from Connaught, the province in which the Tukes had been most active

In 1861 the figure was 53 percent and in 1871 56 percent. Bearing in mind the contrast between English behaviour in general towards the Irish during the Famine, and that displayed by the Tukes and other Friends, it would hardly be surprising if once uprooted, many made for York as a possible haven. Discussing James Hack Tuke's prominent role in Irish affairs, John Ormerod Greenwood referred to the love the Irish people still had for him a quarter of a century later,[41] while further evidence of the continued affection for the man was recorded by his great nephew, the late Mr. Anthony Tuke:

> My late wife and I went to stay at Carna (North West of Galway in Connemara) in the 1930s, and when we arrived at Mongan's Hotel there the proprietor asked whether by any chance I was related to the 'great' Mr. Tuke, as he called him. When I claimed that honour he fell on our necks, and told us that when he was a small boy his father lifted him on his shoulder so that he could see Mr. Tuke pass by in his carriage. He told us with great emphasis that the Quakers were the only people who gave out their relief without any strings, as we should say today.[42]

This evidence may partly account for the surprisingly large number of Irish immigrants to a city which offered no obvious source of employment. The Irish were not welcomed, they were forced to live in hostile and squalid surroundings, few stayed for long and those that did can hardly be said to have assimilated or improved their position in the period. Their accommodation, condemned before they arrived, continued to be occupied by successive waves of immigrants and their descendants. They continued to settle in Irish neighbourhoods until the slums were finally cleared in the late 1920s and the communities eventually dispersed. Appropriately enough, but probably by coincidence, tenants from the Long Close Lane and Hope Street Unhealthy Area Scheme were rehoused in Tuke Avenue. Many had the same names as their early Irish predecessors. Details of their incomes, rents and family circumstances indicate that many of the area's inhabitants – whether or not they were of Irish descent – still suffered the stifling effects of poverty and living in an urban slum. Many were unhealthy. Most were semi– or unskilled workers – usually agricultural or general labourers. Many were unemployed and many, like their impoverished predecessors, were in weekly receipt of relief from York's Guardians of the Poor. The poverty of the immigrants endured from generation to generation.

Notes:

1. *York Courant*, 20 May 1847.
2. J. Smith, *Report to the General Board of Health on a Preliminary Enquiry into . . . the Sanitary Condition of York* (London, HMSO, 1850).
3. *Courant*, 21 October 1847.
4. T. Laycock, *Report on the State of the City of York*. First report of the Royal Commission for Enquiry into the State of Large

Towns and Populous Districts, *P.P.* (1844), vol.xvii.
5. B. S. Rowntree, *Poverty: A Study of Town Life* (London 1903).
6. There were other smaller concentrations of Irish in the city. The parish of St. Mary Bishophill Junior briefly contained in 1851 a temporary settlement of Irish Ordnance Survey workers, highly skilled men who do not appear to have mixed in any way with the main Irish community. It is likely that they were Protestant. Fulford Barracks also contained a varying number of Irish, depending on which regiments were stationed in York. By 1871 there was also a sizeable Irish settlement in the parish of St. Helen on the Walls, the immigrants being largely concentrated in one small court, 'Gill's Yard', off Aldwark, near Bedern. 82 Irish were crowded into nine of the ten small cottages there, and Aldwark itself housed another 39 immigrants, while 30 others occupied two additional yards off the street.
7. York Board of Guardians' *Minute and Letter Books*, March 1847.
8. Laycock, *Report on State of York*, pp.7–8.
9. York Health Department Records, Documents relating to Britannia Yard (renamed Alexandra Yard), Hill's Yard and McQuade's Yard Clearance Area, 1933.
10. *York Gazette*, 4 August 1849.
11. *York Herald, 6 November 1852 and 4 June 1853; Gazette*, 15 December 1849.
12. For details of these and other habitual offenders see Frances Finnegan, *Poverty and Prejudice: A Study of Irish Immigrants in York, 1840–1875* (Cork, 1982), Chapter 9.
13. *Gazette*, 15 April 1848.
14. *Ibid.*, 1 April 1848.
15. *Ibid.*, 24 March 1849. An almost identical case was reported in the *Gazette*, 5 December 1868.
16. Frances Finnegan, *Poverty and Prostitution, A Study of Victorian Prostitutes in York* (Cambridge, 1979).
17. Letter from Samuel Tuke to Jonathan Pim, dated 26 August 1847. Quoted in *Memoirs of Samuel Tuke*, 2 vols. (London 1860), vol.ii, pp.323–4.
18. See, for example, Stephan Thernstrom, *The Other Bostonians: Poverty and Progress in the American Metropolis, 1880–1970* (Harvard, 1973).
19. Leeds Diocesan Archives, Catholic Education Statistics, 7 July 1868, St. Winifred's and St. George's Missions.
20. Bar Convent Archives, vol.45, St. George's School Day Book, March 1869. Another entry in the Headmistress's Log Book (31 July 1866) stated: 'Children above nine years old who attend school daily are exceptional cases; for the great majority, the remainder of their school life consists of odd days or half–days spent in school, whenever they have the will or leisure to come . . . The Reverend Manager's earnestness in seeking the absentees in their homes and in endeavouring to secure the co–operation of the parents has been unceasing'.
21. For further details of this family, see F. Finnegan, *Poverty and Prejudice*, pp.161–2.

22. See, for example, *Gazette*, 8 March 1856; 9 November 1867; 25 January 1868; 13 June 1868; 6 April 1868; 26 October 1867; 14 March 1868.
23. John Foster, *Class Struggle and the Industrial Revolution* (London 1974), p.243.
24. See, for example, *Gazette*, 5 April 1845; 3 May 1845; 10 May 1845; 14 June 1845; 27 June 1846; 7 September 1850.
25. *Ibid.*, 7 November 1846.
26. *Ibid.*, 1 December 1860.
27. *Ibid.*, 5 October 1850.
28. *Ibid.*, 7 April 1849.
29. *Herald*, 11 January 1851. Maria Edgeworth, in a particularly apt explanatory footnote to this expression, states: 'The mere English reader, from a similarity of sound between the word *kilt* and *killed*, might be induced to suppose that their meanings are similar, yet they are not by any means in Ireland synonymous terms. Thus you may hear a man exclaim – *'I'm kilt and murdered!'* – but he frequently means only that he has received a black eye, or a slight contusion'. Maria Edgeworth, *Castle Rackrent* (1800) reprinted (Oxford, 1964), p.18.
30. *Gazette* and *Herald*, 26 April 1851.
31. Smith, *The Sanitary Condition of York*, p.16. In the same year, Thomas reported to the Board of Health that the Irish in Bedern (about 370 people) lived in 'low cellars underground, with a few shavings, where the people live upon a little Indian meal . . . they are nearly naked and, of course, when anything happens the parish is their only refuge. They are always at the Relieving Officer's door, and of course, a great deal of money is spent'. Two years later the Inspector of Nuisances described the court as 'in a filthy and unwholesome condition', with the two privvies used by about 300 persons being 'foul and offensive'.
32. Quoted in John A. Garrard, *The English and Immigration: A Comparative Study of the Jewish Influx, 1880–1910* (Oxford, 1971), p.51.
33. *The Friend*, June 1847, Quoted in *Memoirs of Samuel Tuke*, vol.ii, p.401.
34. *Courant*, 20 May 1847.
35. *Ibid.*
36. *Ibid.*, 13 January 1848.
37. York Ragged Schools, *Third Annual Report*, 1851. Quoted in *Gazette*, 26 April 1851. The actual proportion of Irish criminals in this censual year when maximum identification of offenders' birthplace is possible was 26.3 percent.
38. Letter from Samuel Tuke to Jonathan Pim, dated 26 August 1847, quoted in *Memoirs of Samuel Tuke*, vol.ii, pp.323–4. Tuke wrote: 'the comparison between the disposition to crime in Ireland and England is not so very much in favour of the latter as we have been wont to think. I have seen a great deal lately of your Connaught men, from County Mayo in particular, and I really believe they are in as good a moral state as the class of labourers in this country. I have not met with a man who was not anxious to work, and their strong

social attachments interest me much. I was afraid we should have had children left in our fever hospital, deserted by their parents; but no such thing has occurred. Drunkenness is very rare amongst them and I found one morning at our Post Office that seventeen of them had been there from 9 to 1 o'clock and had obtained Post Office Orders for from 5/– to 50/– to send to their poor friends in Ireland. These are your *reckless* countrymen'.

39. *Courant*, 5 August 1847.

40. James Hack Tuke, *A Visit to Connaught in the Autumn of 1847: Distress in Ireland* (London, 1847). The letter continued; 'I have already said that these "reckless" creatures are generally frugal . It may be safely asserted that their general conduct has been sober and inoffensive. The obtaining of means for their own and their families' present and future support has evidently been the great object of their pursuit . . . These are the people who require to be taught by our English labourers the principle and habit of self-reliance'.

41. John Ormerod Greenwood, 'Friends and Relief,' p.25, in *Quaker Encounters*, vol.1. For example, 'Goodbye gentlemen,' said an armed English landlord as he watched Tuke's party move off, 'You're the only people here who can travel without fear of being shot . . .' 'Every time I took my eye off the horses', his driver told the groom, 'I see Misther Tuke leppin' along the road, and leppin' over walls, and leppin' up and down off the car.''

42. Letter to F. Finnegan from Mr. Anthony Tuke, Andover, 3 February 1975, in the possession of the author.

ENGLISH WORKING–CLASS RADICALISM AND THE IRISH, 1815–50

John Belchem

A lively controversy is now developing about the extent of the rish presence in English popular radicalism in the first half of the ineteenth century. As has long been appreciated, some of the most alented radical leaders and journalists were of Irish stock, but this ells us little about the political attitudes and allegiances of the rowing number of Irish immigrants in early industrial England. Were hey prominent in great movements like Chartism, or were these exiles f Erin hermetically sealed off from such class–based protest? Did hey join O'Connor's mobilization of the 'unshorn chins, blistered ands and fustian jackets' of the north, or did they loyally follow he policy of O'Connell and the leaders of the specifically Irish ssociations and eschew the Chartist challenge?[1] I cannot hope to nswer such questions as these. What I wish to underline is the mportance of the controversy, and to examine the other side of the ssue – the attitude of the English radicals to the Irish.

The recent call for a reassessment of Irish involvement in nglish protest is the product of a new approach to the study of opular movements and forms an integral part of a wider re–evaluation f the strength of the working–class challenge in early industrial ngland. Traditional studies, based on the most readily accessible ources, have tended to spotlight the major leaders of collective ction, the formal organizations of protest and the pronouncements of ne 'official' ideologues. In searching for material about the epresentative protester, the typical pattern of activity at grass–oots level and the motivating ideology of the rank and file, students f popular protest, like historians of pre–revolutionary absolutism, ave discovered considerable divergence between central proclamation nd local practice. This is particularly the case with the new breed f Chartist local studies in which the focus has shifted away from the articularities of the socio–economic structure to an examination of ne various forms of protest culture and activity in the community.[2] uch studies have revealed a quite remarkable eclecticism in working–lass political and social behaviour at the local level, with a onsiderable overlap of personnel in supposedly discrete if not ctually competing movements. The distinctions which national compartmentalizing historians seek to impose on working-class behaviour were quite simply not observed by the ordinary members of popular movements.[3] Thus it is surely no longer sufficient for historians to maintain that the Irish immigrants kept distant from Chartism because such was the official policy of O'Connell and the leaders of the Irish associations, a proscription endorsed by the Catholic clergy. Admittedly there was no formal association between the Chartists and the Irish until after O'Connell's death, but as the local studies show, informal association between the Chartists and the Irish was common, particularly in the smaller manufacturing towns and villages. At this informal local level the injunctions of O'Connell were no more of a barrier to joint action than the official 'no politics' rule of the trade unions.[4] In the rapidly expanding industrial townships of the north, where the Irish were not a single out-group facing a stable population, but simply one such group among many, the exiles of Erin did not stand apart in a subculture of their own. As Dorothy Thompson maintains, it was precisely because they were such typical inhabitants of the industrial areas that the Irish participated so fully in the great protest movements of the early nineteenth century.[5]

This important revisionist claim has wide implications for the social historian, particularly as the extent of Irish integration and involvement in radicalism so often serves as a litmus-test for questions about class formation and consciousness during the transition to industrial capitalism. Even with a demagogic Irishman at its head, it is frequently maintained, Chartism failed to enlist the support of the Irish immigrants, decisive proof this of the weakness of the Chartist challenge and the absence of any pervasive sense of class capable of overriding religious, national, ethnic and other divisions.[6] It would be folly to pretend that this view – and all that it implies – can now be overturned completely. Given the uneven nature of England's industrial development, the sectionalism of the working class must be conceded, as must the political apathy of many of the population, let alone the existence of the beer-swilling, male chauvinist, xenophobic English worker who chose not to spend his spare time dancing with the Owenites or studying in the educational classes at his local Chartist branch, but in wife-beating and in brawls with immigrant Irish workers. But it is precisely against such overwhelming and perennial obstacles and prejudices that the achievements of any radical movement should be judged, and the achievements were substantial in the period 1815–50. One way of appreciating this is by studying the attitude of the radical movement to Ireland and the Irish.

The radical movement which emerged in post-Napoleonic England represented a significant advance on the pattern of traditional or 'pre-industrial' popular protest. The sub-political attitudes and ambivalent generalized beliefs which had underpinned the popular chauvinism, intolerance, rough social justice and xenophobia of the eighteenth-century crowd had disappeared, along with the whole backward-looking *mentalité* which had sought to secure redress not through reform but through the restoration of a happier, doubtless ythical, age. From 1815 through to the collapse of Chartism, the orking class recognized that democratic control of the state was an ssential means to the improvement of their condition, and looked to niversal civil and religious liberty' to achieve this end. This was major 'ideological' advance: only a generation earlier, 'No Popery' ad been by far the most popular cry.[7] Even with the onset of ubstantial immigration from the 1820s, as proto–industrialization in eland collapsed into de–industrialization,[8] there was to be no eversion to the old attitudes. 'Ireland', the *Trades Free Press* oted in 1827, 'innundates us with her miserable poor to gradually ush tens of thousands "from their stools" . . . multitudes are daily oured upon our shores ready to invade the work of every labourer and perative.' But the trades refused to fan any anti–Irish feeling or raise again the old cry of 'No Popery'. Instead, the *Trades Free ress* promoted working–class support for Catholic Emancipation and a rogramme of reform in Ireland which would 'provide employment at home those hordes of human beings who now seek it at any price abroad.' "No Popery" in its practical results', the paper explained, 'is – No eace for Ireland – no capital – no employment – wretchedness – cklessness – emigration – invasion – and alternate destruction to ll.'[9] Thereafter the radical appeal for social justice to Ireland as remarkably persistent, precisely because a programme of Catholic mancipation, repeal, tithe abolition, poor relief, security of tenure nd the like, implied a cessation of Irish immigration and competition the English labour market. The depth of distress in Ireland, obbett castigated middle–class liberals and Evangelical 'saints', attered far more than the fate of nationalist revolt in Spain or reece or the lot of the colonial slave.[10] The fears of English orking–class radicals that Irish coercion and low living standards ould be extended to themselves, intensified as they observed 'the ttered garments and forlorn looks of the impoverished and oppressed ibernians on their first arrival in this country'.[11] Their response as not to ostracize the immigrants, but to seek their support in a ampaign to secure political power and economic well–being for the orking class. Thus, at the same time as they advocated reforms in eland to stem the flow of immigration, the radicals were determined incorporate the Irish immigrants in their demand for fundamental arliamentary reform and self–determination throughout the kingdom.

The incorporation and mobilization of such a large group as the ish immigrants was, indeed, a top priority for the two great leaders the radical platform, Henry Hunt and Feargus O'Connor. Under their adership working–class radicalism developed as an open challenge to e state, with the radicals hoping to overawe government not by ctual insurrection, as the United Irishmen and others had planned uring the underground war years,[12] but by the display of overwhelming opular support. This strategy of 'forcible intimidation', later so kilfully adapted to middle–class ends by O'Connell's Catholic ssociation in the 1820s and the reform unions during the Reform Bill risis, originated with Hunt and the working–class radicals of the ost–Napoleonic era. It was then that Hunt established the radical mass platform – 'constitutional' protest open to all for 'constitutional' programme demanding the recognition of the politica rights of all.[13] Greatly impressed by Hunt's ability to draw th crowds, the Spenceans or 'revolutionary party' cast aside thei conspiratorial plotting in order to build up a 'General Union of th Non–Represented of the United Kingdom of Great Britain and Ireland', scheme promoted in their aptly–named journal, *The Shamrock, Th Thistle and The Rose.*[14] With numbers the name of the game, Hunt wa particularly keen to gain Irish support. Speaking at Smithfiel where Protestant martyrs had once been burned, he insisted that th radical programme must be extended to include Catholic Emancipatior and then announced the publication of an *Address from the People Great Britain to the People of Ireland* advocating 'Political Union i the cause of Universal Civil and Religious Liberty.' This was les than a month before the Peterloo massacre, an event which – literal – cut across the plans of Hunt and the Spenceans for a huge, fina radical demonstration in London which, they hoped, would attract som 20 – 30,000 Irish immigrant workers.[15]

During the next major period of radical activity Irish issue and Irish involvement were of crucial significance. Heated deba over the Catholic Emancipation settlement of 1829 lifted the movemer out of the torpor of the 1820s and encouraged Hunt and the Radic Reform Association to mount a new campaign. This renewed demand fo the full radical programme hardened into opposition to the Whig Refor Bill as the Radical Reform Association was replaced by the Nation Union of the Working Classes and Others.[16] Unlike the better know middle–class political unions of the time, the N.U.W.C. was to reac new heights of militancy once the Reform Bill was passed, a reflectio of the mounting anger of its large Irish membership at the repressiv policies pursued by the 'reforming' Whigs in their administration Ireland, where the 'land and tithe' war had flared up again. Such wa the concern with Irish matters that in October 1832, repeal of th Union was embodied in the Objects and Laws of the N.U.W.C.[17] A fe months later it was the Irish Coercion Act of 1833 which final persuaded the N.U.W.C. to adopt a policy of outright confrontatio with the government by calling a national convention. The governme prohibited the convention, and the N.U.W.C. disintegrated, but th intense anger over the Irish 'Polandizing' Act was never quashed.[18] Indeed it marked the beginning of that rapidly intensifyin disillusion with the 'bloody and brutal' Whigs and the reforme parliament in general which was to bring the Chartist movement in being. Disenchantment with Daniel O'Connell completed the proces the break of 1837 establishing Chartism's independence and working class character. O'Connell's political trimming had been attacked Hunt back at the time of the Catholic Emancipation settlement,[19] an more recently by O'Connor on the occasion of the Lichfield Hous compact.[20] In 1837 O'Connell's obeisance to political economy and th philosophy of the New Poor Law, together with his hostility towar trade unionism, so angered working–class radicals that they resolve on a policy of complete independence, not just from the Whigs, b from all parliamentary radicals. To a considerable extent, the debate over the Irish immigrants revolves around their response to this acrimonious but crucially important split.

This brief glimpse into the 'pre–history' of Chartism surely suggests an essential interweaving of English and Irish interests and endeavour, indicative of an all–embracing class loyalty. It was not, however, until the very last phase of Chartism that the Irish leaders in Dublin were prepared to endorse such co–ordinated activity. In 1848, with O'Connell dead, and with the Irish Confederation reshaped by Lalor's social radicalism and invigorated by news of successful revolution in Europe, the Dublin leaders changed tack and actively encouraged immigrants in England to effect a rapprochement with the Chartists.[21] Ironically in this open, official form, the alliance was to prove detrimental to the working–class challenge and to the interests of the Irish in England.

The operation of this alliance in Lancashire has been studied in some detail, since this was where the change in Irish official policy had the most noticeable impact[22] – Liverpool, not previously noted as a Chartist centre, occupies the largest single file in the Home Office Disturbance Papers for 1848. The failure of the alliance in Lancashire and throughout the country serves as a dramatic reminder that in terms of strictly 'instrumental' politics, of securing specific goals and political demands, the working–class radical movement in early Victorian England never had any prospect of success.[23] The alliance of 1848, the desideratum of every radical leader since 1815, revealed once and for all the inutility of the mass platform at the very same time that it provoked the most decisive mobilization of the nineteenth century *against* the working class.

In 1848 Chartist efforts were still concentrated on the mass platform and the strategy of forcible intimidation.[24] Although the movement was a mere shadow of the great agitation of the late 1830s, the militant support of the Confederates in Liverpool and throughout the north revitalised the otherwise rather effete Chartist rhetoric of menace. Once again, however, strong central direction was not forthcoming. As in 1839 and 1842, the Chartist Convention, a potential anti–parliament, displayed an enervating lack of self–confidence at the critical juncture. Following the 'fiasco' of the 10 April demonstration and the discrediting of the national petition, it is perhaps not surprising that the Chartist leadership hesitated before applying more 'pressure from without'. Having been outflanked on Kennington Common and embarrassed by their own petition, the Chartist delegates questioned both the legitimacy and the expediency of escalating their agitation. The constitutionalists within the movement were quite confounded by the absence of the requisite display of righteous and overwhelming public opinion, while the con–frontationalists had prepared themselves for repression and resistance, not public ridicule. Feargus O'Connor responded to this unfortunate and unforeseen turn of events by renouncing mass agitation altogether. Heartsick of appearing more insurrectionary than he actually was, O'Connor dismissed the bluster of the platform in favour of discussion of 'the labour question'. It was a sad irony that

O'Connor should deal such a blow to 'protest' Chartism at the ver
time when the Irish, whom he had always regarded as a necessar
component of the Chartist challenge, were at last at the ver
forefront of radical agitation and in no mood to demobilize.

The Irish in England were quite unperturbed by the procedura
problems which so beset their Chartist allies. Their leaders i
Dublin, no longer restrained by O'Connell's proscription of physica
force, were now seeking to emulate the success of the continenta
revolutions, and they were quick to realise the possibilities of som
diversionary operation in England which would detain the forces c
order. News from across the Irish Sea – first the conviction of Joh
Mitchel, editor of the *United Irishman*, then the suspension of Habea
Corpus, and finally Smith O'Brien's rising – so impassioned th
Confederates in England that they hastened across the threshold fro
implicit to explicit violence. By so doing, they disturbed th
Chartists and strained the alliance.

The Chartists, it must be stressed, did not repudiate physica
force. They applied 'forcible intimidation' with an open commitme
to physical confrontation quite beyond anything O'Connell ha
permitted in Ireland, as the capitulation at Clontarf had show
Violence, indeed, figured as prominently in the history, martyrolog
and popular consciousness of English radicalism as it did in th
anti-O'Connellite, radical republican tradition of Irish national
ism.[25] The great Irish rebellion of 1798 was as hallowed by th
Chartists as by the Irish themselves. Taking heed of the lessons c
that tragic 'year of liberty', the Chartists appreciated the need fo
maximum organization and involvement in any popular uprising. Th
Chartists, then, used the mass platform to prepare themselves for wha
social scientists would call 'internal war' – that is, highl
organized political violence with widespread popular participatio
Should constitutional platform agitation fail to coerce th
government, then physical force was to be employed, but from
position of strength, with the legitimacy of such action in no dout
whatsoever, and with the mass organization necessary to guarante
success already well established. Operating within this framewor
even after the events of April, the Chartists were critical of th
kinds of political violence displayed by their Irish allies, whethe
it be the spontaneous unorganized 'turmoil' which followed news c
Mitchel's trial or the elitist 'conspiratorial' plotting whic
developed soon after.[26] Still hoping to overawe the government b
mass mobilization, the Chartists were determined to guard against an
partial, premature or ill-prepared physical move.

The vehement response of the Irish immigrants to Mitchel'
conviction cut across Chartist plans for a great demonstration on Wh
Monday, when meetings were to be held throughout the land, at all c
which an exact count of heads was to be taken. These meetings on 1
June were to be the great moral demonstration so far denied th
Chartist mass platform in 1848, and an opportunity to make good th
discredited petition.[27] *'Attend in your Thousands'*, the poste
advertising the Bolton demonstration enjoined, *'and let the Physica*

Force Tyrants know that you are determined to have the Charter and Repeal'.[28] With all their energies and hopes directed towards the Whitsun demonstration, Chartists throughout the land were most disturbed when news of Mitchel's transportation brought the Irish immigrants on to the streets in unruly nocturnal processions and led to much loose talk about 'private assassination and Moscowing'.[29] In London, where there were particularly violent clashes with the police around Clerkenwell Green, the Chartists tried hard to align the vehemence with discipline and organization.[30] On 4 June, Ernest Jones, the foremost strategist of forcible intimidation, addressed a mass meeting on Bishop Bonner's Field. As a relatively recent recruit to Chartism, Jones was particularly anxious to avoid earlier errors and weaknesses, not least the false and debilitating division into moral and physical force camps. Moral force and physical force, Jones always contended, were 'twin cherries on the stalk', the essential point being that 'by showing a bold physical front, they would prevent the necessity for physical action'. 'Without organization', Jones insisted, 'a people is a mob; but with it, it becomes an army'.[31] Thus on 4 June he cautioned the crowd against any hot-headed impetuosity, partial outbreaks or rioting and exhorted them to enrol in Chartist and Confederate organizations. 'Show us your organization', Jones exclaimed, 'and you will have a glorious opportunity on the 12th':

> Only preparation – only organization is wanted, and the Green Flag shall float over Downing Street, and St. Stephen's. Only energy is wanted – only determination – and what will be the result? Why? That John Mitchel and John Frost will be brought back, and Sir George Grey and Lord John Russell will be sent to change places with them.[32]

After Jones had left the meeting and the crowd had begun to disperse, a vast police force, concealed in a nearby church, emerged with ferocious violence.[33] This police brutality was a portent of the government's determination to crush what remained of the Chartist challenge. The Whitsun demonstration was declared illegal, the Executive were prohibited from presenting a Memorial to the Queen, and warrants were issued for the arrest of Jones and other leading Chartists. 'The reign of terror is established', Harney expostulated, 'we live under Martial Law.'[34]

Anger at the arrest of Jones and other leaders, the prohibition of public meetings, and the general tightening of repression, pushed the Chartist stalwarts towards physical force. This was the all too familiar, tremulous path to insurrection in England. The strategy of forcible intimidation relied upon the threat of popular insurgency, but in the past the radicals had never actually progressed to widespread 'internal war.' Instead, the threshold of violence had been crossed only by an ardent embittered few who had turned to 'conspiracy' out of despair at the falling off of mass support and out of anger at the onrush of repression. Superimposed on this dispiriting pattern in 1848, however, was the excitement generated by the Irish situation. While the news from Ireland propelled the

Confederates towards conspiracy, the very strength of feeling evinced by the Irish in England probably delayed still further the hesitant Chartist drift towards violence. The furore over events in Ireland helped to keep alive the otherwise forlorn hope of mounting some great display of popular support, of counteracting the ignominious failure of the platform. In July, two new papers appeared – Bernard Treanor's *Truth Teller* and James Leach's *English Patriot and Irish Repealer* – in a final effort to succeed where Jones had failed in channelling anger and indignation into open organization and effective 'pressure from without'.[35] By this time, however, a secret Confederate system of organization and communication was well established, quite outside any public Chartist framework.

When the suspension of Habeas Corpus in Ireland was announced on 22 July large crowds gathered in several major towns, completely unannounced, to march in procession through the streets, the assemblies at Birmingham, Manchester and Bolton following an identical format.[36] Only in Liverpool, where the magistrates had kept the flourishing Confederate Clubs under strict surveillance, had the authorities expected any such show of force.[37] Thereafter events are much more difficult to unravel. Informers in London and in the north reported moves towards greater secrecy in Chartist and Irish circles as:

> measures are being arranged to cause an outbreak in the North of England the moment any demonstration shall take place in Ireland – and this outbreak, they expect, will become general throughout the land.[38]

Then came the news of Smith O'Brien's 'rising' in Tipperary which raised the emotive question, 'IS IRELAND UP?'[39] In an environment in which insurrectionary language was not immediately suspect and in which some system of secret organization existed, the informer–cum-provocateur found his task all the more easy. It was at this stage that Thomas Powell, the infamous spy, began taking detailed notes.[40] Encouraged by Powell, a small group of London Chartists and Confederates drew up plans for a rising on 16 August, on which date of course, they were duly apprehended by the authorities.[41]

The provincial ramifications of this August 'conspiracy' await detailed study. In the north, where the magistrates had instituted a ban on all confederated clubs, the move towards greater secrecy did not necessarily imply a commitment to insurrection.[42] Indeed there is evidence to suggest that some Chartists were still at odds with the Irish over the use of violence.[43] But it would seem that Manchester was intended to be the centre of co–ordinated insurrectionary activity on either 15 or 16 August.[44] On the night of the 15th, the Manchester magistrates decided to strike a 'decisive blow', and arrested 15 Chartist and Confederate leaders, eight of whom were Irish. This was the beginning of an exhaustive round–up of working–class activists, the Manchester magistrates sending a bill before the Grand Jury at Liverpool listing 'all the leading agitators who have for some time past infested this City and the neighbouring Towns'.[45]

The August conspiracy cannot be considered a serious challenge to the state in this 'year of revolution'. The Chartists had failed to exploit the full physical possibilities of their alliance with the Irish: the alliance, indeed, had exposed the fatal contradiction in radical strategy. Sensing the magnitude of the power confronting them, the Chartists insisted on legitimacy, organization and preparation, and were critical of the bellicosity of their Irish allies. But such solicitude proved self-defeating, as the fixation with legitimacy and large-scale organization caused delay and squandered the 'excitement' of the hour. In the end, a few ardent stalwarts were left to engage in a contest which had become even more hopeless and unequal.

The alliance, then, did not strengthen the working-class challenge in early Victorian England. In truth, it probably benefited the government far more than the Chartists. It was the Irish connection which allowed the government to introduce a particularly rigorous piece of repressive legislation. The stated intention of the Crown and Government Security Act was to curb the rhetoric emanating from Ireland following the formation of the Confederation and the publication of Mitchel's *United Irishman*, but the legislation had a much wider application. By bringing an end to the fundamental distinction which even Pitt and Sidmouth had recognized, between the written word (a felony) and the spoken word (a misdemeanour), this 'Felon Act' served as an effective gagging act to restrain the Chartist platform in the summer of 1848.[46] Furthermore, it was the spectre of the Irish, quite as much as the dread of the revolutionary contagion spreading across from the continent, which brought such an accretion of strength to the forces of order in 1848, allowing the ruling class to mount a massive display of its monopoly of legitimate violence. Borderline occupational groups, shopkeepers, clerks and the lower middle class in general, hurried to enlist in the ranks of the special constabulary as the press highlighted the 'Irish' threat.[47] 'The true character of the present movement is a ramification of the Irish conspiracy', *The Times* commented on the morning of 10 April:

> The Repealers wish to make as great a hell of this island as they have made of their own.[48]

The prompt conviction of Ernest Jones demonstrated that the courts, like the press, saw no distinction between Chartist 'constitutional' agitation and the rhetoric and violence of the *mêleés* in Clerkenwell and the East End.[49] As far as the press was concerned, Chartism had been transmogrified on Clerkenwell Green. In 'The Song of the Seditionist', *Punch* portrayed the Chartists revelling in rapine, pillage and massacre.[50] *The Times* was appalled by 'that extravagance of wild sedition which, for want of any other adjective, must be denominated "Irish"'. London, the paper warned, was endangered by 'the Irish love of knife, dagger and poison bowl'.[51] The press, indeed, played the Irish card on all possible occasions. William Cuffay, the veteran black radical and leader of the August conspiracy in London, was an easy target for the cartoonists, but *Punch*, like *The Times*, preferred to concentrate on the Irish element and always referred to the conspirators as 'MOONEY, ROONEY, HOOLAN, DOOLAN'.[52]

By exploiting the emotive connotations of the term 'Irish', the press and the establishment generally hit upon a crude but effective means both of stigmatizing Chartism and of fragmenting the working class. In vain, working-class papers like the *English Patriot and Irish Repealer* protested at what it labelled 'The Old Original Dodge Divide and Govern!'[53] Indeed, the volume of anti-Irish propaganda was to increase dramatically in ensuing years.[54] The dissemination of such material was an integral part of that process of 'liberalization' which John Foster has charted in Oldham, where the Anglo-Irish political solidarity of the 1840s was to give way to anti-Irish riots in the early 1860s.[55] The resurgence of popular Protestantism in mid-Victorian Britain, the proliferation of anti-Catholic and anti-Irish disturbances in the 1850s and 1860s, and the consequent defensive segregation of the Irish communities in the northern towns, can perhaps all be traced back to 1848 and the determination of the ruling class to use any means to proscribe the working-class challenge once and for all.[56] Thus it would seem that in so far as the identity of interests and active co-operation of the English working class and the Irish immigrants is concerned, the mid nineteenth century remains an important – and distressing – watershed in labour history.

Notes

This paper was presented to the Ninety-Seventh Annual Meeting of the American Historical Association, Washington, DC, December 27–30, 1982

1. For an introduction to the controversy, see D. Thompson, 'Ireland and the Irish in English Radicalism before 1850', in J. Epstein and D. Thompson (eds.), *The Chartist Experience* (London, 1982); J.H. Treble, 'O'Connor, O'Connell and the Attitudes of Irish Immigrants towards Chartism in the North of England 1838–48', in J. Butt and I.F. Clarke (eds.), *The Victorians and Social Protest* (Newton Abbot, 1973); and R. O'Higgins, 'The Irish Influence in the Chartist Movement', *Past and Present*, no.20 (1961), pp.83–94.
2. See E. Yeo, 'Christianity in Chartist Struggle, 1838–42', *Past and Present*, no.91 (1981), pp.109–39; and the various local studies in Epstein and Thompson.
3. For a stimulating critique of traditional 'compartmentalized' labour history, see F.K. Donnelly, 'Ideology and early English working-class history: Edward Thompson and his critics', *Social History*, vol.1 (1976), pp.219–38.
4. R. Sykes, 'Early Chartism and Trade Unionism in South-East Lancashire', in Epstein and Thompson.
5. Thompson, 'Ireland and the Irish', pp.123–4. For a contrasting view of the Irish in the north, see J.M. Werly, 'The Irish in Manchester, 1832–49', *Irish Historical Studies*, vol.xviii (1973), pp.345–58; and for the different experience of Irish immigrants later on in Victorian London, see L.H. Lees, *Exiles of Erin* (Manchester

1979).
6. This applies to most general studies of Chartism from M. Hovell, *The Chartist Movement* (Manchester, 1918) to J.T. Ward, *Chartism* (London, 1973). See also the new textbook by E.H. Hunt on *British Labour History, 1815–1914* (London, 1981), pp.158–76.
7. G. Rudé, *Ideology and Popular Protest* (London, 1980), pp.133–57; and his *Protest and Punishment* (Oxford, 1978), pp.13–26 and 52–58.
8. B. Collins, 'Proto–industrialization and pre–Famine emigration', *Social History*, vol.7 (1982), pp.127–46.
9. 'Ireland', *Trades Free Press*, 29 July 1827; and 'English Writers Upon Ireland, and English Prejudices – the Question of Catholic Emancipation', *ibid.*, 5 August 1827.
10. 'London Tavern Humbug', *Cobbett's Weekly Political Register*, 21 June 1823; and 'West India Islands', *ibid.*, 3 January 1824.
11. See the speech by George Dewhurst at a public meeting of the working classes at Blackburn, reported in *Trades' Newspaper*, 7 January 1827.
12. A.W. Smith, 'Irish Rebels and English Radicals 1798–1820', *Past and Present*, no.7 (1955), pp. 78–85; and M. Elliott, 'The "Despard Conspiracy" Reconsidered', *ibid.*, no.75 (1977), pp.46–61.
13. For the mass platform and the strategy of forcible intimidation, see J.C. Belchem, 'Henry Hunt and the evolution of the mass platform', *English Historical Review*, vol.xciii (1978), pp.739–773, and 'Republicanism, popular constitutionalism and the radical platform in early nineteenth–century England', *Social History*, vol.vi (1981), pp.1–32; and T.M. Kemnitz, 'Approaches to the Chartist movement: Feargus O'Connor and Chartist strategy', *Albion*, vol.v (1973), pp.67–73.
14. T.M. Parsinnen, 'The revolutionary party in London, 1816–20', *Bulletin of the Institute of Historical Research*, vol.xlv (1972), pp.266–82.
15. J. Belchem, 'Henry Hunt', pp.756–58; I.J. Prothero, *Artisans and Politics in Early Nineteenth–Century London* (Folkestone, 1979), pp.113–14.
16. Prothero, pp.275–99.
17. 'N.U.W.C.', *Poor Man's Guardian*, 6 October 1832.
18. See the reports of N.U.W.C. meetings in *ibid.*, 23 February – 18 May 1833.
19. See for example Hunt's letter to O'Connell, 8 March 1829, in *Cobbett's Weekly Political Register*, 14 March 1829.
20. J. Epstein, *The Lion of Freedom: Feargus O'Connor and the Chartist Movement, 1832–42* (London, 1982), pp.8–21.
21. J.H. Treble, 'The Irish Agitation', in J.T. Ward (ed.), *Popular Movements c. 1830–50* (London, 1970), pp.174–79.
22. W.J. Lowe, 'The Chartists and the Irish Confederates: Lancashire, 1848', paper presented to the American Historical Association Conference, Washington DC, December 27–30, 1982 – I understand that Professor Lowe has submitted a longer version of this to *Irish Historical Studies*. I also pay considerable attention to Lancashire in an earlier paper on 'English Working–Class Radicalism

and the Irish 1815–50', *North West Labour History Society Bulletin*, vol.8 (1982–83), pp.5–18.
23. For the distinction between goal–orientated 'instrumental' politics and value–orientated 'expressive' politics, see F. Parkin, *Middle Class Radicalism* (Manchester, 1968), pp.34–40.
24. For a general analysis of Chartism in 1848, see J.C. Belchem, '1848: Feargus O'Connor and the collapse of the mass platform', in Epstein and Thompson. For an excellent study of events in London, see David Goodway, *London Chartism* (Cambridge, 1982), pp.68–96.
25. This radical republican tradition is now attracting considerable attention: see T. Garvin, 'Defenders, Ribbonmen and Others: Underground Political Networks in Pre–Famine Ireland', *Past and Present*, no.96 (1982), pp.133–55, and M.R. Beames, 'The Ribbon Societies: Lower–Class Nationalism in pre–Famine Ireland', *ibid.*, no.97 (1982), pp.128–43.
26. For the classification of political violence as turmoil, conspiracy or internal war, see T.R. Gurr, *Why Men Rebel* (Princeton, 1970), pp.9–13. See also W.H. Maehl, 'The Dynamics of Violence in Chartism: A Case Study in Northeastern England', *Albion*, vol.7 (1975), pp.101–19.
27. 'Proclamation of the Provisional Executive Committee of the N.C.A.', *N[orthern] S[tar]*, 27 May 1848.
28. Posting–bill enclosed in Mayor of Bolton, 12 June 1848, in H[ome] O[ffice Papers: Public Record Office] 45/2410 (1)A.
29. Reports and enclosures in Mayor of Nottingham, 7 June, and Mayor of Birmingham 29 May and 7 June 1848 HO 45/2410 (3); Lewis Levy in [Records of the] Met[ropolitan] Pol[ice Officers: Public Record Office] 2/65; and *The Times*, 2 June 1848.
30. *The Times*, 31 May – 2 June 1848; *NS*, 3 June 1848; and the letters from Faulk and other government reporters claiming damages for the injuries inflicted on them by the intemperate police in HO 45/2410 (2) and MetPol 2/66. See also D. Large, 'London in the Year of Revolutions, 1848' in J. Stevenson (ed.) pp.195–7 *London in the Age of Reform* (Oxford, 1977), pp.195–7.
31. For a useful selection of speeches by Jones in 1848, see J. Saville, *Ernest Jones: Chartist* (London, 1952), pp.97–108.
32. *NS*, 10 June 1848.
33. MetPol 2/66 includes a file of complaints about police behaviour on 4 June, all from non–Chartists.
34. 'Martial Law', *NS*, 17 June 1848.
35. *Truth Teller*, nos.1–3, 29 July – 12 August 1848; *English Patriot and Irish Repealer*, nos.1 and 2, 22 and 29 July 1848.
36. Mayor of Birmingham, 27 July – 1 August 1848, HO 45/2410 (3)P; Lt. Gen. Arbuthnott 26 July, and Clerk to the Magistrates, Bolton, 28 July – 1 August 1848, HO 45/2410 (4)AB. Similar reports were received from Loughborough, Stockport and Edinburgh.
37. Report of the Committee of Magistrates, 8 July, Rushton, 24 July, and the Mayor of Liverpool, 25 July and 3 August 1848, HO 45/2410 (1)A. See also Lt. Gen. Arbuthnott, 2 August 1848, HO 45/2410 (4)AB, and *The Times*, 24 and 26 July 1848.

38. J. Paterson, 24 July 1848, MetPol 2/62. See also W. Dawson's reports enclosed in Duke of Portland, 21 July – 10 August 1848, HO 45/2410 (1)A. For more details of spies and informers in 1848, see J.C. Belchem, 'The Spy-System in 1848: Chartists and Informers – an Australian Connection', *Labour History*, no.39 (1980), pp.15-27.
39. Several Chartists and Confederates were brought before the courts for their speeches at a London meeting advertised with banner placards, 'IS IRELAND UP?', see the reports of the trials in *NS*, 2 and 23 September 1848.
40. See Powell's evidence at the examination of W. Dowling, *NS*, 26 August 1848.
41. 'Reports of Anticipated Disturbances on Wednesday Night', HO 45/2410 (2).
42. See for example the police reports of the private discussions at Hannah Scholefield's house in Rochdale, in W. Heton, 5 September 1848, HO 45/2410 (1)A.
43. Lt. Gen. Arbuthnott's reports, 14 and 15 August 1848, HO 45/2410 (4)AB.
44. For a convenient review of the evidence, see F.C. Mather, *Public Order in the Age of the Chartists*, (Manchester, 1959), pp.24-26.
45. Manchester, Electric Telegraph Company, 16 August and Mayor of Manchester, 22 August 1848, HO 45/2410 (1)A.
46. *Parliamentary Debates*, 3rd. series, vol.xcviii, 7-18 April 1848.
47. For details of 'Swearing in of Special Constables, protection of Public Buildings etc' see MetPol 2/65.
48. *The Times*, 10 April 1848.
49. 'The Trials', *NS*, 8 and 15 July 1848.
50. *Punch*, vol.xiv (1848), p.240.
51. *The Times*, 2 June and 8 July 1848.
52. *Punch*, vol.xv (1848), 154-55; *The Times*, 18 August and 29 September 1848.
53. 'Another Shot at the Press Gang!', *English Patriot and Irish Repealer*, 5 August 1848.
54. As Sheridan Gilley has shown, after the late 1840s it was the malign aspects of 'Paddy' that were stressed in cartoons and literature, displacing the idealized and benign elements of the stereotype, see his 'English Attitudes to the Irish in England, 1780-1900' in C. Holmes (ed.), *Immigrants and Minorities in British Society* (London, 1978).
55. J. Foster, *Class Struggle and the Industrial Revolution* (London, 1974), chapter 7.
56. For an interesting analysis of the Irish in the north after 1850, see N. Kirk, 'Ethnicity, Class and Popular Toryism, 1850-70', in K. Lunn (ed.), *Hosts, Immigrants and Minorities* (Folkestone, 1980).

IRISH INFLUENCE ON PARLIAMENTARY ELECTIONS IN LONDON, 1885–1914: A SIMPLE TEST

Alan O'Day

The supposed influence of the Irish Catholic community in the parliamentary elections of the boroughs of England and Scotland during the period 1885–1914 has exercised a sustained fascination. However there is as yet no close study of the electoral behaviour of the Irish or of their ability to swing the balance in parliamentary contests only a handful of efforts to assess the impact of Irish voters in restricted localities and usually limited to one or two elections Most attention has centred on the admittedly pivotal general elections of 1885 and 1886. Neglect, in this instance, arises from the often rehearsed deficiencies of the source material. It is difficult to state with precision the size of the Irish electorate, the degree to which they participated in successive elections even when formally qualified, and how and why they divided themselves politically. Yet the task is not beyond evaluation as long as it is recognized that only approximations can be offered.

Beween 1885 and 1914 the franchise qualifications and constituency boundaries remained largely unchanged. Interpretation of the rules, population shifts, and the total size of the electorate did not stay static, but the period is suitable for internal comparisons Before 1885, there was only a relatively small Irish Catholic electorate in British boroughs. The legislation of 1884 and 1885 greatly increased the number of voters, made balloting easier and more convenient, and created an electoral system of representation based on the single–member constituency. It was the last, the new constituency arrangement, which perhaps more than anything else created a different set of opportunities and concerns. The new constituencies were usually artificial divisions. Many recent writers have stressed that the single–member seat was a factor in the resurgence of the Conservative party's electoral position, particularly in the English boroughs. It also seemed that Irish voters might exert a disproportionate influence on the outcome of many contests, because in relatively small units they would hold the balance between the Conservatives and Liberals.[1] The effect of Irish votes appeared especially vital in London and industrial Lancashire.

By 1885 there was a very considerable Irish Catholic community in Britain. Before the Great Famine of the 1840s, there were over 400,000 Irish–born living in Britain. The Famine swelled these numbers, and by the 1880s the Irish community numbered somewhere in the order of 1,250,000 to 1,500,000 in Britain with a further increase evident by 1914. But not all of these were Irish–born. After 1861 the Irish–born element was decreasing, and the ethnically Irish community was increasingly built on the foundations of men and women who had always lived in Britain.[2] Nor were the Irish evenly distributed. Few lived in rural districts; nearly all were urban dwellers. Liverpool, Glasgow and most of the northern industrial cities had notable concentrations of Irish, equalling as much as a quarter of the population in a few centres. London, however, contained the largest absolute numbers, having an estimated 350,000 by 1900.[3] Within the cities, particularly London, the distribution was uneven. Although equalling perhaps ten per cent of the metropolis, they constituted over ten per cent of the electorate in no more than possibly five parliamentary constituencies.[4] Nowhere did they total twenty per cent of the electorate. In only one constituency in Britain were Irish voters sufficiently numerous to return one of their own to Parliament (the Scotland Division of Liverpool), but in many places they hoped to have a decisive effect on the outcome between British parties.

Indeed, impressive claims were registered for the influence of the Irish vote, especially in the aftermath of the general election of 1885. The Irish Nationalist party trumpeted its ability to decide the representation of nearly a hundred seats in Britain even before the legislation of 1884 and 1885.[5] Following the general election of 1885, party spokesmen insisted that the Conservatives had secured nearly forty constituencies which Liberals otherwise would have won but for the Irish vote.[6] The Irish Nationalist League of Great Britain had been very active during the election, and had acted as the medium for the organization of the Irish vote. Just before the first ballot, parliamentary elections then being spread out over two to three weeks, Parnell issued a manifesto calling on the Irish in Britain to vote against the Liberals, with fewer than a handful of named exemptions to this dictate.[7] Despite some contemporary doubts, and the marked inability of the Liberals in 1886 with Nationalist assistance, to recapture more than the odd seat (one being in London) allegedly lost because of Irish votes in 1885, the orthodox view became that Parnell's declaration had turned the result in some twenty–five to forty constituencies. The principal caveat, stated nearly forty years ago, did not deny the power of the Irish vote, but attributed its shift to the Conservatives in 1885 at least as much to the influence of the Catholic Church, which was worried about its schools, as to Parnell.[8]

During the past two decades the purported electoral power of the Irish has been treated critically. Compelling doubts have been aired about the ability of the Irish Catholic community to affect the outcome of elections. The evidence has been chiefly of two kinds – general and inferential and from studies of specific localities.[9] Reservations about the Irish factor fall under four broad headlines:

(1) sociological explanations; (2) anti-Irish reaction 'backlash'; (3) the decisive part which British parties played in elections and the exclusion of the Irish from their ambit; and (4) the bias of the electoral registration system. These categories are not mutually exclusive, and virtually all commentators have employed the full range to demonstrate the weakness of the Irish position.

Sociological explanations have commanded wide respect. The argument stems from the view that electoral participation is highest in stable communities where individuals are most completely integrated into society and accept its value system. Irishmen fail by this yard-stick on three grounds – they belonged to the poor stratum of the community; they were relatively disorganized; and they were frequently politically disaffected, or did not possess a strong attachment to the dominant political culture of urban Britain. Paul Thompson has put the case neatly:

> Irish influence was further weakened by poor organization. Insufficiently assimilated to join in a large measure in metropolitan political life, they were nevertheless equally insufficiently alien to develop the political features of a well organised minority, with it own culture, press and communal institutions.[10]

It seems, then, that the Irish lacked the appropriate characteristics to make a political impact.

Although the sociological analysis has a seductive appeal, it is ultimately unsatisfying. Henry Pelling, like Thompson, finds little real muscle in Irish electoral influence in London constituencies – something as evidently true at the end as at the beginning of the period.[11] But the Irish were, as John Denvir observed in the 1890s and has been confirmed elsewhere, making perceptible strides in the direction of upward social and economic mobility.[12] By the turn of the century many Irishmen were involved in trades unions. Even much earlier the London Irish has shown a marked propensity to constitute themselves into stable households and communities.[13] That tendency was increasingly evident after 1910. Moreover, the Irish Nationalist party established a network of organizations to mobilize the political activity of the Irish community, while Gladstone's adoption of Home Rule for Ireland in 1886 probably facilitated a greater degree of integration into the host culture.[14] Pre-eminently, though, the case falls on the notion that the Irish community lacked cohesion and an organisational apparatus. In fact, it had the ideal vehicle in the Catholic Church which by general acknowledgement played a great part in, and exercised immense influence over, communal life.[15] The Church had political as well as social and religious functions. And, if the sociological case is to be sustained, the Irish community should have been more politically effective by 1914. That did not happen at parliamentary level though Irishmen in larger numbers were forging their way into various local offices.

Secondly, it has been supposed that where there was a significant concentration of Irish there was a considerable anti-Irish sentiment. Its existence is undeniable. The situation in Liverpool is so well–known as not to warrant repetition here.[16] Similarly, in Glasgow and in many industrial cities of northern England, Irish votes tended to have a cancelling effect, with many people aligning themselves with the party which seemed to oppose Irish claims.[17] London, though, was a social and political maelstrom where the Irish were only one of many ingredients. There is little evidence for a meaningful political 'backlash' in the metropolis. It was no more than a minor factor in London.

In the period of the Third Reform Act, it was necessary for voters to seek to be placed on the electoral register. Modern scholars have rightly emphasized the crucial role of the political parties in getting voters registered, defending their position on the rolls and/or having them removed from the register. Parties paid attention to potential electors on whom they could depend for support. Irishmen were sometimes viewed by the Liberals – obviously the Conservatives had no wish to encourage Irish voters – as 'somewhat fickle' and therefore did not receive as much attention from party agents.[18] Hence, Irishmen tended to be underrepresented on the electoral registers. Outside of certain instances, mainly in the northern cities, evidence for this contention is a bit thin. After 1885 Liberals in London had little cause to worry about the reliability of the Irish. Never was this truer than for the two general elections of 1910, when there were ample reasons to encourage Irish registration. In any case, the Irish Nationalist party and the Catholic Church had sufficient grounds for getting Irishmen registered and provided an organizational structure for the purpose.

The belief that the registration system itself was heavily loaded against the Irish has had the nearly universal assent of modern writers. Although there has not been a specific study of how the registration regulations affected the Irish community, it has seemed logical that as a mainly working–class group Irishmen must have suffered the consequences of a system loaded against the lower orders. Registration was geared to settled, married men who did not move frequently and were sufficiently prosperous not to claim poor relief.[19] There has been a general agreement that the system tended to exclude many working–class men. Recently, however, these confident assumptions about the bias of the registration regulations have been severely shaken. Duncan Tanner has demonstrated that the voteless towards the end of the period were almost certainly young unmarried men, often belonging to the middle–classes.[20] The bias against the working–class was comparatively insignificant and in London, particularly in poorer districts containing many Irish, lodgers were able to register in impressive numbers. Irishmen resided in settled communities, were participating in upward mobility and increasingly enjoyed the general affluence of the age.[21] The London community, in particular, received the middle–class migrant from Ireland.[22] Females had always immigrated in numbers approximating those of men, and by the turn of the century actually constituted the majority of the flow from Ireland. By the turn of the century, the Irish community was not made up of mainly young, unmarried, frequently moving men. The bias against the Irish in London of the registration system must have been comparatively slight, and cannot be counted a major cause of their political impotence.

Fortunately, there is another means available for analysis of the weakness of the Irish community in parliamentary elections in London. Dr. Pelling's *Social Geography of British Elections 1885–1910* provides some valuable raw material. His examination for the eight general elections (1885, 1886, 1892, 1895, 1900, 1906, and two in 1910) divides the constituencies of the London County Council area into three categories based on 1891 figures.[23] He classifies constituencies as (A) those with a prosperous, predominantly middle or upper–class electorate; (B), where the predominance of electors was neither middle–class nor working–class but mixed; and (C) predominantly working–class areas. He acknowledges that a few constituencies only narrowly fall into the group to which they have been assigned, but overall his categories are remarkably useful.

There are eighteen constituencies in category A (Battersea, Clapham; Camberwell, Dulwich; Chelsea; Finsbury, Holborn; Hackney, North; Hampstead; Kensington, South; Lambeth, Brixton; Lambeth, Norwood; Lewisham; Marylebone, East; Marylebone, West; Paddington, North; Paddington, South; St. George's, Hanover Square; Strand; Wandsworth; and Westminster). These constituencies exhibit a uniformly high Conservative voting preference throughout the period. Only two returned Liberals in 1885 and none did so in 1886, 1892, 1895 or 1900. Only four went Liberal in the huge landslide of 1906, but at the general elections of January and December 1910, these reverted to Conservatives. Pelling listed only the percentage of the total poll gained by Conservatives (Unionists), but when his information is supplemented by the actual difference in votes between the parties in category A, the impression is reinforced that these ordinarily were safe seats. Aside from female domestics, who did not have the ballot, Irish numbers in category A areas were small and could not affect the result. If the Irish voted Conservative in 1885, itself an uncertain proposition, they were of little importance in the outcome.

Category B contains fifteen constituencies (Deptford; Fulham, Greenwich; Hackney, Central; Hackney, South; Hammersmith; Islington, East; Islington, North; Islington, South; Kensington, North; Lambeth, Kennington; St. Pancras, North; St. Pancras, South, St. Pancras, West and Woolwich) and was socially mixed. Liberals experienced sustained difficult in capturing these seats, taking only six in 1885; two, though only narrowly , in 1886; four in 1892; none in 1895 and 1900; gaining most in 1906 but slipping back to about half by December 1910. In terms of differences in actual votes, the margin tended to be narrower than in category A constituencies but almost always wider than the notional Irish vote. There were relatively few Irish voters in most category B seats and in the four constituencies (Kensington, North; Hackney, South; Fulham; and Woolwich) where they were thought to be of some significance, they were unable to hold the balance. In each of these four constituencies the Unionist proportion of the poll increased in 1886. Kensington North was estimated to have an Irish electorate equal to six to ten per cent of the total, yet it went Liberal only in 1892 and 1906.[24] Indeed, in both general elections of 1910 the seat was won handily by the Conservatives, which, contrary to Dr. Pelling's assertion, is scarcely likely to be a consequence of Irish defections from the Liberals. The Irish, therefore, were insufficiently numerous in the crucial category B seats to be a major factor in whether they went Liberal or Conservative. In fact, the Irish had very little influence in such seats.

The remaining category – C – contains twenty–four constituencies which are mainly working–class and concentrated largely in East and South London. The list includes Battersea; Bethnal Green, N.E.; Bethnal Green, S.W.; Camberwell, North; Camberwell, Peckham; Finsbury, Central; Finsbury, East; Islington, West; Lambeth, North; Newington, Walworth; Newington, West; St. Pancras, East; Shoreditch, Haggerston; Shoreditch, Hoxton, Southwark, Bermondsey; Southwark, Rotherhithe; Southwark, West; and the Tower Hamlets constituencies of Bow and Bromley; Limehouse; Mile End; Poplar; St. George's–in–the–East; Stepney; and Whitechapel. London's Irish were heavily concentrated in the category C seats and formed more than ten per cent of the electorate in at least four, as well as being a significant element in several others. As might be anticipated, Liberal fortunes were higher in category C seats, though not so impressive as would be supposed from the class distribution. Nevertheless, few of these constituencies were marginal, most being safely anti–Conservative (Unionist) by 1906. Where the Irish were densely concentrated, they could not have been a very potent independent variable at the general elections of 1885 and 1886, nor could they, had they so intended, have turned Conservative deficits into victories from 1906. At Whitechapel, Conservatives took ony 45.6 per cent of the poll in 1885 and 40.8 per cent in December 1910; at St. George's, the comparable percentages are 49.7 and 42.2; Poplar, 34.1 and 35.1; Limehouse, 60.5 and 45.4; Rotherhithe 54.3 (increased to 60.3 in 1886) and 42.9; and at Bermondsey 49.4 (rising to 52.8 in 1886) and 42.9. The pattern elsewhere is broadly similar. The variations, notably at the beginning of the period, clearly are attributable to local factors rather than to the Irish acting as a self–contained group.[25]

The Irish certainly existed as voters and were present in some numbers in certain constituencies, but they could not significantly alter the outcome of elections even had they acted as a unified bloc up for auction. Irish votes were not a united bloc available for barter anyway, but were part and parcel of the local, mainly working–class environment where they existed. Some Irish probably did move to the Conservatives in 1885, but they were overwhelmingly Liberal thereafter. But, either way, they could not swing results by changing sides or abstaining, and were generally part of the anti–Conservative electorate. Excepting some possible 'backlash' effect in 1886, anti–Irish voting was not a significant feature of election results, for very few constituencies in London could be turned on a small number of votes.

An absence of a genuinely competitive political environment had consequences for the organization of the Irish community and its relations with British parties. There was relatively little incentive for either the Irish leadership or British party agents to make continuous exceptional exertions at registration in ensuring that voter turn–out was maximized. London's election results did not hinge on such efforts. Irishmen were not excluded as some sort of deliberate ploy because they were unreliable. Also, the Liberal (or in a few instances at the end of the period Labour) party was firmly established as the Irish community's party in parliamentary elections. While the progressives were generally sympathetic to Ireland's claims and to those of the London Irish as members of the working–class, they did not have to be responsive to each and every facet of the community's outlook. The Irish really had no weapon to use on the Liberals (Labour), which at least freed the latter from an excessive sense of need to appease Catholic wishes at every turn. Irish powder was rather wet: there was little real alternative to sticking with the anti–Unionist coalition.

The single–member constituency has been seen as a means by which the importance of Irish votes was enhanced.[26] In practice, the opposite was the case. Parliamentary constituencies, as they have existed since 1885, are too large as units for even a sizeable politically–conscious group like the Irish to thrive in. In contrast, Irish influence in local affairs has been more evident and parties correspondingly responsive to the special interests of the Catholic community. The slow rate of advance of Irish leaders at parliamentary level in post–1885 Britain can be attributed to the nature of the system rather than to the quality of politician springing from the Catholic community.[27] With the Irish experience in mind, there should be little wonderment that the post–1945 immigrants have found penetration of Parliament virtually impossible. Nor is it surprising that they, like the Irish, have been little more than a ripple in the outcome of parliamentary elections.

Notes

1. See C.H.D. Howard, 'The Parnell Manifesto of 21 November 1885, and the Schools Question', *English Historical Review*, vol.ccxlii (January 1947), pp.42–43.
2. Derived from J.A. Jackson, *The Irish in Britain* (London,1963), p.11.
3. See P. Thompson, *Socialists, Liberals and Labour* (London,1967), pp.25, 355.
4. *Ibid.*, p.26, plus my count.
5. Parnell to A. Webb, 11 November 1883, T.C. Harrington Papers, National Library of Ireland, MS 8581 (1).
6. *The Times*, 11 December 1885.
7. *Ibid.*, 23 November 1885.
8. Howard, 'The Parnell Manifesto', pp.42–51.
9. See A. O'Day, *The English Face of Irish Nationalism* (Dublin,

1977), pp.110–13; J.McCaffrey, 'The Irish Vote in Glasgow in the Later Nineteenth Century', *Innes Review*, vol.xxi (Spring 1970), pp.30–6; P.J. Waller, *Democracy & Sectarianism* (Liverpool,1981), pp.58–70.
10. Thompson, *Socialists, Liberals and Labour*, p.26.
11. H. Pelling, *Social Geography of British Elections 1885–1910* (London,1967), p.58.
12. J. Denvir, *The Irish in Britain* (London, 1892), pp.398–9; L. Lees, *Exiles of Erin* (Manchester,1979), p.242, passim.
13. Lees, *Exiles of Erin*, pp.123–63.
14. For this suggestion, see, M.A.G. Ó Tuathaigh, 'The Irish in Nineteenth–Century Britain', *Transactions of the Royal Historical Society* (1981), 5th. Series, vol.31 (1981), pp.171–72.
15. See J. Hickey, *Urban Catholics* (London,1967), pp.144–7.
16. The best account is in Waller, *Democracy & Sectarianism*.
17. See McCaffrey, 'The Irish Vote in Glasgow', pp.30–36.
18. M. Oldroyd to W. Runciman, 11 November 1901, W. Runciman Papers, University of Newcastle–upon–Tyne.
19. N. Blewett, 'The Franchise in the United Kingdom, 1885–1918', *Past & Present*, no.32 (December 1965), pp.27–56.
20. D. Tanner, 'The Parliamentary Electoral System, the "Fourth" Reform Act and the Rise of Labour in England and Wales', *Bulletin of the Institute of Historical Research*, vol.lvi (November 1983), pp.205–19.
21. Jackson, *The Irish in Britain*, p.94.
22. *Ibid.*, p.192.
23. Pelling, *Social Geography of British Elections*, pp.26–59.
24. *Ibid.*, p.41.
25. *Ibid.*, pp.42–56.
26. Howard, 'The Parnell Manifesto', p.42.
27. My earlier comparison with the American Irish community seems very wide of the mark. See O'Day, *The English Face of Irish Nationalism*, p.125.

A TALE OF TWO CITIES: COMMUNAL STRIFE IN GLASGOW AND LIVERPOOL BEFORE 1914

Tom Gallagher

It is not hard to see why Glasgow and Liverpool have been most closely identified in the popular imagination with communal friction between Irish immigrants and British workers. Both cities were the main reception centres for millions of Ireland's inhabitants, pushed out of their island by hardship and famine and drawn by the Industrial Revolution.[1] The biggest Irish communities grew up in those western cities which also enjoyed close kinship ties with Protestant Ulster. In cities which grew too quickly to be successful melting pots, it was not only the Irish Catholic newcomers and their British hosts who lived in uneasy proximity. The arrival of Protestant Ulstermen, who were often hostile to their Catholic fellow–countrymen, also greatly complicated matters. The communal tensions of nineteenth–century Belfast were transmitted to Lanarkshire and Liverpool due to 'an unceasing ebb and flow of workers moving to and from Belfast, the Mersey, and the Clyde'.[2] For Erich Strauss, these three cities formed an 'industrial triangle', but the nature and extent of communal unrest in the three of them were not identical. Liverpool and Glasgow managed to avoid the full–scale sectarian warfare which periodically engulfed their Irish sister–city, producing large–scale casualties and permanently dividing Belfast into two rival camps.

Yet in Glasgow and Liverpool, sectarianism was generated by different causes, some of which receded in importance to be replaced by new ones. At various times, economic rivalry between different segments of the working–class, religious disputes, and the Irish Question exacerbated community relations, sometimes separately, at other times in combination. Although the apostles of sectarian unrest viewed their circumstances in simple terms, sectarianism was a complex phenomenon, taking a variety of forms in industrial Scotland, so that the contrasts between Glasgow and Liverpool were considerable. There were, nevertheless, underlying similarities to the communal disputes that scarred these cities as well as important differences.

Employment and Discrimination

Glasgow, a much older city than Liverpool, had deeper traditions on which to draw that make explicable its frosty reception of Irish immigrants. Unlike Liverpool, which already looked outwards to the Empire by 1800 and was isolated from its hinterland, Glasgow entered the industrial age as an archetypally Scottish city. It had been influenced by the Reformation and was transformed by the Industrial Revolution, two events responsible for widening a cultural and developmental gap between Scotland and most of Ireland which had not been so noticeable when both had lain outside the English state. Against these considerations, the shared Celtic lineage of their two peoples counted for little. In 1779, anti-Catholic riots occurred in Glasgow and other Scottish towns, and only in 1793 did the Scottish Relief Act end the penal laws against the Catholic population already repealed in England and Ireland.[3] Much later, in 1867, Bishop Gray explained to Henry Manning, the visiting English prelate, that there was little common ground between them:

> The Scottish people are animated by a strong hereditary hatred of Catholicity; nor is the feeling of the country favourable to Irish settlers . . . The religion, the history, the character and habits of the two peoples show many elements not of difference only but antagonism . . .[4]

Liverpool was not burdened by these ancient prejudices and was situated in one of the few parts of England not wholly converted to Protestantism at the Reformation. Catholicism survived east of the port in Preston and Wigan, and among the landed gentry and their retainers. But before the onset of Irish immigration, the shape of things to come was clear by 1798, when nearby Manchester played host to the first Orange Lodge in England.[5] Until the 1830s, Manchester rather than Liverpool was the power-base of the anti-Catholic Orange Order, founded in County Armagh in 1795 and dedicated to upholding the British Protestant constitution.

Liverpool became more fertile ground for Orangeism with the formation of a large Irish community in the 1830s. A steady stream of new arrivals turned into a human torrent in the mid-1840s, when over one million starving peasants fled after the failure of the Irish potato. 300,000 Irish people arrived in Liverpool during the first half of 1847 alone.[6] Many moved on, but many stayed, so that by 1851 23% of the city's population was Irish-born, making up an estimated 33% of the working class.[7] Uneducated, penniless, many speaking only Gaelic, and some disease-ridden, they were an alien and unwelcome force which transformed the demography of Liverpool, strained the city's facilities to breaking-point, and created many new social problems. Prejudice against both the Irish and their offspring coloured the political life of the city well into the next century, but still they came, Liverpool being the main gateway from backward and exploited rural Ireland to industrial England. By the 1890s, Liverpool was the largest Roman Catholic diocese in England, with over 400,000 people, one-fifth of the total Catholic population.[8]

Irish immigration to the west of Scotland was more gradual than to Lancashire. The Famine did not overwhelm the amenities or living space in Glasgow as it did in Liverpool. For this, there are at least two reasons. First, the province of Ulster, always the chief source of Irish immigration to Scotland, had been spared the worst results of the Famine. Second, the industrial economy of west-central Scotland was at the peak of its expansion and was able to absorb large amounts of cheap unskilled labour.

The Famine thus had a less devastating effect on the social fabric of Glasgow, and the backlash against the Irish from the established community was slower in making itself felt, traditional prejudices notwithstanding. Nevertheless, the Irish were thoroughly disliked and feared in both cities for the problems which they brought in their wake. Not the least of these was disease. Typhus was sometimes called 'famine disease' or 'Irish fever', and its association with the Irish hastened the emergence of distinct ghettoes or 'Little Irelands'. Some of the Irish rejected the housing standards of the native poor and were condemned for their unhygienic habits. The expectations of most immigrants were set by what was commonplace in Ireland, but Ireland was much poorer than Britain.[9] The prominence of the Irish in the statistics of crime was another cause of complaint, although their offences were mostly of a minor kind – drunkenness, petty theft, and offences against the person, sometimes committed in mitigating circumstances.[10] Drunkenness was identified as a singularly Irish vice. Even John Denvir, an eloquent defender of Irish immigrants, conceded that 'drink more than poverty has been the curse of the Irish'.[11] In Glasgow, however, drink may have been less of a stigma than in England, since the Scottish working-class drank heavily as well.[12]

Although their numbers and resources were limited, English Roman Catholics could have done more to welcome their pauperized co-religionists. The divisions of class, culture and nationality proved greater than the bonds of shared religion.[13] Although ten priests died in Liverpool while tending the sick in 1847, Lancashire Catholics did not go out of their way to ease the immigrants into British society. Like the Scottish Catholic clergy up to the 1860s, they may have even felt that the Irish were temporary visitors who would eventually abandon an uncongenial exile in Britain for the greener pastures of America.[14]

Many Englishmen viewed their arrival as a social disaster, and residential segregation set the Irish apart from the host population in all the British cities in which they settled in any numbers. Irish and British prejudice both encouraged this Victorian form of apartheid. Writing in the *Glasgow Free Press*, a correspondent warned of the danger of association with Protestant Scotsmen: '(they) will poison and corrupt our hearts, they will, by degrees, make us cold and indifferent about our religion and duty to God'.[15] In Liverpool, such introversion was even more noticeable, given the watertight nature of residential segregation along religious lines. As a curate attached to St. Francis Xavier's, Liverpool, in 1880, the poet-priest Gerard

Manley Hopkins found that what distinguished the Liverpool Irish from Irishmen he had known in Glasgow was their hostility to the city.[16] Yet the Liverpool Irish produced their own Catholic bourgeoisie, based on the retail trade and the professions, much earlier than the Glasgow Irish, and by 1886 had elected their own M.P. and a growing band of councillors.[17]

Strangers in a strange land tend to congregate out of a feeling of kinship and for protection. Forming communities in exile, Irish districts retained a separate identity even when a majority of the inhabitants were locally–born. The immigrant communities were well–defined and, within them, Irish nationalism, Irish culture and the Catholic faith were carefully nurtured.[18] Thus the term 'Irish' applied in many instances to people of Irish extraction as well as birth, certainly down to 1914. Second or third generation Irish, who were counted as English or Scottish in the census returns, often retained the attitudes and traditions of their Irish parents or grandparents. They were also likely to retain the same job or remain in the same lowly social position.

Most members of the Irish community were disproportionately concentrated in the ranks of the semi–skilled and casual labour force in construction, transportation, dockside labour, food distribution, railway construction and domestic service.[19] The Irish in Britain were not upwardly mobile in their urban environment, compared with the Irish in America or the British Jews. This picture may have to be qualified a little for the west of Scotland, where Irish immigrants secured work in the mills and mines from which they had been barred in the north of England. This was a consequence of the rapid growth of Scottish industry during the years of heavy immigration, and the reluctance of Scots to work in the mills and coal–mining on terms that immigrants willingly accepted.[20] Many of these more enterprising immigrants changed their religion and shook the dust of the exile community from their feet, certainly in Glasgow. In 1880, with a community corresponding to one quarter of a million people, there were only six Catholic students at Glasgow University, five in medicine and one in law.[21] Over twenty years later, the Hibernophile *Glasgow Observer*, identifying the most prominent Catholic layman in the city, declared that 'by common consent', this was not a son of Erin but James Brand, K.C.S.G., a building contractor – and a convert.[22]

The uprooted Irish stood on the bottom of the social ladder, and they provided much of the human raw material for the growth of industrial Britain. Friedrich Engels wrote that 'the rapid extension of English industry could not have taken place if England had not possessed in the numerous and impoverished population of Ireland a reserve at command'.[23] This was appreciated by the more far–sighted in the governing class. In 1829, Sir Robert Peel stated that it was unwise to 'condemn too precipitately the incursion of Irish labourers into England. We must . . . consider well the advantages as well as the disadvantages of cheap labour'.[24]

The arrival of the newcomers often generated swift resentment among the local working–class, and it was economic rivalry rather than religious or cultural differences which usually, in the first instance, brought Irish immigrants and the local proletariat into conflict, whether in Lancashire or the west of Scotland. There were numerous complaints at every social level about the Irish share of poor relief in areas of heavy immigration.[25] Immigrants also took a sizeable share of employment designed to aid the native poor: the Edinburgh–Glasgow canal and the Caledonian canal were intended to provide employment for distressed Highlanders; in fact they employed a greater number of the Irish.[26]

It was the Irishman's readiness to toil longer, harder and for less remuneration which elicited the bitterest response from British workers. Coming from a rural society, in which money still did not have much meaning, the Irish depressed real wages and conditions by working longer for lower rates of pay. In Scotland, this was particularly true of the Lanarkshire coalfield where, as late as the 1880s, Keir Hardie could complain about the Irish colliers who had 'a big shovel, a strong back and a weak brain', came straight from 'a peat bog or a tattie field' and produced 'coal enough for a man and a half'.[27]

Coal owners and iron–masters in west–central Scotland also deliberately employed Irish workers (and Highlanders) as strike–breakers. Sometimes they went further. There is evidence that employers sponsored sectarian infighting by recruiting an Irish workforce composed of rival 'Orange' and 'Green' segments, and then setting them down in the same area.[28]

In Glasgow, with its high ratio of skilled jobs, there was less economic friction since the poorly educated immigrants could not compete for them. The same applied to their better educated sons and grandsons, who were unable to find a foothold in the shipyards, engineering works, or even the Co–operative Society, where freemasonry was strong, and in trades where craft unions were able to ensure that jobs passed down almost as a family heirloom.

In Greenock, on Clydeside, and the adjacent town of Port Glasgow, the labour market was more fluid due to the predominance of unskilled labour. Here Catholic and Protestant workers from Ireland worked in uneasy proximity in the sugar refineries and on the quays. In terms of the nature of their workforce, and their mercantile rather than industrial base, these towns resembled Liverpool far more than Glasgow.

Economic rivalry in Liverpool was at its fiercest after the Famine. The occupational structure of the city comprised a far higher percentage of unskilled and menial jobs for which the Irish were in a position to compete. Unlike Glasgow or even Belfast, Liverpool was a mercantile and commercial port rather than an industrial centre. Casual labour predominated, and it was notoriously difficult to organize workers due to religious differences, and the fact that worker was competing with worker for jobs that would be scarce in time of depression. Trade unionism was weak in Liverpool throughout the Victorian era, and was therefore unable to offer an alternative rallying point to religious and political demagoguery, feeding off working-class divisions.

Also lacking in Liverpool were friendly societies, a strong Co-operative movement and other working-class organisations that signified the existence of a common proletarian culture.[29] Instead, sectional bodies like the Orange Order, freemasonry, and religious fraternities attracted different groups of Liverpool workers. In Liverpool (and even more so in Belfast), Orangeism, with its mixture of religious loyalty and patriotism, gave a sense of identity and selfconsciousness to different layers of workers and, in some instances, may have preceded the Labour Party as a bridge between them. Membership was open to Protestants only, and it is no coincidence that Orangeism really took off in both Glasgow and Liverpool during the very decades when the entry of the rural Irish was becoming really noticeable.

There is no firm agreement among historians as to when Orangeism became a permanent element in the Glaswegian working-class. I.G.C. Hutchinson has suggested that the Order was at a low ebb in the city until the 1870s,[30] while Ian Wood has pointed to references in government documents which show that Orangeism was active in working-class areas of the west of Scotland throughout the 1850s and 1860s.[31]

The Order was certainly encouraged by the presence of a well-established Ulster Protestant community in Glasgow. This was less true of Liverpool, since much of the city's religious strife flowed from unhealthy indigenous sources, and may only have been initially generated by the Ulster link. Two events illustrate the influence of proximity to Ulster on communal relations in Glasgow. In the late 1850s, the return of Clydeside shipyard workers from Belfast was followed by a visible upswing in the fortunes of the Orange Order. The shipyard workers were the most intensely Orange section of the Belfast proletariat and, by the 1870s, the same was being said about shipyard workers living in Partick and Springburn. These Glasgow districts were not adjacent to ones of high Catholic density, which suggests that Orangeism may have developed from the Belfast connection. This Belfast influence recurred in 1912, when Harland and Wolff, the Belfast shipbuilders, founded a new yard at Govan on the Clyde. They brought many workers from Belfast, at a time when Ulster political feeling over Home Rule was at fever pitch. These workers supported the local football team of Glasgow Rangers, located at nearby Ibrox, and within a decade Rangers had become exclusively Protestant and was locked in furious rivalry with Glasgow Celtic, a team closely linked with the Catholic minority, although it signed on Protestant players.[32] No doubt local conditions were already ripe for this contest, but it is significant that the movement of labour prepared the way for popular factionalism in the sphere of recreation, which long remained the chief legacy in Glasgow of more wide-ranging communal divisions.

Religion

Antagonisms in the workplace were intensified by religious differences, and thus given a longer lease of life. Most of the Irish immigrants to Britain held fast to a religion which was regarded as a menace to Protestant England and its liberties. Widespread and genuinely felt opposition greeted each of the laws removing the restrictions on Roman Catholicism between 1778 and 1829. The supremacy claimed by Rome over the whole of the Christian Church was angrily rejected by the national and voluntary churches of Britain. 'Popery' signified this rejection of Rome, but the word had an impact beyond its narrow literal meaning. In patriarchal Victorian Britain, the priest was depicted as a subversive menace to the family, through his ability to undercut the role of the father and husband and gain sway over his womenfolk.[33] The frenzy inspired by anti–Catholic propaganda about the confessional in Lancashire during and after the 1830s shows how raw a nerve this was.

'No Popery' crossed the barriers of class, district, and denomination, and drew in adherents from the most respectable to the most abject corners of British society. Encompassing a senior member of the Royal Family, army officers, churchmen and an enthusiastic working–class membership, Orangeism was a vigorous force according well with certain Victorian ideals and prejudices. In 1845, opponents of Popery had a field–day when Peel's government tripled its annual grant to the senior Irish Catholic College at Maynooth and put it on the Consolidated Fund, thereby removing it from the list of estimates that came under annual discussion.[34] The award was fifty years old, dating from the confiscation of church funds by the French revolutionaries, and was early recognition of Roman Catholicism as a stabilising element in Irish society. Yet it led to Gladstone's resignation from the government, and Macaulay's support for the measure contributed to the loss of his Edinburgh seat in 1847.[35]

The fiercest backlash from Protestant anti–Catholics was accorded to the restoration of the Catholic hierarchy in 1850. This was dubbed 'papal aggression' because of the triumphant manner in which it was announced by Wiseman, the new Archbishop of Westminster. Even the Whigs, led by Russell, the Prime Minister, were influenced by the chauvinist mood of the country to condemn Rome's impertinence. Riots quickly ensued in Liverpool and Birkenhead and in the cotton towns of south–east Lancashire. There were further disorders in the late 1860s, in the wake of Fenian bombings, as Gladstone prepared to disestablish the Church of Ireland. The chief culprit was William Murphy, a fanatical preacher who left a whirlwind of destruction in his wake in the north and midlands. Thousands were drawn to his meetings, but Murphy was banned from Liverpool and Glasgow by the city authorities, because he posed a threat to public order.[36]

Murphy's name indicated his Irish origin. He came from Limerick and had a counterpart in Patrick McMenamin, who disrupted the peace in Greenock and on Merseyside before being arrested in 1855 for brawling in a Liverpool brothel.[37] Many of the most anti–Catholic clergy of the mainland established churches had an Irish background, the most influential being the Ulster–born Anglican, Hugh M'Neile. In the 1830s and 1840s, he gave the Anglican church in Liverpool a strong Evangelical tinge, and worked hard for the Tory cause. M'Neile was also an inveterate opponent of the ritual use of incense, an offertory, or the wearing of a surplice or vestments by High Church clerics. To Evangelicals like himself, these 'ritualists' were crypto–papists, and the small but steady stream of Anglican converts claimed by the Catholic Church from Newman and Manning onwards made ritualism of more than theological importance. This was nowhere more true than in Liverpool, where, before 1914, fringe preachers like George Wise and John Kensit derived mass support by condemning religious 'error' nearer home than Rome. The issue of ritualism led to the mass picketing of churches, and to violent confrontations in Liverpool even beyond the Victorian age.

A local socialist, Frank Rose, wrote in 1907 that 'the main question in Liverpool has from time immemorial been only the struggle between a live Italian priest and a dead Dutchman'.[38] This description did not apply in Glasgow, and it is not difficult to see why. Here, and in Scotland as a whole, the Presbyterianism of the Church of Scotland and of the 'Free Churches' which had broken away in the 'Disruption' of 1843 was judged to be immune from Roman contagion. Ritualism created little or no stir, given the Bible–based character and deductive temper of Scottish popular religion.[39]

The 'Kirk' had played a strong role in the eighteenth–century Enlightenment, one of whose cornerstones was religious toleration. This tradition must have stood for something, even in the 1840s, when some clergymen feared that Ireland's population of eight million seemed about to swamp Scotland's 2.8 million.[40] By 1861 the Irish comprised 6.7% of Scotland's population compared to 3.6% of England's, and some adherents of the Kirk such as the gifted writer, Hugh Miller, and John Hope, an Edinburgh lawyer and member of the Church of Scotland, were already speaking out against the Catholic Irish influx. But the most frank exponent of 'No Popery' in official circles was 'the brilliant, flamboyant and erratic' Rev. Dr. James Begg, of the Free Church of Scotland.[41] Like Hope, Begg combined 'No Popery' and a belief in social reform in equally ardent proportions.[42] Begg maintained that 'it was essential for the church not merely to succour the casualties of society but to uphold a just social order.'[43] He protested against the Highland clearances, called for a legislative body and a Secretary of State for neglected Scotland and campaigned for better working–class housing. He also pressed for the inspection of convents, which was the chief plank of ultra–Protestant campaigners after the 1860s, and was endorsed by 800 members of the Glasgow Stock Exchange in 1870.[44] Such backing graphically highlighted how anti–Catholicism united the weak and the mighty, while Begg's career is a salutary reminder that anti–Catholic preachers were not all reactionary ultras at the service of the blackest Toryism.

A booming economy, the high emigration of restless and

energetic Scots to the Empire, and the weakness of nationalism kept community tensions within manageable proportions in Glasgow. Papal interference and Jesuit intrigues in international and British politics (important issues in English anti-Catholicism), did not loom so large north of the border, perhaps because Scotland no longer had an independent state of her own. Scottish Protestantism was less negative and defensive than the Established Church in the large industrial cities of Lancashire, possibly because it had greater popular support and the religious environment was more secure. When the Scottish Catholic hierarchy was restored in 1878, there was no backlash on the English scale of 1850.[45] None of the anti-Catholic M.P.'s, whose brief was to protect the Protestant constitution in the House, represented Scottish seats. When D.H. McFarlane, a Liberal, became the first Roman Catholic to be elected for a Scottish seat in 1885, his success passed off with little comment.[46] Perhaps the nineteenth-century Kirk was too preoccupied with its own internal schisms and rival church-building programmes to spare energy and time for combating the menace of Rome.

Education, however, was one area of community importance in which Catholic and Protestant clergy collided. From 1873 to 1928, local education boards were elected by a form of proportional representation, and leading Protestant and Catholic churchmen were regularly returned as candidates. In the first election, held in 1873, the Rev. H.A. Long, an Episcopalian and the main clerical exponent of 'No Popery' in Glasgow, topped the poll. Presbyterian clergy took little active part in Glaswegian politics but, in the face of some Liberal pressure for disestablishing the Church of Scotland, the Established Church began to align itself more closely with the Tories. By the end of the century there was an open pact between establishment Presbyterians and Tories over Board elections, but education was not such a sectarian issue during the mid-Victorian era.

Protestant politics in Liverpool were more volatile because religious affiliation was at the heart of political and social life to a greater degree than in Glasgow. Liverpool's residential segregation along religious lines was far more complete than Glasgow's, where no districts were exclusively populated by Catholic immigrants. In Liverpool in 1909, riots over rival religious processions led to hundreds of families fleeing the districts in which they were a religious minority. The chief instigator of this sectarian warfare was pastor George Wise, one of the few Protestant crusaders successfully to make the transition from preaching to politics. During the early 1900s he exemplified the importance of territoriality in the ordinary social relations of Liverpool, by holding provocative meetings and processions in an area where the Catholic bishop's residence, two convents and three churches were sited. Wise asserted that priests 'lived with harlots' and 'got the poor to feed their bastards', comments which incited disorder, and in 1903 he was gaoled for two months.[47] When his outbursts became too much even for the local Tory Party, which had long before turned sectarianism into an effective vote-winner, Wise defied the party machine and formed an Independent

Protestant party which won three council seats in 1903.[48] The party quickly split, however, over Wise's attacks on the Tammany boss of Liverpool, Alderman Salvidge, and by Wise's confrontation with a rival demagogue in the south of the city.

Such internecine warfare has doomed most fringe Protestant forays into local politics to failure, and would–be emulators of Wise in Glasgow were kept in isolation up to 1914 and beyond by the sheer rancour of their extremism.[49] But Wise made the transfer from itinerant preacher to regular minister of a Dissenting congregation, carving out a fiefdom in parts of inner Liverpool, and his Protestant Reformed Church, before 1914, organized a whole range of activities, including education classes, women's groups and social outings.[50] It was, however, chiefly in whipping up sectarian feeling, by incendiary statements and provocative assemblies, that Wise won notoriety in the 1900s, undermining whatever measure of peaceful co–existence had been achieved in the decades before.

Glasgow largely escaped the vicious street–fighting associated with Liverpool, although it had its share of mini–riots and faction fights connected with Orange or St. Patrick's Day demonstrations. The Partick district witnessed a fierce anti–Catholic riot in 1875, but such disorders were rare, possibly because the leaders of rival communal groups emphasized a need for discipline among their followers, and when trouble did arise it was not unknown for an apology to be offered to the offended community. Perhaps such restraint was regarded as simple commonsense in a city like Glasgow where, by 1914, some 700,000 people lived in its three central square miles, the densest concentration of population in Europe.[51]

Political Behaviour

How were the politics of Liverpool and Glasgow affected by these communal tensions? Politically these cities evolved along very different lines in the nineteenth century, despite the importance to both of Irish immigration, religious questions and later Irish Home Rule. With post–1868 Lancashire in mind, Henry Pelling suggested that 'the greater the proportion of Irish immigrants, the larger the tendency in the working–class to vote Conservative',[52] but this only applied in Glasgow to the election years of 1886 and perhaps 1900.

For much of the Victorian era, Liverpool's ingrained communal divisions had a greater impact on electoral politics than the enduring class struggle, the extension of the franchise or economic changes. Even before the shock of the mass influx of Irish peasants in the late 1840s, the Tories had established control of the city council, in 1842, and then retained it for over another century, except for 1892–95. While the Tories were associated with the defence of local interests, the Liberals were gravely hampered by the party's identification with the anti–slavery campaign, which had the direst consequences for Liverpool, the source of half of the slave ships. The arrival of the Irish made the Tories almost invincible with the policies of maintaining the Constitution, the established churches in

Britain and Ireland and militant Protestantism.

In 1868, after the second Reform Act, the Tories swept most of industrial Lancashire, including Liverpool, by appealing to the religious and anti-Irish prejudices of the newly enfranchised skilled workers. The Fenian bombings and the proposed disestablishment of the Church of Ireland were live issues in working-class neighbourhoods, and it was the small men of local society, often the Tory trinity of publican, bookie, and butcher, who manned the party machine and knew which issues to exploit.[53] The Lancashire Liberals lacked this local feel (in Liverpool, they would not possess it until our own time), and could only watch helplessly the Tories play with consummate skill on working-class sensibilities, and adopt proletarian customs or rituals for partisan ends. A fine example of Tory opportunism came in 1872 when, while visiting Manchester, Disraeli was inducted into the Orange Order by the Orange lodges of Salford. He rose to the occasion by observing that 'it was one of the greatest distinctions I ever received, and I hope I shall be a loyal brother'.[54]

It was in Liverpool, however, that the Tories raised the manipulation of the Protestant working-class and its traditional allegiances into a form of art. 'Tory Democracy', which stressed some of the rights as well as the duties of labour, along with devotion to Church, Crown, and Empire, was the recipe for virtual one-party rule from the 1880s onwards. The 'parson and squire' type of Toryism, commonplace elsewhere, was quite redundant on Merseyside, where the party was run by a succession of Tammany-style bosses. The greatest among them was the brewer Archibald Salvidge, who controlled Liverpool Toryism from the 1890s until his death in 1928. Salvidge's base was the Workingman's Conservative Association (W.M.C.A.) which, like the Orange Order in Ulster, united the political and leisure activities of its working-class membership and was confined to Protestants. When the Irish Home Rulers presented the main opposition on the council after 1900, religious sectarianism was openly fanned to keep the Tory working-class vote intact. Protestant militants made the Church Discipline Bill, which aimed to outlaw ritualism and to discipline clergy suspected of Roman Catholic tendencies, a live issue for working-class Tories. No Tory candidate could afford to be suspected of softness on this issue.[55] In 1900, Walter Long, a member of Lord Salisbury's cabinet, withdrew from the Liverpool West Derby seat when he fell foul of Tory zealots for Protestantism.

Salvidge defied old-fashioned Tory notables, unhappy with the Liverpool model, for many years to come. The radical-conservative movement he built up in Liverpool in part anticipated Fascism, and in key respects was alien to mainstream English Conservatism.[56] Salvidge was a rather bogus figure, married to a Roman Catholic and financially insolvent by the end of his life.[57] The Tory F.E. Smith, later Lord Birkenhead, a lower middle-class protégé of Salvidge, used Liverpool as a launching pad to national politics, and confidently assured a Liverpool election audience in 1906 that 'my Protestantism is not of recent growth', when in fact he was an unbeliever.[58] Smith and Salvidge mobilised thousands of their followers to resist Irish Home

Rule before 1914, even though they were probably most concerned with the domestic and short–term consequences of the crusade against Home Rule. It was through the Ulster issue, F.E. Smith wrote in 1913, that 'perhaps we have our one and only chance of destroying it (the Parliament Act of 1911) by counter–revolutionary means'.[59]

In nineteenth–century Glasgow, politics were far less turbulent, and there were no adventurers or machine bosses to give colour to elections in the city. For much of the Victorian era, the local Tories were nearly as weak as the Liverpool Liberals, and sectarianism was never able to influence decisively political affairs. Perhaps the Orange cause was checked because its Hibernian foes were not especially visible in Glasgow politics.

A high degree of residential mobility and the consequent failure to meet property qualifications kept many Irishmen off the electoral rolls after the 1880s, thus greatly reducing their political effectiveness.[60] By 1883, the 300–strong Jewish community had a councillor in Glasgow, but the 80,000 Irish had none.[61] In Glasgow, as in other centres of the Irish diaspora in Britain, Ireland and the quest for Home Rule were the dominant preoccupations of most politically–aware Irishmen. Yet the absence of total ethnic ghettoes in Glasgow inhibited the rise of a strong voting machine as in Liverpool. It was not until 1897 that Patrick O'Hare was elected the first Irish Catholic councillor. Ironically his Springburn seat was one in which the Irish community was not numerically dominant.

The inability of the immigrant community to transform Glaswegian politics in the Victorian era made it easier for the dominant Liberal Party to preserve its sway over industrial Scotland. The loyalties that bound many enfranchised Scottish workers and middle–class people to the Liberals were not of a nature to be snapped by religious intolerance. The Liberals benefited, and Tories suffered, from the effects of the widespread system of Scottish education and the relatively democratic structure of the Presbyterian churches: Scottish Liberalism did not defer to the local aristocracy, and was marked by a dislike of landlordism, a belief in the desirability of the freedom of the individual, as justified by his essential rationality,[62] by a widespread desire for political equality through the extension of the franchise, and, more generally, by support for the freedom of small nations and for free trade, which particularly appealed to the commercial classes who traded outside the Empire.[63]

The widespread dissemination of these attitudes in the midst of an expanding economy helps to account for the Liberal's outright domination of Scottish politics between the first and third Reform Acts. In Glasgow, Toryism was so weak that forty years elapsed before the party won a seat in 1874, but the egalitarian impulses which gave rise to the term 'Scottish Democracy' coexisted uneasily with the imperial and military roles of so many Scots in the high noon of Victorian expansion. The Scottish political consensus finally collapsed in 1886, as a direct result of Gladstone's Irish Home Rule Bill.[64] Other longer–term issues contributed to this process, like the disputes between radicals and moderates over the pace of reform, and especially over the proposed disestablishment of the Church of Scotland. Gladstone so alienated both sides to this religious dispute that some leading radicals joined forces against him, including the former Chartist, Duncan McLaren, who lined up with the old guard in the new Liberal Unionist Party. In the general election held later in 1886, the Tories made only two gains in the whole of Scotland, but seventeen Liberal Unionists were returned, the Liberals losing two-thirds of their seats in the west of Scotland. The fact that Gladstone offered Scotland nothing at all in his first Home Rule Bill also accounted for these defections, and there is no doubt that, on its own, the Irish Question had a massive political impact on Glasgow in 1886. Some of the reasons for the split may seem spurious or exaggerated now, but the 1886 debate did not take place in a calm atmosphere, and the degree of local opposition to Irish Home Rule may be explained in terms of Glasgow's geographical proximity to Ulster and the existence of a large Ulster Protestant community there, the feeling that any change in the status of Ireland would leave the undefended coastline of the west of Scotland vulnerable to foreign invasion, and the linked concern that Ireland's departure from the British orbit would weaken imperial unity and thus jeopardise Scottish trade with the Empire.[65]

Scotland, like the rest of the capitalist world, was in the midst of a severe recession during the first Home Rule crisis, which may also serve to explain why its local impact was far greater than during the second Home Rule crisis of 1912–14, which coincided with economic prosperity. In 1886, the collapse of the Irish economy was predicted if Gladstone's Bill were to be passed. Unskilled workers, many of whom had been enfranchised by the third Reform Act of 1884, were persuaded to believe that mass Irish immigration to the west of Scotland would follow Home Rule and threaten their livelihood.[66] But the political drama rarely spilled over into major communal violence on the streets of Glasgow. This was despite the activities of the Irish Loyal and Patriotic Union which, along with the Scottish Protestant Alliance, exploited anti-Catholic propaganda in 1886 to rally support for the Unionist cause. These tactics were rebuked by the editor of the *Scotsman*, Charles Cooper, a Catholic Unionist, who must have feared the view of his press colleague, James Henderson, the owner of the *Belfast Newsletter*, that 'if we can stir up the religious feeling in Scotland, we have won the battle'.[67] Ultimately, these Anglo-Irish troubleshooters of 1886 were more pleased with their propaganda work in England than in Scotland, and complained of 'the great hold Gladstone had over the Scottish mind', especially in the east, where the Liberals held firm.[68]

The more serious second Home Rule crisis of 1912–14, when Protestant Ulster was turned into an armed camp to resist the measure, had surprisingly little impact in the west of Scotland. In 1910, F.E. Smith described the Home Rule issue as 'a dead quarrel for which neither the country nor the [Unionist] party cares a damn outside of Ulster and Liverpool'.[69] There was a distinct feebleness about the

Scottish response to the call for a Unionist *jihad* in 1912. In October, only 3,000 turned out in Glasgow for Carson, compared with the 150,000 who had awaited his arrival at the Liverpool pierhead a few days before.[70] In the two elections of 1910, most Glasgow workers were swayed by the 'Peers versus People' arguments of Liberal speakers, and voted enthusiastically for the reform of the House of Lords and an assault on aristocratic privilege.[71] It meant little to them that Andrew Bonar Law, party leader and Tory champion of Ulster resistance, was a Glasgow industrialist.[72] When he lost his Manchester seat in December 1910, it was to Liverpool and not to his native city that he turned, and he was elected for South–West Lancashire (the very seat, encompassing Bootle, that had rejected Gladstone over Irish church disestablishment in 1868).

Liverpool responded emphatically to the Ulster drama because it mirrored its own municipal quarrels, and enabled the rival Tory and Irish machines to reinforce the communal allegiances that made Liverpool so different from those elsewhere in England.

Outside Ireland, the island's fate was of most concern to the Home Rule movement in Britain, which directed most of the Irish immigrant vote in the thirty years up to 1914. Known first as the Irish National League and, after 1898, as the United Irish League, the movement survived the split over Parnell in 1890 and was a formidable electoral force wherever the Irish were concentrated. This was nowhere more true than in Liverpool, in which social demography enabled the Irish of birth and origin to elect T.P. O'Connor for the seat of Liverpool Scotland in successive general elections after 1886. At its peak, the Home Rule movement in Liverpool had 17,000 members, and it shared the running of the city with the Liberals in 1892–5 and later superseded them on the council as the city's second biggest party.[73] The Home Rule caucus was an authentically Liverpool movement rather than a British outpost of Irish Nationalism. Local politics sustained the party far more than events or issues relating to Ireland, and immersion in the affairs of local government enabled it to establish its independence from the Irish Parliamentary Party and the executive of the United Irish League. The upshot was that after the creation of the Irish Free State in the 1920s, it was able to survive the demise of the Irish Home Rule Party everywhere else.

In Glasgow, however, the Home Rulers had no pretensions to municipal power and usually held fast to the U.I.L. policy that 'the Irish vote should not be committed to any British Party, Tory, Liberal or Labour, but directed where the interests of Ireland demanded such action'.[74] The longstanding leader of the Home Rule movement in Glasgow was John Ferguson, a Protestant Ulsterman, who had settled in the city in 1860. His influence, and the respect in which he was held, are evidence that in Glasgow, the movement managed to avoid becoming a mouthpiece for the Catholic Church. Relations between the clergy and the ward politicians could be tense when the priesthood, acting on episcopal instruction, urged their congregations to make political choices on the educational issue rather than Ireland. In 1892, Bishop Whiteside of Liverpool placed an English Unionist on the list of Catholic candidates for the School elections, an act which the Home Rulers interpreted as a declaration of war. Refusing to support him, they put three of their own candidates, each of whom was elected, and secured the defeat of all six of the bishop's.

Decisively worsted, Whiteside never publicly opposed the Irish nationalists again and rarely entered municipal politics.[75] He can be compared with Archbishop Charles Eyre of Glasgow, the city's first prelate under the restored hierarchy from 1878 to 1903, who also kept a low profile, often exercising much influence behind the scenes. Eyre preferred a confessional party in local politics, which could be seen in embryo in the Catholic slate in education elections, but this was not the Catholic middle or artisan classes, and the Irish Question loomed too large in the minds of his flock.[76]

Labour

Irish workers may have been used as strike–breakers, especially in the first half of the nineteenth century, but since they were often the first to feel the turn of the screw, many were also prominent in the radical struggles of the period. John Doherty, Feargus O'Connor, Michael Davitt, and Richard McGhee were the best–known Irishmen to be involved in British radicalism. In late Victorian Britain, however, the Irish immigrant played a relatively minor part in the development of a new party of labour.

In those craft unions where there was some recognition of the need for a reformist party, the Irish were not esteemed and the outlook of Glasgow trade–unionists towards them was 'racist'.[77] When two Ulstermen, Edward McHugh and the free–thinking Protestant Richard McGhee, began to build up the National Union of Dock Labourers in Glasgow and Liverpool after 1889, they failed to break down the political isolation of the Irish in these ports. McGhee, for all his radicalism, was an Irish Home Rule M.P. from 1896 to 1900 and from 1910 to 1918. He had come to Glasgow as a young man in the early 1870s and obtained an engineering apprenticeship.[78] It is remarkable that with such a background he made common cause with the lowly Catholic immigrants, but later he was influenced by the prevailing politics of the ghetto. Supporting a Labour candidate was seen as a betrayal of Irish nationalist aspirations, which could only be fulfilled if votes were to be directed towards the Liberal Party, as it was most likely to push through Home Rule at Westminster. The stubborn adherence of even second and third generation Irish workers to Home Rule and the Liberals exasperated those Labour pioneers who collided with the well–oiled Home Rule machine in Britain. Few went quite so far as Bruce Glasier who, after much fruitless missionary work for the labour cause among the Irish at home and in Britain, was driven, in the privacy of his diary, to extolling one of their worst detractors, the Protestant Truth Society leader, John Kensit, who was killed in Liverpool in 1902: 'I esteem him as a martyr. He had real enthusiasm and courage as an agitator and was I think a good man. I feel honest sympathy with his anti–Romanist crusade'.[79] More recently, James Kellas has concluded from an examination of the Mid-Lanark by-election of 1888 that 'it was the attitude of the Irish working-class which prevented the emergence of a strong Labour movement in Scotland until Irish Home Rule was achieved'.[80]

But the performance of the early Socialist movement was usually just as lacklustre in areas of Scotland in which immigration or the Irish issue counted for very little. Furthermore, the Irish did not always perform true to form and did aid the Labour cause at key moments. In 1906, the Labour Party won one of its first two Scottish seats in Glasgow Blackfriars, in which the Irish vote was the highest of any Scottish seat.[81] Here the deciding factor was the decision of the influential Home Government branch of the United Irish League to defy headquarters and campaign for Labour rather than the Liberals.[82] Much earlier, local Home Rulers had demonstrated in an even more significant way that the leaders of the Glasgow Irish were prepared to be less ghetto-bound and more open to radical persuasion than immigrant communities in other British cities.

In 1881, Michael Davitt took up the land question in Glasgow, advocating nationalisation and a taxation of land values.[83] These Home Rulers made common cause with Highlanders, championing the cause of the crofters against absentee landlords. Joint meetings were held, the Irish community collected funds for the Highland land leaguers, and one of the five candidates elected to Parliament in 1885 was D.H. McFarlane, for Argyllshire. McFarlane, a Roman Catholic, had earlier sat for an Irish constituency. These involvements dented the isolation of the Glasgow Irish, chimed in with the traditional anti-landlord views of the Scottish working-class, and produced a greater sympathy between the Irish and the proletarian Highland community in Glasgow.[84]

Over a quarter of a century elapsed before there was another leftward initiative from the Glasgow Irish community, but this later gesture had more significance in the long-term, since it began the shift in voting allegiances which, by the 1920s, had brought the Irish community solidly into the Labour Party.[85]

In 1906, the Catholic Socialist Society was founded by an ex-miner and Home Ruler, John Wheatley. Unhappy with the lack of democracy inside the U.I.L. and drawn to Socialism, Wheatley established a *modus vivendi* with the Catholic authorities, and won over a growing nucleus of immigrants to the belief that adherence to the Catholic faith and belief in Socialism were not incompatible.[86] His achievement has been summed up in the following way: 'As far as can be seen, this is the only instance in Europe of a formal Catholic socialist movement emerging from within Catholic ranks and not being condemned but in fact tacitly accepted by the ecclesiastical authorities'.[87]

Before 1914, the Glasgow Left, dominated by the Independent Labour Party (I.L.P.) was evolutionary in character. Anti-clericalism was largely absent, and John Wheatley was not the only exponent of radical Christianity to shine in its ranks. In Liverpool the movement was thoroughly orthodox and, indeed, intellectually staid, but it was quite unable to break the stranglehold of the Workingman's Conservative Association and the Home Rulers over the divided working-class. For long periods, nationalism and sectarianism swamped the town, and it was only in 1911 that a functioning Labour group emerged on the Council.[88] So unreceptive were the Catholic Liverpudlians that, on occasion, Labourites were tempted to appeal to Protestant prejudice.[89] In 1913, when the Glasgow I.L.P. raised large sums of money for the victims of the Dublin lock-out against James Larkin's Irish Transport and General Workers Union, the Liverpool party failed to show its solidarity, even though Larkin hailed from the port.[90] In 1907 Labour came near to capturing Liverpool Kirkdale at a by-election but, in the event, it had to wait until the 1920s to capture any of Liverpool's twelve seats. The Tory steamroller was unstoppable, and it was a bitter Ramsay McDonald who remarked to Archibald Salvidge at the count that 'It is astonishing how in Liverpool, whatever the issue appears to be at the start, you always manage to mobilise the full force of Orangeism. We will never do any good here until that power is broken.'[91]

Conclusion

No other cities in these islands, Belfast excepted, gave rise to the same level of communal tension as Liverpool and Glasgow. The citizens of these bulging nineteenth-century metropolises were divided up on religious grounds as a result of immigration too rapid and socially dislocating to be easily absorbed, even during an era of unparalleled expansion. Nonetheless, the Glaswegian and Liverpudlian disputes between Catholic immigrants and the Protestant majority took different forms, and often arose from different causes.

Immigrants did not shape Glasgow's politics as they did in Liverpool, and were a subordinate element in political and economic affairs until after 1914. Given their marginal position in the life of the city, they had less opportunity for collision or confrontation with the majority. Those disorders which did occur revealed two Glasgows, but these were less frequent than in Liverpool. Even when they seemed inevitable, as in 1878, when the restoration of the Catholic hierarchy coincided with the collapse of a major Glasgow bank, they were sometimes avoided altogether. Liverpool rarely provided such an anti-climax.

Closer geographically to Ulster, Glasgow was more directly affected after 1870 by the growing tension between the two parts of Ireland. The dethronement of the Glasgow Liberals in 1886 is the most graphic example of Ulster's influence on the adjacent west of Scotland. But the Scots in that region showed surprisingly little solidarity with the Ulster majority on kinship grounds and, despite the rhetoric of the occasion, were moved far more by economic or defence considerations than by Irish ones to reject the Liberals in 1886.

Liverpool's tensions were more intense, and the Irish conflict, while feeding the flames, was not the primary cause of local discord. Much of the worst sectarian violence occurred when the Irish Question was in abeyance. Indeed, much of the recurrent unrest in the city stemmed from the religious segregation of communities and from the nature of the labour market, which encouraged intense competition among workers for short–term jobs. If emigration from Ireland had been spread out over a longer time rather than being so compressed into the late 1840s, rival religious ghettoes might have been less commonplace, and more ethnically mixed neighbourhoods might have emerged to provide the social stability that eluded Liverpool for so long.

Given the history of division, it is ironic that the Liverpool Irish were more easily comparable with the Protestant working–class majority than with the Presbyterians in Glasgow. Socially and economically, there was far less separating them. But the size of the Irish community gave them greater visibility and that, together with their ability to compete in the job market explains the backlash against them in Liverpool. Cultural and religious differences were reaffirmed in the city long after they had lost their cutting edge in the other centres of heavy Irish settlement, Manchester, London and Tyneside. In a city in which church attendance was low within both the Roman Catholic and Anglican communities, religious passions gripped large numbers of citizens, and more than any other phenomenon, demonstrated what little common ground there was between workers in their rival ghettoes.

This distinctive exploitation of religion makes it far more appropriate to describe Victorian Liverpool rather than Glasgow as a sectarian city. The longstanding alliance between the Anglican Church and the Tory Party in nineteenth–century England took its own peculiar form in Liverpool. Aggressive Evangelical clergymen adopted strongly chauvinist positions on many of the issues with a vital bearing on community relations. After 1900, they were overtaken by Dissenting clergymen who made the succeeding decade one of the most turbulent in the city's history. The multiplicity of denominations (reflecting the fact that Liverpudlians had strong English, Irish, Welsh and Scottish antecedents), far from turning the city into a melting–pot, bred suspicion and antagonism. Liverpool was so turbulent and faction–ridden that some of the worst disputes giving rise to public disorder, like ritualism, did not arise from the sectarian divide at all but were confined to the main church of the Protestant majority.

Liverpool's real division would not have proved so enduring if there had not been political forces ever ready to manipulate them. Political parties were far more unrestrained and destructive on the Mersey than on the Clyde. The exaggeration of communal differences was turned into a supreme vote–winning device by the Workingman's Conservative Association, which dominated so much of Liverpool's politics in the sixty years following its creation in 1868.[92]

The levelling effects of the 1914–18 war, the eclipse of the Irish Question, the advance of secularism, and the break–up of the ghettoes by way of urban redevelopment applied a balm to Liverpool's wounds. While the city is far from being at peace with herself today, her sectarian past has been buried more completely than Glasgow's. At first sight, this may seem puzzling, given that sectarian and ethnic disputes on the Clyde usually simmered on the back burner and rarely boiled over into the spectacular violence commonplace in Liverpool. Only after World War I did the Catholic minority in Glasgow begin to compete for jobs, services and general recognition in the manner of their co–religionists in Liverpool. This gave rise to friction, especially since the community was coming of age and reaching political maturity at a time of economic depression. The fact that the epicentre of the unfinished Anglo–Irish dispute had shifted to the part of Ireland geographically closest to Scotland also gave old tensions a new meaning.

Thus the tradition of Red Clydeside coexisted uneasily with the Orange and Green allegiances of much of the Glasgow working–class. The rolling–back of sectarianism in both cities was mainly due to economic change and new relationships bred by war or the spread of materialism – not the result of conscious and direct efforts by politicians. It was the misfortune of Liverpool, in particular, that for so long those of its politicians who were street–wise about sectarianism were least inclined to use their knowledge for the benefit of their city and all its people.

Notes

I would like to thank Mr. Joseph Fisher and his staff at the Glasgow Room, Mitchel Library, Glasgow for the help given to me while doing research on this subject in 1982.

I am particularly grateful to the British Academy for providing me with an award from its Small Grants Research Fund in the Humanities that enabled me to carry out the research on which much of this chapter is based.

1. According to the 1851 census, Dundee had a slightly higher percentage of Irish–born inhabitants (18.9%), than Glasgow (18.2%) but it was a much smaller centre and hardly counted as a 'metropolis'.
2. Erich Strauss, *Irish Nationalism and British Democracy* (Methuen, London, 1951), p.234.
3. Christine Johnson, *Developments in the Roman Catholic Church in Scotland, 1789–1829* (John Donald, Edinburgh, 1983), pp.18, 29–33.
4. Quoted in J.F. McCaffrey, 'Roman Catholics in Scotland in the 19th and 20th centuries', *Records of the Scottish Church History Society*, vol.21 (1983), pp.283–4.
5. N. Kirk, *Class and Fragmentation: Some Aspects of Working–class life in south–east Lancashire and north–east Cheshire* (unpublished Ph.D. Thesis, University of Pittsburgh, 1974), p.362.
6. Frank Neal, 'The roots of violence', *The Tablet*, I May 1982.
7. *Ibid.*
8. *Catholic Herald*, 5 May 1921.
9. E.H. Hunt, *British Labour History, 1815–1914* (Weidenfeld &

Nicholson, London, 1981), p.160.
10. *Ibid.*, p.163.
11. John Denvir, *The Irish in Britain* (Kegan Paul, Trench, London, 1892), p.299.
12. Owen Dudley Edwards, 'The Irish in Scotland', in D. Daiches (ed.), *A Companion to Scottish Culture* (Edward Arnold, London, 1981), p.185.
13. Hunt, *British Labour History, 1815–1914*, p.162.
14. McCaffrey, 'Roman Catholics in Scotland', p.238.
15. *Glasgow Free Press*, 2 January 1864, quoted in A.B. Campbell, *The Lanarkshire Miners, A Social History of their Trade Unions* (John Donald, Edinburgh, 1979), p.192.
16. Quoted in P.J. Waller, *Democracy and Sectarianism, A Political and Social History of Liverpool 1868–1939* (Liverpool University Press, Liverpool, 1981), p. 25.
17. By 1892, the Liverpool Irish community had furnished eight members of the Irish Parliamentary Party at Westminster: Denvir, *The Irish in Britain*, p.432.
18. Hunt, *British Labour History, 1815–1914*, p.159.
19. M.A.G. Ó Tuathaigh, 'The Irish in Nineteenth–Century Britain: Problems of Integration', *Transactions of the Royal Historical Society*, 5th. Series, vol.31 (1981), p.154.
20. Hunt, *British Labour History, 1815–1914*, p.165.
21. Rev. D. McRoberts, 'The Archdiocese of Glasgow', *Glasgow Observer and Scottish Catholic Herald, Scottish Survey 1878–1955*, p.vii.
22. *Glasgow Observer*, 19 March 1904.
23. F. Engels, *The Condition of the Working Class in England in 1844* (1936 ed.), quoted in Strauss, *Irish Nationalism and British Democracy*, p.123.
24. Strauss, *Irish Nationalism and British Democracy*, p.123.
25. Hunt, *British Labour History, 1815–1914*, p.162.
26. *Ibid.*
27. Hardie quoted in David Howell, *British Workers and the Independent Labour Party 1886–1906* (Manchester University Press, Manchester, 1983), p.142.
28. Sydney and Olive Checkland, *Industry and Ethos, Scotland 1832–1914* (Edward Arnold, London, 1984), pp.88, 94.
29. Joan Smith, 'Labour Tradition in Glasgow and Liverpool', *History Workshop*, vol.17 (Spring 1984), p.47. The fact that the Co–operative movement in Glasgow employed mainly non–Catholics may have had more to do with its presence within the skilled working–class than with blatant religious discrimination.
30. I.G.C. Hutchinson, *'Politics and Society in Mid–Victorian Glasgow 1846–86'*,(unpublished Ph.D. Thesis, University of Edinburgh, 1974), pp.397–8.
31. Ian Wood, 'Irish Immigrants and Scottish Radicalism, 1880–1906', in I. McDougall, *Essays in Scottish Labour History* (John Donald, Edinburgh, 1979), p.69.
32. For the sectarian nature of Glasgow soccer rivalry and its early

20th. century origins, there is Bill Murray, *The Old Firm, Sectarianism, Sport and Society in Scotland*, (John Donald, Edinburgh, 1984), esp. pp.84–5 where he gives a cautious appraisal of the view that the arrival of Harland and Wolff at Glasgow in 1912 was the key event in the growth of sectarian enmity in Glasgow football.

33. G.F.A. Best, 'Popular Protestantism in Victorian Britain', in R. Robson (ed.), *Ideas and Institutions of Victorian Britain* (G. Bell, London, 1967), p.134.

34. J.E. Handley, *The Irish In Modern Scotland* (Cork University Press, Cork 1947), p.93.

35. *Ibid*, p.107 but other reasons for his defeat are advanced by W. Ferguson's *Scotland: 1689 to the Present* (Oliver & Boyd, Edinburgh, 1968), p.323. Macaulay regained his Edinburgh seat in 1852.

36. Worth consulting for Murphy is W.L. Arnstein 'The Murphy Riots: A Victorian Dilemma', *Victorian Studies*, vol.19 (1975), pp.51–71. The impact Murphyism had on respectable society is touched upon by Patrick Joyce in *Work, Society, and Politics, The Culture of the Factory in later Victorian England* (Harvester, Brighton, 1980), p.259.

37. A.L. Drummond and J. Bulloch, *The Church in Victorian Scotland 1843–1874* (The Saint Andrew Press, Edinburgh, 1974), pp.73–4.

38. Quoted by Waller, *Democracy and Sectarianism*, p.230.

39. J.G. Kellas, *The Liberal Party in Scotland, 1885–1895* (unpublished Ph.D. Thesis, University College London, 1961), p.16.

40. McCaffrey, 'Roman Catholics in Scotland', p.276.

41. For this description of Begg, see H.J. Hanham, 'Mid–Century Scottish Nationalism, Romantic and Radical', in W. Robson, *Ideas and Institutions of Victorian Britain* (G. Bell, London 1967), pp.153–4.

42. G.I.T. Machin, *Politics and the Churches in Great Britain 1832 to 1868* (Clarendon Press, Oxford, 1977), p.254.

43. Drummond and Bulloch, *The Church In Victorian Scotland 1843–74*, p.134.

44. Handley, *The Irish In Modern Scotland*, p.121.

45. On 13 April 1878, a copy of the Pope's letter confirming the restoration of the hierarchy was burned on Glasgow Green in the presence of several thousand protesters; the authorities had the military on stand–by but in the event it was not needed: David Daiches, *Glasgow* (Andre Deutsch, London, 1977), pp.138–9.

46. The son of a Caithness magistrate, D.H. McFarlane was elected MP for Argyllshire as an Independent Liberal; defeated in 1886, he regained the seat in 1892 as a Liberal and held it until suffering another defeat in 1895.

47. Quoted by Waller, *Democracy and Sectarianism*, p.200. Also useful on Wise is an article by R.S.W. Davies, 'The Liverpool Labour Party and the Liverpool Working Class, 1900–39', *North West Labour History Society*, vol.6 (1979–80), pp.2–14; and A. Shallice, 'Orange & Green and militancy: Sectarianism and Working Class politics in Liverpool, 1900–14', in the same issue, pp.15–32.

48. Wise was debarred from re–contesting his seat in 1906 because, in the meantime, he had become an ordained minister. Waller, p.209.

49. The historian Sir Charles Petrie, son of the Tory leader on

Liverpool council at the turn of the century, described Wise as that 'combination of Uriah Heep and Titus Oates': Waller, *Democracy and Sectarianism*, p.313.
50. Davies, 'The Liverpool Labour Party and the Liverpool Working Class', p.10.
51. Checkland, *Industry and Ethos*, p.185.
52. Henry Pelling, *Social Geography of British Elections 1885–1910* (Macmillan, London, 1967), p.284.
53. Joyce, *Work, Society, and Politics*, p.276.
54. *Ibid.*, pp.257–8.
55. John Campbell, *F.E. Smith, Lord Birkenhead* (Jonathan Cape, London, 1984), p.88.
56. An historian who sees Liverpool Toryism as a precursor of fascism is Norman Stone. See his *Europe Transformed 1878–1919* (Fontana, Glasgow, 1983), p.127.
57. Waller, *Democracy and Sectarianism*, pp.179, 313. But Salvidge pledged that 'no Roman Catholic priest had ever crossed the threshold of his door'.
58. Campbell, *F.E. Smith*, p.125.
59. *Ibid.*, p.340.
60. J.F. McCaffrey, 'The Irish Vote in Glasgow in the Later Nineteenth Century', *Innes Review*, vol.21, no.I (1970), pp.30–6.
61. Hutchinson, Thesis, p.486.
62. Kellas, Thesis, p.30.
63. *Ibid.*, p.30; see also Joan Smith, 'Labour Tradition in Glasgow and Liverpool', p.34.
64. Gladstone grew more responsive to Irish political aspirations while still joining with much of England in resisting the claims of the Roman Catholic Church. After the declaration of papal infallibility, he was to conclude that Roman Catholicism and modern civilization were incompatible.
65. The reasons for Glasgow's opposition to Home Rule in 1886 are set out in Howell, *British Workers and the Independent Labour Party*, p.142, and by Kellas, Thesis, pp.42–3.
66. Howell, *British Workers and the Independent Labour Party*, p.43.
67. D.C. Savage, *The General Election of 1886 in Great Britain and Ireland*, (unpublished Ph.D. Thesis, King's College London, 1958), p.462.
68. *Ibid.*, pp.483–4.
69. Quoted in Waller, *Democracy and Sectarianism*, p.249.
70. Bernard J. O'Connor, *The Irish Nationalist Party in Liverpool 1873–1922*, (unpublished M.A. Thesis, University of Liverpool, 1971), p.111.
71. Joan Smith, 'Labour Tradition in Glasgow and Liverpool', p.45.
72. Bonar Law had strong Ulster family connections as well as personal ties with Canada. These probably intensified his hard line over Irish Home Rule. If these linkages had not intruded into his Glasgow background, it is likely that this low-key and colourless politician would not have displayed such extremism before World War I. Perhaps a useful comparison might be made with Campbell-Bannerman,

the Glasgow businessman who supported Home Rule and was Liberal Prime Minister 1906–1908.

73. O'Connor, *The Irish Nationalist Party in Liverpool*, p.250.

74. Anthony Hepburn, 'Political and Industrial Relationships', *Glasgow Observer and Scottish Catholic Herald, Scottish Survey, 1878–1955*, p.xv.

75. However in the local elections of 1906, the Liverpool Home Rulers actually backed their sworn enemies the Tories over the education question. Here was the first major sign which showed them to be more concerned with their religion than their nationalism: O'Connor, *The Irish Nationalist Party in Liverpool*, p.88.

76. The importance of the Irish Question may be shown by the fact that Coatbridge and Airdrie, lying to the east of Glasgow in the north Lanarkshire coalfield, boasted the largest branch of the Irish National League anywhere in Britain during the 1890s: Campbell, *The Lanarkshire Miners*, p.203.

77. Checkland, *Industry and Ethos*, p.90.

78. For McGhee's background, there is E.L. Taplin, 'Irish Leaders and the Liverpool Dockers: Richard McGhee and Edward McHugh', *North West Labour History Society*, vol.9 (1983–4), pp.36–44.

79. *Diaries of J. Bruce Glasier*, 8 October 1902, Liverpool University Library.

80. Kellas, Thesis, p.297.

81. Dundee was the other Labour gain in 1906. Here there was a large and politically aware immigrant community, but it was firmly under the control of the Home Rulers.

For a very useful article looking mainly at the Irish in Dundee but with a wider applicability than its title suggests, see William Walker, 'Irish Immigrants in Scotland: Their Priests, Politics and Parochial Life', *Historical Journal*, vol.15 (1972), p.649.

Also valuable is his monograph *Juteopolis: Dundee and its Textile workers 1885–1923* (Scottish Academic Press, Edinburgh 1979).

82. One pioneering article has put the 1906 Blackfriars result into perspective by showing how in previous decades, the local Home Rulers had been far from monolithic in their political behaviour. See Ian Wood, 'Irish Immigrants and Scottish Radicalism, 1880–1906', in Ian McDougall (ed.), *Essays in Scottish Labour History* (John Donald, Edinburgh, 1979), pp.64–89.

83. Davitt and the other land reformers were much influenced by Henry George, the U.S. agrarian radical and philosopher. The connection is ably delineated in T.W. Moody, 'Michael Davitt and the British Labour Movement', *Transactions of the Royal Historical Society*, 5th. Series, vol.3 (1952), pp.53–76. See also D.W. Crowley 'The Crofters Party 1885–1892', *Scottish Historical Review*, vol.35 (1956), pp.110–26; and Howell, *British Workers and the Independent Labour Party*, pp.135–6.

84. For a detailed overview of how the land question brought Irish nationalists and early Scottish nationalists into contact both in Scotland and North America, there is James Hunter, 'The Gaelic connection: the Highlands, Ireland and nationalism, 1873–1922',

Scottish Historical Review, vol.54 (1975), pp.179–204.

85. Elsewhere I have sought to examine the close but sometimes fractious relationship that emerged between the Irish immigrants and their descendants on the one hand and the Labour Party in Scotland on the other after 1918. See my 'Scottish Catholics and the British Left 1918–1939', *Innes Review*, vol.34, no.I (Spring 1983), pp.17–42.

86. Part of the reason Wheatley escaped the wrath of the Church could have been to do with the long sway of the Home Rule movement among Glasgow Catholics which may already have predisposed some clergy to welcome their involvement in a more British–orientated cause – even though the bulk would have preferred a less radical cause to be the agent that weaned them away from Irish preoccupations. See also Sheridan Gilley, 'Catholics and Socialists in Glasgow, 1906–1912' in Kenneth Lunn (ed.), *Hosts, Immigrants and Minorities: Historical Responses to Newcomers in British Society 1870–1914* (St. Martins, London and New York, 1980).

87. McCaffrey, 'Roman Catholics in Scotland in the 19th and 20th centuries', p.293.

88. Joan Smith, 'Labour Tradition in Glasgow and Liverpool', p.33.

89. Waller, *Democracy and Sectarianism*, pp.265–6.

90. Joan Smith, 'Labour Tradition in Glasgow and Liverpool', pp.42–3.

91. Stanley Salvidge, *Salvidge of Liverpool* (Hodder and Stoughton, London, 1934), p.90.

92. Waller, *Democracy and Sectarianism*, p. 18.

A COMPARATIVE VIEW OF THE IRISH IN EDINBURGH IN THE NINETEENTH CENTURY

Bernard Aspinwall and John F. McCaffrey

I

The Scottish Background

The Irish immigrant was in the almost impossible position of being unable to become Scottish. In the United States he might hope to start as an equal American in the making, but that was a remote prospect in Edinburgh or Glasgow.[1] The essence of Scottishness was Protestantism and its culture of work, thrift and sobriety. It was opposed to any priestly or other social caste who did not oil the wheels of urban industrial 'progress', an attitude captured by the *Presbyterian Review* in its assertion of July 1833 that 'the Romish church has contrived to retain the Irish in thraldom at once of ignorance and crime (and) . . . has resisted the adoption of all political ameliorations, or infused them with such a venomous trait as to make them productive or evil rather than of good'.[2]

Given this Scottish perception of Irish Catholics, immigrants were unlikely to win acceptance. Reinforced by a revitalised Evangelicalism, religious tracts, travel books and novels, Scottish Presbyterianism was unable to compromise with sin. Every value nearest the Presbyterian heart was outraged by the Irish, so that Irish immigration, particularly after the Famine, presented a major problem. In particular, it threatened to postpone the advent of the Kingdom here and now: the millenarian hope would be thwarted. The injection of these poor feckless characters into the Scottish economy of grace and industry undermined the quality of Scottish life. They believed in miracles rather than personal effort, and upheld an undemocratic religion which did not educate the masses. The growing power of the priesthood was further reinforced by the support of Maynooth. The solution was an awakened active Protestantism: 'no rest for ourselves and for our children till every college, convent, monastery and church of Anti–Christ has disappeared from the land. It must be a time of up and doing'.[3] Such statements before the advent of the massive Irish immigration indicate the fear of Irish organisational success in an apprehensive Scottish community.

Irishmen were therefore regarded as incapable of success, especially when measured in terms of material progress, because an obscurantist religion and culture, a sort of inherent national defect, held them down. G.K. Chesterton saw this in a different light: 'the

Irish are not in the least unsuccessful', he wrote, 'unless it is unsuccessful to wander from their own country over a great part of the earth, in which case the English are unsuccessful too'. One of the places they wandered to was Edinburgh. Curiously enough, in the light of Chesterton's observation, this was a city which contained a very high proportion of English wanderers during the nineteenth century, and the resulting combination of contrasts, of a mediated imperialism on a subject, ancient capital and on a lowly, unsung and unskilled helot class, explains something of the city's mixed character. Irish settlement and absorption in Edinburgh is the story of thousands of personal accommodations to the demands of a new environment in a redefinition of individuality and aspirations. The problem with immigration studies is that groups have to be examined in aggregates so that they become 'the Irish', just as if, as Chesterton also says, they existed only in the plural 'like the measles'. But their story has to be considered as the sum of individual experiences. Unfortunately, the individual leaves few records to allow us to see much of the substance behind the shadows thrown by statistical categories, and the more one looks at the statistics the more one realizes that only individual case histories could do justice to the whole. This essay is no more than an attempt to sketch a collective view, and the individual may be obscured.

II

The Irish Presence

Irish immigration into Edinburgh began at the turn of the nineteenth century. It became part of an already existing movement of Celts into Scotland's capital, since migratory Highland workers had long been employed as labourers, servants, porters, sedan carriers and water caddies.[4] As Irish reapers ousted Highlanders in Lothian agriculture, familiarity with the locale produced permanent settlers. The construction of the Union Canal (completed in 1822) connecting Edinburgh with Glasgow drew further labour. Although never large in comparison with Irish settlements in the industrial towns of western Scotland, the Irish population of Edinburgh grew under the impulse of the search for subsistence and economic opportunity. During the 1820s, building schemes, demands for general labour to meet the needs of an expanding city, and the construction of the Scottish railway network continued to suck in Irish labour. By the 1830s, the Irish were largely replacing Highlanders on the lowest rungs of the economic and social ladder. By then, too, they were attracting increasingly adverse comment: with the bankruptcy of Edinburgh in the early 1830s and the downturn in building activity, the Irish were increasingly regarded as an additional social burden.

The *Report on the Irish Poor* spoke of the great numbers who poured into Edinburgh after 1825. Remarkably indifferent to their appearance, in public they stood out. Their main abodes were in the Old Town – the Grassmarket, Cowgate, St. Mary's Wynd, Leith Wynd, and the Westport. There they lived mainly by labouring, especially for masons and contractors, some dealing in old clothes, others supplying domestic coals. Many of them monopolised the ranks of scavengers and street lighters. Because they worked for very little they overtook the Highlanders.[5] In the late 1830s they comprised a large proportion of the 10–11,000 Roman Catholics estimated by the Religious Instruction Commissioners to live in and around the city.[6] Reports of clashes over Orangeism indicate that there must have been a proportion, as in Glasgow, who were Protestants. In 1832, 26,965 of the 35,554 Irish-born in Glasgow were estimated to be Catholics.[7] The high proportion of non-Catholics in Glasgow, however, may have been due to the greater opportunities for textile workers from urban Ulster to gain employment in the burgeoning cotton trade of the west, an attraction absent in Edinburgh, in which job opportunities consisted of more casual work in service and labouring occupations. The 1841 Census reported 7,100 Irish-born in the county of Edinburgh, and most of these must have been in the city. In 1851 there were 12,514 Irish-born in Edinburgh and Leith. This was the highest number recorded in the nineteenth century, and was due to the Famine exodus. Thereafter, their numbers stabilised and receded. In 1861 the Census recorded 8,816 Irish-born in Edinburgh city; in 1871, 8,031; in 1881, 7,875; in 1891, 6,950; in 1901, 7,023; in 1911, 5,360; and by 1921, 6,382. The higher figures estimated at between 11,000 and 14,000 by witnesses at the Religious Instruction Inquiry in the later 1830s included children born in Scotland but, even so, comparison with the Irish-born totals shows that there was a substantial pre-existing group of Scottish Catholics in the city, made up of Highlanders and some Catholic gentry and their retainers.[8]

Irish immigration into Edinburgh, therefore, curved upwards in the 1820s and 1830s, sharpened under the impulse of the Irish Famine by the 1850s, and thereafter, in an expanding city (comparisons are difficult, for the census areas of the city do not correspond as the city boundaries were enlarged in this period), settled at between 7,000 and 8,000 during the late nineteenth century. It is no accident that the sharpest clashes between the host society and its newcomers occurred in the 1850s and 1860s, when the threat of swamping was at its greatest, and Scottish institutional and cultural life was being eroded. However the scale of Irish immigration into Edinburgh was less spectacular than in the towns of industrial Scotland, where Glasgow had nearly 53,000 Irish-born by 1871, a figure which would have been much higher if their children had been included. Nevertheless, Edinburgh's Irish, like their fellows in other towns, represented a significant group of at least 4% to 5% of the city in the middle of the century and, because of culture, religion, appearance and nationality, formed an easily identifiable group. They shared in the querulous observation made in the 1871 Census that 'this very high proportion has undoubtedly produced deleterious results, lowered greatly the moral tone of the lower classes, and greatly increased the necessity for the enforcement of sanitary and police precautions wherever they have settled in numbers'.[9] Thus their reputation gave them a prominence out of all proportion to their numbers.

An examination of the Irish role in Edinburgh can be instructive, because it allows for a study of their development in that other Scotland so often lost to sight in the vast industrial and commercial expansions of the nineteenth century. Edinburgh belonged to the Scotland of small or traditional towns, with agricultural hinterlands, which were changing under the pressures of commercialism and population growth and were increasingly affected by anonymity and urban problems, but in subtler, slower and certainly less–dramatic ways than Glasgow and the industrial west. As late as 1841, the population and employment figures show that at least half and probably more of Scotland was still an older country, not heavily industrialised and urbanised, and as yet not obliterated by new factories and industrial conflict.[10]

An examination of the Edinburgh Irish also shows that they were not the only – in the Registrar–General's blunt phrase – 'aliens'. Indeed, only once in the nineteenth century did the Irish–born figure as the largest group of outsiders in Edinburgh: this was in the unusual census years of 1851 and 1861, after the Famine, when they accounted for 6% and 5% of Edinburgh and Leith, compared with 4.4% and 4.3% born in England. Otherwise they were always numerically overshadowed by the English–born. In 1841 the English–born outnumbered the Irish–born in Edinburgh; and by 1871 the English–born were growing at an increasing rate, while the Irish–born remained pretty constant or declined. In 1871 the English had 8,847 to 8,031 Irish; in 1881, 11,514 to 7,875; in 1891, 13,144 to 6,950; in 1901, 17,229 to 7,023; in 1911, 18,951 to 5,360; and in 1921, 28,187 to 6,382. Edinburgh, a capital city with its university, an administrative and legal centre, and an increasingly important banking and insurance nexus, attracted people from all classes from south of the border. As the hub of government and finance from the turn of the century, it has continued to do so.

Edinburgh, therefore, was a city used to drawing in from governing groups as well as attracting workers to service their needs. Its occupational profile shows how much of a capital city it was, living on government, the press, education, law and the Church. As the driving force of the intellectual life of the nation, it was already declining by the 1830s and 1840s. But the demands of a visiting population of rentiers and wealthy landowners and a legal and ecclesiastical establishment conscious of the progress in living standards and liberal sentiment in the nineteenth century created its own small demand for new services, for carrying its messages and personnel, and for cleaning its face. Edinburgh thus remained a part of that older, more slowly adjusting Scotland, while its rawer, younger contemporaries made the running in the industrial central belt.

This can be seen in its employment pattern. The New Statistical Account saw Edinburgh as a retail city, supplying the houses of the gentry and professions. Its biggest manufactures lay in coach building and bookprinting, with other ventures only in candle, soap and glass-making, in brewing and distilling, and in shawl and linen manufactures.[11] In the 1831 Census, in comparison with Glasgow, it was heavily represented in retail, trade and handicrafts (12% to 9% of the population), capitalists and professions (4% to 1.3%), labourers and other (4% to 2.2%) and, above all, in domestic servants (8% to 4.4%), and only underrepresented, as might be expected, in manufacturers of machinery (0.4% to 9.5%). This pattern continued throughout the century. Taking 1871 as typical for the latter part of this period, Edinburgh's employed population was proportionately greater in the professional, domestic, commercial and indefinite classifications, and much less in the manufacturing: 1.7% were lawyers, over six times Glasgow's proportion; 17.7% were domestic servants, compared to 6.6% in Glasgow; those employed in producing books were greater by nearly three times (3.9% to 1.4%). Edinburgh also had a small but significantly higher proportion employed in house-building and furniture-making, and, despite Glasgow's greater mercantile wealth, 5.1% of Edinburgh's population were returned as being of independent means, compared wth 1.3% in Glasgow. What Edinburgh lacked of the new Scotland was in machine and tool manufacture, general factory workers and labourers, and in the large nineteenth-century staple industries of textiles and iron and steel.[12]

Immigrants had to fit into this pattern of employment, seizing their chances as they came. Thus they slotted into those general service, domestic service, portering and cleansing roles which had been filled by cheap Celtic labour before them - the Highlanders.[13] However a small but significant section, always noted by contemporaries, established themselves in small-scale retailing, dealing in provisions, spirits and old clothes. This group's overall experience of transfer to urban Scotland in the nineteenth century was qualitatively different from that abrasiveness of change experienced by the populations of miners, ironworkers and factory operatives in the west of Scotland and Forfar. This, and the fact that their numbers were small, presented less of a 'swamping' threat to the host community (a community which prided itself, anyway, on its Whiggish, enlightenment tradition by the 1840s), and might account for the relative absence of any large-scale and continuous communal conflicts of the sort which scarred western Scotland. Though Edinburgh mobs could be roused by any hint of a foreign, Catholic threat and had burned down Bishop Hay's house in 1779, and although Irish or Catholic properties could be attacked in nineteenth-century Edinburgh (the convent of St. Margaret had its windows smashed on occasions), Irish settlement occurred on a lower key in Scotland's capital than elsewhere,[14] and the jobs and workers they threatened, those of the Highlanders, were not such as to command any widespread reaction or support from skilled trades.[15]

III

Churches and Institutions

Yet Catholic Emancipation, the Famine influx, the Fenian activities of the 1860s and 1880s and the Home Rule debate kept the Irish issue firmly before the public mind.[16] Some historians have suggested that Paul Cardinal Cullen, the Archbishop of Dublin, hijacked the Irish tradition for the Counter–Reformation. The clerical emphasis upon the providential role of the Irish in sustaining and spreading Catholicism throughout the English–speaking world served to preserve clerical leadership, establish a rapport with the laity and underwrite policy in Rome. Beamed through Scotland by allegedly less–than–gentlemanly Maynooth clergy, Catholicism was no longer defensive.[17] The shortage of priests meant that Scottish cities were dependent upon the devotion of Irish priests,[18] whose presence and seemingly absolute power emphasised the alien nature of the Church. The parish and all that it entailed heightened the status of the priest and bishop: the arrival of His Lordship at the end of the parochial mission to confirm was a grandiose occasion. The introduction of Perpetual Adoration, the Stations of the Cross and confraternities channelled Irish religious enthusiasm into areas controlled by the priest.[19] Congregational singing of new hymns, frequently written by wealthy Scottish converts, further consolidated this sacerdotal control. As contemporary Catholic literature indicates, *Irish* Catholics were not encouraged to be Irish. There was a sense, as David Noel Doyle has described it, of beleaguered alienation among the Irish.[20] There was a remarkable activity of the Catholic laity, but it was largely uncritical. The continual arrival of poor Irish into Glasgow and, to a lesser extent, into Edinburgh perpetuated group poverty. The preoccupation with immediate practical needs distracted attention from alternative or long–term solutions.

The Scottish Vicars Apostolic had little sympathy for Irish nationalism. In 1848, Bishop Murdoch of Glasgow saw the solution to the threat of Young Ireland as 'a skinful of bullets'.[21] The quiet, unobtrusive faith of such Catholic clergymen was deeply disturbed by the effusive and volatile Irish immigrant. The social eruptions and the 'inferno–like' quality of Scottish slums, noted by numerous visitors, emphasized the passing of their old comfortable order.[22]
Two notable exceptions, Bishop Gillis in Edinburgh and the Rev. Peter Forbes in Glasgow, saw little necessity of hiding their faith: in urban Scotland, all men were equal. Although concerned for their charges, some bishops hoped that they would soon go away and that life might resume its former even tenor. Irish immigrants placed tremendous strains upon the limited resources of the Scottish Church. In Glasgow, to help finance the purchase of the Dalbeth estate, an auxiliary bishop and a priest were sent on an unsuccessful begging tour of the United States.[23] The clergy were more concerned with

maintaining the status quo than with the conversion of the upper and aristocratic classes, and they were overwhelmed by the problem of reaching, let alone winning, the poorer souls. Anxious not to appear as the domineering clerics of popular bigotry, and keen to encourage the new converts to find a role, the bishops resigned themselves to supporting prudent lay initiatives.[24] Bishop Gillis enthusiastically endorsed these developments. He, more than the rest, was in touch with the English Catholic 'Second Spring' and with the enterprising Liberal Catholic Bishop Dupanloup in France.[25] Glasgow went more warily.

But some Catholics did welcome emigration as a positive good, and it was promoted by several leading Catholic clergy and laity in Glasgow and Edinburgh. The Association of St. Margaret, founded in Edinburgh in 1849, encouraged not only education, savings and life insurance schemes but also emigration. Significantly, Robert Monteith, the outstanding lay convert to Catholicism and staunch advocate of a British identity for the Irish in the Catholic community, was associated with Augustus Stafford O'Brien, M.P., the Earl of Lincoln and Charles Buller as promoters of emigration schemes. Opening up opportunities abroad stabilised society at home: humanity and self–interest coincided in that reforming endeavour. In this vein of Irish amelioration, the Catholic Caroline Chisholm and her husband addressed gatherings in Scotland in support of their family colonisation scheme in Australia.[26] For many Irish people, Edinburgh and Glasgow were merely staging posts *en route* to a final destination: the pilgrim people of a pilgrim church. The later experience of Michael MacGowan and Patrick MacGill, the writer, was part of a long tradition. The Glasgow Irish Catholics emigrated to New Zealand, to the prairies of Texas and Wisconsin, and even to Florida, where a model colony failed in the 1880s. Like the dreams of the American Bishop Spalding and many others, these idyllic moral commonwealths were doomed to failure. The future lay with the metropolis. The remarkable entrepreneurial success of the Glasgow Irish Donahoe brothers, who became millionaires in California, and the radical hopes of James Connolly of Edinburgh, could only be achieved in the city.[27] Either way, the countryside held out little prospect to the emigrant. As yet, there are no studies comparable to those of Stephan Thernstrom and others of American cities, but Glasgow especially seems to have had a considerable rate of turnover of population. Textile workers were in heavy demand in America during the first half of the century,[28] and Bishop Murdoch complained that 'the best of our people continue to cross the Atlantic. By and by we will be left a congregation of beggars'.[29]

Thus a new sense of Catholic community in the urban setting was vital. Historically, Scottish Catholicism had drawn its post–Reformation strength from the Highlands, islands and north–east. A pastoral strategy was needed in response to persistent Protestant reproaches about the debasing nature of Catholicism. There was a need for organisation and discipline. The climax to the organisational revolution came with the restoration of the Scottish Hierarchy in

1878. The discipline followed from education, temperance and a new spirituality. As one priest wrote to the Bishop of Edinburgh, Irish ignorance and unwillingness to learn were astonishing.[30] Their conversion to a new kind of urban Catholicism was an awesome task.

The Catholic commitment to education through day and Sunday schools was to become immense. The tireless support of religious orders of nuns and laymen emphasised the dedication to social and eternal salvation. Following unsuccessful attempts to secure the Irish Christian Brothers, the Marists and Jesuits arrived to teach in the Glasgow schools in 1857–59. They did not, however, establish schools in Edinburgh.[31] They provided upward social mobility and leadership for the Glaswegian community and, following the Education Acts of 1872 and 1918, Catholicism began its considerable social advance which has only been recognised in recent years.

Temperance activity among the immigrant community was another inspiration of the drive to respectability. Although Edinburgh had a fair interest, the real strength of the movement lay in Glasgow. The beginnings of the Catholic Temperance Association in 1839, consolidated through the successful visit of Fr. Mathew three years later, improved the Catholic image and relations with Protestants. Soon there were some 3,000 enrolled in the society. After this burst of enthusiasm, zeal waned until Archbishop Eyre established the League of the Cross in every Glasgow parish. Its meetings, halls and picnics contributed to a sense of cohesion and self–improvement. The acquisition of habits of thrift was to lead in the end to home ownership, the vote and greater Catholic influence.[32]

The new spirituality imparted in Glasgow and Edinburgh by the parochial missions boosted Catholic morale. The increased status of the parish priest, the strength of the parish sense, the renewed enthusiasm for colourful devotions in improved, more ornate churches gave a richness to many poor lives. The emotional fulfilment of celebrations of the greater feasts, with their popular hymns, proved effective to maintain links with the mass of the faithful. This outlook was strengthened by Bishop Gillis's visit to Bishop Dupanloup in France, where Dupanloup was renewing his people in this way. In Glasgow, the close connections with America made the revivalist techniques of both Catholics and Protestants well known and accepted.[33] The common parochial experience was central to the formation of an Irish identity.

There was one important difference from the American experience, that the emergence of a Scottish Catholic press was slow and erratic. As the taste for public lectures grew and the Catholic Young Men's Society developed, so an audience of literate people appeared. Parish libraries were established. That of St. Mary's, Glasgow, took the *Dublin Review*, *Rambler*, and *Brownson's Quarterly Review*, as well as many newspapers. After the disastrous *Free Trade* episode, it was 1885 before the *Scottish Catholic Observer* was founded as a national organ for Catholic news.[34] Before that date, the Scottish Catholic community was held together by common attitudes rather than by a conscious, publicly–articulated policy.

By then Catholic apologetic had somewhat improved. After the earlier, violent physical and verbal responses, more mature views came to the fore. Where fighting and crude threats, as in the *Orthodox Journal*, had been the means of striking a blow for the old faith and fatherland, subtler approaches were obvious by mid-century.[35] Under the influence of Robert Monteith and Charles Waterton, the eccentric Yorkshire naturalist, the Rev. Paul McLachlan of the Eastern District produced a restrained statement of Catholic claims: 'The Church conquers in the long run by humility and holiness, and every stimulant [i.e. angry response] given by any of us to a harsher spirit, though it may "serve a turn", runs up somehow an account at compound interest against our holy things'.[36] This was a great advance towards intellectual and social maturity.

Organisations were a means of giving form to the Catholic community. In Edinburgh, the foundation of the Association of St. Margaret in 1849 provided a platform for Irish Catholic loyalty to the Church and Scotland:

> Catholicism will exhibit itself as truly Scottish and patriotic . . . while everything will be done so as to nourish affectionate loyalty to our bishops and clergy. We shall have something independent alike of O'Connell and Lord Shrewsbury – and something to unite the poor spinner of Glasgow with the chief and clansmen of the north. We shall have a little Catholic government and parliament in the land without the folly of squabbling and factions.

The achievement was remarkable, as the *Rambler* saw. Yet, by comparison England was a Catholic country: 'If ever there was a principle and body of men existing in a kingdom but not of it, it is Catholicism and Catholics in Calvinistic and Puritan Scotland'.[37]

The ascendency in Scottish Catholicism of wealthy, aristocratic converts gave a rather conservative tone to the Catholic community. Bishop Gillis promoted a vigorous medieval revivalist style. He and the other bishops were heavily dependant for funds upon their aristocratic and monied patrons: the convert lawyer, Campbell of Skerrington, gave a school to Edinburgh, and James Robert Hope-Scott furnished reproductions of Raphael to another.[38] This, and generous benefactions to church building, the support of religious orders and their ability to promote an articulate, positive image of Catholicism, reinforced their position within the Catholic community.

Some Irish immigrants emerged as men of substance. Usually they were drawn from those who provided services for Irish Catholics: doctors, shopkeepers, construction firms, and the like. From these families in the next generation came the teachers whose children entered the professions. The Irish complexion remained, but it was rather restrained. Unlike in America, the bishops were native Scots, and Scotland did not become part of an Irish ecclesiastical empire.[39] Ironically, the only Irishman appointed to a Scottish see, the Rev. James Lynch of the Irish College, Paris, proved – as coadjutor Bishop of Glasgow in 1866 – to be a disaster. His outspoken Irish character, which coincided with the vigorous nationalism of the Glasgow *Free*

Press and the visit of the firebrand nationalist priest, Fr. Patrick Lavelle, distressed the Scottish clergy. Attempts like Lynch's to harness the Scottish Church to Ireland and Cullen failed. The decisive episcopal influences were those of the Scottish–Canadian, Gillis, in Edinburgh and the Englishman, Charles Eyre, in Glasgow. The Irish role after the supression of the unruly *Free Press* was supportive and self–improving: an Irish parishioner of St. Patrick's, Anderston, Glasgow, gave a loan of £1,000 for a school in 1872. As in Ireland, and elsewhere, the Irish defined their identity largely on terms laid down by the clergy.

The new clergy emerging from Maynooth stiffened the clerical influence in Scotland. Narrowly confined to the spiritual, pastoral and administrative duties of parish life, the priest tended to become middle–class. Apprehensive at the possibility of any social disturbance, the clergy did not envisage social reform as beneficial, either to them or to their flock: it distracted the individual from spiritual concerns, particularly the salvation of his own soul. But the League of the Cross, a temperance body, was established in every parish of the archdiocese of Glasgow at the very moment that Catholics were beginning to better their condition. They were becoming school teachers in fair numbers, and beginning to build Pugin–the–younger churches, adding extensions, elaborate decoration and the like. Some of the Catholic Irish acquired lace–curtain respectability. Coincidentally, the Church of Scotland also experienced something of a liturgical renewal which naturally led to accusations of Romanisation during the period 1865–91.[40]

IV

Leadership: Clerical and Lay

In all these ways the transition from a mainly peasant, pre–Famine culture to an anonymous urban one in Edinburgh was perhaps made easier for the bulk of Catholic immigrants by the nature of Catholicism in the city, for the only organisation which could give them cultural cohesion was the Church. In Edinburgh, Roman Catholic organisation, as in the west of Scotland, had been small–scale, used to dealing with the needs of Highland Catholics and intent on getting on with its Protestant neighbours. But it also had what Glasgow lacked, a solid core of Catholic gentry who could give their religion status with Presbyterians.[41] Catholic priests in Edinburgh were part of a more cosmopolitan religious world, and moderate Presbyterians had a tradition of vague sympathy with the Catholic claims.[42] Although zealots like Dr. Begg and John Hope flourished in Edinburgh, and the activities of the Scottish Reformation Society, slum missionaries, and tract distributors heightened tensions during the mid–Victorian period, they never had the field to themselves, unlike in the west of Scotland. Indeed, there was a group of Edinburgh public men, priding themselves on their broad–mindedness, who were always ready to support any effort to integrate the Irish immigrant into the life of the city, even if for no better reason than the self–interested one that in such an insanitary city they desperately needed hewers of wood and drawers of water. Thus when educational reformers like Dr. Guthrie tried to impose Protestantism on Scots and Irish ragged children alike, a group of prominent citizens helped Bishop Gillis to set up a counter joint–denominational venture in the United Industrial Schools.[43]

As in other Scottish towns, priests found their resources stretched and experienced conflicts over Irish and Scottish attitudes to religion and nationality, and the precise mixture of the two that was acceptable.[44] However, they never suffered the intensity of the Glasgow *Free Press* split in their clerical ranks, or at least were better able to contain it. Moreover the immigration figures show that they had a much more manageable number of Irish to deal with, located in certain identifiable areas of Edinburgh. This population did not fluctuate wildly with each successive census as the clergy tried to plan their future strategies for investment in building and schools. For the Catholic Irish, pre–Famine Ireland was a country in which priests and churches were already hard–pressed to meet the needs of the population. Professor Larkin has estimated that by 1850 the ratio of priests to the Catholic population of Ireland (1:2,100) had barely improved since 1800. Before and during Cullen's ascendency in the Irish Church, efforts were made to provide more churches and to cure the traumas of social upheaval through a more regularised spiritual life suited to the rootlessness of the Irish, now with no settled peasant or small–town community tradition to fall back on. By 1870, due to such efforts, there was one priest to every 1,250 Catholics in Ireland, and Mass attendance and devotional observance had markedly increased as a result of better organisation.[45]

Much the same pattern of challenge and response occurred in Scotland, and cities like Edinburgh, with less population pressure to absorb, showed a similar development. Figures for individual parishes and cities are notoriously difficult to obtain, so much has to be done by piecing fragmentary evidence together.[46] Historians like P.F. Anson and contemporaries like Bishop Gillis put the number of Edinburgh Catholics (not all of them Irish) at about 14,000 during the 1830s, but the First Report of the Commission on Religious Instruction provided a more cautious estimate of about 12,000 in 1837. Taking the latter to give a more favourable result, and dividing by the number of priests working in Edinburgh (five in all, including the bishop), gives a ratio of one priest to 2,400 Catholics. The 1851 Religious Census is difficult to interpret. It records four churches in existence for Edinburgh and the burgh of Leith but gives an attendance at Sunday Mass less than for the 1837 Inquiry. Yet by 1851 the figures show a sharp rise in Irish immigration into the city, so that there must have been an increase in the number of Catholics. An additional complication is that the latest modern estimates give only 10,600 Catholics for Midlothian as a whole. As Edinburgh had increased its complement of priests to eight by 1852, the ratios were either getting better or at least keeping pace. By the 1870s we are on firmer ground. In 1879 the Archdiocese of Edinburgh and St. Andrews was estimated to have 42,230 Catholics served by 43 priests, 12 of them in the city. This gives a ratio of 1:1,005 and as it covers a wide area of variations, the ratio is, therefore, likely to have been better in the city, a more compact unit. These rough estimates suggest that the clergy had doubled their provision for the increasing Irish population of Edinburgh between 1830 and 1870.

Much of this was due to the work of priests like Gillis, who became coadjutor Bishop to Bishop Paterson in 1838 and succeeded him in 1852. Bishop Gillis was unlike his more cautious Scottish colleagues, who were unwilling to commit themselves to overspending and loathe to indulge in any expansion of devotional life and ecclesiastical structures. He was a getter and a spender, with the philosophy that Catholicism bedecked in full Roman panoply was the surest way to recommend his religion to the minds and hearts of his countrymen. He laboured hard to raise money in France for churches (not always in the most appropriate areas for his mainly poor flock), and in the process he collected religious orders to provide service, stability and status for his people. The result was that by the 1880s Edinburgh was served by five churches in what was, by then, a stabilising population.[47]

Unlike the Irish in Glasgow, the Edinburgh Irish had a bishop aware not only of the Scottish scene but of the European, and one ready to think for the future and, like his parishioners, to take a chance. Bishop Gillis was a flamboyant character who provided a refuge for Irish men and women in Edinburgh; to his outgoing generosity, they could respond. Born and educated in Canada, his range of contacts in France and Scotland was wide, his sympathies and outlook European, and his sense of social place among his compatriots unflurried. He saw the need for schools and parochial organisation to give the slum dwellers of the Old Town a sense of their own dignity and place. Active among the upper reaches of Scottish society, he nevertheless enlisted their support to provide schools and organisations to draw all his flock together in common ventures of social uplift. The educational and social work of the orders of nuns introduced into the city in the 1830s enabled Gillis to remain in touch with Edinburgh's upper–class and labouring Catholic populations. Gillis established self–help societies like the Holy Gild of St. Joseph (1842) and the Catholic Association of St. Margaret (1849) which provided sickness and funeral benefits, savings societies, prizes for good housekeeping and efforts at home ownership. Such ventures recommended his labours to Presbyterian Scots engaged in similar efforts with communal self–help to thwart radicalism and social disorder, exemplified for so many of them by the Irish horde. Thus they could be disarmed: 'even the bitterest enemies of such establishments (as St. Margaret's Convent) have invariably made an exception in favour of the Sisters of Charity'.[48] By the 1870s and 1880s, the *Catholic Directories* for Scotland were recording the fruits of such labours with pride: parochial associations of many sorts strengthening the spiritual attachment of the Catholic population, reading societies, libraries and discussion groups, even the Catholic Boys Brigade in St. Mary's parish. Moreover, the Edinburgh Irish were relatively better provided with elementary schools for the poor than other cities, and efforts were made to staff them with qualified teachers. In this, priests like Gillis used their contacts with sympathetic Protestants, who included Dr. William Chambers and the historian John Hill Burton, in efforts to establish the rights of Edinburgh's Irish to considerate treatment in the public institutions of the city. They were also in favour of using religious orders such as the Jesuits (introduced in 1859) as a mobile army to provide religious services where needed, and to increase the piety of the faithful through parochial missions.[49]

Such efforts stabilised Irish immigrants and allayed fears of them as a radical disruptive force. Gillis aimed to create social harmony by building bridges in the local community. Speaking on the need for an increased spirit of self-help to fight slum conditions, he declared: 'dare to measure if you can the cancerous spread of this social ulcer and tremble at the idea of your own accountability while you reflect that with you *and those along with you in the higher ranks of life* (author's italics) lies the remedy of this evil'.[50] Such a message, though defensive and conservative, was, for the time, realistic. It was paternalist, but in the positive sense that it treated its recipients not as agents to be acted upon but as individuals who could themselves take part in and gain pride in the process.

V

Reactions and Compromise

The violent social, institutional and cultural changes in towns like Edinburgh, with its mounting evidence of social misery, squalor, disease and vice, demanded a response. Along with Glasgow and some of the larger English industrial cities, Edinburgh was notorious for its squalid dens, high mortality, proneness to epidemic and all the general signs of alienation, visibly manifest in drunkenness and street brawls. 'If the citizens are as saturated with the Darwin theory as they are with the odour of whisky we might almost expect that in the course of time they would be transmuted into whisky bottles!'.[51] This was said of Glasgow; from the number of its dram shops, the same could have been said of Edinburgh. Edinburgh's death rates and propensity to epidemics induced by poverty were especially marked out for notice by medical reformers like W.P. Alison, who was informed by Dr. Kay, one of the English Poor Law Commissioners, that 'the only parallels he had seen to the wretchedness of the Irish and low Scotch population of Edinburgh are in the Irish of Manchester and the weavers of Spitalfields'.[52]

Unemployment and underemployment worsened the situation. Dr.

George Bell, in his investigations of the wynds of Edinburgh in 1849 and 1850, observed that 'it takes at least nine men to make a tailor. Edinburgh cannot muster enough of men to make the tailors it contains'. The vagaries of service demand were increased by newcomers: 'paupers are imported into, as well as bred in, the town. We might here trace a bitter sentence about the Irish who are forced over in crowds to deepen the dye of our pauperism'. They also pressed in on scant social services. In September 1847 Bell noted that 379 out of 511 fever victims in the Edinburgh Royal Infirmary were Irish, concluding that 'the migratory Irish are a pestilence as well as a pest'. Nevertheless, Bell acknowledged that this was part of a wider malaise in which the lowest Scotch were even worse off than the Irish poor. 'If drunkenness is the vice par excellence of Great Britain, it is to an intense degree the vice of Scotland. The Scotch are one third more drunken than the English, and half more drunken than the Irish'.[53] The 1861 Census pointed to appalling social contrasts in Edinburgh: the city had the greatest number of large–roomed houses in Scotland, but also crammed some 13,209 families into one–room dwellings piled on top of each other in cramped closes. Of this number, 1,530 one–room dwellings each housed from six to fifteen persons! The Rev. Dr. John Lee, of the Old Parish Church, confessed to the Commissioners on Religious Instruction in 1837 that he had never witnessed such wretchedness as existed in his district in the Old Town.[54] However, bad as their conditions might be, the Irish were a rung above the very lowest Scots. Contemporary observers noted that the Irish in these districts had something, something which the lowest Scotch had lost, which gave them a lifeline – a greater attachment to religion. They might not have been constant attenders at church, but their link with Christianity gave their lives meaning. 'They adhere tenaciously to a religion . . . because adherence to it is a matter of principle and, perhaps, because it is the only legacy left them by their predecessors'. Attachment to parochial organisations, designed to create social harmony and encourage devotion, may be sneered at as an emasculation of their natural radicalism, but it could also be cherished by the community, even by its non–observing members, as a determination to express that radical legacy. Even the implacable Hugh Miller overcame his loathing to acknowledge, in his usual shrewd way, what his acute powers of observation told him, that: 'the Irish of Edinburgh differ in one very important respect from the hapless and disreputable class below them . . . (compared with the churchless proportion of Scots) they . . . are represented on its Sabbath day streets. The man who stands beside the door of their chapel will not fail to be struck by their vast inferiority . . . their ragged working clothes, stained by the soil of their week–day labour; and their general aspect indicating the depression of ignorance and poverty. And yet they are the better for their religion, even though that religion be Popery. Bad as penance and the Confessional are, they are morally superior to the non–confession of our degraded Scotch'.[55] Lee made the same point in his own way. In his parish, Catholics and Seceders were the best attenders.[56]

Much of the Catholic organisation which gave identity and cohesion to Irish immigrants in Edinburgh may have been socially conservative in aim, like the avowedly non-party Gild of St. Joseph. However, by the 1850s even Gillis was forced to move from this non-political stance and adapt the Gild as a pressure group for securing Catholic interests. In consequence, radicalism, though muted in the small-scale milieu of Edinburgh, existed in the form of a sense of identity and of a visible presence expressed in organisation, in institutions, and in mortar.

These tensions were exacerbated by the emergence of vigorous anti-Catholic tracts, newspapers and lectures, particularly in the 1850s.[57] Scots sympathisers with liberalism and nationalism, especially with their anti-Catholic forms in Italy, were outraged by the massive growth of the Irish Catholic presence and strength within Scottish cities. Two world views were in conflict. The Scottish Presbyterian saw an international Catholic conspiracy to spread its faith throughout the English-speaking democratic world. Catholics saw their plight as part of the crusade against the Papal States. Although some Scottish Catholics joined the Papal Zouaves, the vast majority believed that they fought for the rights of the Pope's Temporal Power by strenuously espousing the cause of Ireland. Pastorally and locally, this was a far more effective and meaningful cause. The League of St. Sebastian, in support of the Temporal Power, boasted only 30 members in Scotland in 1871, but Irish nationalist organisations were far more enthusiastically supported. As Newman saw, the locality was everything in judging a faith. Angel Gabriel Orr, Alessandro Gavazzi, and numerous former priests or imposters visited Scotland to harangue and to attack the faith of the Irish,[58] and riots not infrequently followed.

Disturbances also followed the advent of Irish Protestant Orangeism. Glasgow, with its heavy urban concentration of industrial labour, experienced far more conflicts than Edinburgh. From their earliest days, there had been more Orange Lodges in Glasgow than in Edinburgh, and although efforts to boost their membership had met with little initial success, they had expanded considerably by the early nineteenth century.[59] Catholic Ribbonmen were equally ready to assert themselves, particularly in the west, and despite episcopal pressures they contributed to the intensification of religious hostilities.[60] In 1835, 100 Ribbonmen marched from Glasgow to Airdrie, where a riot ensued. In 1869 serious rioting occurred in Glasgow, following several days of provocation by flute bands, and fighting raged through the Saltmarket and the East End for six hours. Fifteen people were arrested. Street-preaching by Protestants in Glasgow and by Jesuits in Edinburgh intensified resentments,[61] and these raw feelings are indicative of the lack of an adequate Catholic apologetic in Scotland and illustrate the generally lower socio-economic standing and educational attainments of the Catholic community.

Given the petty bigotry, the Irish were naturally angry in their sense of their political impotence. In the face of seemingly liberal and Protestant double standards, as in the matter of British iscrimination between Irish and Italian nationalism, their antagonism nd distrust were greatly reinforced.

The Protestant reaction of the early twentieth century perhaps prang from a wider subconscious realisation that the confident rusading vision of the nineteenth century was over. The economic ase of the west of Scotland was eroding, and new forces were emerging n the wake of social change and the enfranchisement of the Catholic nasses in 1884 and 1918. Numerically, Catholicism seemed to be rowing with the continued influx of immigrants, and the sense of the hreat to Protestant cultural standards was intense.[62] The great nflux of Polish Catholics and Jews intensified this sense of cultural risis. The First World War, the considerable native–born Scottish migration and the failure of the overwhelmingly Protestant rohibitionist crusade in Glasgow in 1920 meant that the ideal ommonwealth of the Scottish Presbyterians would not be realised. The ise of Socialism further threatened the old Protestant entre–reneurial ethos: the work ethic had served its purpose.

To counteract these Irish Catholic influences, the Free Church mployed lecturers, under the auspices of the Protestant Institution f Scotland, to address meetings against the insidious influence of atholic schools. Numerous meetings were held in Edinburgh and Motherwell.[63] The fear of being swamped, which was further increased y the declining Scottish birthrate, became a common theme at the eneral Assembly of the Free Church between 1916 and 1929: 'the peril s that our Protestant Church will be swamped by an alien population aving no sympathy with Scotch (sic) history, tradition or custom' 1928). Indeed 'the invasion of the Irish is likely to produce far nore serious effects upon the population of Scotland than even the nvasion of the warlike hordes of Saxon, Dane and Norseman' (1929).[64] 'he parallels with the United States were not lost on these 'resbyterians: they were standing at Armageddon and battling for the ord.

This crisis of identity was bound to spill over into issues vhich concerned the temporal aspirations of the Irish, and their conomic position in the public life of the city. The interaction of nese themes had a long history. Daniel O'Connell's expression of rish aims received a rapturous reception from Edinburgh radicals in 835, and in 1889 Parnell was similarly feted, given the freedom of he city, and received an address from local workers.[65] Tensions aused by Orangeism were there in the nineteenth century,[66] but never ith the intensity witnessed in the west of the country. Bishop Gillis was constrained to appeal publicly to his fellow–citizens gainst the insults with which he and his clergy were assailed when hey stepped out of their presbytery doors daily in the 1850s, but hat was a result not of Orangeism but due to emotions whipped up by nti–Catholic rabble–rousers like Gavazzi. On the whole, the Irish cted as most members of lowly or easily entered occupations, such as eneral labourers and scavengers did in politics elsewhere – taking art where they could hope for some improvement in their lot. In the xcitement of the threatened Chartist rebellion in 1848, the Irish achieved a sort of rapprochement with Edinburgh suffrage radicals, a were involved in the riots with police and in the proposals to form Chartist National Guard, which led to trials for sedition.[67] Moreover, the efforts made by the Edinburgh Trades Councils in 1860s to support organised labour and to protect craftsmen a labourers received support from the Labourers' Union, which contain a large Irish element. This suggests a growing political feeling o more enduring sort. Moreover, the greater organisation of the Ir vote in Scotland, which developed in the 1870s and 1880s, gener swung Irish elements in cities like Edinburgh behind Liberals.[68] Jame• Connolly's appeal to the labourers of Edinburgh vote for their class interests and throw over leaders who had beco bourgeois and parliamentary therefore fell on deaf ears. Appealing the Irish voters in the city to see Liberals and Conservatives as two halves of the same whole, he wrote: 'perhaps they will real that the Irish worker who starves in an Irish cabin and the Sc worker who is poisoned in an Edinburgh garret are brothers with o hope and destiny'. It was foolish to denounce tyranny in Ireland a vote for it in Britain: 'the landlord who grinds his peasants on Connemara estate, and the landlord who rack–rents them in a Cowg slum are brethren in fact and deed'.[69] But as R.Q. Gray has argu the skilled mass of workers in Edinburgh was only slowly gropi towards a wider class–consciousness by the 1890s, and the mass general labourers, united not by workplace but by their deaden environment, could hardly be expected to become a revolution vanguard.[70] Connolly, like Maclean in Glasgow, inspired the Sociali of the committed few, but the great mass of Scottish labourers, alone those from Irish backgrounds, never voted for them or press their solutions on their political leaders.[71]

Nevertheless support for Irish nationalism was a sort radicalism, and who can speak categorically about the individua views, and how he translated his personal aspirations into intere and ideals as a social as well as a national struggle? Merely to an Irish voter was to support social justice, given the status of mass of Irishmen in Ireland and in British cities. Given too, strength of the land question as a radical social issue in Edinbur with the formation there of the Socialist Land and Labour Leag voters could see a vote for Home Rule as being a vote for better tim for Irishmen. Irish National League politics had some contacts w Labour organisation and were able to support industrial struggle.[7 The effort to separate Socialism and nationalism was always struggle, never clearcut one way or the other. The increas discussion of the need to keep a nationalist priority over soc issues in the 1890s and 1900s ran like a motif through the Irish pr in Scotland, suggesting that there was real tension on this matt As early as 1892 the Irish newspaper the *Glasgow Observer*, (or *Catholic Herald* in its Edinburgh guise) was ready to admit t Irishmen could turn to labour reforms once Home Rule had be gained.[73] Irish voters were a small element in Edinbur parliamentary politics, so they generally must have fallen in with dominant pattern which was to return Liberals in the constituencies where they were most concentrated – Edinburgh Central, Edinburgh East, and Edinburgh South (where Unionists only ever succeeded in 1895 and 1900). Only Edinburgh West, the residential centre, was solidly Unionist. In Edinburgh, as in the west of Scotland, the Irish voted according to sectional interest, suspicious of Liberal promises and of the effects of the House of Commons on Irish members' loyalty to Ireland.[74] Thus the general movement of Irish voters towards the Labour Party after 1918 must have sprung out of pre–existing conditions in the decades before 1914.

The minority position of Labour in local politics in twentieth–century Edinburgh is a wider reflection of the smaller proletarian element in the city and, in turn, of the smaller Irish tradition among the working classes. However, if public life in Edinburgh was less abrasive than elsewhere in Scotland in the nineteenth century, paradoxically it could have been the threat of labour and Socialist confiscation and the loss of accepted values after the First World War which stimulated the curious twentieth–century attack on the Irish in general and Catholics in particular. Edinburgh, as the seat of the main Protestant denominations, and as a literary centre for writers on contemporary Scotland, saw a surprising amount of anti–Irish and anti–Catholic hysteria in the 1920s and 1930s. As in Liverpool and Glasgow, Edinburgh rather uncharacteristically saw the emergence of a strongly–based town council group called Protestant Action, led by John Cormack, which scored quite high percentages in the local polls in 1934, 1935 and 1936. Perhaps it was the switch of Irish votes to Labour in the 1920s and 1930s which lay behind this, because Cormack ran on a populist platform vying with Labour, with the spice of an 'anti–foreign elements' demagoguery thrown in.

In 1923, the General Assembly of the Church of Scotland also gave credence to a report entitled *The Menace of the Irish Race to Our Scottish Nationality*. In 1935 the Catholic Archbishop was driven to protest to the government and the national press that he and his fellow priests could hardly stir out of doors without being daily insulted, while their parishioners were being molested,[75] complaints which uncannily echo the protest of Bishop Gillis in the 1850s. The situation paralleled that of the 1850s: the need for religious assertion and aggression against the foreigner to contain the threat from within to Scottish life. However, the anti–Catholic disorders of the 1850s had been mounted by a confident and aggressive group at a time of visible civic deterioration and large–scale Irish presence, whereas the events of the 1920s and 1930s occurred in a radically altered setting. The frenzied nature of the times and the loss of economic security led to a search for national roots to provide stability in a period of social and cultural change. The interesting thing, however, is that it should have happened when large–scale Irish immigration was a thing of the past. Edinburgh's Irish–born were the older migrants, and their numbers were not being added to in any appreciable way by younger recruits. The Edinburgh Irish had taken on something of the ethos of the capital and lived under its shadow.

Cormack's movement never expanded, and fizzled out because it could not be sustained on an anti-foreigner, anti-alien basis. Such an animal of any size no longer existed. Only Catholics did, and not all of them looked to nineteenth-century immigration for their roots. By the 1930s, very few of the religious representatives of the host community gave much credence to Protestant attacks. Writers like Compton Mackenzie, Moray McLaren, Bruce Marshall and George Scott-Moncrieff were by now intent on stressing Catholic Edinburgh's historic origins in pre-Reformation Scotland and, by and large, the residual Irish elements were content to let them do so.

The drive to respectability did not mean an end to violence, although it took different forms in different cities. Riots and disturbances occurred at frequent intervals throughout much of the nineteenth century, but in Glasgow rather than in Edinburgh. Orangeism and Ribbonism were mainly responsible. With a greater presence in Glasgow than in Edinburgh, the Orange Order made some headway in organising Glaswegian working-class antagonism towards the Catholic Irish. Even so, numbers remained relatively small. But the popular outrages which the Orange and Green confrontations provoked in the wake of St. Patrick's Day and the Twelfth were persistent in the west.

The bonds of Irish tribalism in the Scottish Victorian city were reinforced by the new stringent laws on mixed marriages.[76] They exacerbated the considerable suspicions of Catholics and Protestants. As the Catholics moved into the growing Labour Party, led by Secularists and Presbyterian social gospel ministers, so the propertied Presbyterian elite toughened its adherence to the Conservatives. The conservative nature of Catholicism, however, ensured that the clash remained constitutional and relatively restrained. Red Clydeside was hardly the norm.

In the past there had been some elements totally and violently opposed to the status quo. Although there may well have been emotional support for the ultimate goal of such men, Glasgow provided surprisingly few political activists. In Glasgow and the west, the few Ribbonmen were effectively checked by the parish missions: the emphasis upon individual morality, if not the direct assault on such bodies, was decisive. A tiny element supported the Fenians in 1867-8 and in the 1883 attack on the Tradeston gasworks.[77] Later, there was some support for James Connolly in his extreme Socialist position, and Jim Larkin helped to organise the Glasgow dockers. Countess Markievicz visited Glasgow in 1919 and 1923, when she produced *Poblacht na h-Eirean*, which became *Eire-Irish Nation*. It was still necessary to articulate Irish grievances within a traditional framework. As Markievicz said of a pamphlet she had written in Scotland to Charles Diamond, the editor of the *Scottish Catholic Observer*: 'I gave all Connolly's important points in his own words and justify them from the Encyclical (*Rerum Novarum*)'.[78] Others found more conventional ways to Socialism. The Irish became staunch supporters of the infant Labour Party, developing a close relationship which continued to recent times. Interesting characters like Paddy he Cope' took the ideals of the Scottish Co–operative movement back Donegal with some success, while Patrick MacGill wrote moving and tense accounts of Irish navvy life in Glasgow and the west of cotland.[79] Like his contemporary, Michael MacGowan, and the earlier onahoes, MacGill later found fulfilment in America. They succeeded leaving.

Those who remained found other outlets and satisfactions. In articular, the development of the Edinburgh Hibernian football club om 1869 by Fr. Hannan and his C.Y.M.S. branch encouraged nitation.[80] Glasgow Celtic followed later, with Archbishop Eyre and ichael Davitt as vice–presidents: Ultramontanism and constitutional ationalism united. In addition, parochial functions, *soirées* and llies provided group satisfaction. Choir competitions, picnics and king associations all consolidated that community parallel to the rger host community. The Irish Catholics in Scotland came to be sulated in a cradle–to–grave community which only decisively altered Catholics achieved greater social mobility and opportunities in the ake of the welfare state. By then, the old parish structure was umbling under the hammer of urban renewal. Vatican II pushed the anges still further. With the decline of the traditional Scottish eavy industries, particularly from the 1950s, and the virtual end of ontinued Irish immigration, including that of the clergy, a profound ansformation had taken place.

The tensions in Glasgow stand in marked contrast to the rather ore assured Catholic posture in Edinburgh. There is a pronounced fference between Compton Mackenzie, Bruce Marshall and George Scott–oncrieff, with their confident attitudes, and the troubled, tense riting of Patrick MacGill. The petty bigotry and snobbery of the est of Scotland which emerges in MacGill's books suggest a repulsive ost community. Preoccupied with superficial appearance, with onspicuous consumption and superior social station, this Scottish stablishment saw the Irish Catholic community in the light of these nattractive attributes. They were astounded by the loyalty of the oor Irish to their culture, to their national identity and especially their religion: 'that irrevocable instinct', as A.J. Cronin called [81] The attendance of the Irish community at Mass and the acraments was not the only test of their faithfulness. Even Paddy acGill loved to hate his clericalised church. So did James Connolly. hey had that quality, that 'something, which surges up, which is in s blood, his bones, his very marrow, something he will never be rid , which will haunt him till the instant of his death'.[82] That was s Irish religious identity. It is a fitting comment on the Irish xperience in Edinburgh and Scotland in general. They were in the cottish Victorian city but hardly of it, and yet adapted to it ccording to the special local urban patterns of economic and social rcumstance which made Edinburgh and Glasgow so different from each ther.

Notes

1. See for example R.A. Burchell, *San Francisco Irish 1848–18* (Manchester University Press, Manchester, 1979); C. Shanabru *Chicago's Catholics: The Evolution of An American Identity* (Univer of Notre Dame, Notre Dame, 1981); M. Funchion, *Chicago's Ir Nationalists 1881–1890* (Arno Press, New York, 1976); P d'A. Jones a M.G. Holli, (eds.), *Ethnic Chicago* (W. Eerdmans, Grand Rapi Michigan, 1981), Similarities with the Scottish scene appear in Handlin, *Boston's Immigrants 1790–1865* (Harvard University Pre Cambridge, Mass., 1941); D. Clark, *The Irish in Philadelphia* (Tem University Press, Philadelphia, 1973); B. Laurie, *Working People Philadelphia, 1850–1880* (Temple University Press, Philadelphia, 19 Detroit is somewhere between the two extremes: See J.E. Vinyard, *Irish on the Urban Frontier: Nineteenth–Century Detroit, 1850–18* (Arno Press, New York, 1976). An overall view of the vast a increasing literature is D.N. Doyle and O.D. Edwards (eds.), *Amer and Ireland 1776–1876* (Greenwood Press, Westport, Connecticut, 19
2. *Presbyterian Review*, vol.4 (July 1833), pp 18–19. See a vol.2 (January 1832), pp.378–93; vol.3 (1833), pp.1–26; vol.6 (183 pp.496–517, vol.10 (1837) pp.197–421: vol.12 (1840), pp.430–54: vo (1844), pp.86–124; and also *United Presbyterian Magazine*, vol.15 March 1871). For something of the persistent attitude towards Ir and Catholics see *Reformed Presbyterian Magazine*, 1 August 1867 a 1 December 1879.
3. *Presbyterian Review*, vol.l8 (1845), p.283. Also vol (1838), pp.42–59, and vol.l3 (1840), pp.209–225; vol. l7 (184 p.ll8. The international conflict is best seen in R.A. Billingt *The Protestant Crusade, 1800–1860* (Harper, New York, 1938); D. Bow *The Protestant Crusade in Ireland, 1800–1870* (Gill, Dublin, 197 J.M.S. Careless, *Brown of the Globe* (Macmillan, Toronto, 1939) Senior, *The Fenians in Canada* (Macmillan, Toronto, 1978); Carwadine, *Transatlantic Revivalism: Popular Evangelicalism in Brit and America 1790–1865* (Greenwood Press, Westport, Connecticut, 19
4. D.F. MacDonald, *Scotland's Shifting Population* (Jackson, So Co. Glasgow, 1937), p.81.
5. *P.P. Royal Commission on the Irish Poor*. Appendix G. 18 vol.xxxiv, pp.92–100.
6. *P.P. Royal Commission on Religious Instruction (Scotla First Report 1837*, vol.xxi, pp.13–4.
7. J.E. Handley, *The Irish in Scotland* (Cork University Pre Cork, 1943), pp.307–8; J. Cleland, *Enumeration of the Inhabitants the City of Glasgow* (Glasgow, 1832), p.260.
8. C. Johnson, *Developments in the Roman Catholic Church Scotland 1789–1829* (John Donald, Edinburgh, 1983), pp.153–5.
9. *Census of Scotland, 1871, General Report*, p.xxxiv. figures here and hereafter drawn from the Census Reports 1831–19
10. I. Levitt and T.C. Smout, *The State of the Scottish Work Class in 1843* (Scottish Academic Press, Edinburgh, 1970), pp.6 estimate that some 65% of the population still lived in towns of fe

that 5,000 inhabitants and in the countryside, and that the majority of occupations were still rural, traditional and non-factory.

11. *New Statistical Account of Scotland, Edinburgh* (Edinburgh, 1845), pp.650, 668.

12. Figures calculated from *Census Reports*.

13. See A. Dickson and W. Speirs, 'Changes in Class Structure in Paisley, 1750–1845', *Scottish Historical Review*, vol.lix (1980), pp.54–72 for a similar movement in the west of Scotland.

14. *History of St. Margaret's Convent, Edinburgh* (John Chisholm, Edinburgh, 1886), p.62. Also Handley, *Irish in Scotland*, pp.304–311 and J.E. Handley, *The Irish in Modern Scotland* (Cork University Press, Cork, 1947), pp.98–116.

15. In the 1890s James Connolly made the same point about the old city areas being inhabited by general labourers whom he found unsuited for Socialist promptings, unlike industrial Leith. However, the subtleties in this process are complex. Being so heavily unskilled it was general unions like the Labourers' Union, with a numerous Irish element in it, that affiliated to the Edinburgh Trades Council in the 1860s in the search for labour solidarity. I. MacDougall, *The Minutes of Edinburgh Trades Council 1859–1873* (Scottish History Society, Edinburgh, 1968), p.xix.

16. Besides Handley, see P. Quinlivan and P. Rose, *The Fenians in England 1865–1872* (John Calder, London, 1962); K.R.M. Short, *The Dynamite War: Irish-American Bombers in Victorian Britain* (Gill, Dublin, 1979).

17. D.E. Bowen, *Cardinal Cullen and the Shaping of Modern Irish Catholicism* (Gill, Dublin, 1983); E.R. Norman, *The Catholic Church and Ireland in the Age of Rebellion, 1859–73* (Macmillan, London, 1965); J.L. Spalding, *The Religious Mission of the Irish People and Catholic Colonisation* (New York, 1880); A.J. Thiebaud, *The Irish Race in the Past and the Present* (New York, 1878).

18. B.J. Canning, *Irish-born Secular Priests in Scotland, 1829–1927* (Greenock, 1979).

19. B. Aspinwall, 'The Formation of the Catholic Community in the West of Scotland', *Innes Review*, vol.33 (1982), pp.44–57. For a different emphasis see W.M. Walker, 'Irish Immigrants in Scotland: their Priests, Politics and Parochial Life', *Historical Journal*, vol.15 (1972), pp.649–67.

20. D.N. Doyle, *Irish-Americans, Native Rights and National Empires* (Arno Press, New York, 1976), pp.334–37.

21. Bishop Murdoch to Bishop Kyle, 20 August 1848, Scottish Catholic Archives, Edinburgh, Blairs Papers.

22. Margaret Fuller, *At Home and Abroad* (1856, reprinted, New York, 1971), p.159, and J. Griscom *A Year in Europe* 2 vols. (New York, 1823), vol.2, p.416.

23. Murdoch to Kyle, 21 April, 8 June 1846; Murdoch to Bishop Smith, 18 October 1848; Archbishop F.P. Kenrick to Murdoch, 13 June 1848, Blairs Papers.

24. Murdoch to Kyle 21 September 1848; R. Monteith to Rev. P. McLachlan, 14, 20, Aug. 1848, 13 Jan. 1850, Blairs Papers.

25. Bishop Dupanloup to Bishop Gillis, 7 April 1857, and sever letters from French laity, Gillis Papers, Edinburgh Archdiocesa Archives. Christianne Marcilhacy, *La Diocèse d'Orléans sou L'Episcopat de Mgr. Dupanloup 1849–1878* (Plon, Paris, 1962) pp.28 et seq.

26. R. Monteith to Rev. P. McLachlan, 22 June, 25 December 184 16 and 22 January 1848; A. Stafford to McLachlan, 26 December 184 Blairs Papers. B. Aspinwall, 'Before Manning: Some Aspects of Britis Catholic Social Concern Before 1865'', *New Blackfriars*, vol.61 (1980 pp.113–27, and 'David Urquhart, Robert Monteith and the Catholi Church: A Search for Justice and Peace, *Innes Review*, vol.31 (1980 pp.57–70. *Tablet*, 10 May 1851. E. Mackenzie, *Memoirs of Mrs Caroline Chisholm* (Webb, London 1852); Margaret Keddle, *Carolin Chisholm* (Melbourne University Press, Melbourne, 1950).

27. Michael MacGowan, *The Hard Road to Klondike* (Routledge Kegan Paul, London, 1962): James Handley, 'Unpublished manuscri life of Patrick MacGill', in the possession of B. Aspinwall. O emigration see *Catholic Observer*, 29 August, 12 September 1885 o Florida: *Exile*, 16 November 1884, on Texas: The *Observer* carrie several letters from emigrants through 1887–94. James Patric Shannon, *Catholic Colonisation of the Western Frontier* (Yal University Press, New Haven, 1957). J.F. Maguire, *The Irish America* (Longmans, London, 1868), p.273.

28. S. Thernstrom, *The Other Bostonians* (Harvard University Press Cambridge Mass. 1973). Also Ray Ginger, 'Labour in a Massachusett Cotton Mill 1853–1860' *Business History Review* vol.28 (1955) pp.67–91

29. Bishop Murdoch to Dr. Smith c/o Archbishop Hughes, New York 1848. Blairs Papers.

30. Rev. Paul McLachlan to Bishop Carruthers, 8 March 1847, Blair Papers.

31. B. Aspinwall, 'The Formation of the Catholic Communit . . . *History of St. Margaret's Convent* shows the educationa impulse in Edinburgh had been developed by the Ursuline Nun introduced by Bishop Gillis in the 1830s.

32. *Scottish Temperance Journal*, December 1839; March 1840; July August 1841; May 1844; James E. Handley, *The Navvy in Scotland* (Cor University Press, Cork 1970), pp.335–337. Also see *Tablet*, 16 Jun 1849 and 25 May 1861 which notes 2,500 in the St. Alphonsus paris temperance society; *League of the Cross Magazine*, March 1844 on th Edinburgh A.G.M.; and March 1855 for the article by Rev. Lord Alfre Douglas entitled 'For God and St. Patrick'; *Scottish Temperance Leagu Journal* 22 March, 26 July 1879, 7 July 1894.

33. B. Aspinwall, 'The Formation'; C. Marcilhacy, *Le Dioces . . .* pp.280–300; R. Carwardine, *Transatlantic Revivalism: Popula Evangelicalism in Britain and America, 1790–1865* (Greenwood Press Westport, Connecticut, 1978); Jay P. Dolan, *Catholic Revivalism: Th American Catholic Experience* (Notre Dame University Press, Notre Dame 1979).

34. Parish Records, Glasgow archdiocesan seminary, St. Peter' College, Glasgow. Also see O.D. Edwards, 'The Catholic Press i

cotland since the Restoration of the Hierarchy', in D. McRoberts ɘd)., *Modern Scottish Catholicism, 1878–1978* (John S. Burns, Glasgow, 979), pp.156–82.

5. Cf. *Weekly Orthodox Journal*, 15 October 1836 for a ferociously olent outburst; R. Monteith to Rev. P. McLachlan, 29 June 1848, lairs Papers. McLachlan wrote numerous restrained pamphlets efending Catholicism.

6. R. Monteith to Rev. P. McLachlan, 14 August 1848, Blairs Papers.

7. 'Catholicism in Scotland: The Association of St. Margaret', *ambler*, vol.3 (April 1849), pp.597–99. Also vol.7 (June 1851), .541.

8. *Tablet*, 6 September 1879 and 13 June 1872.

9. The major metropolitan sees were invariably under Irish ishops: V.A. McClelland 'A Hierarchy for Scotland', *Catholic istorical Review* vol.56 (1970), pp. 474–500; D. McRoberts, 'The estoration of the Scottish Catholic Hierarchy in 1878', in D. lcRoberts (ed.) *Modern Scottish Catholicism*, pp.3–29. On Lavelle see .E. Bowen, *Cardinal Cullen and the Shaping of Modern Irish atholicism* (Gill, Dublin, 1983); S. Gilley, 'The Catholic Church and evolution in Nineteenth Century Ireland', in Yonah Alexander and Alan 'Day (eds.), *Terrorism in Ireland* (Croom Helm, London, 1984), pp.121–6.

0. *Tablet*, 27 January 1872. In Edinburgh see *Tablet* 22 November 873. The similarity with Ireland is apparent in S.J. Connolly, *riests and People in Pre-Famine Ireland 1780–1845* (Gill and lacmillan, New York, 1982), pp.264–78 and Desmond J. Keenan, *The atholic Church in Nineteenth Century Ireland* (Gill and Macmillan, ublin 1983). Cf. B. Aspinwall, 'The Formation . . . ' and John M. arclay 'The Renaissance of Public Worship in the Church of Scotland' *tudies in Church History*, vol.14 (1972), pp.339–50 and A. Cheyne, *The ransformation of the Kirk: Victorian Scotland's Religious Revolution* The Saint Andrew Press, Edinburgh, 1983).

1. *The History of St. Margaret's Convent* mentions Colonel and Mrs. lacDonnell, Mr. Menzies of Pitfodels, Mrs. Colonel Hutchison, Lady ordon, Mr. Fletcher of Dunans, Dr. Strain, among others. See also andley, *Irish in Scotland*, pp. 196, 197, 201–212 for David Doud. eorge Scott-Moncreiff, *Catholic Edinburgh* (CTS, Glasgow, 1956), p.28 uoting a nineteenth-century account: 'The Roman Catholics are both a umerous and respectable body of professing Christians and their astors men of liberal and enlightened minds'.

2. I.A. Muirhead, 'Catholic Emancipation in Scotland', *Innes eview*, vol.xxiv (Spring and Autumn, 1973) pp.26–42 and 103–120. W. anna, *Memoirs of Thomas Chalmers*, 4 vols. (Constable, Edinburgh, 850–52) vol.iii, pp.231–240, 512–519. Chalmers had preached a sermon ı Edinburgh in December 1817 which some of his fellow clergy disliked ecause it could be interpreted as favourable to Catholicism: 'I am old that Bishop Cameron was present and was greatly delighted'. Rev. . Davidson to Rev. H. Grey. 30 December 1817, in Chalmers Papers CHA.4 6–18), New College Library, Edinburgh. Sir John Joseph illon, proponent of Catholic relief measures and a member of the

Catholic Committee of Great Britain found Edinburgh Presbytery mor receptive to his lobbying on behalf of Catholic claims. B. Aspinwal 'Was O'Connell necessary? Sir John Joseph Dillon, Scotland and th movement for Catholic Emancipation', in D. Loades (ed.) *The End* *Strife* (T & T Clark, Edinburgh, 1984).
43. *Explanations Regarding the Establishment of the Unite Industrial Schools* (Edinburgh, 1847); Handley, *Irish in Moder Scotland*, pp.198–201.
44. J. McCaffrey, 'Roman Catholics in Scotland in the Nineteent and Twentieth Centuries', *Records of the Scottish Church Histor Society* vol.xxi (1983), pp.275–300.
45. E. Larkin, 'The Devotional Revolution in Ireland 1850–75 *American Historical Review*, vol.77 (June 1972).
46. Figures here estimated from the following: *R.C. on Religiou Instruction, First and Second Reports, New Statistical Accoun Catholic Directories for Scotland* (annually from 1830s to 1890s), F Howie, *Churches and Churchless in Scotland* (David Bryce & Sor Glasgow, 1893) J. Darragh, 'The Catholic Population of Scotland sinc the year 1680, *Innes Review*, vol.iv (Spring 1953), pp.49–59, and 'Th Catholic Population of Scotland 1878–1977, *Innes Review*, vol.xx (Autumn 1978), pp.211–47; P.F. Anson, *Underground Catholicism i Scotland* (Standard Press, Montrose, 1970), *Census of Religious Worshi and Education, Scotland*. Reports and Tables (London 1854). On th 1851 Census in Scotland see D.J. Withrington, 'The 1851 Census c Religious Worship: with a note on Church Accommodation in mid–19t Century Scotland', *Records of the Scotish Church History Societ* vol.xviii (1974), pp.133–48.
47. McCaffrey, 'Roman Catholics in Scotland', p.288.
48. *History of St. Margaret's Convent*, p.43 and pp.41–9 generall
49. *History of St. Margaret's Convent*, p.62. B. Aspinwall, 'Th Scottish Dimension: Robert Monteith and the origins of modern Britis Catholic Social Thought', *Downside Review*, vol.97 (1978), pp.46–6 and 'The Second Spring in Scotland', *Clergy Review*, vol.66 (1981) pp.281, 290 and pp.312–19. For missions in New York showin interesting parallels at the same time see J.P. Dolan, *The Immigrar Church* (John Hopkins, Baltimore, 1975).
50. Aspinwall, 'Scottish Dimension', p.6l.
5l. Cuthbert Bede, *A Tour in Tartan Land* (London, 1863), p.67.
52. W.P. Alison, *Observations on the Management of the Poor Scotland and its effects on the health of Great Towns* (Edinburgh 1840), pp.12–13. H. Miller, *My Schools and Schoolmasters* (Johnson Hunter, Edinburgh, 1854). Also M.W. Flinn (ed.), *Report on th Sanitary Condition of the Labouring Population 1842* (EUP, Edinburgh 1965), e.g. pp.97–9.
53. G. Bell, M.D., *Day and Night in the Wynds of Edinburg* (Edinburgh 1850), pp.15, 22. In the early 1830s it was estimated th there was one licensed premises for every 15 families in the Old Tow of Edinburgh, *P.P. Select Committee on Drunkenness, 1834*, vol.vi pp.533–4.
54. *R.C. On Religious Instruction, First Report*, pp.335–6, 337.

5. Handley, *Irish in Scotland*, pp.130, 135–7.

6. See note 54 above.

7. E.g. *The Scottish Protestant* and other papers which surfaced in ne period. J.E. Handley, *The Irish . . .* pp.232–62.

8. *Tablet*, 27 July 1872. On Gavazzi and Orr, *Tablet* 26 July, 9 ugust 1851; *Four Patriotic Orations by Fr. Gavazzi, the Eloquent arnabite* (Glasgow 1851): his *Fifth, Sixth, Seventh and Eighth rations* (n.p., n.d.); R.S. Sylvain, *Clerc, Garibaldien, Prédicant des eux Mondes, A. Gavazzi, 1809–89* 2 vols. (Centre Pedagogique, Quebec, 962).

9. *P.P. Select Committee on the origin, etc... of Orange nstitutions in Great Britain 1835*, p.xvii, especially Appendix 6; 1.R. Beames, 'The Ribbon Societies: Lower Class Nationalism in Pre–amine Ireland'. *Past and Present*, no. 97 (1982), pp.128–43.

0. *Glasgow Herald*, 24 July 1835, 18, 19, 22, 24, 25 March 1879: *orth British Daily Mail*, 15, 18, 19, 22, 24 March 1879.

1. *Scottish Protestant* 1851–52: Report of the *General Assembly of ne Free Church*, 1902, 1904, 1905 expressing concern at Catholic open ir services in Edinburgh and elsewhere.

2. See the 1911 Census returns of foreigners in Scotland showing n eightfold increase of non–Irish foreign born in Scotland over the revious fifty years. *Report on Alien Immigration* C.7113 (1893); *nterdepartmental Report on Physical Deterioration* Cd.2210 (1904); oan Smith, 'The Labour Tradition in Glasgow and Liverpool', *History Vorkshop Journal*, no. 17 (1984), pp.32–56.

3. *Report to the General Assembly of the Free Church of cotland, 1905 and 1910.*

4. *Report ot the General Assembly of the F.C. Church*, 1928 and 929. The fears about declining birthrates run through all the eports for 1916–1921.

5. Although the Lord Provost and the minority of Town Councillors oycotted Parnell's reception, the Unionist press deplored the mbarrassments caused by its own *enragés*: 'They have assailed him with avagery that has naturally produced a reaction in his favour.' *ilasgow Herald*, 22 July 1889. The enthusiastic and select audience athered to great Parnell at the Corn Exchange prepared themselves by ommunal singing which included a version of Scots Wha Hae, starting Scots Wha has wi' Gladstone fought'. . . and ending 'see approach roud Balfour's Power, Chains and Slavery.' *North British Daily Mail*, 2 July 1889.

6. *Select Committee on the Origin, etc, of Orange institutions in ireat Britain*, lists only two lodges in Edinburgh.

7. L.C. Wright, *Scottish Chartism* (Oliver & Boyd, Edinburgh, 953), p.197; A. Wilson, *The Chartist Movement in Scotland* (M.U.P. Aanchester, 1970) pp.222, 230.

8. On this topic see, J. McCaffrey, 'Politics and the Catholic Community since 1878', *Innes Review*, vol. xxix (1978), pp.140–155 and Roman Catholics in Scotland'. Also I.S. Wood, 'Irish Immigrants and cottish Radicalism 1800–1906', in I. MacDougall, *Essays in Scottish abour History*, (John Donald, Edinburgh, 1978) and 'John Wheatley, the

Irish and the Labour Movement in Scotland', *Innes Review*, vol. xx (1980), pp.71–85. W.M. Walker 'Irish Immigrants in Scotland: the priests, politics and parochial life', *Historical Journal*, vol. x (1972), T. Gallagher, 'Catholics in Scottish Politics', *Bulletin c Scottish Politics*, no.2 (Spring 1981), pp.21–43.

69. C.D. Greaves, *The Life and Times of James Connolly* (Londo 1960), p.50. Connolly's effort to gain a seat on the local parochi board in the 1890s foundered on Irish support for the candidature c the local priest representing community and continuity. Greaves p.53.

70. R.Q. Gray, *The Labour Aristocracy in Victorian Edinburg* (University Press, Oxford, 1976), *Glasgow Herald*, 25 July 1892: 'Th Irish voter is the most migratory of the enfranchised community an his name is therefore frequently absent from the roll when hi services are wanted'.

71. N. Milton, *John Maclean* (Pluto Press, n.p., 1973), p.130. Als O.D. Edwards and B. Ransom (eds.), *James Connolly, Selected Politica Writings* (Cape, London, 1973).

72. Wood, 'Irish Immigrants, Scottish Radicalism', pp.76–77.

73. Files of the *Glasgow Observer* for this period, e.g. 8 Jun 1892; also 16 April 1892 and 16 July 1892. The number of times th need for electoral unity was stressed shows some awareness of th possible divisions.

74. *Scotsman*, 24 September and 1 October 1900: and 18 Novembe 1909. Also *North British Daily Mail*, 2 and 4 July 1892 for th assiduous Liberal courting of the Irish vote in St. Patrick's parish Edinburgh.

75. Details culled from Edinburgh and Glasgow newspapers of th time. See also T. Gallagher, 'Scottish Catholics and the Britis Left', *Innes Review*, vol.34 (1983), pp.17–42, and his 'Catholics i Scottish Politics.' Also Compton MacKenzie, *Catholicism and Scotlan* (Routledge, London, 1936), pp.166–185.

76. See *Glasgow Herald*, 22 November 1907: *Report to the Genera Assembly of the Free Church* 1908 and 1909. For an interesting vie on the reassertion of tribal/family loyalties see Susan E. Hirsch, *Th Roots of the American Working Class: The Industrialisation of Craft in Newark, 1800–60* (University of Pennsylvania, Philadelphia, 1978) pp.133–34.

77. P. Quinlivan and P. Rose, *The Fenians*, and K.R.M. Short, *Th Dynamite War*.

78. Jacqueline Van Voris, *Constance de Markievicz* (University c Massachusetts, Amherst, 1967), pp.98, 260, 327, 336.

79. P. MacGill, *The Rat Pit* (Caliban Books, London, 1982 ed.) an his *Children of the Dead End* (Brandon Books, Dingle, Kerry 1982 ed.) Patrick Gallagher, *My Story: Paddy the 'Cope'* (The Co-op, Dungloe n.d.). Sir John Joseph Dillon had been active in encouraging the Iris wavers to press their legal rights to better wages and condition Aspinwall, 'Was O'Connell Necessary. . .'

80. See G. Doherty and P. Thomson, *100 Years of Hibs* (J. Donal Edinburgh, 1975) and J.E. Handley, *The Celtic Story* (S. Paul, Londor

1960).

81. A.J. Cronin, *Shannon's Way* (Gollancz, London, 1975 ed.), p.71.

82. A.J. Cronin, *The Green Years* (Gollancz, London, 1945), p.238. A similar passage occurs in *Shannon's Way*, pp.46–7.

THE IRISH PRESS IN VICTORIAN BRITAIN

Owen Dudley Edwards and Patricia J. Storey

The history of the newspaper press in the nineteenth century is littered with the bodies of newspapers started with high hopes and varying aims which failed for an equally varied number of reasons like insufficient capital, local indifference to the cause supported and the strength of rival newspapers. In the eighteenth century the provincial newspaper press consisted of 'scissors and paste' journals normally produced by the local printer, who added local advertisements to news from the London papers. In the early nineteenth century editorial comment and local news crept in, and rival papers were established to represent different political views. Some large towns like Newcastle–upon–Tyne and Liverpool could support several papers neutral or strongly partisan; in other towns only one, generally non-party, paper satisfied demand. In the early 1830s, however, the debate over political reform encouraged papers to take sides, which in turn encouraged the establishment of new papers to represent rival views. The reduction of newspaper stamp duty from 4d. to 1d. in 1836 made more newspapers economically viable; and in the mid–1850s the final abolition of the Taxes on Knowledge (the advertisement tax in 1853 and stamp duty in 1855) meant that daily publication became feasible in England outside London. Improvements in communications through railways and the telegraph system, the development and rapid spread of a good shorthand system for reporting (Pitman's) and technological advances in printing, helped make the second half of the century the high point in the history of the provincial newspaper press. Among the many local papers begun in these years to represent specific political parties or interest groups were an increasing number aimed at Catholic and/or Irish readers. Outside London these were started in areas where massive Irish immigration meant a large potential readership interested in Catholic and Irish affairs: Lancashire, Glasgow and later, the north–east of England.

The problems in charting Irish newspapers in Victorian Britain are endless but highly instructive. This essay is about the Irish Catholic press. The extensive Irish Protestant community in British journalism was served by existing British newspapers, though from time to time an Irish Protestant group sought and even won control of

British organs, the most famous and most disreputable instance being the Irish Protestant seizure of control of *The Times*, to throw its energies and reputation into the 'Parnellism and Crime' articles of 1887. The disclosure of key Government agents in Irish revolutionary ranks to strengthen the newspaper's case before the Special Commission, the exposure of the Pigott forgeries, on which *The Times's* most sensational charges against Parnell depended, and the great speeches of counsel (including Michael Davitt), may obscure the extraordinary achievement of the Catholic Unionist J. Woulfe Flanagan and his fellow-Irish Protestants in taking advantage of the inexperience of the youthful *Times* editor, George Earle Buckle, and the senility of the manager, J.C. Macdonald, to enmire the newspaper in their own Irish Unionist obsessions. What Woulfe Flanagan and his associates achieved was the broadening of the newspaper's Irish preoccupations beyond all sensible proportions.

Individual Irish Catholic nationalists on secular British journals did something like the same thing, and the Frank Hugh O'Donnells, the Justin McCarthys, and the T.P. O'Connors won more attention for Ireland. Sometimes these careers included editorship, as with Justin McCarthy on the *Evening Star* in the 1860s, or ownership, as with T.P. O'Connor for the *Star* (no relation to McCarthy's), the *Sun* (no relation to anyone else's), *M.A.P.* and *T.P.'s Weekly*, from the 1880s into the new century. But any long-lasting success in winning greater sympathy for Irish nationalist aspirations had to be relative. An editor who allowed Irish preoccupations to dominate his journal to the exclusion of significant British and foreign news would lose his place, an owner in similar circumstances would lose his journal. The determinant was the extent to which the journalist was a journalist first and a nationalist afterwards. Britain saw careers comparable to those of James J. O'Kelly and John Devoy on the *New York Herald*. Both were life-long votaries of Irish nationalism, but O'Kelly carved out a reputation as a crack reporter in the 1870s where Devoy, in 1880, was dismissed; O'Kelly knew when to mute his Irish obsessions and Devoy never did.

The Irish journalist might expect greater acceptability for his national preoccupations in the Catholic press. Many British Roman Catholics greatly disliked the Irish Catholic propensity for swamping Catholic communications with Hiberniana, with its corollary of more and better places for the Irish clergy and laity in Britain. The difficulty was that the Irish brought the numbers, and circulation was vital to survival. Before the enormous Irish intake to Britain with the Great Famine, an Irish-tinged image, preferably redolent of Daniel O'Connell, was deemed desirable. The *Tablet* commenced its first issue – that of 16 May 1840 – with a letter of benediction from O'Connell on its masthead dated three days before ('I am rejoiced to find that the Catholics of Great Britain and Ireland have at length in London an organ to communicate to the public facts of importance to the religious liberty of all classes . . .'), and the *Edinburgh Catholic Magazine*, resuming its career after a cessation of a few years, in February 1837, led off its articles with 'Justice to Ireland' (new series, vol.1, no.1, pp.1–5), with its third article also devoted to Ireland. The *Dublin Review*, founded in 1836, is the prime example, with O'Connell among its three co-founders, the Rev. C.W. Russell of Maynooth exercising super-editorial powers of recruitment and censorship, the name being chosen in spite of its London publication to show its dissimilarity from the *Edinburgh Review* (which, however, *was* published in the city of its title), and the motto a gallant but unsuccessful attempt to provide a slogan in the Irish language. (*'Éire go Bráth'* (Ireland forever) was clearly what was intended but what appeared was *'Éire go Brát '* whose clearest meaning is either 'Ireland unto a flag' or 'Ireland unto a shroud'.)

These early publications, however, quickly acquired an English personality, including the *Edinburgh Catholic Magazine*, which dropped the first word of its title from the issue of April 1838, when the Shetland-born editor James Smith moved even farther south: the *Magazine* expired in December 1842. The *Tablet* and the *Dublin Review* attracted Irish journalists to the editorial staff: the *Tablet's* founder, the convert Frederick Lucas, became M.P. for Meath in 1852, and played a noble fruitless part in Irish politics till his death in 1855. But the *Tablet* and the *Dublin Review* fell under the domination of the see of Westminster under Henry Edward Manning and Herbert Vaughan. This did not mean a hostility to Irish national aspirations, save in their more extreme form: Manning was exceptional among Catholic converts in his affection for the Irish masses, as well as in his desire to keep Irish M.P.s in play as a pressure-group for British Catholic interests. Nor was the journals' hostility to theological liberalism inimical to most Irish, although it conflicted with the liberal spirit in which O'Connell had hailed the *Tablet* and founded the *Dublin Review*. But their history after the death of O'Connell and Lucas is an English history: the Irish in Britain read them, but did not run them.

The Irishness of British journalism was largely a first-generation matter, often with an early career in Irish journalism behind the literary invaders. Marcus Lee Hansen's 'third-generation' law of American immigrants is that the first generation arrives, the second assimilates and the third from its security indulges in nostalgia for the homeland: the significant Irish impact on Victorian journalism was almost always in the first generation. Again, the Irish in Britain, especially the literary Irish, liked to tell themselves their new domicile was temporary: for many, journalism kept the dream of return alive. This had more serious consequences in Scotland than in England. English politics was the seat of power over Ireland: an interest in English public questions developed out of an absorption with the masters with the intent of shaking or swaying their power. Scottish issues did not stand by any Irish road to power in Dublin or London; hence Irish periodicals in Scotland starved their Scottish readers. The Irish Catholic press in Scotland showed little sense of obligation to the Scottish Catholicism which was its official reason for existence.

This could hardly have pleased native or convert Scottish

Catholics, when confronted by it so forcibly in the shape of the *Exile* founded by Patrick Shiels in 1884, or the Glasgow *Observer* which followed it in 1885, supplanting it under a succession of three Irish editors of whom the third, Charles Diamond, became owner as well as editor in 1894. But it must hardly have surprised them. The Scottish Catholic hierarchy was not restored by Rome until 1878 when Cardinal Cullen died and could no longer fill the new sees with his family or friends, as in other parts of the British Empire. England had her Roman Catholic bishops in place when Cullen obtained an Irish see for himself in 1850, but the subsequent years saw many a covert and overt battle in Catholic journalism as elsewhere. Cullen was in harmony with the Irish emigrants in seeking key places for Irishmen, even if the emigrants often differed from him in politics. The struggle between liberal and Utramontane elements in English Roman Catholicism often unsettled fledgling newspapers, and ecclesiastical fears of Acton and Newman might make a way for seemingly orthodox Irish journalists whose conservatism in theology masked a highly radical Irish nationalism.

The *Universal News* is a case in point. It was founded, in December 1860, by the Very Rev. Frederick Canon Oakeley, out of the British Roman Catholic alienation from British literary support of the Italian *Risorgimento*. Newspapers, of which the most enduring would be the *Universe*, sprang into being more because normal newspapers had become abhorrent to Catholics, in dealing with the issue of the Papal States, than because of any sense of positive need to provide a Catholic newspaper. Up to 1860, ordinary British newspapers, supplemented by Irish newspapers and the *Tablet* and *Dublin Review*, had fulfilled readership requirements. Italian violence, and its protracted character, made for a new situation. Canon Oakeley was but one of many ecclesiastics to rise to the occasion. His own credentials were aristocratic and Oxonian: born about 1803, the sixth son of Sir Charles Oakeley, Bart., he was a Fellow of Balliol 1827–45, and a Prebendary of Lichfield 1832–45, when he was converted to Roman Catholicism. He was made Canon of Westminster in 1852. His first editor was the former editor of the Tipperary *Examiner*, A.W. Harnett, whose successor, John Francis O'Donnell, also followed him to the *Universal News*. By 1869 the weekly had fallen into the hands of Christopher Clinton Hoey, a former slater who had written with success for architectural journals, but whose politics had been shaped by that vigorous and disreputable organ of Irish nationalism, the *Irishman*, edited and subsequently owned by Richard Pigott. Pigott's subsequent career as pornographer, forger and perjurer has undermined his nationalist credentials, but his lively impudent sheets inspired lively and impudent patriotic imitation. He had brought to a fine art the practice of sailing near the political wind without risking Government prosecution. In Clinton Hoey's hands, the *Universal News* delicately shifted from inquiries as to how the British would like it if the Italian national liberation they advocated against Austria, Naples and Rome were to be imitated in Ireland, to firm demands for this liberation. Clinton Hoey's pages became havens for Fenian poets, notably the youthful Michael Davitt, and expired in 1869 in a welter of furious controversy with Bishop Ullathorne of Birmingham, who denounced its support for Fenianism and was threatened with a libel action in response. Ullathorne won in the end, though driven to tears before his congregation; distributors banned the paper, a salutary indication of the pitfalls ahead of the journalist serving an immigrant community whose chief organisation was clerical. Hoey died in London in 1885 at the age of 54.

Clinton Hoey arguably deserved what he got, though his commitment to revolution was probably no more serious, if more principled, than his mentor Pigott's. Literary Fenianism had much in common with what Sean O'Casey called 'the shadow of a gunman'. But Fenianism required something more direct, especially in its early years. As Clinton Hoey put it in his description of the journal in his grasp for the *Newspaper Press Directory* published by C. Mitchell and Co. for 1867, 'The week's news is carefully given, and is not a mere record of intelligence'. It was essential to please and instruct local audiences who might have little in common besides their religious and geographical origin. Audiences had to be won, and agents obtained, in a variety of the provinces. Clinton Hoey had succeeded by catering for a Lancashire Fenian audience, as in his dubious fortune in drawing poetry from Davitt, and in his impact on Birmingham. Ullathorne, the former cabin–boy, saw in Fenianism a movement to destroy the religion of his flock. He had already worsted a spiritual danger in the shape of Sir John Emerich Edward Dalberg Acton's *Home and Foreign Review* earlier in the decade, but Fenianism was probably more serious to him than the fencing of bad baronet and gallant cabin–boy. Acton's disdain for the Irish was an insurance against his permeation of their ranks with his theological liberalism: the pupil of Pigott was more likely to win an Irish following than the pupil of Döllinger. Manning was using as a stick with which to beat British Protestant complacency his cry, 'show me an Irishman that has lost his faith, and I will show you a Fenian', arguing, as Burke had argued before him, that Catholicism stood in the way of revolutionary Irish opposition to British rule; but the famous words, originally uttered on 13 January 1867 before Ullathorne and the Birmingham Catholics (*Catholic Opinion*, 30 January 1867), were quickly taken in the converse meaning, that Fenianism brought with it religious apostacy. Ullathorne had no intention of indulging that process by undue freedom of the press.

The system of politico–religious agencies for newspaper distribution, had long been basic to Ireland. Irish Catholic journals in Britain followed this route from 1860 onward, much depending on the good will of the local ordinary. The newspapers and their clients were often caught up in baroque personal and religious controversies among the clergy: Acton and Hoey were not the only journalistic thorns of Ullathorne. Under the editorship of E.S. Purcell, the *Westminster Gazette* flourished from December 1866 for ten years by Manning's contrivance but without his official sanction, and Ullathorne was irritated about its freedom of gossip to start hares in Manning's interest. It was an old Irish principle in journalism to place scandal–hunting and taunt–sharpening talents at the disposal of the highest bidder, – even the great fictionist William Carleton was such a mercenary – and Catholic prelates found it served their turn in the heady atmosphere before the Vatican Council. But this also made local enemies, leading to circulation stoppages. The historian is also frustrated by the efforts of such literary activists to cover their tracks: the *Westminster Gazette* had so restricted an estimate of the things that are Caesar's, that it deposited no copyright copies at the British Museum. The paper finally expired in acute financial crisis: Manning was unable to rescue Purcell, but destroyed his own reputation for posterity by compensating the ruined journalist with the assignment of his official biography. Purcell and Clinton Hoey were more vulnerable than a straightforward editorial line of much more unrepentant radicalism. But the years of Palmerstonian equipoise, Gladstonian equivocation, and the Disraeli Odyssey to the top of the greasy pole did not set a cultural pattern of inflexible adherence to a line. The Irish followed suit. The problem was exhibited by the Dublin *Nation*, which trained so many Irish in British journalism. Fenianism was anathema, but Fenian balladry increased sales. Hence the Fenians found their greatest enemy in the *Nation's* A.M. Sullivan, and their most popular bard in his brother T.D. This was no familial feud: the Sullivans, any more than their Healy relatives, did not feud. Brotherhood is business in Bantry. But the cautious diversification was characteristic of Irish journalism, and confusing to their British hosts. Some like Manning sought to recruit the subtlety, to the danger of their own reputations. Some withstood it, like Ullathorne. But the ambiguities inherited by Irish journalism in Victorian Britain from the Sullivans and Pigotts increased with the complexities of life in Britain. Opposition to literary radical nationalism reflected Ullathorne's fears for the damnation of his flock, or irritation at Hibernian obsessiveness and greed, or a mingling of variations of these. Before the arrests and trials of the staff of the Fenian *Irish People* in Dublin in 1865, the range of possibilities was still wider.

The *Irish People* followed the principle of Fenianism, with a secret and an open organization, the latter designed to fan fires of national sentiment and draw the warmest supporters into the secret activity. But the newspaper had vaguely to promise that action would take place at some time. It was an invitation to Government to intervene with secret agents, and these entered the Fenian ranks through such obvious channels with sinister results for the editorial officers of the *Irish People*. But there were more conspiracies afoot than one. The Fenians were notable for working for recruits through public–houses, the drink increasing the potential recruits, and literary Fenianism was also often more concerned with public audience than real private commitment. Local agents wanted to spread revolution; other local agents wished to divert moneys collected to their private use. In Britain all of these factors obtained, as with the National Brotherhood of St. Patrick and its supporting London weekly, the *Irish Liberator*. John Denvir, [writing decades later in his *The Irish in Britain* (London, 1892), pp.178–79], presented the matter in the clear-cut myth foisted by Fenian historiography on posterity. The Brotherhood, organized in London in April 1861, was intended to win Irish independence through Irish unity, not an agenda capable of the speediest fulfilment. The issue of physical force was brightly dealt with: 'A member of the National Brotherhood of St. Patrick, by learning the use of arms, does not forego any of his social rights'. The secret organization would then recruit its numbers from the open organization. But the effectiveness of this, and the issues at stake, remain opaque in the extreme. This report in the *Irish Liberator* could be a cunning announcement of secret recruiting and rallying-cry to Fenians against repressive clerics, or it could be the noisy rust of a parish pump (19 December 1863):

> STALEYBRIDGE (O'CONNELL) BRANCH. The members of this branch have made arrangements, according to their bye-laws, to hold a tea-party in their meeting-room (the Old Repeal Room), on Saturday evening, Dec. 26th, the proceeds to be devoted to purchasing books for the library. On last Sunday, one or two priests of this locality made another of their fierce attacks against the Association, specially directing their censure towards members of this branch, forcing us to the disagreeable necessity of defending ourselves and refuting their undoubted accusations. It is true, we at first resolved to have the said tea-party on the Saturday preceding Christmas Day, but we very justly re-reconsidered the matter, and decided not to have it in Advent, but on the Saturday after Christmas Day. The clergy stated from the altar that it was not through religious motives we adjourned it, but to induce members of the congregation to purchase tickets for what they were pleased to class a tea-party and ball; which is untrue . . . The Archbishop of Warsaw has set a noble example to the priesthood of every down-trodden and oppressed nation, and we feel assured our Holy Father, Pope Pius, will not denounce us as criminals, for seeking to redress the intolerable wrongs of our cruel enemy. We will hold our tea-party, and confidently appeal to the wisdom of our countrymen and countrywomen to decide for themselves what course they shall take.

It bears five signatures, where most reports carry one.

Peasant Irish Catholicism had two languages: one for the gentry and the public, another for itself. Ribbonism had flourished by secret formulae and passwords which meant different things to the ignorant and the informed; satire, especially Gaelic satire, often meant the reverse of what it asserted. The tea-party could be a fund-raising for purchasing guns, while the ball might be an immediate insurrection which had been vetoed. The improved conduct of the Irish might refer to readiness to organize for violent insurrection. The Poles had recently risen in insurrection against Russia, and Pius IX had unsuccessfully employed volunteers under Mgr. de Mérode against Piedmont-Sardinia at Castelfidardo. But the whole thing may have simply been a means by which Catholic workers relieved the monotony of their drab lives in industrial England by dreaming romantic adventures and defying the terminological inexactitudes of English curates (who, on their side, may have been more concerned about sexual than national liberation). The tempest raged; but it may never have transcended the teapot.

Certainly the other branch despatches were, as Denvir noted, far-flung, and reflected the extent of the *Liberator's* hold by means of the Brotherhood. On 19 December reports also came in from Pimlico, Soho, High Holborn, Chelsea, Ratcliff Cross, Tottenham Court Road, Finsbury, High Street, Regent Street, Paddington, Fulham, Manchester Central, Newcastle-on-Tyne, Edinburgh, Sheffield and Westminster. They reported fiery oratory, tea-parties, balls and three-hour denunciations of Castlereagh (possibly in belated celebration of the fortieth anniversary of his suicide), but their main significance appears social, with the fullest allowance for the 'open' organization's shop-window and the astuteness of its codes. Tottenham Court Road seems fairly characteristic:

> The usual weekly meeting was held on Sunday last, at the Ship Tavern, Tottenham-place, Tottenham-court-road; Mr C. O'Callaghan in the chair. After the reading of several articles from our national organs, and a new agreement with our landlord for a considerable reduction in our rent, the meeting adjourned until Sunday next, at eight o'clock p.m.

The reading of newspapers, Irish and British, to the audience was a longstanding method of communication in the culture of Irish peasants, many with an imperfect hold on literacy and the English language. The *Irish Liberator* thus addressed a much wider audience than its circulation figures, if known, would indicate, but this was financially disastrous. It meant that far fewer copies were purchased, and that Irish newspapers from Ireland had a greater appeal in an exiles' gathering, like the *Nation*, the *Irishman*, and the *Irish People*. Still, the *Irish Liberator* seems to have been conceived with an oral rendition in mind. Its periods were well rounded, and its anti-British sarcasms cast-iron.

The *Irish Liberator's* case raises a nice point about the immigrant press response to developments in Britain. The Irish revolutionists abroad associated themselves for opportunistic or idealistic reasons with local politics, as in Mitchel's association with the American Confederate States, Sir Charles Gavan Duffy's premiership of Victoria, and John Devoy's involvement with the United States Republican party. Daniel O'Connell had given a spectacular inspiration for this in his apostleship of antislavery, and in the United States, the *Irish World* and the Boston *Pilot* were identified from 1870 to 1890 with support for American radical and liberal dissent. The *Irish Liberator* is an analogous case. In its brief career from 3 October 1863 to 16 January 1864 it alternated between fierce, if vague, calls for Irish Revolution and, vociferous support for Richard Cobden, in terms which almost seemed a romantic idealisation of true English radicalism. It goes far beyond any crude search for allies, and recalls Feargus O'Connor of the *Northern Star*, the famous Chartist. Where the *Universal News*, after the Fenian trials and insurrections, became a Fenian paper masquerading as a Catholic journal, the *Irish Liberator*, before them, was showing at its demise every sign of being a Cobdenite weekly in Irish revolutionary clothing.

It is often very difficult to assign authorship to newspaper editorials, but if internal evidence is any guide, the moving spirit behind the *Irish Liberator* was Thomas Cashen, Secretary of the Irish Liberator Newspaper Company (Limited). He was much assisted by a sub-editor, Maurice Sarsfield Walsh, who, however, was on a tour to raise shareholders and sale agents for the newspaper by the time of its last appearance. Cashen may not even have been the Secretary's real name as Edgar Wallace, an experienced reporter, remarks in *The Four Just Men*, a limited company supplies an excellent alias. 'Cashen' itself is not conspicuously Irish, but Manx. Cashen's last official action was to announce a meeting of the Directors at the Coach and Horses, 81 High Holborn, for Tuesday, 19 January 1864, after which no more is heard of the paper. His Directors may not have relished his newly-found enthusiasm for Cobden, Bright and G.J. Holyoake, the last of whom had been printed in the newspaper with or without his permission. Trouble may also have been aroused by the *Irish Liberator's* vehement advocacy of the cause of the enslaved Blacks in the American Civil War, coupled with denunciations of the support for the Confederacy from 'John Mitchell [sic] and William Smith O'Brien' the week before. The journal vociferously agitated the land question in international, historical and vehement terms, though to no more radical ultimate end than peasant proprietorship: but this might have evoked harsh comment since to pure Fenianism the land was divisive of the national issue.

The failure of the *Irish Liberator* led some of its creators to lay more successful siege to the *Universal News* after the great crisis of Fenianism in 1865–67. Clinton Hoey as poet and student of architecture, a labourer emancipated by literature, may have been an easier prospect for gentle persuasion than the former editors of the Tipperary *Examiner*. An altogether different figure was Denis Lane of the *Universe*, not so much a type of Cockney journalism – the designation supplied by Irish nationalist critics – as of petty-bourgeois Irish Catholic business. Lane was the London commercial expression of the phenomena which Professor Emmet Larkin has exhibited as evidence of the devotional revolution in Ireland after 1850, the traffic in objects which stamped the purchaser as a Catholic of religious adherence and respectability of life. He 'adopts the plan', he assured readers of the *Universe*, of 'having his work well executed, and charging the lowest possible prices, consistent with fair and just remuneration to those he employs'. This last showed the distinction between his work and that of the average Victorian entrepreneur: his clientele was partly drawn from ex-members of the labouring class, from those whose relatives were still in it, and those still in it themselves. He needed a reputation as a good employer. His Protestant counterparts might be employers as good or better, but they were not under such pressure from their clients to exhibit it. There was enough memory from Ireland of 'gombeen men' who preyed on their own kind for

Lane to wish to seem very scrupulous. He was to the fore with offers to print cards, mortuary papers, raffle cards, agreements, specifications for architects, pamphlets and circulars; he laid before his public lives of St. Paul of the Cross, declarations of the principles of Catholicism, methods of reciting the beads of the five wounds of Jesus Christ, and the Little Rosary in honour of the Immaculate Conception of the Blessed Virgin Mary.

He entered on the *Universe* with public support from the Roman Catholic hierarchy, headed by Wiseman. It is unclear how much backing he received, and from whom Wiseman and his associates needed him, and his readiness to publish at one penny meant that he reached the mass Catholic audience they desperately wished to make aware of the Catholic case on Italy. Beyond this Lane surrounded his proceedings in mystery. A significant survey of the Catholic press in Britain through history was compiled by Frederic Canon Husenbeth for *Notes and Queries* (reprinted, *Catholic Opinion*, 30 January 1867) but Husenbeth bitterly reported that:

> Of the Catholic newspaper *The Universe* . . . I can give no particulars. Application was made to the editor for information, first through a friend, and afterwards directly, but no notice was taken of either application.

There was more to this than Denny Lane's belief that no business was likely to be obtained from the readers of *Notes and Queries*. The *Universe* was certainly not wholly written by Lane himself: indeed, if prose styles convey a message, the author of the launch announcement. wrote virtually nothing of the paper (in decided contrast to Cashen). Lane paid his men, and probably drew on volunteer priests. His subvention from the hierarchy came through advertisements of causes dear to the hearts of the bishops, such as the new St. Peter's Pence Association to raise funds for the beleaguered Pope, firm advice to clergy as to the support of the paper and stocking of Lane's other products, publication of the ecclesiastical calendar, of episcopal and Papal documents and of subscriber lists from bodies like the Syrian Catholic Committee. It is probable that he drew on the see of Dublin as well as on that of Westminster from the first: his first issue quoted extensively from Archbishop Cullen on the subject of mixed schools and mixed marriages, both of which he condemned, ascribing the latter to 'the prospects of influence, earthly power and riches' with no allowance whatever for the gentler emotions. The reprint of episcopal speeches is evidence of links with the diocesan chancellories. Lane may not have made a formal bargain: the furtherance of his merchandise would have been a *quid pro quo* for his generosity of space to the bishops and their causes. Where a bishop was concerned with Irish political or social questions, Lane obliged him: John MacHale of Tuam had his letter to Lord Palmerston on the Partry evictions reprinted. Otherwise, attacks on the government's Irish policy arose from general denunciation of its anti-Papal European policy, and certainly few Irish nationalists could consider Lane's scribe to be mealy-mouthed. On 8 December he editorialized on Palmerston, the Prime Minister, and Lord John Russell, the Foreign

Secretary, charging conspiracy on the part of the British and French cabinets. This was much stronger meat than the *Universal News* would provide when it began its career a few weeks later. Harnett, on 29 December 1860, radiated a civil apologetic. Yet both were saying the same thing: that Catholics should stand together in Parliament on the Papal States and on Naples, whose King, Francis II, had been driven into exile earlier in the year.

They were far from sure of their men. Acton, then Whig M.P. for Carlow, was hardly to be relied on. But where the *Universal News* talked vaguely of unity arising from questions of conscience as transcending the dictates of party to which the Catholic M.P.s would normally subscribe, the *Universe* spoke arrogantly of 'the Catholic party'. It continued to do. 'This journal is the only cheap organ of the Roman Catholic party in the kingdom', it told readers of Mitchell's *Newspaper Press Directory 1867*. 'It takes the ultramontane or High Church side', it continued, either in a cunning manoeuvre to make Roman Catholic divisions analogous to the Anglican, or in sheer ignorance of the meaning of 'High Church'. Ireland continued to be subordinate to European issues, although supplying ammunition. On 22 December 1860, the *Universe* denounced all the evils of the day as the commercialism of 'The Modern Idea':

> The Modern Idea, the offspring of MARTIN LUTHER, the assertor of the rights of intellectual licence, and HENRY THE EIGHTH, the assertor of the rights of man's brutal passions, baptized in the blood of thousands of innocent martyrs, and named by the curses of heartbroken needlewomen and starving Irish peasants, has had for its sponsors the Whigs, and for its *preux chevalier* NAPOLEON THE THIRD. . . .But unfortunately for the success of the Whigs and the Modern Idea, there is a GOD, . . .

Lane's anonymous scriveners, clerical and lay, simply reiterated a simplistic and sensational view of affairs to arouse Catholic voters, and so much the worse for Catholic M.P.s who had not shown themselves the *Universe*'s men. They were a little cautious about letting Ireland move from the status of example to issue. The real issues were European. The *Universe* would make no concession on Papal questions.

Thus began the most successful wooing of the Irish masses in Britain and their fellow–Catholics by an Irish newspaper controller. Silent, small, secretive, Denny Lane was wholly unlike the journalists of thunder and lightning in the tradition of O'Connell and O'Connor. But he represented the most significant and enduring form of Irish association with British journalist – the small capitalist, lobbyist, pressure–maker, entrepreneur, and stylist of the new Catholic bourgeoisie. In size, resolution, business capacity and ability to whip up pens of venom to his aid he anticipates the future, the days of that similarly proportioned Irish newspaper–owner of Cork and Dublin, William Martin Murphy.

Lane was not a clericalist, save in a business sense. The *Universe*'s violence against the cash nexus of the 'Modern Idea' was appropriate from an owner who made his creed neither the master nor the martyr of his pocket, but its firm accomplice. Other Irish men of the press found themselves unable to work out a *modus vivendi* with non–Irish ecclesiastics. Wiseman, who was of Irish ancestry, and Manning, who conspicuously preferred the Irish either to his fellow–Oxonians or to the progeny of the recusants, had enough pull on Irish loyalties to keep dissension within bounds. But there was clearly an Irish expectation of preferential treatment from the British Roman Catholic authorities, and in Scotland, where native Catholicism was much more proletarian than its English counterpart, competition for jobs and influence sharpened between the emigrants from Banffshire and the Western Isles to the Lowlands, and the newcomers to the same central belt from Ireland. This expressed itself in the career of the first long–lasting Scottish Catholic weekly, the Glasgow *Free Press*.

The journal was founded in 1851, but its quarrels with the Scottish Vicars Apostolic only burst into full flame with the rise in its ranks of Augustus Henry Keane, an Irish former clerical student who became editor in 1862 before his thirtieth birthday. Keane promoted scurrilous campaigns against Scottish–born clergy, whom he accused of misappropriation of funds, inattention to duties, inefficiency, incapacity and reception of promotion on grounds of blatant favouritism. There was some hint of Scottish priests' fears of the newspaper's sympathy for the Brotherhood of St. Patrick, which they had already condemned. The Scottish Roman Catholic authorities feared being drawn into Irish political quarrels by Irish immigrant pressure, and were quicker to distance themselves from Irish nationalist crusades than their English brethren. The kernel of the problem was that the Scots feared to make any concessions, suspecting these would be the prelude to a general successful Irish assault on their ecclesiastical power; the Irish carried grievances far beyond any possible level of compromise. The ease with which the *Free Press* trumpeted charges with only the faintest shadow of a factual basis suggests that Keane and his subordinate Peter McCorry, who succeeded him in 1865, wanted absolute victory, whose only justification was the number of their fellow–Irish. The deciding factor may have been a class one: coming from a society ruled by a superior caste, they had no intention of deferring to superiors of a social origin little superior to their own. Keane had studied in Rome as well as in Ireland, and it may have been that his experiences in either place had given him a conviction of the power of agitation and intrigue; it certainly led him to dismiss the Vicars Apostolic whom he opposed as parochial time–servers with no claims for respect. McCorry was even more violent. In England it was the bishop of humblest origin, Ullathorne, who sustained the brunt of Irish journalistic opposition. A common factor in both quarrels were controversial visits from the parish priest of Partry in Galway, the Rev. Patrick Lavelle, whose suspected Fenianism alarmed both Ullathorne and the Scots. Keane was briefly successful in mobilising Irish priests in the West of Scotland to protest against their lack of preferment, but under McCorry the situation became impossible. Manning was brought in, and in 1868 the *Free Press* was condemned by the ecclesiastical authorities and ceased publication.

Keane himself went on to become Professor of Hindustani at University College, London, made important contributions to linguistics and ethnology and seems to have died outside the Roman Catholic faith. McCorry after the demise of the *Free Press* ran the *Irish Catholic Banner* in 1868 but again was condemned for the vehemence of his attacks on the Scottish clergy and saw his editorial charge end in its turn. Although James Edmund Handley (Brother Clare), author of *The Irish in Modern Scotland*, was normally zealous in the extreme in the defence of his ethnic group, he could make little defence of Keane and McCorry, who seem to have believed a Scottish Catholic priest to be a contradiction in terms. The icily judicious account of Keane and the *Free Press* in the *New Catholic Encyclopedia* by Monsignor David McRoberts (whose articles are invaluable, if not always absolutely accurate, surveys of their subjects), argues that 'The *Free Press* incident is important in the development of the Church in modern Scotland: the very real threat of schism it produced made it clear that the Church in Scotland badly needed reorganization. The result was the reestablishment of the Scottish hierarchy in 1878.' McRoberts's comment on schism must be taken seriously: had Keane and McCorry been more restrained in their agitation of a real grievance, and less openly determined to concede nothing in their denunciations of the Scottish Catholic clergy, they might have made a very ugly break. McRoberts made clear in his contribution to *Modern Scottish Catholicism*, edited by himself (Glasgow, 1979), that the dangers of Irish domination of the Scottish Church actually held back the restoration of the Scottish hierarchy until Cullen, who alone could have carried through such a design, was dead. As Handley states, the spiral of Scottish–Irish rivalry in Catholic affairs had been longstanding in Scotland before the foundation of the *Free Press*, and while the Irish were more aggressive and less defensive than he is wont to suggest, the Scots often showed themselves uneasy, suspicious and grudging towards their co–religionists. To the end of the century the Irish repaid them by largely freezing them out of discussion in the Irish–dominated organs of Scottish journalism. The Scottish Catholics, both clerical and lay, were often obliged to throw themselves on the mercy of the non–Catholic press repudiated by all the Catholic newspapers in England.

The third important centre after London and Glasgow was Liverpool, where Michael James Whitty, a native of County Wexford, founded the *Liverpool Daily Post* in 1855, and in it advocated Catholic views. These were not to everyone's taste, and in October 1859 the short–lived *Lancashire Free Press* was launched by a former sub–editor of the *Daily Post*, the future Fenian Stephen Joseph Meany, who went to America the following year. The *Free Press* was discontinued in April 1860, but on 9 June 1860 it was replaced by the *Northern Press*, launched ostensibly by James G. Plunkett, and edited by S.B. Harper, a convert from Anglicanism. They aimed at making it the organ of Catholics in northern England, and declared that the interests of the Irish race are ours, 'for Irish and Catholic are to us the same'. A basic problem was revealed four months later when Whitty wrote in the

Daily Post (23 October 1860) that the *Northern Press* was conducted with considerable ability but its principles were vile and English Roman Catholics refused to read it – 'it is eternally abusing Victor Emmanuel, Garibaldi and the "Daily Post"'. At the end of the year a *Northern Press* (29 December 1860) editorial declared that, despite difficulties, the paper had survived free of party bondage.

In March 1863 a new series of the paper was launched, published by Richard Campbell, in which the blame for the failure of earlier enterprises was laid on those to whom they had been entrusted (*N.P.*, 21 March 1863). The following month the paper's title was changed to the *Northern Press and Catholic Weekly Times*. A break in the files in the British Museum Newspaper Library from 1863 to 1869 and the appearance and disappearance of the paper from the pages of *Gore's Liverpool Directory* suggest its fortunes were at a low ebb for much of the 1860s. However, it survived to be acquired in or by 1869 by a respected Liverpool priest, Fr. James Nugent (1822–1905). Nugent, born in Liverpool but of Irish parentage and sympathies, was a temperance advocate, the first Catholic chaplain of the borough gaol at Walton, and founder of the Catholic Institute, Hope Street, and the Boys' Refuge in St. Anne Street, (Denvir, *Life Story*, p.64; *The Times*, 28 June 1905). The first number of the *Northern Press* received by the British Museum since 1863 was No.CI of a 'New Series', dated 6 February 1869, and printed at the 'Boys Refuge Printing Works'. From September 1870 the paper's title was simplified to the *Catholic Times*, and from 1870 to *c.* 1873/74 it was edited and managed by the Irish Nationalist John Denvir, who had been closely involved with Nugent in the late 1860s when he was secretary of the 'Association of Providence for the Protection of Orphan and Destitute Boys', i.e. Nugent's Boys Refuge.

Denvir recalls in his *Life Story of an Old Rebel* that he was left in charge of the *Northern Press and Catholic Times*, while Nugent went to America for nine months. At that time it had a small circulation, and was not a paying concern, but when Nugent returned the paper was in a healthy state (Denvir, *Life Story*, pp.153–9).

In 1876 the *Catholic Times* was merged with *Catholic Opinion* which had been founded in London in 1867. Edited by Fr. William Lockhart from 1867–73 it was used between 1873–76 by Herbert Vaughan, Bishop of Salford, as an educational supplement to the *Tablet*, but in 1876 he transferred it to Fr. Nugent. Denvir records that when Vaughan became Bishop of Salford (1872), he was very sympathetic to Nugent and proved a useful ally as Manchester, though smaller in terms of Catholic population, was important in publication terms as a centre for a number of large manufacturing towns (Denvir, *Life Story*, p.158). Vaughan's attitude must have made a pleasant change for Nugent and Denvir after the difficulties created by Canon Fisher, the 'anti-Irish' Vicar-General of the Diocese of Liverpool, when they sought access to Bishop Goss of Liverpool, whose sermons they wished to use in the *Catholic Times* (Denvir, *Life Story*, pp.156–7).

Soon after the merger, the *Catholic Times and Catholic Opinion* was claiming a circulation of over 25,000 copies per week (advt., Mitchell's *Newspaper Press Directory*, 1877) and it survived under this title until 1933 when it reverted to being simply the *Catholic Times*. In 1884 Patrick L. Beazley (1859–1923) began his long editorship of the paper. The *Catholic Times* was apparently financed privately until 1897 when, probably due to ill-health, its then proprietor, another Liverpool priest, Fr. John Berry, Principal of the Catholic Institute in the 1890s, who had taken the paper over from Nugent, sold it and his monthly *Catholic Fireside* to a limited liability company, The Catholic Publishing Co. Ltd., for 19,993 paid-up £1 shares and £7 cash – the cash presumably being provided by seven other shareholders who subscribed for one share each (PRO: BT31 7747/55377). Whatever the reason for the sale, Berry remained a Director of this company and its successor of the same name, formed in 1907, until at least the end of the first World War (PRO, BT31 7747/55377, and Companies Registration Office, London, Co. No.100987) and his principal associates also stayed unchanged in these two decades: Charles J.P. O'Dowd, an Irish journalist, who was Secretary and Managing Director; two other Liverpool-based priests, William H. Leeming and Alfred Jeanrenaud; and Thomas P. Maguire, a Liverpool solicitor.

A different type of limited liability company to the small one owning the *Catholic Times* is the broad-based kind represented by the Catholic Printing and Publishing Co., which started another Lancashire Catholic paper, the Preston *Catholic News*, in February 1889, with the declared aims of asserting Catholic principles, defending the Catholic Church and representing Catholic thought and opinion (*C.N.*, 16 February 1889). The Newcastle *Irish Tribune* accused it of being anti-Irish, and when canvassing for advertisements to have claimed that its circulation was chiefly among English Catholics, who were superior to mere Irish Catholics (*I.T.*, 12 October 1889). Certainly the news columns of the *Catholic News* are full of Catholic news while ignoring the Irish Nationalist items which filled the *Irish Tribune*. The names of shareholders listed in 1889 also bear out the suggestion of English, not Irish, Catholic backing. These shareholders included not only a broad range of Lancashire merchants and tradesmen but also a number of women, and went comparatively far down the social scale, to 'Warder', 'Asst. Storekeeper' and 'Postman', who held one £5 share each in 1889 (PRO: BT31 4299/27901). One interesting omission in this list of shareholders is the local Catholic clergy – one priest, Robert Gradwell of Claughton, Garstang, held 20 shares, but he is the only member of the clergy listed in 1889, albeit an important one locally.

The company went into liquidation in 1893, but the paper survived: ironically, in view of the *Irish Tribune's* anti-Irish allegations, it was brought by the *Tribune's* founder, Charles Diamond, who did not want to see any useful Catholic publication collapse (*C.N.* 18 November 1893). Diamond set up a new company, the British Catholic Printing and Publishing Co. Ltd., to take over the business and offered 1,000 £1 Preference Shares for subscription by Catholics who wanted the paper to remain non-political, but only 64 had been taken up by seven shareholders by July 1896 (*C.N.*, 28 October, 18 November

1893; PRO, BT31 5614/39099).

The type of venture represented by the *Catholic News* was a common one in the history of nineteenth–century journalism: a group of men deciding to start a paper and forming a limited company in order to spread the risks among a large number of men and women who, committed to the cause the paper was to represent – whether a political party, Catholicism, Irish Nationalism – could be persuaded to take one or more shares – generally £1 or £5 in value, although the full purchase price would not have been paid at once – and all too often after a short time the capital would be found to be insufficient and the company would have to be wound up.

Another example of such a venture is the *Catholic Press*, started in London in 1887 by the Catholic Press Association Ltd. with 73 shareholders including 23 Catholic priests and three Irish bishops. Despite its distinguished backing the paper lasted less than a year, and A. Hilliard Atteridge, the company's managing director, who also acted as its liquidator, wrote many years later to another journalist, that the *Catholic Press* 'stopped for want of capital just as it was beginning to make way'. (Atteridge to Thomas Jeffs, 8 September 1901, PRO: BT31 14877/24839).

The North East of England produced a paper which provides an interesting contrast to the Catholic papers of Lancashire and London, the *Irish Tribune*, started by Charles Diamond in Newcastle in December 1884. Diamond was born in County Derry in 1858 but moved to Newcastle in or soon after 1878, working as a spirit traveller and paper merchant before turning to journalism (*I.T.* 23 July 1892). Despite its large Catholic, and especially Irish Catholic, population, Tyneside does not seem to have produced any Catholic journals, possibly because there was no room for yet another paper in the varied and thriving Newcastle press, or because the existing papers satisfied demand, or because, until Diamond came on the scene, no Catholic had both the desire and ability to start such a venture. Whatever the reason the Irish Catholics seem to have had to wait until 1884 before a paper aimed specifically at them was launched.

From the first the *Irish Tribune* was an Irish Nationalist paper. The first editorial declared that no 'representative National Journal' was published in Britain at this time and it was the *Tribune*'s aim to fill this gap and become 'the organ of Irish national thought in this country, to represent and possess the confidence of all Irishmen – priests and laymen, labourers and merchants, rich and poor – who on the broad national platform can meet and work together.' (*I.T.*, 13 December 1884). The news columns of the paper included Catholic and Irish news from all round the country, with particular prominence being given to reports of branch meetings of the Irish National League of Great Britain.

Local response to the new paper may be judged from the announcement on 21 February 1885 of a special local edition for Northumberland and Durham with increased local news. Clearly the paper had achieved sufficient circulation to be worth printing more than one edition, and the Tyneside Irish wanted it to be their one weekly paper with all the Tyneside news. To obtain their support, it needed to fulfil the dual role of local newspaper and Irish Nationalist newspaper. Its success was reflected in its *claimed* circulation of 20,000 subscribers in England and Scotland only three months after it was launched (*I.T.*, 14 March 1885) and its survival for at least a decade while so many of its contemporaries, which failed to provide both local news *and* support for a cause, collapsed. The *Tribune* also secured the blessing of the Catholic hierarchy, receiving a letter of approval from the pro–Irish Edward Bagshawe, Bishop of Nottingham, in November 1885 which was published together with the announcement that the *Irish Tribune* would be issued in the four central towns in the diocese of Nottingham (Nottingham, Leicester, Derby and Lincoln) with a special column of diocesan news.

The paper's progress may be judged by the increase in the number of publication offices listed in the imprint – Newcastle, Nottingham and Glasgow had been joined by London, Liverpool and Manchester in June 1886 – and by the rising number of wholesale and retail agents for the paper listed in it from time to time (e.g. 5 June 1886, 1 January 1887). 1887 saw the addition of a Catholic children's column, 'Catholic Legion', conducted by 'Guardian' and June 1887 saw a change in size with eight larger pages replacing twelve smaller ones.

On 4 August 1888 the *Irish Tribune* published an interesting letter from Diamond. Referring to statements by Pope Leo XIII that a Catholic newspaper is a perpetual mission and by the Archbishop of Tunis, Lavigerie, that 'to found or sustain a Catholic journal . . . is as necessary as to build a church', Diamond described himself as the publisher of three Catholic weeklies, two of which (the *Irish Tribune* and the *Glasgow Observer*) were now in days of comparative calm, while the third, a new London venture (the *Weekly Herald*), only some twenty weeks old, was bidding fair to surpass them in both circulation and as an advertising medium. The *Irish Tribune* had cost him £2,000 in the first year and a half and made him a host of enemies; the *Glasgow Observer*, which had been under his control since 9 July 1887, had cost the local limited liability company which started it in 1885 £2,000 in two years, but was now a success. The Catholic press in Britain, he declared, existed despite Catholic apathy.

The *Irish Tribune* passed through the Parnell crisis, moving from a declared belief up to the last moment that Parnell would be vindicated, to an immediate response after the divorce court proceedings that Parnell must resign – if Home Rule was to be won he must clear out, he could not just lie low and keep silent (*I.T.* 22 November 1890). The *Tribune* continued to follow this line in the weeks that followed and in late December/early January ran a coupon poll asking 'Do you think Charles Stewart Parnell has any longer the right to pose as the Irish Leader?'. According to the result published on 24 January 1891, 4,756 readers replied No, 346 Yes.

In the early 1890s the *Tribune* became less of a local paper, more of a Catholic one, and the temperance cause began to figure more prominently its columns. The decline in its general quality was possibly because of Diamond's withdrawal from Newcastle. He had been actively involved in local Irish political life in the 1880s, being president of one of the Newcastle I.N.L. branches in 1884, but with the growth of his other newspaper interests after 1887 and his removal first to Glasgow and then to London, the paper lost that personal touch which had first helped it to succeed. By 1895, the *Tribune* had become far more Catholic, Irish and literary, less general and all-round. This, however, may also have been a reflection of general developments in the provincial press. More people now looked to daily newspapers, whether morning or evening, for their news, and expected their weekly paper to provide family reading for the weekend rather than an epitome of the week's news. Increasingly weekly papers were either attached to a daily paper (whereas, not so many years before, many dailies had succeeded in life because they were attached to successful weeklies), or represented a special interest.

Diamond began to expand his newspaper interests in 1887 when he moved to Glasgow to edit the struggling *Glasgow Observer*. The *Observer* had been founded in 1885 in competition with Patrick Shiels' *Exile* (1884–5 – on this episode see Edwards, 'Catholic Press in Scotland', *Innes Review*, vol.xxix, no.2). The *Exile* had been the first Catholic weekly published in Scotland since the demise of the *Glasgow Free Press* and the short-lived *Irish Banner* in 1868. Diamond probably saved the *Glasgow Observer* from an early grave and in 1894 became its proprietor, changing its title to the *Glasgow Observer and Catholic Herald* at the beginning of 1895.

In 1888–89 Diamond also started the *Weekly Herald* and the *Catholic Educator* in London and the *Manchester Citizen*. In 1893 the *Weekly Herald* was renamed the *Catholic Herald* and the *Manchester Citizen* became the *Manchester Catholic Herald*. The *Catholic Educator*, a journal for Catholic teachers, only survived until September 1894.

In July 1892 Diamond was elected to Parliament as M.P. for County Monaghan. He stayed in Parliament for only three years, not being re-selected as candidate in 1895. From then until his death in 1934 he concentrated his energies on journalism. By then his New Catholic Press Company in England and Scottish Catholic Printing Company in Scotland owned nearly forty weekly newspapers. Much of this chain was built up in the 1890s.

Mitchell's 1890 *Newspaper Press Directory* includes an advertisement (p.148) for the Catholic Press Company of Great Britain which owned the *Irish Tribune*, Newcastle, the *Manchester Citizen*, the *Weekly Herald*, the *Catholic Educator* and the *Glasgow Observer*. It had offices in London, Manchester, Newcastle, Glasgow and Dublin. Three years later the *Dundee* and *Edinburgh Catholic Heralds* had been added to the list (Mitchell's *NPD*, 1893). *Walker's Press Directory*, 1897, lists either Diamond himself or the Catholic Press Company as the proprietor of not only these papers (minus, of course, the *Catholic Educator*) but also of a *Catholic Herald* or *Catholic News* for Birmingham, Blackburn, Bolton (no proprietor is given), Bradford, Bristol, Cumberland (Carlisle), Hull, Leeds, Liverpool and Wigan in England and of the *Lanarkshire Catholic Herald* (Coatbridge) and

Clydesdale Catholic Herald (Greenock) in Scotland. A letter dated 5 April 1897 written on Catholic Press Company headed notepaper reveals further changes (PRO, BT31 5614/39099). In Newcastle the *Irish Tribune* had been replaced by the *Tyneside Catholic News*. This was probably a simple title change which took place *c.*, 1896 – there are no copies of either paper in the British Museum between the last known extant copy of the *Irish Tribune* dated 27 December 1895, and the first of the *Tyneside Catholic News*, No.715, dated 7 January 1899 – as with a number of Diamond's other papers, the issue numbers are confusing rather than helpful. This letter also reveals that the Catholic Press Company had acquired the *Aberdeen Catholic Herald*, started in 1893 by J.J. Moran. Not included separately in any of the 1890s newspaper directories or in the notepaper heading, but allegedly started in 1894, was the *Welsh Catholic Herald*, Cardiff (Mitchell's *NPD*, 1903, p.94 advt.; the earliest copy in the British Museum is No.196, 14 February 1902). This process of starting or buying up newspapers continued into the twentieth century, with 32 titles being listed in the Catholic Press advertisement in Mitchell's 1910 *Directory*.

Most of Diamond's papers were local editions of either the London *Catholic Herald* or the *Glasgow Observer* with perhaps only the Manchester, Newcastle and Preston papers from among the English provincial ones and the *Aberdeen Catholic Herald* in Scotland being able to claim a genuinely separate existence at least for part of their lives. It would seem that Diamond had concluded that, however much common content there might be, it was better to have a local paper, in name at least, for each main area of circulation rather than one *Catholic Herald* or *Catholic News* or *Irish Tribune* circulating throughout the country – people were more likely to buy their local paper than an anonymous *Catholic News*.

Diamond at least seems to have found a recipe for success in Catholic weekly journalism, which he was to continue using during the early years of the twentieth century.

Conclusion

The mass migration of members of the Irish nomadic, labouring and tenant–farming classes in the Victorian era was accompanied by an exodus of the intellectuals and *literati*, sometimes enforced. Many of the latter played a part in journalism. Their proportions may well have been the same among the Irish in Britain as in the wider world, and by 1900 they included illustrious names like Shaw and Wilde. Despite the official Roman Catholic hostility to the Queen's Colleges established in Cork and Galway by Peel, they and the Catholic University produced many more lively and literate students, voracious for careers in the world of letters. Irish links were of assistance, notably in the need in Britain as well as the United States, for candidates to produce output for the Catholic press. The intellectuals and *literati* were not automatically to be relied on to accept a limited status under clerical or other authorities who wished to use them. The conflict naturally arose over mindless hacks who could stifle their journals by mechanical lack of conviction, and also over ideas which distressed employers, readerships and advertisers. The Irish could control their own hacks the best: Lane, Diamond and, in Ireland, Murphy, always seemed to get the men they wanted.

Great difficulty exists for the historian in determining the precise extent of Irish influence. A term like 'editor' or 'owner' could mean virtually absolute control of material, or servility or indifference, or anything between these extremes. Sometimes historians have been baffled as to the dates of even nominal control. The *Dublin Review* has received the most thorough study of all the journals, its administrative history being summarised and articles where possible ascribed by the *Wellesley Index of Victorian Periodicals*, but deep mysteries remain. Nicholas Wiseman was certainly its co–founder and continued as co–proprietor or sole proprietor for many years, but when did O'Connell's connection cease? It may have ended in 1843, it may have lasted, at least nominally, until his death in 1847. He wrote only once for it, a lengthy review–article denouncing Rebecca Theresa Reid's *Six Months in a Convent*, a work of unsubstantiated sensational revelation about convent life after the manner of the more famous *Awful Disclosures* of Maria Monk. Even this may not be entirely his – it was long ascribed to the third co–founder Michael Joseph Quin, who had already written another such essay for the *Review* – but certain aspects of the handling of evidence and the thunderous rhetoric have every mark of O'Connell, whose authorship is firmly asserted by the records. At the very least, it must be the substantial revision and completion by O'Connell of a fragment by Quin. Again, all three of the co–founders were often absent from Britain, Wiseman often being as far as Rome. Russell's supervisory role has been noted: he exercised it from Maynooth, probably following *ad hoc* arrangements made by Wiseman and O'Connell, but he was for a time diverted to Ceylon between 1842 and 1845. Denis Gwynn declared that the journal was 'intended in great measure to counteract the Cisalpine tendencies of the existing *Catholic Magazine*' [*Cardinal Wiseman* (London,1929)], but the *Edinburgh Catholic Magazine* was in abeyance when the *Dublin Review* was founded, and according to Husenbeth the third, fourth and fifth numbers of the *Dublin Review* were actually edited by Smith of the *Catholic Magazine*. Gwynn's deduction may simply be an erroneous reading of conclusions by the co–founders, when the *Dublin Review* had been well launched, that they found Smith too parochial, and that in any case it was excessive for him to continue editing both the *Dublin Review* and the *Catholic Magazine*, which he was in process of reviving. The editorship was taken over by Henry Ridgard Bagshawe who held it from 1837 to 1863, but he certainly did not exercise even full editorial control. His successor, W.G. Ward, clearly was much more decisively in charge, but it is unclear how far his initial years were affected by his Irish assistants, Edward Healy Thompson and John Cashel Hoey, who successively dealt with cultural questions for Ward's first four years. These problems have far more complex counterparts in all other journals of Irish connection.

The question of an ideologically Irish journal was greatly affected by the proximity of Ireland, as ventures across the oceans could not be. O'Connell might seem excessively preoccupied by a Catholic press, but he intended to ensure that any Catholic press was responsive to himself, rather than to conservative Catholic families, influential converts or Pope Gregory XVI. We do not know what individual Irish journalists he set on their way with the clear intention that their fealty would be to him, or where he succeeded in placing them in the several journals he influenced. O'Connell's disciples often revolted, however, especially when they were figures of originality, and his record in dealing with journalists is particularly conspicuous in setting in motion this sort of revolt. Of British journalists, the O'Connellite disciple who most conspicuously set up on his own was the Chartist Feargus O'Connor, but the nature of O'Connor's Chartist journalism was firmly established by the advent of Victoria. The links maintained by O'Connor with more youthful Irish journalists and his influence on radical Irish journalism both in and outside Britain merit serious investigation. After O'Connell's death and O'Connor's descent into insanity, there was little direct attempt to provide a political Irish journalism in Britain in its own right, though the *Tablet* under Lucas fulfilled such a need in part. The Fenians and their allies made some gains, but Parnell's subsequent dictum 'The Fenians made only one mistake. They should never have fought', seems to apply also to their influence on journalism, save where they sought directly to establish a journal. Above all, Irish journals in Britain wishing to exercise political influence could not fight off the competition from Ireland of the Sullivans' *Nation*, Pigott's newspapers and, in Parnell's day, *United Ireland*, although all proved important schools of Irish journalistic education. In sum, the Irish in British Victorian journalism, like the Irish in so many other areas of British life, owed much of their force and fire to their Irish origins, but were never permitted by Ireland to establish a British identity.

'ANOTHER STAFFORD STREET ROW': LAW, ORDER AND THE IRISH PRESENCE IN MID–VICTORIAN WOLVERHAMPTON

Roger Swift

> There abides he, in his squalor and unreason, in his falsity and drunken violence, as the ready made nucleus of degradation and disorder.
>
> Thomas Carlyle, *Chartism* (1839).

In recent years, social historians have devoted increasing attention to the study of the character of Irish immigration in Victorian Britain[1] and of the problems of integration which faced Irish communities in an urban–industrial society.[2] Although Anglo–Irish relations were often more complex and fluid than many contemporaries realised,[3] the Irish presence was frequently resented by the native English,[4] and Anglo–Irish tensions, coloured by a variety of social, economic, religious and cultural factors,[5] sometimes resulted in open violence and popular disturbances.[6] Such incidents, which were frequently described by the provincial press as 'Irish Rows',[7] were often manifestations of the strains and stresses which faced immigrant Irish communities in the Victorian city, particularly in the aftermath of the Irish famine, yet served only to reinforce the popular belief in the Irish predilection for violence and unruly behaviour. Moreover, they were widely regarded by the authorities as a challenge on the part of 'the dangerous classes', in which the Irish bulked large,[8] to the growing ability of provincial police forces to maintain public order in Victorian society.[9] However, the relationship between popular disturbances and the Irish presence in the Victorian city has been the subject of relatively limited research, particularly on the local level, and this article seeks to examine this subject with specific reference to the Irish presence in mid–Victorian Wolverhampton.[10]

I

A small Irish community had developed in Wolverhampton during the late eighteenth and early nineteenth centuries when road improvement schemes, canal construction and the advent of the railways offered employment opportunities. The Irish Famine witnessed a further influx of migrants, principally from the countries of Mayo, Sligo and Roscommon.[11] In 1851, when the population of Wolverhampton totalled 49,985, there were over 6,000 Irish in the town, and by 1871, when the population of the town was 68,291, the Irish population exceeded 12,000.[12] This expanding immigrant community, largely unskilled or semi-skilled, chiefly found employment in local collieries and ironworks, and in construction trades, working as masons, bricklayers, labourers and navvies.[13]

Irish living conditions were generally the very worst in the Victorian industrial slum, and Irish neighbourhoods were frequently characterised by appalling overcrowding, poor sanitation, vagrancy, disease, alcoholism, and general squalor.[14] A similar picture emerges in Wolverhampton where the Irish community lived largely, although not exclusively, in dwellings secreted into the courts and alleyways leading off Stafford Street, Canal Street, and Little's Lane, a poverty-ridden district characterised by grossly overcrowded and insanitary living conditions, and containing a profusion of lodging houses, public houses and beershops. The most notorious enclave within this district was the Caribee Island, described in February 1849 as 'a collection of the most squalid looking houses on the north side of Stafford Street inhabited by the lowest class of Irish. A passage about 100 yards in length and 3 or 4 wide leads into the heart of this loathesome neighbourhood. The passage is stopped at the far end by a cross wall and collection of filth . . . an open gutter passes down the passage between the houses or, rather, the whole is an open gutter'.[15] Although Robert Rawlinson's subsequent Report to the Board of Health on the Sanitary Condition of Wolverhampton showed that slum conditions existed elsewhere in the town,[16] the Stafford Street district acquired an unenviable local reputation: cholera struck with great mortality in 1832 and 1849, and contemporary descriptions of the neighbourhood often pointed to the association between insanitary conditions and the habits of the Irish.[17] Indeed, respectable opinion was particularly critical of the state of the lodging houses in the Irish district, and of the high incidence of vagrancy,[18] and it was not unknown for the Wolverhampton magistrates to dismiss Irishmen charged with vargrancy, on condition that they left the town.[19] Dr. Edward Ballard's Report to the Local Government Board on the Sanitary Condition of Wolverhampton in 1874 suggests that the general character of the Stafford Street district had barely improved during the intervening years,[20] and the Caribee Island remained a fever nest until its demolition in the wake of the Artisans' Dwellings Act of 1875. Some Irish families, however, migrated to other parts of Wolverhampton during the period: indeed, Mark Shaw's recent analysis of contemporary census data suggests that by 1871 the Irish were slightly less concentrated in the Stafford Street district than before, and were present in significant numbers in others of the areas of poorest housing.[21]

The Religious Census of 1851 indicates that there was a high degree of religious pluralism in Wolverhampton, with a strong leaning towards Methodism.[22] However, there had long been a relatively large and well-established Roman Catholic community in the town and, in a recent and illuminating study, James Quirke has suggested that Wolverhampton's importance as a Catholic centre was endorsed in 1804 when the town became the headquarters of the Midland District of the Roman Catholic Church in England and the Vicar Apostolic, John Milner, the formidable and combative English Athanasius' of the Catholic mission, took up residence in Giffard House.[23] By 1851, the Catholic population of Wolverhampton had been swelled by the influx of Irish immigrants, and Quirke has argued that the subsequent growth of the Irish Catholic community at a more rapid rate than that of the well-established and essentially middle-class English Catholic community resulted in some conflicts within the Catholic Church locally during the mid-Victorian period.[24] Nevertheless, in Wolverhampton, as in other urban areas,[25] the Catholic Church faced considerable problems in meeting the spiritual and temporal needs of the Irish poor, including shortages of money and places of worship. When Irish-born Father Patrick O'Sullivan arrived in the town in 1830 he found only one Catholic chapel, in North Street, which held a congregation of 380,[26] and although three additional churches had been built by 1851 to cope with the post-Famine influx of Irish,[27] Catholic priests often complained of their inability to minister effectively to the expanding Irish community. Their concern was justifiable: the Irish newcomers held an emotional and frequently practical loyalty to the Catholic Church, and the Religious Census indicates that religious observance among Irish Catholics in Wolverhampton was considerably higher than religious observance among other sectors of the working-class population. Indeed, 4,435 persons attended the four Catholic churches in the town (which collectively provided for only 1,896 sittings) on Sunday 30 March 1851.[28] However, the pressure of numbers was partly alleviated by the foundation of S.S. Mary and John's Church, Snowhill in October 1851, and St. Patrick's Church, in Little's Lane, Caribee Island, in June 1866. The latter was intended primarily 'to afford accommodation for the Irish Catholics who live in large numbers in the district',[29] and was designed in part to combat the problem of 'leakage' among Irish Catholics in Wolverhampton.[30]

The absence of educational provision for the offspring of the Irish slums was another problem which faced the local Catholic Church, and one to which increasing attention was given. The Wolverhampton Ragged School Union had originally established a school in the Caribee Island in March 1848, but the institution was soon moved to Prince's Alley because the Caribee Island was considered to be 'so unhealthy as to be prejudicial to the health of teachers and children'.[31] Nevertheless, the Catholic Church was instrumental in the establishment of the schools of St. Patrick and St. George in Little's Lane in 1849, and by 1851 the three Roman Catholic day schools in Wolverhampton catered for 745 children – almost one-fifth of all children then receiving some form of elementary education in the town.[32] In 1853, Inspector T. W. Marshall reported to the Committee of Council on Education that the poverty of the Irish often impeded their education: 'the most formidable obstacle which confronts the promoters of Catholic education for the poor, and which has hitherto most obstinately baffled their efforts, is connected with this fact in their social state, that many of the parents profess to be, and often really are, too sorely burdened with poverty either to contribute anything towards the education of their children, or to forgo the scanty earnings by which their premature toil not unfrequently alleviates their own destitution'.[33] Nevertheless, Marshall noted that provision for the education of Catholics in Wolverhampton was improving, despite shortages of space and equipment, and commended the Sisters of Mercy for the quality of their instruction.[34] By 1878, this improvement had been sustained: five Roman Catholic schools were aided by Parliamentary Grant and could collectively accommodate 1,648 children.[35]

The extension of religious and educational provision suggests that the Irish community was becoming more organised and self-assertive in Wolverhampton during the mid-Victorian period, and that the Catholic Church played a crucial role in this process. Nevertheless, the Irish presence was unpopular, particularly among the more respectable sectors of Wulfrunian society who were often quick to denigrate the Irish for their poverty, their squalid living conditions, their alien ways (which included the Gaelic language)[36], and their lawlessness. Indeed, the Irish were held to be responsible for a significant proportion of all crimes committed in the town, particularly during the 1850's. The Annual Returns of people taken into custody by the Wolverhampton police, detailed in the Watch Committee Minutes, indicate, for example, that out of 1907 persons held in custody in 1854, 445 (23%) were Irish; in 1856, 588 Irish people (25%) were held in custody out of 2,377 persons apprehended; in 1857, 428 Irish (19%) were amongst the 2,262 persons apprehended; in 1859, out of 1960 committals, 419 (22%) were Irish.[37] At first sight, these figures suggest that the capacity of the Irish for breaking the law was disproportionate to their size within the community at large. This was not, of course, unusual: Sheridan Gilley has observed that 'the English stereotype of the Irishman . . . rested on a body of social fact, however misinterpreted. The predilection for violence suggested by their street songs was enhanced by slum overcrowding, by a vigorous pub culture, and by the attraction of English working-class mores also disfigured by drunken violence . . . so Irishmen figure in disproportionate numbers in the criminal statistics for casual violence'.[38] Nevertheless, the Stafford Street district was widely regarded as a breeding ground for crime and disorder. Gilbert Hogg, the Chief Constable of Wolverhampton from 1848 to 1857, twice singled out the district in his evidence to Government Inquiries during the period, reporting to Robert Rawlinson in 1849 that he had, at times, 'been compelled to have as many as twenty men parading the streets with cutlasses to assert the supremacy of the law',[39] while in 1853 he informed the Home Secretary, Sir George Grey, that he had frequently been obliged to withdraw policemen from other parts of Wolverhampton to cope with disturbances in the Irish quarter.[40] The Tory *Wolverhampton Chronicle* was also quick to condemn Irish lawlessness: in June 1849, for example, the newspaper reported that 'a great many persons appeared to answer charges of assault, drunkenness and disorderly conduct', adding that 'As usual, Stafford Street furnished its quota',[41] while leaders such as 'Another Stafford Street Row'[42] and 'Stafford Street Disturbance'[43] reinforced popular imagery.

Indeed, it appears that respectable opinion in Wolverhampton was most perturbed by the fact that although the town was becoming increasingly orderly during the mid-Victorian period,[44] there were some serious instances of rioting and, in each instance, the disturbance contained an Irish dimension and stretched the forces of order to the full.

II

Several disturbances, which involved ugly clashes between the Stafford Street Irish and the local police, occurred in 1848 and 1849.

In May 1848, a near-riot ensued in the Caribee Island following an attempt by a policeman, McCasker, to investigate a disturbance early one Sunday morning. The policeman was attacked by a group of Irishmen and was only rescued, with difficulty, by John Fenn, a parish constable. The disorder escalated, and the district remained in a uproar throughout the day, so much so that it was popularly rumoured that troops would be called in to restore order. In the event, order was restored temporarily by the arrival of a large body of police, armed with cutlasses, under the command of John Hatton, the Chief Constable of the Mining District, and his deputy, Gilbert Hogg, who dispersed the crowds of Irish, which numbered over 2,000, despite a bombardment of stones. The police displayed considerable violence in quelling this disturbance and in apprehending some of the ringleaders: William Maxwell, a navvy, was arrested and handcuffed by two officers, Maddocks and Sunderland, and when examined by the Magistrates at the Petty Sessions on a charge of assaulting the police, claimed that he had been unjustifiably attacked by the police, showing the Bench his back, which was black and blue. Gilbert Hogg denied that these injuries had been inflicted by the police, stating that Maxwell had been so violent that it had been necessary to strap him down at the police station where he had inflicted the injuries on himself. The Bench philosophically informed the prisoner that if he assaulted the police he should expect to be beaten, and committed him to prison for two months. In addition, seven Irishmen received similar prison sentences for the initial assault on McCasker, and six men were fined various sums for assaults on other officers.[45]

Two weeks later, P.C. Sunderland, who had been assaulted by two Irishmen in Stafford Street earlier in the year,[46] and who had evidently treated William Maxwell roughly during the Caribee Island troubles, was attacked by a vengeful group of Irish folk in Stafford Street. Additional policemen came to his rescue, and in the resulting fracas an Irishwoman had her arm broken. Several arrests were made, and John Gallacher was convicted of assaulting the police and was fined 20s.[47]

In July 1848, further clashes between the police and the Irish resulted from the refusal of Ramsay, one of the sub-contractors of the Stour Valley Railway Company, to pay the wages of between 50 and 100 Irish navvies in Bywater's Beershop in Stafford Street one Saturday evening. The police were called in to rescue the sub-contractor from the understandably irate workers, but their presence appears to have exacerbated the situation. The navvies turned on the police, and a pitched battle took place in the beershop. Order was only restored by the arrival of a force of 16 policemen under the command of Gilbert Hogg, who cleared the house and escorted Ramsay, who alleged that he had been threatened with murder, to his home. However, unrest continued in the Stafford Street district throughout the week, and on the following Saturday evening brickbats and other missiles were thrown at the police, and two Irishmen were apprehended and sentenced to two weeks imprisonment for assaults on the police.[48]

In January 1849, two policemen, Robinson and Wardle, attempted to arrest an Irishman in the Black Horse public house. The fellow eluded the officers, who chased him down Canal Street into the Caribee Island. The incident brought hundreds of Irish men and women out into the streets, and they attempted to protect their kinsman by hurling mud and stones, and no little abuse, at the policemen. Additional forces were despatched to the spot and, amidst ugly scenes, the police succeeded in apprehending their suspect, arresting several other Irishmen in the process. Order was eventually restored, and four Irishmen were convicted of assaulting the police and were each sentenced to two months hard labour, while two others were each fined £2.[49]

Anti–police disturbances were not uncommon in early Victorian England, and as R. D. Storch has shown, these sometimes contained an Irish element, as in the case of the Leeds anti–police riot of 1844.[50] Moreover popular disorders involving the Irish sometimes contained an anti–police element although on the surface they were attributed to other causes: F. Neal has recently suggested that the so–called 'Garibaldi Riots' in Birkenhead in 1862 were more in the nature of a clash between Irish immigrants and the police.[51] The disturbances in Wolverhampton would appear to fall into the category of anti–police disorders, although lacking the extreme violence which characterised similar disturbances elsewhere. Indeed, they fall into the category of 'B' class disturbances rather than fully–fledged riots.[52]

Nevertheless these ugly disorders may be explained largely in terms of the ideology, organisation and priorities of a developing police force in Wolverhampton during the period. In November 1842 the Staffordshire Magistracy decided to adopt the 1839 County Police Act for the whole of Staffordshire, including Wolverhampton, which henceforth became the headquarters of the Mining District, supporting a force of 30 policemen under the command of John Hatton, the Chief Constable.[53] In November 1848, following the acquisition of borough status by Wolverhampton, the town established a Borough Police Force under the command of Colonel Gilbert Hogg who remained in Wolverhampton until he was elevated to the post of Chief Constable of the Staffordshire Police Force in 1857 and was succeeded by Captain Henry Segrave.[54] During these formative years in the growth of local policing, both the county and borough forces sought to combat crime and disorder in Wolverhampton by closely monitoring working–class life in a variety of dimensions and by entering into the very heart of working–class communities. Continuity of leadership within the police force was a vital ingredient in this process, and Hatton, Hogg and Segrave shared a common ideology about policing which in part stemmed from their military backgrounds. During the 1840s and 1850s successive police forces in Wolverhampton were subject to strong discipline and were organised on paramilitary lines, policemen practising sword drill with cutlasses which were provided to constables at the discretion of the Chief Constable.[55] Moreover successive Chief Constables were provided with a mandate by the Wolverhampton Magistracy and the Town Council to suppress specific forms of petty crime which were often associated with working–class cultural, leisure and recreational activities and, in consequence, the priorities of the police included the regulation of public houses and beershops, the prosecution of drunken and disorderly behaviour in the streets, the inspection and regulation of lodging houses, and the enforcement of Sunday observance. These were by no means serious offences, but they did account for the majority of committals at the Petty Sessions during the period[56] and, in each instance, brought the police into contact with the Irish community, sometimes with violent results.

Thus the legendary association between the Irish and drink made them rather vulnerable to police observation. There were 35 public houses in the Stafford Street district alone, while many Irish immigrants brought alcohol with them from Ireland and sold it, without licence, in local lodging houses: these 'wabble–shops' were illegal but were difficult for the police to detect,[57] and their determination to find breaches of the licensing laws in the Irish quarter made for bad feeling between the police and the residents. This was particularly true following the Beer Act of 1848 which regulated the sale of beer and other liquors on the Sabbath: Hogg requested publicly that landlords should comply with the regulations but, in the Stafford Street district, public houses and beershops tended to stay open until late at night, particularly on Saturdays, thus breaching the new Act. Indeed, the most common cause of friction between the police and the Wolverhampton Irish lay in the consistent attempts by the police to evict persons drinking after time and behaving in a drunken or disorderly manner, although Gilbert Hogg in part attributed this to the reluctance of the Irish to leave public houses for the want of comfort in their own homes, adding 'indeed, many of them have told me, after having been turned out of the public house, and ordered to go home, that the place in which they lived was in such a miserable state that they would rather remain out in the open air if the weather was not severe'.[58] Certainly the majority of committals from the Irish during the period were for drunkenness and disorderly behaviour,[59] mirroring trends in the Irish districts of Liverpool,[60] Manchester[61] and Merthyr,[62] and police interference in the vigorous pub culture of the Irish fired resentment and resulted in assaults on the police and more general disturbances, including those of 1848–9.

Similarly, the tendency of the Wolverhampton Irish to populate lodging houses in the Stafford Street district, where accommodation was cheap, satisfied their love of family and kinship, and was suited to their often intinerant ways, also made them vulnerable to police observation, particularly following the Lodging Houses Act of 1851. Gilbert Hogg held that the crowded condition of these lodging houses 'tends greatly to disseminate vice and demoralization of every kind, and to impart to the young, especially, a total disregard for those decencies of life which prevail among the more favoured classes of society'.[63] Hence the police monitored the district closely, but their presence was resented and was often sufficient to incite violence: indeed, Hogg reported in 1848 that 'these overcrowded lodging-houses pour forth their inmates in almost incredible numbers, attacking a single policeman or two with great ferocity and savageness, but being equally expert in beating a retreat when faced by a sufficient force to repel their lawless proceedings'.[64]

These are but two examples of sources of animosity between the police and the Wolverhampton Irish, and a more detailed analysis may be found elsewhere.[65] Moreover, while it does appear that the priorities of law enforcement agencies in Wolverhampton brought the police into specific contact with the Irish community during the 1840s and 1850s, there is also some evidence to suggest that this was a deliberate policy. First, although there were other unsavoury working-class districts in Wolverhampton, there is no evidence that these areas were as closely monitored as the Stafford Street district. Indeed, the only recorded instances of the use of cutlasses by the Wolverhampton police pertain to troubles in the Irish quarter. Second, it was noted by Sir George Grey in 1853 that convictions for drunkenness and disorderly behaviour in Wolverhampton, which were particularly associated with the Irish, were proportionately higher in Wolverhampton than in neighbouring Birmingham, which possessed a larger and more efficient police force, and a correspondent to the *Wolverhampton Chronicle* suggested that Hogg's force was apprehending as many people as possible for minor offences in order to reduce the cost of policing through fees and fines and to project an image of efficiency.[66] The Irish quarter provided a suitable recruiting ground for such prosecutions. Finally, it is not without significance that when Gilbert Hogg acquired a house in 1854 to serve as an additional police station, it was situated in Stafford Street, thus enabling the police to maintain an unceasing vigil over the Irish community.[67]

Thus the anti-police disturbances in Wolverhampton in 1848 and 1849 must be seen in part as the product of a clash between the police drive to assert its authority in the town and the growing Irish presence which was an obstacle to that drive. As David Philips has suggested, the Black Country police at large found in the Irish a natural target for their attentions, and the Irish reciprocated with attacks on the police,[68] and this would appear to have been the case in Wolverhampton. However, other factors may have contributed to the disorders. In July 1848, John Hatton sought to explain the Stafford Street troubles through the influence of Chartist agitators 'who inculcate contempt of the laws and authorities';[69] however, although this perhaps reflects a fairly predictable explanation on the part of the authorities, there is no direct evidence to substantiate Hatton's allegations. Indeed, although there were altercations between Chartists and the police in the Black Country at the time of the Third Petition, Wolverhampton was remarkably free from such incidents.[70] A more potent factor underlying the anti-police sentiment of the Irish quarter was the actual composition of the Wolverhampton police force, which contained many Irishmen, including the Chief Constable himself, and it is possible that the presence of such men in a policing (i.e. authoritarian) role in the Stafford Street district served to heighten resentment and provided the local Irish with an opportunity to show their dislike of these 'turncoats', as well as to settle old scores and personal and religious animosities. It is also worth noting, moreover, that clashes between the police and the Irish appear to have been less pronounced by the 1860s than during the late 1840s, and it is possible that the disorders of 1848–9 were symptomatic of the relative instability of an emergent Irish community which was adjusting to the norms of urban life, and was particularly conscious of its separate identity and its vulnerability. In consequence, police interference in the culture of the Irish district produced an inevitable but defensive backlash.

III

On 13 July 1850, a serious disturbance involving local Irish navvies occurred in Horseley Fields, Wolverhampton. Riots and randies involving navvies were not an unfamiliar scene during the Railway Age, as Terry Coleman has shown,[71] but this particular disturbance arose from competition between the Shrewsbury and Birmingham Company and the London and North Western Company. The former company has hoped to establish a link between their line and the Birmingham Canal at Horseley Fields, but the L.N.W.R. attempted to prevent this by despatching 300 navvies employed by Hoof, Hill and Moore, the Stour Valley contractors, to the spot. These men, armed with spades and pick-axes, were ordered to prevent employees of the Shrewsbury and Birmingham Company from setting foot on the disputed territory and from transferring any goods from their line to the canal. The latter company duly responded by despatching 200 navvies, similarly armed, and distinguished by red armbands, down the line to meet the challenge of the L.N.W.R. The *Wolverhampton Chronicle* noted that 'no ill feeling was displayed on the part of either body of men, many of whom exchanged smiles and other signs of familiar recognition';[72] nevertheless, fighting broke out between the two groups, with Hill and Moore's men securing a temporary victory.

The authorities had been expecting trouble for several days and, at the request of the Mayor, Robinson, a detachment of the 48th. Foot, commanded by Captain Sykes, had been sent to Wolverhampton to assist the borough police in the event of disturbances.[73] When news of the disorders at Horseley Fields reached Gilbert Hogg, he headed for the scene with a body of fifty policemen and special constables, followed by the military, with bayonets fixed.

When these forces arrived at the railway station, the Mayor read the Riot Act, informing the workmen that 'It is not to be tolerated that hundreds of persons are to come here to assert their rights by brute force',[74] and this action brought a temporary halt to the disorders. Indeed, Hill and Moore's men made a strategic withdrawal up the line near Cannock Road bridge while their adversaries settled down to their dinner, accompanied with ale, in a nearby field. However no sooner had these navvies finished their lunch than they charged up the line and attacked Hill and Moore's men. Waggons were overturned, and ugly clashes took place. The police, cultlasses at the ready, and the troops, bayonets fixed, chased after them. The Mayor again read the Riot Act and, the navvies continuing to fight, the police and troops were ordered to charge.

In the clashes which ensued, several navvies received sabre wounds and a number of Irishmen were arrested. By three o'clock in the afternoon, order had been restored, but the line was so badly littered by debris, including waggons, timbers, and cinders, that train services were delayed until five o'clock in the evening. The Mayor entered into negotiations with the aggrieved parties, who agreed to withdraw their men, and Messrs. Hill and Moore were ordered to enter into recognizances of £500 each to keep the peace in Wolverhampton. The L.N.W.R. and the Shrewsbury and Birmingham Company subsequently resorted to legal means to settle their differences.[75]

The riot was at heart the reflection of the simmering rivalry among railway companies in the West Midlands. Indeed, on 17 July, the *Wolverhampton Chronicle* observed 'for some time past, a series of disputes have taken place between the London and North Western, the Shrewsbury and Birmingham, the Shrewsbury and Chester, and other rival companies, with reference to the working of their respective lines, and the railway fares on some of those lines have been unusually low'.[76] Although these disturbances were regarded in Wolverhampton as further evidence of the Irish love of fighting, the navvies were merely the tools of their employers, and in this sense both armies of navvies correspond with E. P. Thompson's 'hired bands' – mobs manipulated by external interests.[77] Nevertheless the use of Irish labourers by employers for such purposes is not in itself without significance at a time when the Irish were often used to undertake tasks which the native English could not, or would not do, particularly in providing blackleg labour as a strike–breaking measure during industrial disputes.[78]

IV

Religion was a vital ingredient in Anglo–Irish relations during the mid–Victorian period. The terms 'Irish' and 'Catholic' were virtually synonymous in English eyes and, although anti–Irish sentiment was more diffuse than anti–Catholicism,[79] it is evident that the resurgence of popular Protestantism in the wake of the Tractarian Controversy and the re–establishment of the Catholic hierarchy by Pius IX in 1850 provided an additional cutting edge to Anglo–Irish tensions.[80] Indeed, anti–Catholic sentiment contributed to the most serious clashes between English and Irish during the period, notably in Stockport, 1852;[81] in Oldham, 1861;[82] in London, 1862[83] and during the more widespread Murphy Riots of 1867–71.[84] Wolverhampton was not exempted from manifestations of anti–Catholicism during the same period, for two serious disturbances, both involving the Stafford Street Irish, occurred in 1858 and 1867 in consequence of the activities of anti–Catholic lecturers in the town.[85]

During the early 1850s, at the height of the controversy over the restoration of the Catholic hierarchy, Wolverhampton was visited by several anti–Catholic lecturers who warned of the dangers of 'Papal Aggression'.[86] These included the renowned anti–Catholic lecturer, Father Gavazzi, who addressed Protestant audiences in the town in October 1851 and January 1852, when the *Wolverhampton Chronicle* observed that 'Although, from his address being delivered entirely in Italian, he was not understood by the majority of those present, yet from the extraordinary power of his voice, and the clearness of his enunciation, his words (even those delivered in the lowest key) were distinctly audible and . . . (he) was loudly cheered at various portions, especially in those parts when he referred to Cardinal Wiseman and Father Newman'.[87] Nevertheless, these reflections of popular Protestantism were not accompanied by violence.

However, in June 1858, Andre Massena, an anti–Catholic lecturer who styled himself the 'Baron de Camin', obtained permission from the directors of the Corn Exchange to deliver a series of lectures in Wolverhampton on the evenings of Monday, Tuesday and Wednesday, the 28, 29 and 30 June. Massena had recently delivered a similar series of lectures in Walsall and Birmingham which had created considerable excitement and unrest among the Irish Catholic communities in those towns. However, the Wolverhampton authorities were slow to take the necessary precautions to preserve the peace and on 28 June several thousand people, consisting largely of Irish colliers and labourers, some of whom were armed with bludgeons, sticks and stones, surrounded the Exchange and prevented the Baron and his supporters from entering. Fights broke out between Protestants and Catholics and, amid tumultuous scenes, the directors of the Exchange cancelled the lecture. On the following evening, the Baron was escorted to the building by the police, with the intention of delivering a lecture on 'The Jesuits'. However, a number of Irish men and women had purchased some of the cheaper seats in the Exchange and attempted to make their entrance, several of them armed with sticks and other weapons which were confiscated by the police. The appearance of the Baron de Camin, however, was guaranteed to elicit a violent response from the Irish Catholics in the audience: dressed in the habit of a Dominican friar, the Baron stood before a mock altar, complete with candles and crucifix, and surmounted by a large doll which purported to be the representation of a saint. Cries of 'Judas' and 'Turn him out', mingled with hisses and groans, were heard from the Irish contingent, and the police were forced to use their staves to prevent some Irishmen from reaching the platform where the Baron stood. Stones were hurled at the lecturer who, significantly, wore a life–preserver, and who was yet to utter a word.

Meanwhile, a crowd of over 3,000 people, chiefly Irish, had surrounded the Exchange and were hurling volleys of stones at the windows, shattering the glass. The Mayor, magistrates and police also came under fire, some policemen having their helmets dislodged by the missiles, and the Mayor, Moses Ironmonger, decided that the crowd had adopted a menacing attitude and read the Riot Act. Segrave formed the police into a line and the crowds were gradually pushed back. After two arrests had been made, the show of force had the desired effect and the Irish slowly dispersed. Order was also restored inside the building, largely due to the arrival of the Reverend John Kelly, a Catholic priest at S.S. Mary and John's Church, Snowhill, who, in the words of the *Wolverhampton Chronicle*, 'seemed to produce a talismanic effect upon the Irish portion of the audience', exhorting those Catholics present to leave, which they immediately did.

On 30 June, in order to prevent a repetition of the disturbances, the Wolverhampton Magistrates decided to summon additional forces: the local Yeomanry and the Enrolled Pensioners were mobilised, special constables were sworn in, and 120 policemen from the Mining, Pottery and Rural Police Districts were despatched to Wolverhampton under the command of Gilbert Hogg. During the evening, these forces were stationed around the Exchange and, despite the presence of a large number of Irish outside the building, De Camin succeeded in delivering his final lecture before an exclusively Protestant audience who resolved that they would not be beaten by 'an Irish rabble'. The proceedings passed off without incident, and the Baron De Camin left the town to deliver further lectures in neighbouring Bilston.[88]

In the aftermath of these disorders, one Irishman, Patrick Flaherty, was indicted for riot and unlawful assembly. During his trial, the judge, Mr. Justice Hill, expressed the opinion that there had not been a riot in Wolverhampton because the Irish had not adopted an overtly menacing stance, and Flaherty was convicted of unlawful assembly only, and was bound over to keep the peace. This verdict drew an angry response from the *Wolverhampton Chronicle* which charged that 'a serious and formidable riot' had indeed taken place and that, 'but for the prompt measures taken by the Magistrates', more serious disorders would have ensued.[89] Indeed, it was widely held in Wolverhampton that Mr. Justice Hill's comments had undermined the measures which had been taken to preserve the peace during the disorders and which had met with the approval of Hatherton, the Lord Lieutenant of Staffordshire,[90] and the Home Office.[91] Moreover, some ultra–Protestants, claiming that an Irish mob had committed an 'outrage upon our liberties as citizens and Protestants', called for the formation of a Wolverhampton Protestant Alliance,[92] although no such alliance materialised, due largely to the lack of unified opposition to Popery among Anglicans and Dissenters in the town.[93]

More serious were the disorders which accompanied the visit of William Murphy, a member of the Protestant Evangelical Mission and Electoral Union, in February 1867.[94] Before his arrival in Wolverhampton, Murphy had delivered a series of anti–Catholic lectures in Newcastle–under–Lyme which had been attended by disorders involving the Irish Catholic community, and in the light of these disorders the Wolverhampton authorities arranged for a strong police presence at the Agricultural Hall in Snow Hill on the evening of 18 February, when Murphy's first lecture was due to commence. These arrangements notwithstanding, however, thousands of Irish descended on the building during the evening, while others succeeded in purchasing some of the unreserved seats inside the hall. Although the police succeeded in controlling the crowds gathered outside the building, fights broke out inside the hall when Murphy arrived: Irishmen broke up chairs and attempted to reach the platform where the speaker stood, and several policemen were injured in the clashes which ensued. The arrival of a further body of police brought the fighting to a close, but H. J. Brockman, the president of the Protestant Union, decided to cancel the lecture. On the 19 February, the Magistrates sought to strengthen the forces of order by swearing in special constables but further violence occurred during the evening when several thousand Irish gathered outside the Agricultural Hall and proceeded to hurl volleys of stones at the windows. A number of policemen were injured by stones and flying glass, and order was only restored by the arrival of the Volunteers, who pushed the crowds back beyond throwing distance. On 20 February, the Mayor of Wolverhampton, Sir John Morris, resolved to obtain additional civil and military assistance: 200 special constables were sworn in, a force of County Police was despatched from Stafford, and a troop of the 9 Hussars were conveyed by train from Birmingham. These developments were a response to rumours circulating in Wolverhampton that there had been a meeting of Roman Catholics in the Irish district at which it had been decided to send emissaries to their fellow countrymen in other parts of the Black Country for the purpose of driving Murphy from the town, the grand attack being scheduled for Friday 22.Moreover, Morris, Segrave, and some members of the Protestant Union had been the recipients of threatening letters, signed 'Fenian', which threatened their lives if Murphy's lectures were not banned. During the evening, the police and military succeeded in monitoring the four thousand Irish who gathered outside the Agricultural Hall, and Murphy was able to deliver his lecture to an exclusively Protestant audience. But disorders broke out in the Stafford Street district where the Irish, taking advantage of the absence of the police from the area, launched attacks on the homes of known Protestants, smashing windows and insulting passers–by. Captain Segrave despatched a body of police to the scene and order was eventually restored. On the Thursday evening the proceedings were again relatively calm, although four thousand Irish gathered outside the Agricultural Hall to heckle Murphy as he arrived. However, the authorities feared that there would be a concerted effort by the Irish to disrupt the proceedings on the Friday evening and, with Home Office sanction, the Magistrates obtained additional military assistance, a detachment of Hussars being conveyed to the town by special train from Coventry. Additional special constables were sworn in and a further body of County Police was despatched to Wolverhampton by Gilbert Hogg. Sir John Morris also arranged a meeting with the Reverend Kelly who agreed to visit the Stafford Street district in an attempt to discourage the local Irish from taking part in any tumultuous assemblies. In the event, however, disorders did not ensue. Despite the presence of over ten thousand people, largely Irish, and including some strangers to the town, outside the Agricultural Hall the massive presence of police, military, and special constables was adequate to the needs of the situation and, in the words of the *Manchester Guardian*, had the effect of 'overrawing the turbulent',[95] although the *Wolverhampton Chronicle* subsequently stated that 'not the slightest doubt is entertained that, but for the prompt action of the authorities . . . much damage would have been done both to life and property.'[96]

William Murphy left Wolverhampton for the Potteries, where he had arranged to deliver lectures in Longton and Hanley.[97] He did, however, return briefly to the town in May 1867 to give evidence on behalf of Mr. Scott, a local bookseller, who had been prosecuted by the Wolverhampton Watch Committee for selling copies of the tract *The Confessional Unmasked*, the text of one of Murphy's lectures. News of Murphy's arrival in Wolverhampton quickly reached the Irish quarter, and on leaving the police court Murphy was attacked by a crowd of Irishmen who attempted to drag him away to Stafford Street where, the *Wolverhampton Chronicle* later claimed, the Irish community would have taken a more complete revenge. Murphy was dragged to the ground, beaten, and subjected to gross insult, and only with difficulty did the police succeed in rescuing him.[98] This incident marked the last visit of William Murphy to Wolverhampton, although the tumult which had surrounded his presence in the district proved to be the prelude to the extensive disorders which attended his lectures in Birmingham in June, when violent clashes between local Protestants and Irish Catholics necessitated a massive show of strength by the police and the military before order was restored.[99]

Although popular opinion in Wolverhampton held that the disturbances of 1858 and 1867 were symptomatic of the Irish predilection for disorder, the evidence suggests that it had been the extreme anti–Catholic sentiments of the Baron de Camin and William Murphy which had fomented disorder by provoking an Irish Catholic backlash. In this light, the frequent references to 'Irish mobs' and 'Irish rabble' in the columns of the *Wolverhampton Chronicle* are inadequate as explanations for the disorders, although they do indicate something about local attitudes toward the Irish community.

Nevertheless the circumstances surrounding both disturbances illustrate the relative strengths of religious feeling among certain sections of local society. Indeed in the aftermath of the Murphy riots, a prolonged debate was conducted by correspondents to the

Wolverhampton Chronicle whose views reflected local Protestant and Catholic opinion on fundamental issues arising from Murphy's visit. Protestants alleged that William Murphy had been fully entitled to deliver his lectures, and that a determined effort had been made by the local Irish to interfere with civil and religious liberty. Moreover, they held that Murphy's lectures could hardly be regarded as inflammatory since their contents consisted of extracts from Roman Catholic publications with which Catholics were only too familiar, and it was alleged that the disorders indicated that Popery was on the march and constituted an ever–present danger to liberty. In contrast, Father George Duckett, a Roman Catholic priest, claimed that Murphy's lectures had been designed to incite the Irish Catholic population, and ought to have been banned, while even the *Wolverhampton Chronicle* was moved to observe that the situation had been exacerbated by the fact that 'the lecturer is one of their countrymen and is regarded by them in the light of a traitor to the faith in which he was brought up'. Father Duckett further suggested that Murphy and the Protestant Association had constituted a threat to liberty, adding that if the loyalty of Irish Catholics was to be questioned then one had only to recall the great loyalty and enthusiasm evident in the Stafford Street district during Queen Victoria's recent visit to Wolverhampton when 'the body of the people that has been so maligned showed their loyalty, their love, and their affection for her that so benignly rules over us'.[100] Protestations of loyalty to the Crown on the part of the Catholic Church were not unusual during the period: nevertheless the character of this debate and, indeed, the growing number of Protestants who attended the lectures provided by both the Baron de Camin and William Murphy, serve to illustrate the appeal of anti–Catholic propaganda among the most fervent elements within the local Protestant community at a time when Irish immigration served to heighten fears of Roman Catholicism gaining ground. Likewise the large numbers of Irish Catholics who sought to register their protests in 1858 and 1867, not to mention the vociferous Catholic response to Protestant allegations in 1867, are indicative of the communal solidarity of an ethnic minority whose most cherished beliefs had been openly and violently attacked. Indeed, given the fact that the Irish community in Wolverhampton was becoming more organised and self–assertive (a process in which the Catholic Church played a vital part) – in other words, a less–alienated minority – it is possible that part of the explanation for the Irish reaction to De Camin and Murphy lay in the increasing establishment of the Irish community and its more brittle tolerance of insult and affront.

Indeed, in view of the size of the crowds which participated in the De Camin and Murphy disorders, it is surprising that greater violence did not ensue. Violence was minimal. There was no sectarian violence, despite the inflammatory rhetoric of the lecturers. The Irish backlash was largely limited to a mass physical presence rather than wholesale violence, to the stoning of specific targets, and to a natural desire to punish the lecturers. Relatively little damage to property was incurred. That this was so was due as much to crowd restraint on the part of the Irish as to the effectiveness of the measures taken by the forces of order, and it is clear that much of the credit for helping to defuse potentially volatile situations belonged to local Catholic priests who exercised a moderating yet powerful influence over their Irish flock. In the context of the Murphy riots, the experience of Wolverhampton offered a sharp contrast with that of neighbouring Birmingham, where popular violence was exacerbated by the acute anti–Irish sentiment of the police,[101] while the course of the disorders suggests that religious tensions between the English and the Irish were less marked in Wolverhampton than in Birmingham. Indeed, in the aftermath of the Murphy riots, demands by Protestant extremists for the establishment of a Protestant Union in Wolverhampton came to nothing. Nevertheless, both the Baron De Camin riots and the Murphy riots (or, rather, anti–Murphy riots) in Wolverhampton are indicative of the ease with which violence and hostility between sections of the working–class could be stirred up by anti–Catholic propaganda in a town with a substantial immigrant Irish Catholic population.

The attitudes evinced by the Wolverhampton Magistrates during the riots of 1858 and 1867 reflected a dilemma which frequently faced borough justices when anti–Catholic lectures provoked disturbances in mid–Victorian society, namely the need to protect the liberties of the individual by upholding the right to freedom of speech while at the same time seeking to maintain law and order and to protect property and the person when these were threatened by mob action. These were sensitive issues, and difficult questions to resolve, as the multiplicity of disorders associated with Murphy's subsequent lectures illustrated. Nevertheless the Wolverhampton Magistrates were consistent in their approach in both 1858 and 1867, seeking to uphold rights and duties which were, in the context of the immediate circumstances, contradictory. Thus the *Wolverhampton Chronicle* asserted in July 1858 that 'the right of free discussion was unmistakably asserted; and misguided and ignorant men were taught that the law of England will not tolerate the interruption by brute force of a public lecture, even upon the ground that the views about to be expressed by the lecturer are distasteful to the religious feelings of a section of the community'.[102] A similar epitaph, with its implicit anti–Irish prejudice, was prescribed by the same paper in the aftermath of the Murphy riots.[103]

The question of Fenian involvement in the riots of 1867 requires closer examination. William Murphy frequently alleged that Irish opposition to the Protestant Union had been co–ordinated by 'Fenians',[104] a charge which is not without significance in view of the extensive Fenian activity on the English mainland in 1867, when incidents such as the Fenian attempt to seize Chester Castle, the case of the 'Manchester Martyrs', and the escapades at Clerkenwell did much to colour Anglo–Irish relations on a local level.[105] Neville Kirk has suggested that Fenianism, the economic slump, and anti–Catholic propaganda jointly contributed to the revival of anti–Irish sentiment in Lancashire and Cheshire in 1867–68, while Fenian outrages served also to resurrect English fears of the subversive leanings of the Irish.[106] Although the leaders of Wolverhampton's Catholic community vehemently denied such allegations at the annual Roman Catholic Reunion at SS. Peter and Paul's Church in March 1867, finding some support for their views from the Town Council,[107] it is possible that Protestant allegations were not wholly without foundation, although much research has yet to be conducted on Fenianism in the Black Country. Fenianism had a wide base in England, with support on all levels of Irish emigrant society, although it found little support within the Catholic Church.[108] Moreover, when the Fenian raid on Chester Castle was discovered on 10 February 1867, Wolverhampton was one of several large towns which were informed of Fenian activities,[109] which might well suggest that the town was suspected of harbouring Fenians or their sympathisers. There is also some evidence to suggest that the Wolverhampton Irish did support the Home Rule movement.[110] Nevertheless, in the context of the Murphy riots in Wolverhampton, it would appear that if Fenians or their supporters were involved in the disturbances their participation was influenced by religious rather than political considerations. Yet Sir John Morris and Henry Segrave took the threatening letters signed by 'Fenian' seriously enough to summon additional forces to Wolverhampton during Murphy's visit,[111] while Spencer Walpole, the Home Secretary, was questioned on the subject in the House of Commons on 26 February.[112]

V

In February 1874, the *Annual Register* reported that riots had taken place in several boroughs in the manufacturing districts during polling at the General Election.[113] This was the first election to be held in the aftermath of the Ballot Act of 1872, and Wolverhampton, which had once held an unenviable reputation for electoral violence,[114] was not immune from these disorders. Indeed Donald Richter has suggested that 'a Wolverhampton mob routed the local police force and threatened to kill the magistrate who was trying to read the Riot Act'.[115] Although this assertion is not strictly true, there were serious disorders within the Parliamentary Borough of Wolverhampton on 5 February, and here too was an Irish connection.

Wolverhampton was traditionally a Liberal stronghold, and the sitting members , C. P. Villiers and W. Weguelin, were expected to be returned with little difficulty. Indeed the *Wolverhampton Chronicle* reported with some optimism on 4 February that 'It is an agreeable thought that the present election in Wolverhampton is not one in which there is much personal feeling of an objectionable nature called into prominence respecting the claimants for the seats . . . It is therefore a question of principle which is being fought out'.[116]

Nevertheless there was much excitement in the town and on February 3 there had been a hint of things to come during an open air meeting in Queen Square which attracted a large number of working people, including a strong Irish contingent. The meeting was addressed by Mr. Rednall, the President of the Republican Club in Birmingham, Mr. Flanagan, the Secretary of the Miners Association, and Mr. Maddox, the Secretary of the Brass Workers Union. Rednall encouraged the Irish present to vote Liberal, claiming that 'If they would only consider the various measures that had been passed in the House of Commons they would have no difficulty in deciding that it was to the Liberal party that their thanks were due'.[117] Rednall added that before the time of the last government the Irish people had a Church which did not represent the interests of the Irish people.[118] This charge caused mayhem amongst the Irish present, and they began fighting among themselves. Stones were thrown at buildings in the square and the windows of the Liberal Committee Rooms were smashed. The violence increased, and order was only restored by the arrival of a force of police commanded by Henry Segrave.

On Thursday 5 February, polling began quietly enough, but there was some excitement in St. Mary's Ward, which comprised the Stafford Street district, and where it was reported that 'a large number of idlers, chiefly Irish, of both sexes, and a large proportion of them mere youths and girls, amused themselves by shouting and screaming at the different classes of voters as they were brought up to the poll'.[119] Early in the afternoon, news was received of serious disorders at Wednesfield, within the Parliamentary Borough, where there were attacks by English roughs on Conservative supporters. The Mayor of Wolverhampton, W.H. Jones, and the Stipendiary Magistrate, I. Spooner, entered a cab for the purpose of driving to Wednesfield and reading the Riot Act there, but they were held up in Stafford Street where they were pelted with stones by the crowds gathered in the street, and they returned to the Town Hall. Eventually, Mr. Brevitt, Clerk to the County Magistrates for the Wolverhampton district, repaired to Wednesfield, where he twice attempted to read the Riot Act, being greeted on both occasions by a hail of stones from the mob. Disorders had also broken out at Willenhall, also within the Parliamentary Borough, where the Conservatives were again the targets of the crowds, and where fights also took place between the local roughs and a gang of former prize–fighters from Wolverhampton.[120]

Meanwhile crowds of youths began to appear on the streets of Wolverhampton, many of them armed with sticks, and they embarked on an orgy of indiscriminate violence, smashing shop windows, insulting shopkeepers, and abusing passers by. The Wolverhampton police were fully employed at the polling stations in the wards, leaving the town centre at the mercy of the youths. Within a short time, the crowds were joined by an Irish contingent from Stafford Street, some three hundred strong, many of whom wore bits of green ribbon in their hats and chanted 'Home Rule for ever'. It was also noted that many of these Irish youths also wore the blue colours of the Liberals.[121] Gathering timbers and palings from the back of the Agricultural Hall, this division joined in the fun.

Segrave had only 16 policemen in reserve and telegraphed to Birmingham for additional support, 20 members of the Birmingham

Borough Police reaching the town by late afternoon. These forces succeeded in driving the various groups of youths from the town centre, arresting a number in the process, and by 6.30pm when the polls closed, the town centre was quiet, although mayhem still reigned at Wednesfield and Willenhall.

The authorities were quick to point out that Wolverhampton itself had escaped the kind of violence which had occurred elsewhere in the borough, although the costs of damage incurred to property totalled £145.[122] The *Wolverhampton Chronicle* concluded that the disorders were the work of the ignorant, uneducated roughs of the town who had taken advantage of the election to have some fun, adding that the troubles were the consequence of mischief rather than political feeling.[123] Nevertheless, a public enquiry was subsequently held at which considerable criticism was levelled at the police for failing to prevent disorder in the town, although the meeting eventually accepted Segrave's claim that he had done all that was possible under the circumstances and had succeeded in dispersing the crowds once additional forces had arrived in the town.[124] The Watch Committee concluded that 'the disturbances cannot in any sense be called political riots in as much as the parties causing the damage . . . were not men on whom political excitement would have had any effect, but resulted in the banding together of a lot of rough boys, and young men, from the ages of fifteen to twenty-one, with a proportionate number of factory girls'.[125] Henry Segrave added that 'considering the nature of the contest (religious feeling having been introduced), the class of population surrounding the town, and the serious riots that have occurred elsewhere, it is a matter of congratulation that no serious disturbance took place within the town of Wolverhampton'.[126]

There is little evidence to suggest that the disturbances in the Parliamentary Borough of Wolverhampton represented anything other than electoral violence by the mob. In the context of the Irish contribution to these disorders, perhaps the most striking feature to emerge is the relatively small role played by the Irish, for the fact that a few hundred Irish youths joined in more generalised disturbances hardly endorses the more widely accepted view that the Irish were always prepared to take advantage of such opportunities for violence. Indeed, although some Irish youths were among those persons convicted of riot in the aftermath of the troubles, including some known 'roughs' such as Thomas 'Jemmy the Brick' Miller,[127] the majority of persons apprehended were English.[128] In relative terms, the Irish appear to have shown a considerable degree of restraint during the disturbances. Nevertheless, the fact that Irish participants wore green favours and liberal colours perhaps bears testimony to the growing political consciousness of the local Irish community: on a national level, as Ó Tuathaigh has observed, Irish support for the new Home Rule movement in Ireland and identification with the Liberal Party in domestic politics were outstanding features of the political allegiances of the Irish in late Victorian Britain,[129] and the Irish contribution to the Wolverhampton disturbances perhaps provides a minute reflection of such allegiances locally.

In the aftermath of the riots, some local Councillors alleged that police incompetence had been partly responsible for the disorders, and Councillor Weir stated that 'The police force (of 54 men) which the Chief Constable had at his command on the election day, was, in his opinion, quite sufficient to have quelled the disturbances, if they had shown themselves; the reserve force at the Town Hall should have been small, and the show of police larger, in those parts of the town where the disturbances took place'.[130] However, the Watch Committee exonerated the force of blame, concluding that Segrave had deployed his men correctly, under the circumstances.[131] Nevertheless, the disorders exposed, once more, the problems faced by the Wolverhampton police in attempting to quell large-scale public disorders.

VI

The relationship between popular disturbances and the Irish presence provides some insights into the growth and development of the Irish community in mid-Victorian Wolverhampton.

First, the evidence suggests that the participation of the Wolverhampton Irish in serious disorders was largely the product of external pressures exerted upon the Irish community rather than as a result of pressures from within. In particular, police harassment in 1848–9, and the activities of anti-Catholic lecturers in 1858 and 1867, produced an Irish backlash, essentially defensive in character.

Second, although these disorders provide some reflections of contemporary attitudes towards the Irish community locally, it is clear that there was a relatively low level of ethnic tension in Wolverhampton during the period, for there is little evidence of sectarian violence.[132] Why this was so is difficult to ascertain. Indeed, Sheridan Gilley has noted that it has often been difficult to assess the scale of popular prejudice against the immigrant Irish in that whilst anti-Irish riots, and clashes between the English and Irish, were popular in a few places, including Birkenhead, Stockport and Liverpool, they appear to have been rare in most towns.[133] It may well be that minor clashes between the English and the Irish did occur in Wolverhampton's public houses and beershops but were not widely reported by the *Wolverhampton Chronicle*, which, by concentrating largely on purely 'Irish rows', highlighted the relative orderliness of the non-Irish population. It is also possible that the distinct locational patterns of working-class habitations in Wolverhampton contributed to a low level of ethnic tension, with the Irish largely concentrated in the Stafford Street district to the north of the town centre and the English working-class inhabiting the Salop Street district to the south and the Walsall Street area to the east. Moreover, the very nature of Irish employment in Wolverhampton – concentrated as it was in collieries, ironworks, and railway construction – may well have served to reduce rather than increase ethnic tensions. It is also possible, as Mark Shaw has suggested, that the Irish were more fully integrated into local society – more like everyone else – by 1870, thereby diminishing those factors which had once set them apart from the population as a whole.[134] Sheridan Gilley has suggested that outwardly easy relations between the Irish and the non-Irish in some towns is to be explained by the retreat of many Irish from the public gaze into their own little ghettoes, 'islands of a distinctive culture set in an English sea – out of sight and out of mind, save for politics and religion'.[135] While this may well explain Anglo-Irish relations in Wolverhampton during the 1840s and 1850s, when a number of social tendencies acted on and reinforced one another within the Caribee Island district, it is, however, a less-convincing explanation for developments during the 1860s and 1870s. What is clear, perhaps, is that popular attitudes towards the Irish in mid-Victorian Wolverhampton offer a sharp contrast with those evident in the industrial towns of Lancashire and Cheshire where, according to Kirk,[136] the same period witnessed rising ethnic tensions resulting from a variety of social, economic, religious and political factors.

Third, there is much evidence to suggest that the Wolverhampton Irish were becoming more organised and self-assertive during the period. In terms of their participation in popular disorders alone, a sharp yet significant contrast emerges between their response to increasing police surveillance in 1848–9, when it may well be argued that the Irish were an alienated ethnic minority living in an unstable, volatile, and distinct community, with their more organised – and restrained – reaction to the presence of William Murphy in 1867. The Catholic Church played a vital role in the development of the Irish community locally, and by 1870, Irish Catholic loyalty to the Catholic faith was matched in political terms by a growing identification with the Irish Home Rule movement and the rising Liberal Party. Indeed, as E. D. Steele has observed, the leadership of the Irish in late-Victorian Britain based itself firmly on these three institutions,[137] and there were signs of similar allegiances amongst the Wolverhampton Irish by the 1870s.

Although there is much room for further research on the subject of the Irish presence in the Black Country townships during the Victorian period, it would appear that, by the 1870s at least, the Wolverhampton Irish were less alienated, more integrated, and increasingly tolerated in local society than they had been earlier in the nineteenth century. As such, the growth and development of the Irish community in the town parallels the experience of the immigrant Irish in other Victorian cities.[138] Moreover, the experience of the Wolverhampton Irish during the mid-Victorian period is not without relevance to the position of ethnic minorities in contemporary British society.

Finally, Irish disturbances in mid-Victorian Wolverhampton provide some interesting insights into contemporary methods of policing and, in particular, into the ability – or inability – of provincial police forces to contain large-scale popular disturbances. First, it is clear that the Wolverhampton Irish bore the brunt of the drive by the local police to assert their authority and to attain public acceptability, particularly during the 1840s and 1850s. This was by no means unusual: David Jones has recently observed that in Merthyr 'the authorities were ready to place much of the burden for all the violence in Merthyr on Irish men and women',[139] while in Manchester, such was the police fear of serving warrants and making arrests in the Irish districts that they patrolled these areas in large numbers.[140] The evidence from Wolverhampton suggests that the intensive monitoring of the Stafford Street district by the police, and the para-military methods which they initially employed, were in the short-term counter-productive, in that they caused an Irish backlash. Nevertheless, by the 1860s, Wolverhampton was a relatively orderly town, although the growing ability and experience of the police force was only one of many factors which contributed to this general improvement.[141]

Second, whilst it does seem that the Wolverhampton police were becoming increasingly successful in dealing with the welter of petty crimes, including minor brawls and disturbances, it is equally evident from an analysis of the major disturbances involving the local Irish community that they found greater difficulty in controlling large-scale disorders. Indeed, in 1850, 1858, 1867 and 1874 the authorities found it necessary to summon additional forces, both military and civilian, in order to restore public order, albeit during a period when the Home Office was becoming increasingly reluctant to sanction the use of troops by provincial authorities when riot and disorder threatened.[142] David Philips has suggested that Black Country police forces were becoming increasingly adept in riot control during the period,[143] but the evidence from Wolverhampton sheds doubt on this thesis. Crucial to the inability of the Wolverhampton police to contain large-scale disorders was the actual size of the force, which, although increased from 30 to 62 men between 1850 and 1860, barely kept pace with the increase in population between 1860 and 1870:[144] indeed in 1874, Segrave had only 54 policemen at his disposal to cover a Municipal Borough with a population of over 68,000 and a Parliamentary Borough populated by over 130,000. Thus, the experience of Wolverhampton during the mid-Victorian period illustrates the degree to which Victorian authority relied upon the ultimate good sense of the civilian body, including the Irish, when disorder threatened, as well as the continuing dependence of local law-enforcement agencies upon military assistance when breakdowns of public order occurred.[145]

Notes

This study was first published in *Immigrants & Minorities*, vol.3, no.1 (March 1984), pp.5–29, and is reprinted by courtesy of Frank Cass and Company Ltd. It derives in part from an unpublished paper presented at the Seminar in Social History, University of Birmingham, in March 1983.

1. For the classic study of this process, see A. Redford, *Labour Migration in England, 1800—1850* (London, 1926), pp.132–164; See also J.A. Jackson, *The Irish in Britain* (London and Cleveland, 1963); James Walvin, *Passage to Britain: Immigration in British History and Politics* (London, 1984), pp.24–9; 48–60.

2. See esp. M.A.G. Ó Tuathaigh, 'The Irish in Nineteenth–Century Britain: Problems of Integration', *Transactions of the Royal Historical Society*, vol.31 (1981), pp.149–174. For an interesting historiographical essay, see David Feldman, 'There was an Englishman, an Irishman, and a Jew', *Historical Journal*, vol.26, no.1, (1983), pp.185–99.

3. N. Kirk, 'Ethnicity, Class and Popular Toryism, 1850–1870', in K. Lunn (ed.), *Hosts, Immigrants and Minorities: Historical Responses to Newcomers in British Society, 1870–1914* (Folkestone, 1980), pp.64–106.

4. For an illuminating examination of English attitudes towards the Irish, see Sheridan Gilley, 'English Attitudes to the Irish in England, 1789–1900', in C. Holmes (ed.), *Immigrants and Minorities in British Society* (London, 1978), pp.81–110.

5. See, for example, F. Engels, *The Condition of the Working Class in England* (1845, trans. and ed. W.O. Henderson and W.H. Chaloner Oxford, 1958), pp.122–5.

6. J. Stevenson, *Popular Disturbances in England, 1700–1870* (London, 1979),. pp.276–282.

7. See, for example, F. Neal, 'The Birkenhead Garibaldi Riots of 1862', *Transactions of the Historical Society of Lancashire and Cheshire*, vol.131 (1982), pp.87–111.

8. Stevenson, p.300.

9. See esp., D. Philips, 'Riots and Public Order in the Black Country, 1835–1860', in J. Stevenson and R. Quinault (eds.), *Popular Protest and Public Order* (London, 1974), pp.141–180.

10. For further details, see R.E. Swift, 'Crime and Ethnicity: The Irish in Early Victorian Wolverhampton', *West Midlands Studies*, vol.13 (1980), pp.1–5; R.E. Swift, *Crime, Law and Order in Two English Towns during the early Nineteenth Century: the experience of Exeter and Wolverhampton, 1815–56* (unpublished Ph.D. Thesis, University of Birmingham, 1981), pp.420–6.

11. *Select Committee on Public Houses, P.P.* (1852–3), vol.xxvii, p.403, St. 6943.

12. Census returns, 1851 &1871. These figures include English–born members of Irish families.

13. *S.C. on Public Houses, P.P.* (1852–3), p.403, St. 6930.

14. Ó Tuathaigh, *T.R.H.S.*, vol.31 (1981), p.154.

15. *Wolverhampton Chronicle*, 7 February 1849.

16. *Board of Health, Report on the Sanitary Condition of Wolverhampton, P.P.* (1849), pp.1–29.

17. *Sanitary Inquiry, England and Wales, Report on the Sanitary Condition of the Town of Wolverhampton, P.P.* (1840), pp.218–224.

18. See, for example, *Wolverhampton Chronicle*, 18 April 1849; 25 April 1849.

19. For example, in May 1849, Patrick Maley, an Irishman, was brought before the Bench charged with vagrancy. Maley stated that he intended to return to Ireland, whereupon the Magistrates provided him with 2s. 6d. from the Poor Box on condition that he left for Liverpool the following day, and the case was dismissed: *Wolverhampton Chronicle*, 2 May 1849.
20. *Reports to the Local Government Board, Report on the Sanitary Condition of the Municipal Borough of Wolverhampton, P.P.* (1874), pp.13–27.
21. M. Shaw, 'Individual Behaviour and Social Change: the Irish in Victorian Wolverhampton', *W.M.S.*, vol.14 (1981), pp.1–9.
22. *Religious Worship, England and Wales, P.P.*, (1852–3), Summary Tables, vol.cclxxvi, Table F.
23. James Quirke, *The Development of the Roman Catholic Community in Wolverhampton, 1828–67* (unpublished M.A. Dissertation, Wolverhampton Polytechnic, 1983), p.7.
24. *Ibid.*, pp.38–48.
25. See esp. Sheridan Gilley, 'The Catholic Faith of the Irish Slums: London, 1840–70', in H.J. Dyos and M. Wolff (eds.), *The Victorian City: Images and Realities*, vol.ii (London, 1973), pp.837–853; Gerard Connolly, 'The Transubstantiation of Myth: towards a New Popular History of Nineteenth–Century Catholicism in England', *Journal of Ecclesiastical History*, vol.35 (Jan. 1984), pp.78–104.
26. F. Mason, *The Book of Wolverhampton* (Buckingham, 1979), p.25.
27. *Religious Worship, P.P.* (1852–3), Summary Tables, vol.cclxxii.
28. *Ibid.*
29. *Wolverhampton Chronicle*, 15 November 1865.
30. Quirke, Dissertation, p.14. For broader discussions of the problem of 'leakage', see Sheridan Gilley, 'The Roman Catholic Church and the Nineteenth–Century Irish Diaspora', *Journal of Ecclesiastical History*, vol.35, no.2 (April 1984), pp.188–207; John Sharp, 'Juvenile Holiness: Catholic Revivalism among Children in Victorian Britain', *Journal of Ecclesiastical History*, vol.35, no.2 (April 1984), pp.220–38.
31. *Wolverhampton Chronicle*, 6 June 1849.
32. *Education, England and Wales, P.P.* (1852–3), Summary Tables, vol.clxvii, Table P.
33. *Minutes of the Committee of Council on Education* (1853–4), p.1171.
34. *Ibid.*, pp.1198–9.
35. *Report of the Committee of Council on Education, England and Wales* (1878–9), Appendix IV, p.996.
36. There is some evidence to suggest that many Irish people spoke Gaelic. In 1856, a correspondent of the Irish *Nation* reported that many Irish labourers in the Black Country still communicated in their native tongue, both at home and at work: D. Gwynn, 'The Irish Immigration', in G. Beck (ed.), *The English Catholics, 1850–1950* (1950), p.267; in 1849 the *Chronicle* reported that James Conway, an Irishman, who had been brought before the Wolverhampton Bench charged with stealing bread from a shop in North Street, spoke only Gaelic in

court. However, the Magistrates were of the opinion that Conway was seeking to deceive them and duly commited him for trial: *Wolverhampton Chronicle*, 18 April 1849.
37. Wolverhampton Central Library. Wolverhampton Watch Committee Minutes, 1854–49. Annual Reports of the Chief Constable.
38. Holmes, p.99.
39. *Board of Health, Rawlinson Report, P.P.* (1849), p.28.
40. *S.C. on Public Houses, P.P.* (1852–3), p.403, St. 6935.
41. *Wolverhampton Chronicle*, 6 June 1849.
42. *Ibid.*, 5 July 1848.
43. *Ibid.*, 17 January 1849.
44. Swift, Thesis, pp.420–455.
45. *Wolverhampton Chronicle*, 17 May 1847.
46. *Ibid.*, 22 March 1848.
47. *Ibid.*, 5 June 1848.
48. *Ibid.*, 5 July 1848; 12 July 1848.
49. *Ibid.*, 17 January 1849.
50. R.D. Storch, 'The plague of the blue locusts: police reform and popular resistance in Northern England, 1840–57', *International Review of Social History*, vol.20 (1975), pp.61–90.
51. Neal, *T.H.S.L.C.*, vol.131 (1982), pp.87–111.
52. Stevenson & Quinault, pp.141–80.
53. Swift, Thesis, pp.389–404.
54. *Ibid.*, p.418.
55. *Ibid.*, pp.389–420.
56. *Ibid.*, pp.288–321.
57. *S.C. on Public Houses, P.P.* (1852–3), p.397, St. 3826.
58. *Board of Health, Rawlinson Report, P.P.* (1849), p.29.
59. Swift, Thesis, pp.312–321.
60. W.R. Cockroft, 'The Liverpool Police Force, 1836–1902', in S. Peter Bell (ed.), *Victorian Lancashire* (Newton Abbot, 1974), pp.150–6.
61. D. Jones, *Crime, Protest, Community and Police in Nineteenth–Century Britain* (London, 1982), pp.117–143.
62. *Ibid.*, pp.85–116.
63. *Board of Health, Rawlinson Report, P.P.* (1849), p.29.
64. *Ibid.*, p.28.
65. Swift, *W.M.S.*, vol.13 (1980), pp.1–5.
66. *S.C. on Public Houses, P.P.* (1852–3), p.387, St. 6646–6651; *Wolverhampton Chronicle*, 18 Dec. 1850.
67. Watch Committee Minutes, 9 Dec. 1854.
68. D. Philips, *Crime and Authority in Victorian England* (London, 1977), p.274.
69. *Wolverhampton Chronicle*, 28 July 1848.
70. The degree to which the Irish were involved in Chartist agitation is still a matter of debate amongst historians; for example, J.H. Treble, 'O'Connor, O'Connell and the Attitudes of Irish Immigrants towards Chartism in the North of England, 1838–48', in J. Butt & I.F. Clarke (eds.), *The Victorians and Social Protest* (Newton Abbot, 1973), has suggested that the pressures acting upon Irish immigrants caused them to hold apart from Charism; for the counter–

argument, see esp. Dorothy Thompson, 'Ireland and the Irish in English Radicalism before 1850', in J. Epstein and D. Thompson (eds.), *The Chartist Experience* (London, 1982), pp.120–151; for a useful overview, see J. Belchem, 'English Working–Class Radicalism and the Irish, 1815–1850', *North West Labour History Society Bulletin*, vol.8 (1982–3), pp.5–18.

71. T. Coleman, *The Railway Navvies* (London, 1965), pp.93–114.

72. *Wolverhampton Chronicle*, 17 July 1850.

73. *Ibid.*

74. *Ibid.*

75. *Ibid.*, 24 July 1850; See also R. Christiansen, *A Regional History of the Railways of Great Britain: The West Midlands* (London, 1973), pp.87–9.

76. *Wolverhampton Chronicle*, 17 July 1850.

77. E.P. Thompson, *The Making of the English Working Class* (London, 1963), pp.59–83.

78. J.H. Treble, 'The Attitude of the Roman Catholic Church towards Trade Unionism in the North of England, 1832–42', *Northern History*, vol.5 (1970), pp.93–113.

79. Stevenson, pp.276–82.

80. See esp. G.F.A. Best, 'Popular Protestantism in Victorian Britain', in R. Robson (ed.), *Ideas and Institutions of Victorian Britain* (London, 1967), pp.115–42.

81. See Pauline Millward's paper in this volume.

82. J. Foster, *Class Struggle and the Industrial Revolution* (London, 1974), pp.243–6.

83. S. Gilley, 'The Garibalidi Riots of 1862', *Historical Journal*, vol.16 (1973), pp.697–732.

84. W.L. Arnstein, 'The Murphy Riots: A Victorian Dilemma', *Victorian Studies*, vol.19 (1975); See also W.L. Arnstein, *Protestant versus Catholic in mid–Victorian England: Mr. Newdegate and the Nuns* (University of Missouri Press: Columbia and London, 1982), pp.88–107.

85. For further details, see R.E. Swift, 'Anti–Catholicism and Irish Disturbances: Public Order in mid–Victorian Wolverhampton', *Midland History*, vol.ix (1984), pp.88–109.

86. These lecturers included the Reverend Dr. Bryson, of the Scottish Presbyterian Church; Reverend Teodor, who claimed to be a former Romish Archdeacon of the diocese of Poldachia in Silavonia; Reverend Birks, of Kelishall in Hertfordshire; Reverend Miller, of St. Martin's, Birmingham. For further details, see Quirke, Dissertation, pp.22–5.

87. *Wolverhampton Chronicle*, 4 February 1852.

88. *Ibid.*, 7 July 1858.

89. *Ibid.*, 21 July 1858; 28 July 1858.

90. Staffordshire County Record Office, D 260/M/F/6/2, Ironmonger to Hatherton, 5 July 1858.

91. Public Records Office, HO/4120, Walpole to Ironmonger, 2 July 1858; 6 July 1858.

92. *Wolverhampton Chronicle*, 14 July 1858.

93. J.D. Walters, 'The Evangelical Embrace: Relations between Anglicans and Dissenters in the period 1830–1870', *W.M.S.*, vol.14 (1981), pp.32–8.
94. Full details of these disorders are contained in the *Wolverhampton Chronicle*, 20 February 1867; 27 February 1867. See also Arnstein, *Victorian Studies*, Vol.19 (1975), pp.510–72; D. Richter, *Riotous Victorians* (Athens and London, 1981), pp.35–49.
95. *Manchester Guardian*, 27 February 1867.
96. *Wolverhampton Chronicle*, 13 March 1867.
97. *Ibid.*, 3 April 1867.
98. *Ibid.*, 24 May 1867.
99. *Ibid.*, 19 June 1867; see also *Annual Register* (1867), Chronicle, pp.79–82; Arnstein, *Victorian Studies*, vol.19 (1975), pp.56–9; Richter, pp.37–9.
100. For details of this debate, see *Wolverhampton Chronicle*, 27 February 1867; 6 March 1867; 13 March 1867; 20 March 1867; 27 March 1867.
101. B. Weinburger, 'The Police and the Public in Mid–Nineteenth Century Warwickshire', in V. Bailey (ed.), *Policing and Punishment in Nineteenth Century Britain* (London, 1982), pp.69–71.
102. *Wolverhampton Chronicle*, 7 July 1858.
103. *Ibid.*, 27 February 1867.
104. Richter, p.40.
105. See P. Quinlivan & P. Rose, *The Fenians in England, 1865–1872* (London, 1982); W.J. Lowe, 'Lancashire Fenianism, 1864–71', *T.H.S.L.C.*, vol.126 (l971), pp. 156–185; E.D. Steele, 'The Irish Presence in the North of England, 1850–1914', *Northern History*, vol.12 (1976), pp.220–41.
106. Lunn, p.89.
107. *Wolverhampton Chronicle*, 6 March 1867.
108. Ó Tuathaigh, *T.R.H.S.*, vol.31 (1981), pp.169–70.
109. F. Turley, 'Centenary of the Fenian Raid', *The Cheshire Sheaf* (October 1967), pp.45–6.
110. *Wolverhampton Chronicle*, 4 February 1874.
111. P.R.O., HO/45/OS 7991, 1–63, Morris to Walpole, 21 February 1867; *Wolverhampton Chronicle*, 27 February 1867.
112. *Hansard* (Commons), 3rd. Series, vol.clxxv, 1031. 26 February 1867.
113. *Annual Register* (1874), Chron., p.12.
114. Swift, Thesis, pp.432–41.
115. D. Richter, 'The Role of Mob Riot in Victorian Elections, 1865–1885', *Victorian Studies*, vol.xv (1971), p.22.
116. *Wolverhampton Chronicle*, 4 February 1874.
117. *Ibid.*
118. *Ibid.*
119. *Ibid.*, 11 February 1874.
120. *Ibid.*
121. *Ibid.*
122. *Ibid.*, 18 February 1874.
123. *Ibid.*, 25 February 1874.

124. *Ibid.*, 11 March 1874.
125. *Ibid.*
126. *Ibid.*
127. *Ibid.*, 18 February 1874.
128. *Ibid.*
129. Ó Tuathaigh, *T.R.H.S.*, vol.31 (1981), pp.149–74.
130. *Wolverhampton Chronicle*, 11 March 1874.
131. *Ibid.*
132. There were exceptions, of course. In March 1849, for example, an Irishman, Timothy Burke, was tried for the murder of Joseph Higgins in Canal Street, Wolverhampton, in September 1848. During the trial, several witnesses alleged that Higgins had been involved in a fracas outside The Clog public house when a group of Irishmen, including Burke, had threatened to 'kill every bloody Englishman in the street'. Burke was eventually acquitted, although Justice Baron Platt stated that the incident had been 'a reflection of those deadly feuds which were of such frequent occurrence between English and Irish labourers': *Wolverhampton Chronicle*, 21 March 1849.
133. Holmes, p.101; For a recent study of the impact of ethnic tensions and religious conflicts on provincial politics, see P.J. Waller, *Democracy and Sectarianism: A Political and Social History of Liverpool, 1868–1939* (Liverpool, 1981).
134. Shaw, *W.M.S.*, 14 (1981), pp.1–9.
135. Holmes, pp.102–3.
136. Lunn, p.94; see also Michael E. Rose, 'Rochdale Man and the Stalybridge Riot: the Relief and Control of the Unemployed during the Lancashire Cotton Famine', in A.P. Donajgrodzki (ed.), *Social Control in Nineteenth Century Britain* (London, 1977), pp.185–206; Rose suggests that the Stalybridge Irish were obvious scapegoats for disorders which arose from local socio-economic ills.
137. Steele, *Northern History*, vol.12 (1976), p.235.
138. See especially Lynn Lees, *Exiles of Erin: Irish Migrants in Victorian London* (Manchester, 1979), pp.244–50; C. Bermant, *London's East End: Point of Arrival* (New York, 1975), pp.40–74.
139. D. Jones, p.106; for popular attitudes to the Irish presence in South Wales, see also J. Parry, 'The Tredegar Anti-Irish Riots of 1882', *Llafur*, vol.iii, no.4 (1983), pp.20–3.
140. D. Jones, pp.154–5.
141. Swift, Thesis, pp.446–61.
142. Richter, pp.1–18.
143. Stevenson & Quinault, pp.141–80.
144. Swift, Thesis, p.414.
145. Richter, p.167; for a useful study of the relationships between riot and social control during the period, see esp. Victor Bailey, 'Salvation Army Riots, the 'Skeleton Army', and Legal Authority in the Provincial Town', in Donajgrodzki, pp.231–53.

THE STOCKPORT RIOTS OF 1852: A STUDY OF ANTI–CATHOLIC AND ANTI–IRISH SENTIMENT

Pauline Millward

The Stockport riots took place between 28 and 30 June, 1852, at the time of a last major upsurge of anti–Catholicism in England. 'No Popery' in Britain had a long tradition stretching back to the Reformation. Catholic countries, France and Spain, were long–standing enemies, and Catholicism was seen as a threat to the liberties of free–born Englishmen. Feeling was intensified in the nineteenth century by the Act of Union (1801) which brought large numbers of Irish Catholics within the sphere of the Westminster Parliament, and by the Catholic Emancipation Act (1829) which gave Catholics political influence. Yet another cause of nineteenth–century anti–Catholicism was the sudden influx into mainland urban centres of large numbers of poor Irish Catholics fleeing from the potato famine of 1845–9. Moreover Roman Catholics were not the only group which threatened the Established Church. Voluntaries were working against the church/state connection and the writings of certain High Churchmen suggested moves towards Rome (indeed a number,including Manning, were converted).[1] The creation of twelve Catholic bishoprics in 1850 and an unfortunate Pastoral from the new Cardinal Archbishop, Nicholas Wiseman, making what appeared to be territorial claims in England[2] looked like the last straw. Lord John Russell, the Whig leader, made public his letter to the Bishop of Durham condemning the new hierarchy, and in 1851 carried through his Ecclesiastical Titles Bill. These moves brought Russell great public support, but kept anti–Catholic feeling on the boil throughout 1851.[3] A Proclamation issued by Lord Derby's Tory Government on 15 June 1852 (three weeks before a general election) forbade Catholics to process through public streets with symbols of their religion. The motives behind this proclamation are obscure. Disraeli said it was to prevent trouble 'in more than thirty places at least'[4], but the *Manchester Guardian* condemned it as an electioneering device, 'a popularity hunting attack upon Roman Catholic ceremonials' which government 'admirers and imitators' had used to 'stimulate the sectarian passions of the electors for their own selfish purposes'.[5] Whether the motives behind the proclamation were pacific is difficult to say. In Stockport, where vertical ties of religion and nationalism had been strengthened by the Protestant campaign of the preceding months, the proclamation was welcomed by all Protestants, and its effects were disruptive.

I

The proclamation was issued twelve days before the nineteenth annual procession of Stockport's Roman Catholic Sunday Schools was to take place on 27 June 1852. Extra copies of the proclamation together with inflammatory Orange placards urging Protestants not to elect a 'Papist Parliament', and exhorting its readers to 'make aggression on Rome' were posted in the town, and slogans proclaiming 'To Hell with the Pope' and 'Down with the Lousy Irish', were chalked on walls. In spite of this, the Catholics went ahead with their procession, but it was preceded by a body of strong Irishmen, for the majority of Stockport Catholics were Irish, and although priests walked in ordinary dress and almost all religious symbols were avoided, the procession was unwise given the strength of anti-Catholic feeling. It was not generally appreciated that the Catholics had tried to comply with the proclamation, and it was widely felt that the procession should not have taken place.

Nevertheless, the procession itself passed off peacefully, but the next afternoon an effigy of a priest was paraded by members of the Protestant Association. In the evening large-scale fighting broke out in Hillgate, one of the town's main streets, after an incident in the Bishop Blaize public house when a local man, William Walker, who had been turned out of the Bishop Blaize for starting a fight with an Englishman, came back and interrupted a group of Irish dancing to a fiddler. They beat him up, and again he was turned out by the landlord. He later returned with a crowd of English supporters, but the Irish had left. The crowd attacked Irishmen in Hillgate and general fighting between large numbers of Irish and English followed. Fighting was resumed the next night between young Irish and Englishmen, firstly in Hillgate and then in St. Peter's Square. The Square was taken and retaken several times, and windows were broken in a warehouse, St. Peter's Schoolroom and the house of Alderman Graham. There is conflicting evidence about how the windows were broken, but the weight of opinion suggests that the Irish were responsible. Eventually, the Irish were pursued down Rock Row, which led from the Square and which was occupied almost entirely by Irish. The *Stockport Advertiser* reported that the Irish were 'followed into their dwellings, dragged from their hiding places and their beds, furniture and other articles thrown into the street. The windows were completely destroyed, the houses were sacked and they were now tenantless'.[6] The police, the mayor and magistrates arrived after the damage had been done, at the head of a detachment of sixty men of the 4th. Regiment of Infantry from their barracks in Hall Street, Stockport. The Riot Act was read and the disturbances in Rock Row ceased, but the crowd moved on to ransack the town's two Catholic chapels. The Chapel at Edgeley was 'completely sacked and gutted and the adjacent priest's house and vestries in the same condition. The rioters had brought the furniture, etc., out of the chapel and the residence, piled it in the road and set fire to it'. At St. Michael's Chapel 'the furniture had been dragged out, broken up and some of it set fire to'.[7] Once again, the authorities arrived after the destruction had taken place and again the Riot Act was read. On the Wednesday night things were quieter but more Irish homes were attacked.

By Tuesday night 24 Irish homes had been wrecked, an Irishman was dead, 51 Irish were injured and two Catholic chapels had been ransacked, but of 113 prisoners taken, 111 were Irish and only 2 were English. The *Manchester Guardian* reported that the scene on Wednesday morning in the Court House 'cannot be easily described. Within a rail separating the lower end of the court from that where justice is administered were penned together some sixty or seventy youths and men, nearly all Irish, most of whom had bandages and plasters on their heads, faces, hands, and arms and legs . . . others were moaning and bleeding and the whole formed a scene not unlike that of a military hospital after a battle', adding that 'the bloodshed, the violence and the rapine' were 'Protestant handiwork'.[8] Where, it might be asked, were the perpetrators? Indeed during the next few weeks more Englishmen were arrested and eventually ten English and ten Irish were sent for trial at Chester, where only three English but all the Irish were found guilty of riot. One Irishman, Matthew Mulligan, was transported for 15 years for the manslaughter of another Irishman who had received blows to the head during the disorders, although the fatal blow was deemed to have come from his compatriot in the heat of the battle. Sentences for the other Irish ranged from 2 to 15 months imprisonment with hard labour and for the English from 18 months to 2 years imprisonment with hard labour.[9]

II

It is apparent that the nationwide 'No Popery' agitation of 1850 contributed to the riots. In Stockport, however, the resurgence of anti–Catholicism was given an extra dimension by certain Stockport politicians and churchmen who had exploited Protestant fears to their own ends and so intensified the tension between the Irish and English populations.

Stockport politics were in a state of flux. After some years in the political wilderness, the Tories had won one of the town's two parliamentary seats from the Liberals in 1847, and had gained a majority on the local Council in 1848. By November 1852, however, the Liberals were again in control of the Council, and this waning of Conservative power is reflected in their defeat in the election of 1852. The probability of Conservative electoral defeat, suggested by canvass returns, caused increased anti–Catholic activity in the months preceding the general election.[10] One of the two Liberal candidates, J.B. Smith, had been among the minority of M.P.s who had opposed the

Ecclesiastical Titles Bill, and his possible election was regularly cited as inimical to Protestant liberties.

The local newspaper, the *Stockport Advertiser*, which was strongly Protestant and High Tory, was at the forefront of the anti-Catholic campaign.[11] Between March and the election on 9 July 1852, the *Advertiser* published five anti-Catholic editorials, often linking the names of the Liberal candidates to support for papal aggression. Just before the riots and the election, the *Advertiser* declared that 'it would be quite as safe for Stockport to choose a professed Jesuit for its representative as to give its suffrage to Mr. Smith, who refuses to resist the late papal aggression and who will at every opportunity join the Irish Brigade in their intended assault at the citadel of our Protestant religion and national freedom'.[12] Most significantly, in May, 1852, under the heading 'Protestantism and Liberty', it openly attacked Stockport's Irish. 'What is it', thundered the *Advertiser*, 'that so often disturbs the peace of the borough, increases our rates and saps the very foundation of all our charitable institutions, but popery embodied in Irish mobs, paupers and fever patients?'[13]

The *Advertiser* also promoted a Protestant Association, formed in Stockport in December 1850, which stirred up anti-Catholic feeling and was strongly supported by local Tory and Anglican leaders. The Protestant Association had gained notoriety in June 1780, when a campaign against limited concessions to Catholics, spearheaded by its President, Lord George Gordon, had culminated in week-long riots in London.[14] The Association reappeared in 1835, and immediately became an important force in the nineteenth-century anti-Catholic campaign. It addressed all classes, and worked for the repeal of the Relief Act of 1829 and the Maynooth Grant, and was vociferous about the dangers inherent in the growth of Catholicism in social, educational, religious and political terms.[15]

The Stockport Protestant Association was behind the inflammatory Orange placard[16] posted before the election, which was printed by Alderman T. Claye, who was himself a supporter of the Association. The names of prominent citizens who attended Protestant Association meetings were featured in the *Stockport Advertiser*, and the vote of twenty-two of these gentlemen may be traced in the 1847 Poll Books. All but two voted Tory on that occasion,[17] and one of the two who did not was the Liberal Mayor at the time of the riots, John Boothroyd, who attended the First Annual Dinner shortly after his inauguration. A number of local Tory politicians and the Tory M.P., James Heald, also attended Protestant Association meetings, and all but one of the nine local Anglican ministers also attended and sometimes lectured.[18] Links between militant Protestantism and the Tory party had been strengthened after the Emancipation Act of 1829, and G.F.A. Best has suggested that it then 'became necessary for keen Protestants - and politically profitable for keen Tories - to keep the fires of the true faith well stoked beneath a widening range of political public'.[19]

The Protestant minister most active in the anti-Catholic

campaign in Stockport was the Rev. J. Meridyth of St. Peter's Anglican Church. Meridyth was one of a number of Irish–born Protestant clergymen resident in England who were at the forefront of 'No–Popery' activity.[20] He delivered inflammatory anti–Catholic speeches at Protestant meetings in 1851 and 1852, sometimes with the Rev. Hugh Stowell of Salford, another notorious anti–Catholic campaigner. In March 1852, Meridyth wrote to J.B. Smith, the Liberal candidate, demanding to know Smith's views on certain religious issues and, when rebuffed, informed Smith that he would use his influence to procure for Stockport an M.P. who would 'acknowledge his belief in the great leading doctrines of Christianity'.[21] Later, at a meeting for the Tory candidate just after the riots and before the 1852 General Election, Meridyth 'declared that he would not be scared by any threat of personal violence nor by the taunts of being a "political parson". . from throwing himself heartily into the present movement and of using whatever talent or influence he might possess in order to secure the return to Parliament of such a right–minded consistent Protestant representative as Mr. Heald.'[22] Meridyth's activities suggest that the breaking of St. Peter's School windows during the rioting was neither accident nor blind destruction. He and other local leaders had used their influence to stir up anti–Catholic and anti–Irish feeling in the months before the riots, and were partly responsible.

Given the activities of these prominent citizens, it might be asked whether the Magistrates' Inquiry which followed the riots, and which decided who should be sent for trial, was properly conducted. Exactly half (7) of the magistrates were Liberal and half Tory, so no political party dominated the Inquiry. Three of the magistrates had links with the Protestant Association, however, and the Association's fear that it might be implicated in the riots is implicit in the fact that it was represented at the Inquiry by Edward Reddish, a solicitor, who had attended meetings of the Protestant Association and who also represented the Tory Alderman Graham, the proprietors of St. Peter's School and some of the English prisoners. Mr. Gibson, who acted for the Catholic priests and some of the Irish, actually called the printer of the Protestant Association posters, Alderman Claye, as a witness, since he felt that 'no–one who had read the placard could doubt the effect it had on the night of the riot'.[23] But his attempt to raise questions about the poster and the Protestant Association were thwarted by interruptions and objections from both Mr. Reddish and the Mayor. The Mayor advised Alderman Claye not to answer certain questions about the placard which, in any case, he later insisted was not in evidence, and when Mr. Gibson asked Alderman Claye if there was a Protestant Association in Stockport, the Mayor, who himself had links with the Association, said that 'if there was, that could have nothing to do with this Inquiry'.[24] Mr. Gibson then allowed Alderman Claye to stand down. Gibson declared that 'those who excited the people to the disturbances in which life had been lost were the really guilty parties and . . . ought to be discovered',[25] but he was not allowed to pursue this line of inquiry.

The authorities were not only reluctant to deal with the

instigators of the riots, they were also reluctant to apprehend th
English rioters. As Mr. Gibson remarked to the Inquiry, most of th
prisoners were Irish, although only Irish property had been destroyed
and it was 'only through the investigations of Mr. Faulkner assiste
by Alderman Ashton that any evidence had been obtained upon which som
of the English had been apprehended.'[26] Gibson also complained tha
two local Catholic priests, Father Frith, of St. Philip and S
James's Church, and Father Foster, of St. Michael's Church, had bee
obliged to bear the costs of bringing the English to justice. To som
extent these complaints were accepted by the authorities. Gibso
produced the reply to a letter he had written to the Home Secretary
Walpole, asking for assistance. The Government was reluctant t
undertake the prosecution of the offenders, leaving the matter wit
the Catholic priests, although the government offered to 'take upo
itself any reasonable expenses properly incurred by Mr. Frith and Mr
Foster.'[27]

All in all, the response of the magistrates left much to b
desired. So did the performance of the police during th
disturbances. They were not only reluctant to arrest English rioters
but were slow in arriving at the scene of the rioting, with the resu
that, on each occasion, the damage was done before they appeared
Their inefficiency was in part the product of their lack of numbers
Stockport had a police force of only eleven men for a population o
53,835. The trial judge stated that the size of the police force wa
a 'matter of astonishment to him', and concluded that 'It might hav
been perhaps that motives of ill-judged economy had caused this stat
of things'.[28] T.A. Critchley has suggested that reluctance to spen
ratepayers' money meant that many boroughs failed to appoint
sufficient number of policemen during the early Victorian period, an
has concluded that the ratio of police to population in Stockpor
during the 1850s was the 'worst ratio of any borough in the country'
This was appalling in comparison to London, which then boasted on
policeman to every 461 inhabitants.[29]

Shortage of policemen meant that large numbers of specia
constables had to be recruited once the disturbances had begun. Th
Irish and Catholics claimed that some of these special constables wer
not sworn in and that a number were actually rioters,[30] perhap
accounting for the large number of injuries among the Irish prisoners
Reports of both the Magistrates' Inquiry and the trial lend substanc
to these claims. One witness at the Inquiry, William Cadman, son of
regular constable, testified that his father had told him to give
constable's staff to Samuel Royle, a prisoner later discharged by th
Magistrates, and that his father had not seen Royle.[31] Two of the te
English tried at Chester, and one of the three found guilty, wer
acting as special constables. Indeed, fear about the behaviour o
special constables was not confined to Stockport: during th
Birkenhead riots of 1862, 1,000 special constables were sworn in, bu
were not in fact used, because it was felt that they were prejudice
against the Irish and, if let loose, would increase the level o
violence.[32]

III

The apparent failure of justice in Stockport can be ascribed in art to popular support for the rioters. The regular constable who rrested one of the two English taken during the riots, reported that hen he did so the crowd shouted 'let him go . . . he's one of urs',[33] and the Irish Defence Counsel claimed at the trial that printed placards had been posted in Stockport denouncing some of the itnesses who had come forward as perjurers, and giving their names, escription and address'.[34] After the trial, a procession and 'bands f music' were planned to greet the English acquitted at Chester, but ere banned by the authorities.[35]

Popular support for these anti–Catholic and anti–Irish isorders had its origins in a number of local economic, social, ultural and religious conditions. In this light, the rioters emerge ot simply as passive instruments of religious leaders, press and oliticians, but as people who had their own grievances, some of which ere of little importance to their better–off sponsors, and which arrant closer consideration if a real understanding of the Stockport iots is to be achieved.

During the early nineteenth century the rise of the cotton ndustry, and the opportunities for employment it provided, ontributed to the rapid growth of Stockport, and by 1851, 48.8% of he working population of the town was employed in 'new industries'.[36] tockport's growth was not achieved without cost. Police, sanitary, ealth and other facilities were woefully inadequate, and a number of rade depressions, especially in the 1840s, brought hardship.[37] The esperate plight of Stockport workers in 1842 was a major cause of heir participation in the Plug Plot which affected many of the nanufacturing districts.[38] The strike in Stockport lasted for over a nonth and, although Chartists were involved and there were demands for he wage rates of 1840, the evidence suggests that in Stockport 'the urn–out was in essence a hunger movement'.[39] Indeed, on 11 August, tockport's Workhouse was invaded and about 700 seven–pound loaves f bread and around £7 in money were stolen, an event which T.D.W. and laomi Reid have described as 'a pillaging expedition by hungry eople'.[40] There were no further serious disturbances in the town etween 1842 and 1852, despite a harsh decline in trade in 1847–48 hich resulted in two, three and four–day weeks and a 10% cut in ages. This coincided with a large influx to Stockport of poor Irish leeing from the famine, and by 1851, 5,701 of Stockport's population f 53,835 were Irish–born. Alienated and frightened, they found elease from two sources – Saturday night drinking sprees and the Roman Catholic Church.

Contemporary newspapers frequently referred to drunken weekend isturbances in Stockport. These generally took place between the rish themselves, but at times the English were involved, and such ows often culminated in attacks on the police who tried to interfere.

The 1836 *Report on the State of the Irish Poor in Great Britair* suggested that differences between the Irish and the police violent rows between the Irish from different parts of Ireland were long–standing occurrence.[42] Yet, in spite of their differences, I immigrants possessed a strong sense of community, fostered by t common culture and religion, and strengthened in Stockport b Catholic Boys School founded in 1824, a Girl's Guild, and a Sun School founded in 1845.[43]

The Church provided continuity between the old life and new, and the Catholic priest often acted for his congregation secular as well as religious matters. Sheridan Gilley has remar that 'He judged communal feuds and brawls, administered charity, fo jobs for new arrivals and the unemployed, guided his less lite parishioners in their financial transactions and correspondence interpreted to them the political events of the outside world'.[44] too, was often Irish and, though literate, came from a backgro similar to that of his flock, although one of Stockport's two pri was said to be 'the son of an English gentleman'. The Irish id tified with their Church and in turn were closely identified with 'Irish and Catholic are nearly synonymous here',[45] said Stockpo Chief Constable at the Inquiry after the riots. Unfortunately, faith which promoted this sense of identity separated Irish f English. Geoffrey Best's assertion that the Roman Catholic commu was 'as close and segregated a denomination as any in Britain' seems an accurate description of Stockport's Irish Catholic popula in 1852. Even as far back as 1836 a Catholic priest had claimed 'the Irish do not assimilate themselves much to the English',[47] a echoed by a surgeon at Stockport Infirmary who remarked that English do not assimilate themselves to the Irish, and rather fee pride in keeping a superior state of their houses'.[48]

Many Irish immigrants gravitated to the cheapest and n decrepit property in Stockport. Lodging houses were overcrowded, few complied with the 'necessary safeguards to public health wh cleanliness, ventilation and sewerage can afford'.[49] Moreover, of 140 common lodging houses in the borough, 122 had Irish keepers within them lived 1,355 Irish and only 11 English. The 1851 Cen records also reveal Irish household patterns. In Rock Row, where m homes were later wrecked, 217 persons lived in 24 houses and all 11 of the adults were Irish–born. Moreover all but 15 of children, some of whom were very young, had also been born Ireland.[50] It thus seems clear that the street where the most sev rioting took place in 1852 was occupied by recent Irish immigrants lived in crowded conditions separated from their English counterpar

E.P. Thompson has suggested that the Irish in some towns w 'partially segregated in their own streets and quarters' but 'w never pressed back into ghettoes'.[51] In Stockport, however, the I were mostly separated from the English in their own areas. In 183 Catholic priest had observed that the Irish were 'living together certain parts of the town',[52] and this pattern persisted. J.M. W has shown that a similar pattern characterised the Irish settlemen anchester.[53] The 1851 Census further reflects the extent of Irish olation in Stockport during the riot period. In 1815, 1,531 persons ved in the enumeration district which included Rock Row, and, of ese, 74% (1,130) were either Irish-born (986) or the children of ish-born (144) and only 26% (401) were non-Irish.[54] Moreover, ish isolation is also indicated by the fact that there were no more an six mixed marriages in the whole of the enumeration district. If ere was no Irish ghetto in Stockport, a distinct Irish neighbourhood ad developed by the 1850s.[55] At the heart of this neighbourhood lay ock Row, scene of some of the most severe rioting.

Of the 24 heads of family in Rock Row, 6 were women and 14 ere 'Labourers'. Only 4 had jobs obviously connected with the cotton ills. Most of the younger Irish, however, definitely worked in the ills, as bobbiners, piecers, weavers, or throstle-spinners. This, gether with the fact that the rioters were mostly young people, uggests some truth in the *Stockport Advertiser's* claim after the ots that English antagonism towards the Irish had its foundation in ish competition for cheap labour in the mills.[56] But there is ttle evidence for this view in the *Manchester Guardian*, the *tockport Advertiser*, and the papers of the Christie Hat Company, hich was a large employer in Stockport, in the years before the ots. However, in July 1852, Alderman Graham stated that on the econd night of rioting he had spoken to someone 'clad as a labouring an', who had said of the Irish 'there will be no good done with them r they keep the wages down'.[57] Although there is little evidence to upport the claim that the Stockport Irish were popularly regarded as n economic threat, the ten per cent cut in wages during the 1848 epression had coincided with the peak of Irish immigration, and the o could have been associated in the minds of English workers, ereby heightening Anglo-Irish tensions.[58] Moreover, since any wage ould have been better than what the Irish received at home, they were ossibly willing to work for less than the English worker held to be ir wage, but there is little solid evidence that this was the case Stockport.

The English regarded the unemployed Irish as a burden on the oor rate, which also contributed to Anglo-Irish antagonism in tockport. But English fears about the drain on the Poor Rate were ften exaggerated. In 1848 an amendment to the Poor Law had given removeable status to those resident in a parish for five years, but is was of little use to the Irish who flooded into Stockport in the te 1840s. They might be relieved a few times as casual poor, but fter that would be returned to Ireland. During 1846, 42 Irish were emoved, whilst 73 removals took place in the first quarter of 1847,[59] nd a Select Committee Report of 1854[60] shows that Stockport continued ith its policy of Irish poor removal. What is more, those returned Ireland represented only a small proportion of needy Irish. ccording to Henry Coppock, Stockport's Town Clerk, the Irish epeatedly said that they 'would rather die here than be removed ere', and were 'driven to shift for themselves'[61] rather than apply r relief and risk removal.

Vagrancy was often cited in the local press as another aspe of the Irish problem. Thus a Police Report of January 1849 blame Irish beggars for much of the crime in Stockport.[62] Coppock evidence suggests that this problem was largely the result of offici policy. Many of the poor Irish immigrants in the later 1840s ha little choice: they must beg or starve. The vagrant, however, wa thought a threat to the existing social order, and David Jones ha suggested that 'To many Victorians the vagrant was the most glarin affront to the trinity of work, respectability and religion. He wa the epitome of uncivilised self-indulgence, lacking in bo "industrious habits" and "independence" and without a home in eith the material or spiritual world'.[63] Thus the increasing number Irish vagrants in the later 1840s may have exacerbated tensio between the English and Irish populations in Stockport.

Not all the Irish were driven to begging for a living. Pre famine Irish who had lived in a particular parish continuously f five years had to be supported, and the Census figures suggest th about half of the 1851 total of 5,701 Irish-born had settled Stockport before 1841. The new Irish sometimes brought seriou diseases which had to be treated in local hospitals.[64] Part of th cost of this medical treatment had to be borne by local ratepayer and any increase in rates was hard on some of Stockport's less wel off ratepayers. During the recession of 1850, three hundred wer summonsed for arrears.[65] Hence any expenditure on the Irish, to sa nothing of the threat to health which they represented, may hav contributed to the anti-Irish feeling which was manifest in th disturbances.

However there is little evidence to suggest that the politic leanings of Stockport's working population were a cause of the riot Local Chartists, who had long been in the forefront of working clas political activity in Stockport, took no part in the riots. Indee at a meeting of the South Lancashire Chartists, the delegate expressed their warmest approval of the Stockport Chartists, 'the pacific behaviour forming a contrast to those whose minds wer cribbed, cabined and confined by teachers of darkness rather tha light.'[66] It is not clear how far Chartist attitudes to the rio were connected with Irish involvement in the movement. In 1848, loc Chartists and Irish Repealers had worked together for a time in th hope of achieving their separate ends,[67] although C.A.N. Reid sugges that it is difficult to determine the scale of Irish participation Stockport Chartism, concluding that there were few Irish among thos prominent Chartists whose careers can be traced.[68] Reid has furth suggested, however, that those Irish who were linked with the moveme were among the most prominent Chartists, including Thomas Clark, member of the Chartist National Executive.[69]

Chartism was not the only form of working-class politic activity in Stockport. Many working people had been involved campaigns in support of the Ten Hours Bill and against the Rel System. It is possible that the support of Tories like Ashley an Oastler for these campaigns influenced the cotton operatives in favo

' the Tory Party, and that in 1852 the rioters were expressing Tory ɔlitical preferences which could not be expressed through the ballot ɔx. But this does not appear to have been the case. Thousands athered round the hustings at the 1847 and 1852 elections, yet in 347 the show of hands favoured Richard Cobden, the Liberal, and John est, the Chartist, rather than the Tory, James Heald, while in 1852 ands were raised overwhelmingly for the Liberal candidates, and 'oans and hisses greeted their Tory opponent.[70]

IV

Anti–Irish riots occurred in many towns in mid–Victorian 'itain, including Cardiff in 1848, Greenock in 1851, and Wigan in 352.[71] However John Stevenson has suggested that 'The Stockport ɔts were by far the most destructive of the 1850s',[72] and the ɹestion arises as to why they took place in Stockport and why they ɔcurred in 1852.

Several contemporary explanations of the Stockport riots ressed economic factors. In 1852 the *Annual Register* claimed that ey 'arose from an old feud existing between the English operatives ıd the Irish', the Irish having 'incurred the hatred of the natives the effect of their competition in the labour market'.[73] A similar planation was put forward by the *Stockport Advertiser*, which claimed at the riots were 'evidently more a workman's quarrel than a eologian's quarrel', because the Irish, 'by working more hours and at wer terms, keep down wages'.[74] However, the *Advertiser* had played important part in the Protestant campaign and it was therefore in own interests to play down the religious aspect. Moreover, its ne was so aggressively anti–Irish that its objectivity must be open question.

In contrast, the *Manchester Guardian*, which was by no means a ıpporter of the Irish, avoided the excesses of the *Advertiser* and ıould perhaps be given more credence. The *Guardian* claimed that 'For ɔme time past there has been in Stockport bad feeling between the two asses indicated partly on trade quarrels, partly on national ounds, but chiefly the result of religious differences'.[75] This port lends support to the argument of this paper that the Stockport ɔts were not simply the product of working–class grievances, but can so be connected with the activities of political and religious oupings outside the working class. This was also the view of ɹrtain minority newspapers. The *Star of Freedom* (formerly the *ɔrthern Star*) castigated those who fought the religious wars of hers and remarked that 'for working men to fight the battles of any the sects or parties into which their oppressors are seemingly vided is to be guilty of the most wretched self–abasement'.[76] *The ablet*, a Catholic newspaper, was more specific, blaming the disorders ı the 'Derby Proclamation' which had 'fulfilled its mission' and had een baptised in blood and consecrated by internecine slaughter'.[77]

The Stockport riots have not been examined very closely by

historians, but they are referred to in a number of texts. Mode writers have not been content with the simple-minded explanatio offered by nineteenth-century commentators, although most ha stressed the economic and religious foundations of the riots. Kev O'Connor has remarked that the Stockport riots 'compounded th elements of economic fear, racial fear, and religious hysteria',[78] whilst G.I.T. Machin has suggested that 'the affair became a means expressing antipathy towards Catholicism and resentment at th economic competition of the Irish, who accepted low wages fro employers'.[79] More recently, Neville Kirk has devoted some attenti to the Stockport riots in the setting of Anglo-Irish relationships Lancashire between 1850 and 1870, and has suggested that the increas in the Irish population, the growth of Irish communities, Iris nationalism and religious and political factors, contributed to ethn tensions. Kirk has emphasised the importance of economic fears whic though not always soundly based, 'were real to their holder constituted the material roots of conflict, and were of cruci significance in informing the consciousness of the rioters'.[80]

Kirk's emphasis on economic causes is persuasive, and he use the 1851 Census to support his claim that by the early 1850s larg numbers of Irish were employed in Stockport's cotton industry.[81] However, economic tensions between English and Irish were by no mear inevitable, and Kirk's analysis of the economic motives behind th riots relies heavily upon contemporary press reports issued after th disorders and the evidence of Alderman Graham to the post-ri Inquiry. In the years leading up to the riots, local newspape frequently commented on the ways in which the Irish antagonised th English population, drawing attention to their waywardnes drunkenness, alien religion and unhealthy living condition References to Anglo-Irish economic tensions, however, only emerge after the riots had taken place. Nevertheless, there may have bee tensions beneath the surface, and it is possible that economic fea contributed to anti-Irish sentiment. However there is little dire evidence from Stockport sources to support the suggestion that the were a vital ingredient in the disturbances of 1852.

Indeed, a multi-causal explanation best fits the Stockpo riots, and it is important not to pay too much attention to any or aspect of Anglo-Irish tension. It is evident that although the spa which started the explosion was the Roman Catholic procession on th Sunday before the disturbances, this was simply the catalyst of highly volatile situation.

Stockport had been in the vanguard of the Industri Revolution. Working-class life was hard and unstable, and there ha been several trade depressions in the decade before the riots. Iris immigrants were seen as a burden on the poor rate and a threat to bo public health and the local economy. The fears generated by th situation were exaggerated by the fact that the English and Iris communities lived in clearly defined districts and were furth separated by religion and culture. These pressures probably a contributed to the riots, although they cannot be merely attributed local grievances and deprivation, otherwise disturbances would have occurred more frequently. Similar situations existed in other towns. In Liverpool, 23% of the population was Irish–born in 1851, which caused great strains and tensions in that city, and in 1849 a local magistrate complained of the threat to finances, health and moral welfare which the Liverpool authorities believed were posed by Irish immigration.[82] It might be reasonable to have expected that more serious rioting would have taken place in Liverpool or in Manchester, where the cultural, economic and social pressures which the Irish exerted were very similar to those evident in neighbouring Stockport.[83] It is necessary, therefore, to look for some extra dimension.

The inadequacy of Stockport's regular police force cannot of itself have been of vital importance, otherwise large–scale disturbances might have occurred more frequently. Nevertheless, because of their small numbers, the police found it difficult to contain the initial disorders. Auxilliary forces were called in, and the role of certain special constables was an important element in the riots: not only did they fail to contain the rioters, they actually took part in the disturbances. Their activities can, however, only be linked to events which took place after the riots had started and, although they may have prolonged the rioting, they cannot be blamed for the outbreak of the disorders.

Religion was clearly linked to the outbreak of rioting. National anti–papal feeling was an important element in licencing popular anti–Catholicism, but there were outbreaks of national 'No–Popery' in 1829 and 1845 which did not lead to riots in Stockport. Perhaps the key is provided by G.I.T. Machin, who has suggested that the difference between 1850 and earlier 'No–Popery' activity was the fact that 'the government now joined the crowd'.[84] In Stockport,not only was anti–Catholicism promoted by the activities of Lord John Russell and the Derby Government, but local government also 'joined the crowd'. Before the Catholic procession, the local press and religious and political leaders, often pursuing political as much as religious ends, went to extreme lengths in support of the Tory–Protestant cause, and reinforced the impression that Catholics and Irish were a threat to liberty and freedom. Indeed commenting on the excesses of the Stockport activists, the *Manchester Guardian* remarked that 'In no locality has the flame been more systematically and recklessly provoked'.[85] Stockport's particular political situation may have tipped the scales. Many of the respectable inhabitants involved in the political campaign were active in the Protestant Association which raised the temperature on the day after the procession.

In sentencing the English found guilty at Chester, the judge compared the Stockport riots with the Gordon riots. Indeed, George Rudé's analysis of the Gordon riots might equally apply to those in Stockport. As with their more famous counterpart, the Stockport riots appear to have been 'deliberately fostered by the Protestant Association', whose 'leaders did not scruple to stir up violent feeling against the Roman Catholic minority to achieve their ow ends', but as far as the rioters were concerned, 'behind the slogan of "No-Popery" and other outward forms of religious fanaticism ther lay a deeper social purpose'.[86] In Stockport, this was a desire to d something about the Irish, who threatened an already precariou existence. Stockport's growing population had outstripped it facilities, and in 1852 working-class life was still harsh an insecure. The depression in trade at the end of the 1840s ha coincided with an influx of troublesome, half-starved and unhealth Irish. But the fears generated by this situation were exacerbated b the activities of local and national political and religious leader who, to serve their own ends, promoted anti-Catholic fervour whic they could not, or would not control, and for which they would accep no responsibility.

Notes

1. See Stephen Usherwood, '"No Popery" Under Queen Victoria' *History Today*, no.4 (April 1973), pp.274–279.
2. Philip Hughes, 'The English Catholics in 1850', in G.A. Bec (ed.), *English Catholics 1850–1950* (1950), pp.47–8, quotes from thi pastoral: the Archbishop declared (without making it clear in th first instance that his claim related only to Catholics in a privat capacity) 'until such time as the Holy See shall think fit otherwis to provide, we govern and shall continue to govern the counties c Middlesex, Hertford and Essex as ordinary thereof, and those c Surrey, Sussex, Kent, Berkshire and Hampshire with the islands annexe as administrator with ordinary powers'.
3. E.R. Norman, *Anti-Catholicism in Victorian England* (1968) G.I.T. Machin, *Politics and the Churches in Great Britain, 1832–186* (1977); G.F.A. Best, 'Popular Protestantism in Victorian Britain' i Robert Robson (ed.), *Ideas and Institutions of Victorian Britai* (1967). Best spells out the theoretical, political moral and sexua components of anti-Catholicism.
4. Quoted in G.I.T. Machin, *Politics and the Churches*, p.238.
5. *Manchester Guardian*, 3 July 1852.
6. *Stockport Advertiser*, 2 July 1852.
7. *Manchester Guardian*, 3 July 1852.
8. *Ibid.*
9. For further details of the disorders, see the reports of th trial and Magistrates' Inquiry, held in the weeks following the riots which appeared in the *Manchester Guardian*, 3, 7, 10, 14, 17, 21, 24 28, 31 July 1852, and 14, 18 August 1852. See also the *Stockpor Advertiser*, 2, 9, 16, 23, 30 July; the *Manchester Courier*, 3, 10, 3 July; *Tablet*, 3, 10, 17, 24, 31 July 1852, and 7, 14 August 1852 Henry Heginbotham, *Stockport Ancient and Modern*, vol.1 (1882), pp.104-106, also contains a useful account. Of less value is the descriptio of the riots which appeared in W. Astle, *History of Stockport* (1922) pp.137–141. Astle was editor of the *Stockport Advertiser*, and hi

account depends largely on that source.
10. The papers of J.B.Smith held in Manchester Central Library include a letter from a Liberal supporter who claimed that 'the Tories are beginning to be desperate'. They also include canvass returns relating to the 1,826 votes pledged for the election of two M.P.s. There were 360 pledged to Heald, 559 for Smith and 596 for Kershaw, the other Liberal. The canvass suggested that 88 of the votes not pledged were favourable to the Liberals and 135 were against. If the latter, together with a further 57 'doubtful' votes are credited to Heald, he emerges with 552 votes. The remaining 39 votes were neutral, so it was unlikely that Heald would be elected.
11. During 1851 it had set the scene by furnishing stories about 'seduction by a Romanist subject', 'Jesuits in the neighbourhood', and a priest wheedling fortunes out of the dying.
12. *Stockport Advertiser*, 17 June 1852.
13. *Ibid.*, 14 May 1852. Kevin O'Connor, *The Irish in Britain* (1972), pp.2–6, describes a history of similar sentiment dating back to the thirteenth century. See also M.A.G. Ó Tuathaigh, 'The Irish in Nineteenth–Century Britain', *Transactions of the Royal Historical Society*, vol.31 (1981), pp.149–174.
14. See George Rudé, *Paris and London in the Eighteenth Century: Studies in Popular Protest* (1974), pp.268–92.
15. G.I.T. Machin, *Politics and the Churches*, p.96.
16. It is perhaps worth mentioning that the Orange Order, which in this period played an important role in Anglo–Irish tension in a number of towns, including Manchester and Liverpool, had a minor role in Stockport. It is mentioned just once in the local press. In July 1851 at the height of the anti–Catholic campaign, when the Irish were particularly vulnerable, the *Advertiser* reported that the 'Loyal Orangemen of Stockport held their annual festivity . . . the proceedings passed off in an agreeable manner without that annoyance from the Irishmen which seems to be becoming remarkable in other towns': *Stockport Advertiser*, 18 July 1851.
17. Five used a second vote. The other candidates were two Liberals and a Chartist. In every case the Tory voters supported Richard Cobden rather than the other Liberal, James Kershaw, presumably because Kershaw was a Voluntary opposed to the church/state connection so dear to the hearts of Protestant Association members.
18. The names and parishes of these ministers are listed in *Slater's Lancashire Directory* (1851).
19. G.F.A. Best, 'Popular Protestantism in Victorian Britain', in Robson (ed.), *Ideas and Institutions*, p.139.
20. See Sheridan Gilley, 'Protestant London, No–Popery, and the Irish Poor, 1830–1869', *Recusant History*, vol.10, no.4 (January 1970), pp.210–30; Frank Neal, 'The Roots of Violence', *Tablet*, 1 May 1982, pp.420–22.
21. Meridyth's letters and Smith's reply are included in J.B. Smith's Papers, held in Manchester Central Library.
22. *Stockport Advertiser*, 9 July 1852.
23. *Manchester Guardian*, 24 July 1852.

24. *Ibid.*
25. *Ibid.*, 28 July 1852.
26. *Stockport Advertiser*, 30 July 1852.
27. *Tablet*, 14 August 1852.
28. *Manchester Guardian*, 14 August 1852.
29. T.A. Critchley, *A History of the Police in England and Wale* (1967), pp.67–68. Even later in the century Stockport's policing wa still poor. Critchley also comments (p.129) that in 1871 Stockport' police force was reported as 'inefficient' by the Inspectors c Constabulary.
30. This claim appears in the Shrewsbury Catholic records' *Histor the Diocese of Shrewsbury* (1892); *Tablet*, 3 July 1852; *Mancheste Guardian*, 18 August 1852.
31. Reported in the *Manchester Guardian*, 31 July 1852.
32. See F. Neal, 'The Birkenhead Garibaldi Riots of 1862', *Th Transactions of the Historic Society of Lancashire and Cheshire* vol.31 (November 1982), pp.87–111, and Sheridan Gilley, 'The Garibald Riots of 1862', *Historical Journal*, vol.16 (1973), pp.720–24. Fo further illustrations of the problems of policing anti-Catholi disturbances in Victorian Britain, see W.L. Arnstein, *Protestan versus Catholic in mid-Victorian England: Mr Newdegate and th Nuns* (1982), pp.88–107; D. Richter, *Riotous Victorians* (1981), pp.35-50; R.E. Swift, 'Anti-Catholicism and Irish Disturbances: Publi Order in mid-Victorian Wolverhampton', *Midland History*, vol.ix (1984).
33. *Manchester Guardian*, 17 July 1852.
34. *Ibid.*, 18 August 1852.
35. *Stockport Advertiser*, 20 August 1852.
36. Philip Hughes, 'The English Catholics in 1850', in Beck (ed.) *The English Catholics*, p.60.
37. W. Cook-Taylor, *Tour of the Manufacturing Districts o Lancashire* (1842), pp.180–221, describes Stockport during a recessio and provides graphic details of the suffering of its inhabitants.
38. See, for example, F.C. Mather, 'The General Strike of 1842', i J. Stevenson and R. Quinault (eds.), *Popular Protest and Public Orde* (1974), pp.115–40.
39. T.D.W. Reid and Naomi Reid, 'The 1842 "Plug Plot" in Stockport' *International Review of Social History*, vol.xxiv, Part 1 (1979), p.72.
40. *Ibid.*, p.65.
41. *Report on the State of the Irish Poor in Great Britain, P.P* (40), vol.xxiv (1836) Appendix on Stockport, pp.85–87.
42. R.E. Swift, 'Crime and Ethnicity: The Irish in Early Victoria Wolverhampton', *West Midlands Studies*, vol.13 (1980), pp.1–5 argue that the police in Wolverhampton maintained an 'intensive presence in Irish areas and the 'Irish quarter provided the police with eas pickings'. Thus the high recorded incidence of Irish law-breaking i that town was partly due to the activities of the police themselves.
43. J. Robinson, 'Catholicism in Edgeley', p.3 and p.5, Undate manuscript held in Stockport Reference Library.
44. Sheridan Gilley, 'The Roman Catholic Mission to the Irish i London', *Recusant History*, vol.10, no.3 (October 1969), p.140.

detailed account of the relationship between the Irish priest and his flock is also contained in W.J. Lowe, 'The Lancashire Irish and the Catholic Church 1846–1871: The Social Dimension', *Irish Historical Studies*, vol.78 (September 1976), pp.129–155.

45. *Manchester Guardian*, 7 July 1852. For good studies of the forging of Irish Catholic culture see Lynn Hollen Lees, *Exiles of Erin: Irish Migrants in Victorian London* (1979), Chapter 7, pp.164–212, and Sheridan Gilley, 'The Catholic Faith of the Irish Slums: London 1840–70', in H.J. Dyos and M. Wolff (eds.), *The Victorian City: Images and Realities*, vol.II (1973), pp.837–853.

46. Geoffrey Best, *Mid–Victorian Britain 1851–75* (1971), p.186.

47. *Report on the State of the Irish Poor in Great Britain, P.P.* (1836), p.87.

48. *Ibid.*, p.86.

49. *Manchester Guardian*, 20 September 1851.

50. 1851 *Population Census*, Stockport, Enumeration District 3–D Middle Ward.

51. E.P. Thompson, *The Making of the English Working Class* (1963), pp.478–80.

52. *Report on the State of the Irish Poor in Great Britain, P.P.* (1836), p.87.

53. J.M. Werly, 'The Irish in Manchester 1832–49', *Irish Historical Studies* vol.xviii, No.71 (March 1973), pp.345–358.

54. 1851 *Population Census*, Stockport.

55. Neville Kirk, 'Ethnicity, Class and Popular Toryism, 1850–1870' in K. Lunn (ed.) *Hosts, Immigrants and Minorities* (1980), p.87, also argues that, although the Irish were not segregated into ghettoes, two Irish neighbourhoods existed in Stockport by 1851.

56. M.A.G. Ó Tuathaigh, p.161, has suggested that economic competition was often a factor in tension between English workers and the immigrant Irish. Nevertheless, it does seem that the *Stockport Advertiser's* claim after the event may not have been entirely objective. It had been one of the main instigators of the religious discord which was a major factor in the riots, and perhaps had a vested interest in turning attention away from this aspect.

57. *Stockport Advertiser*, 9 July 1852.

58. N. Kirk, 'Ethnicity, Class and Popular Toryism', in K. Lunn (ed.), *Hosts, Immigrants and Minorities* (1980), pp.85–6 examines the situation in a number of north–west industrial towns, and argues that English workers believed the Irish lowered wages and, although Kirk considers that these beliefs were not always soundly based, he suggests that they were of great importance to anti–Irish sentiment.

59. The Sixth Report from the Select Committee on Settlement and Poor Removal , *P.P.* (1847), Appendix no.3, Evidence of Stockport's Town Clerk, Henry Coppock, p.330.

60. Select Committee on Poor Removal , *P.P.* (1854), vol.xvii, p.131, p.140, p.632, p.634.

61. Select Committee on Poor Removal, *P.P.* (1847), pp.114 and 115.

62. *Manchester Guardian*, 27 January 1849. See also David Jones, *Crime, Protest, Community and Police in Nineteenth–Century Britain*

(1982), pp.181–182, for a discussion of Irish vagrancy in the late 1840s.
63. *Ibid.*, p.178.
64. Between 1849 and 1852, newspaper reports linked the Irish in Stockport with outbreaks of cholera, smallpox, typhus and 'malignant Irish fever'. See, for example, *Stockport Advertiser*, 17 August 1849; 26 July 1850; *Manchester Guardian*, 4 June 1851; 24 March 1852.
65. Reported in the *Manchester Guardian*, 9 January 1850; 30 January 1850.
66. C.A.N. Reid, *The Chartist Movement in Stockport* (unpublished M.A. Thesis, University of Hull, 1974), p.373.
67. E.g. *The Manchester Guardian*, 23 August 1848, reported that extracts from the *Irish Felon* and the *Northern Star* were read at a Chartist meeting in Stockport.
68. C.A.N. Reid, Thesis, p.310. There is some historical debate about the extent of Irish involvement in the Chartist movement. For each side of the argument see, for example, J.H. Treble, 'O'Connor, O'Connell and the Attitudes of Irish Immigrants towards Chartism in the North of England, 1838–1848', in J. Butt and I.F. Clark (eds.), *The Victorians and Social Protest* (1973), pp.33–70; and Dorothy Thompson, 'Ireland and the Irish in English Radicalism before 1850', in James Epstein and Dorothy Thompson (eds.), *The Chartist Experience: Studies in Working–Class Radicalism and Culture, 1830–60* (1982), pp.120–151.
69. C.A.N. Reid, Thesis, p.310.
70. *Manchester Guardian*, 10 July 1852; *Stockport Advertiser*, 6 August 1847; 16 July 1852.
71. See Kevin O'Connor, *The Irish in Britain*, p.32 and G.I.T. Machin, *Politics and the Churches*, pp.227 and 243.
72. John Stevenson, *Popular Disturbances in England, 1700–1850* (1979), p.280.
73. *Annual Register* (1852), p.90.
74. *Stockport Advertiser*, 9 July 1852.
75. *Manchester Guardian*, 3 July 1852.
76. *Star of Freedom*, 17 July 1852.
77. *Tablet*, 3 July 1852.
78. Kevin O'Connor, *The Irish in Britain*, p.32.
79. G.I.T. Machin, *Politics and the Churches*, p.238.
80. Neville Kirk, 'Ethnicity, Class and Popular Toryism', in Lunn (ed.), *Hosts, Immigrants and Minorities* (1980).
81. *Ibid.*, pp. 84 and 96.
82. Accounts and Papers. Poor: England and Wales, Ireland, Scotland Session 1 February–1 August 1849. HC.1849 (342) vol.xlvii, 579.
83. See John M. Werly, 'The Irish in Manchester, 1832–49'. *Irish Historical Studies*,, vol.71 (1973), pp.235–58.
84. G.I.T. Machin, *Politics and the Churches*, p.218.
85. *Manchester Guardian*, 3 July 1852.
86. George Rudé, *Paris and London in the Eighteenth Century; Studies in Popular Protest* (1974), p.278, p.289.

IRISH AND CATHOLIC: MYTH OR REALITY?

ANOTHER SORT OF IRISH AND THE RENEWAL OF THE CLERICAL PROFESSION AMONG CATHOLICS IN ENGLAND, 1791–1918

Gerard Connolly

> Take an Irishman wherever he is found all over the earth, and any casual observer will at once come to the conclusion, 'Oh! he is an Irishman, he is a Catholic!' The two go together.[1]

Not too long ago this well–known boast of the firebrand Dominican, Tom Burke, proclaiming the virtues of Ireland's Catholic nationhood, would have caused little comment.[2] Far from it, the link between Irish men and women and their majority religious affiliation has usually appeared self–evident to everyone. There is little evidence even now that this link has lost its fascination among scholars, for the claim that Catholicism played a critical part in the formation of Irish society is still without serious question.[3]

Yet while Ireland's essential Catholicism remains an indelible feature of the Irish identity, at home or abroad, the understanding of its nature has not survived unchanged. Historiographical fashions are sometimes short–lived, but recent studies of Irish religious behaviour suggest that the religion of Irish people before the Famine of 1846–49 may not translate quite so neatly as was once imagined into the language of modern Catholic conformism. Indeed, if conformity be strictly defined in terms of Tridentine conformism, there is every reason to suppose that it does not.[4]

The notion of Catholics in Ireland on the eve of the Famine unacquainted with the discipline of Tridentine conformism will be a familiar one to those who have followed the unfolding debate upon the evolution of modern Irish society.[5] How far the description 'non–practising Catholics'[6] (a term originally deployed by Emmet Larkin) describes a majority of Irish Catholics before 1846 is unclear.[7] There can, however, be little doubt that a considerable number of Irish men and women did fit this description,[8] and that these non–practising Catholics were numerous in the population from which emigrants were drawn.

Irish immigration into England and Wales showed a slow but steady rise throughout the first two decades of the nineteenth century, but was given a savage boost after the end of hostilities with France.[9] Between 1820 and 1830, assisted by the post-war introduction of cheap crossings, the numbers reaching the textile weaving towns of northern England climbed so far that by 1834 the Irish-born and their descendants formed around a fifth of the population of Manchester and had established immigrant communities in Ashton-under-Lyne, Stalybridge and Leeds,[10] and in the midlands and the north-east.[11] These migrants, often young, and including some families as well as the usual preponderance of single males, originated in the rural and neighbouring northerly counties of Ireland in and around Ulster, where a contracting domestic textile industry, falling agricultural prices, landlessness and pressure from population increase compelled many to seek their living elsewhere.[12] The majority of Irish emigrants to London before 1830 hailed from Leinster, but in the decade before the Famine the main area of origin was Munster.[13] The Famine and its aftermath saw the peak of Irish emigration to Britain and, while the population outflow to London was still mostly from Munster, Irish emigration to northern England was from Leinster and the bordering counties of Connaught.[14] It is not easy to provide a rule of thumb for so slippery a subject as Irish emigration, but the evidence suggests that most Irish emigrants to England came from the central and eastern districts of Ireland.[15]

Recent studies have, however, identified as the regions varying widely in their religious observance the Irish north-west, west and south-west, and these were marginal contributors to emigration almost until the early twentieth century.[16] Does this imply that most of the Irish arriving in nineteenth-century England did not have quite so much in common with Emmet Larkin's pre-Famine generation of non-practising Catholics as has been presumed?[17] Did Ireland export a greater proportion of modern 'devout' Catholics from Leinster and Munster to sustain, as legend has it, a flagging native Catholicism in England?[18] These questions do not lend themselves to ready answers. All the same, it is important to ask, as the Catholicism of the migrants was an essential feature, perhaps *the* most essential feature, in virtually every assessment of Irish life abroad.

Standards of religious observance among baptized Catholics on the British mainland during the century of Catholic expansion in the wake of the 1791 Relief Act have never been submitted to profound investigation.[19] The notion of widespread Irish abstention from Catholic ritual in England is one that has remained very much on the dark side of the moon.[20] Local instances of high or low levels of performance of religious duties have caught the eye, and it might seem that there exists little beyond haphazard and isolated observation, but it is still possible to construct a provisional picture from the anecdotes and patchy statistics now available.[21]

Possibly the most thorough scrutiny of Irish immigrants on the British mainland is the study of Victorian London's Irish community by Lynn Lees.[22] It is a competent and thoughtful assessment, and though her treatment of Catholicism is marred by her preoccupation with the ground rules of American urban sociology,[23] it is to her credit that she squares up to the problem of bringing order to conflicting accounts of immigrant religious habits in nineteenth–century London. To the bold question, 'What proportion of London Catholics participated actively in the rituals or organisation of their church?', she provides the convincing reply that 'the rate of participation remained low'.[24] According to her statistical surveys and estimates,[25] regular Catholic practice in Victorian London never much exceeded 30%, on average, of the total baptized population,[26] while at the beginning of the period, Easter Duty may have encompassed as few as 10%.[27] Lees herself is quick to acknowledge that these figures place Irish Catholics very much behind their English Protestant counterparts in any comparison of churchgoing behaviour,[28] and this in London, to which most migrants were drawn from the more 'practising' Catholic counties of Ireland.[29]

Of course, this is a very one–sided summary of Lees. Her account of the probable scope of Catholic practice has a great deal more to it than crude statistical reductionism, and while not pretending to be exhaustive also gives a proper place to the mitigating elements of this story.[30] But the evaluation of Irish Catholic practice in London, quite independent of Lees, by Jean Lesourd,[31] is equally unfavourable. His conclusions are a good deal better based upon quantitative data than hers, but are strikingly similar.[32] Modern Catholic practice, measured as Tridentine discipline, remained sluggish among the metropolitan Catholic population in the mid–nineteenth century by comparison with the north of England, and possibly attracted no more than a third of the total number of baptized Catholics.[33]

There is also non–statistical evidence of a low level of Catholic religious participation among the London Irish.[34] Both Lees and Lesourd quote serving Catholic clergy in the thick of it, and although these missionaries may have exaggerated the size of Irish non–attendance at Mass, they understood better than any the difficulty of mounting a successful mission to the non–practising immigrant. The same complaints were made by clergy throughout the British mainland, especially after 1820.[35]

In summer 1835, William Bond, an English missioner, educated at the English College at Lisbon, travelled home via Ireland to take up his first posting, the meagre and demanding mission of Swansea, in South Wales.[36] While in Ireland, Bond observed at close quarters a native funeral of the more edifying variety, and was so moved by this demonstration of popular devotion that he wrote to his former Rector at Lisbon, Edmund Winstanley, describing his uplifting experience.[37] Regrettably, Bond also related his sobering, down to earth feeling on arriving to minister to the 4–500 mostly immigrant Irish in his congregation at Swansea:

> The chapel is small and in a most dilapidated state, part even of the roof has already given way. Some money has been collected to build a new one but I feel it will scarcely suffice to cover the expenses we shall be obliged to go to in repairing the old one. My salary is about 75 pounds annual. (To myself I say I am truly miserable). I tremble at every step I take, and how long I

> shall remain in this state, God only knows, but if I continue long I shall without doubt make my humble petition to his Lordship, to free me from my anxiety and give me some other employment. I do my best however to keep up my courage and spirits. My Revd. friend, you have had a great deal of experience with the Irish, give me some advice. They come to me and say they have not confessed for 2, 3, or 4 years, and yet they have nothing to tell you. I question them and yet all you can get from them is that they don't say their prayers or come to chapel. What is to be done with them?[38]

In fairness, Bond was wet behind the ears, and a rather whimpering creature, unsuited to the rough and tumble of the urban missioner's life.[39] But though his predicament is open to more than one interpretation, a picture of ostensibly casual Irish piety not necessarily connected with regular church attendance can be gleaned from his disgruntled remarks, and it will strike a chord with those who have examined other sources for the study of Irish Catholicism on the ground at this time.[40] Derek Homes suggests that in nearby Cardiff, where the Catholic mission had a similar constituency, something like 25% of the total Catholic baptized population performed their Easter duty between 1841 and 1861, despite the improving efforts of resident missioners.[41]

Of a more robust frame of mind was another Lisboan, Thomas Rimmer, charged with the mission at Nottingham.[42] Again writing to Edmund Winstanley in 1840, Rimmer shows the leanings of the missioners, particularly those employed among the urban poor, faced with the mass indigence caused by a local recession.[43] He was far from hostile to the Chartists active among his congregation, and assured his old superior that he would soon become 'a Radical' had he to work amid the poverty endemic in Nottingham.[44] The Irish were the centre of his attention, and he was sufficiently respected among them to be called to intervene in marital disputes.[45] He summarized the general religious situation in Nottingham in 1840:

> Nottingham contains about 60,000 inhabitants. The Catholic body amounts to 1,000 English and Irish. I speak of those who attend chapel. Also there are many Irish who do not attend.[46]

According to later estimates of religious practice in the Diocese of Nottingham by Garret Sweeney, there was an awesome number of baptized Catholics who had set aside all visible allegiance to Catholicism by the final decade of the nineteenth century.[47] Jean Lesourd thinks that the situation was somewhat less drastic, but he has calculated that fewer than half the baptized Catholic population practised between 1851 and 1878.[48]

The extenuating circumstances of Irish absence from Catholic services have all had a generous airing; unfamiliarity with native Catholicism in England and Wales; lack of confidence in its clergy; initial want of chapels and failure to recognise them as valid Catholic churches; the oft-quoted embarrassment of having no decent clothes.[49] But however plausible any one of these might be, considered in isolation, none of them offers more than a very partial explanation as to why a staggering number of baptized Catholic Irish men and women in Britain neglected to avail themselves of obligatory Catholic ritual. What is needed is a detailed study of just how extensive and serious was the problem of Irish non–practice on the English Mission in the first fifty years of sustained immigration from Ireland,[50] by reference to standards of Catholic observance in the heartland of the Mission, the increasing urban concentration of native and immigrant Catholics in northern England.

Certain conclusions, however, already seem clear. First, among Irish immigrants in the boom towns of northern England – Manchester, Liverpool, Wigan, Huddersfield, Leeds, Bradford, Sunderland and Newcastle – possibly fewer than 30% were acquainted with the discipline of modern Tridentine conformism between 1790 and the early 1840s.[51] Second, this situation contrasted sharply with levels of Catholic practice among native English Catholics; some parts of Lancashire were turning into communities of almost total adherence, with an average possibly as high as 70% for the English Catholic population of northern England.[52] Third, and hardly surprisingly, rapid Irish immigration between 1820 and 1830 pushed the baptized Catholic population of the ecclesiastical division in the north from about 119,000 in 1814 to 190,000 in 1832, diluting and reducing overall levels of Catholic practice in the north and provoking a crisis on the Mission.[53] In fact, so grave was the emergency that it gave rise to private fears among English missioners of Irish immigration causing a sacramental collapse in the crucial theatre of missionary activity.[54] Finally, that this did not happen, and that from the early 1840s onwards there began a gradual though limited recovery, restoring practice levels to roughly half the total baptized population beyond the huge intake from the Irish Famine, has to do as much with the personal heroism of English–born missioners as external circumstances, or the employment of Irish clergy seconded to the Mission.[55]

This, then was the experience of the English Mission between the last decades of the eighteenth and the first half of the nineteenth century. A glimpse of how this translated into the lives of the missioners themselves can be had by way of the stories from the front line.[56] As early as 1806, Rowland Broomhead, in Manchester, expressed amazement at discovering so many Irish who did not frequent the Sacraments; some of them up to forty years away from their last Confession or Eucharist.[57] His successors, meanwhile, by 1828, on the eve of celebrating the public triumph of Catholic Emancipation, found less room for astonishment than consternation over the fact that perhaps as few as one in seven of the baptized Catholic population of their chapels in Manchester actually attended services.[58] At Ashton–under–Lyne, the missioner, James Fisher, had built a church to seat 1,000 amid an Irish population of 4,000, but found it regularly less than half full – and himself very much out of pocket.[59] John Briggs, appointed Vicar Apostolic in the Northern District in 1836, and before that Coadjutor Bishop, administered Confirmation to thousands of Catholics throughout the late 1830s and described himself as taken aback at the number of Irish, 'rounded up' by the local clergy, who were of advanced age even for this adult ceremony.[60] A confidence to Paul Cullen, later known to have become hard–bitten on this subject, in 1842, reveals the Catholic clergy in Liverpool of the opinion that barely a tenth of their overwhelmingly Irish–baptized Catholic population (supposedly of 100,000) practised to any recognizable degree.[61] By contrast, sometime earlier, the missioner in Newcastle, James Worswick, had occasion to record with some puzzlement his encounter with an apparently Catholic Irishman who had never been with a priest![62] Small wonder then that upon opening St. Patrick's in Irish Town on the outskirts of Manchester, to serve probably the largest immigrant ghetto outside of London or Liverpool, the Irish missioner Daniel Hearne's initial problem was to fill it.[63]

Much of the evidence presented by Catholic clergy to the Commissioners investigating the Irish poor of the mainland in 1834 tells a similar story.[64] The reports of (Irish) Christian Brothers, drafted into England to help remedy what some English missioners thought the scandalous state of immigrant religious practice in the towns, are equally explicit about the magnitude of the problem.[65] Even information relative to success for the missioner, 'conversion' on a pronounced scale, serves also to highlight the size of the remaining task as well as leaving one to wonder how many 'converts' in nineteenth–century parlance were actually converts from another creed:

> By sending out the poor boys on Sundays to instruct poor people in lots of different directions, we were able to impart instructions to about 2,000 each week. So numerous were the conversions that the priests could not conveniently attend all.[66]

In view of the concentration of the Catholic baptized population in the north and what has been said already of London, it would seem, therefore, safe to argue that the fortunes of Catholics in northern England describe the experience of the Catholic community countrywide.[67] In short, immigration from Ireland reduced a thriving native Catholicism in England, at least momentarily, to a rather sorry state, and this in the very area of its established strength, practice: thereby threatening the long–term credibility of Catholicism on the British mainland as a religion of regular observance.

So much, then, for the persistent blarney that has Irish men and women revitalise, in the nick of time, a moribund Catholicism over the water in a heathen land. The truth was quite the contrary. There was, however, more to the problem than the often grim statistics. These are no more than a rough guide, and this same analysis also provides clear evidence of an upturn in practice as the English Mission began to get to grips with its task.[68] Certainly by the latter half of the century, this improvement, most visible in the north, had gone a good way towards making immigration a major element in transforming the expectations of Catholics throughout mainland Britain. Within the space of little more than fifty years, Catholics in England acquired a self–confidence unthinkable at the onset of the nineteenth century; hence the outrageous notion of the conversion of

England; much of it, and its direction, due to the impact of immigration from Ireland. W.J. Lowe's recent assumption that a conversion of religious habits on a scale which prompted Emmet Larkin to speak of a 'devotional revolution' among baptized Catholics in Ireland had no parallel among immigrants settled in the Lancashire towns of Victorian England may be correct.[69] But his discovery of levels of practice variously around 40% to 60% in Liverpool, Widnes, St. Helens and Preston between 1855 and 1871 looks like progress compared with the first quarter of the century rather than the failure which he seems to suggest.[70] And while it would be taking a liberty to describe this modest turn–about as a 'revolution', this is not a reason to undervalue the achievement of the English Mission.[71] In Ireland, where the Catholic population was nearly halved, the clergy achieved spectacular success, in persuading Irish men and women to attend services more regularly by the last decades of the nineteenth century.[72] In England, faced with a corresponding eightfold increase in baptized Catholics during the same period, the gains were understandably rather less pronounced.[73] In view of the different circumstances, however, both the Irish and English churches had equal cause for satisfaction.

Admittedly, further south unambiguous evidence of revival is a great deal more difficult to find. Jean Lesourd insists that London's Catholic community never attained the levels of practice notable in the north, settling at around 30% of the baptized Catholic population and, in so far as it is possible to judge, remaining thereabouts until the end of the nineteenth century.[74]

Other sources support this.[75] More pertinent, perhaps, is the likelihood that an average ratio of practice of 50% to 60% for the community as a whole represents, give or take temporary fluctuations, the broad limit of the Catholic restoration.[76] It would seem that the upward trend of recovery reached a plateau during the 1880s, when Catholic concern over what was dubbed 'leakage' became a matter of public debate within the community, and at that level, religious practice stuck there.[77]

This, in summary, was the state of Irish Catholic practice on the major part of the British mainland in the nineteenth century. There is plenty missing from the picture by way of definition, and this is not the only possible overview of events. But as Geoffrey Elton has said, the historian's task is not to pine after theological truth but to seek to strike the balance of reasonableness. There can be no doubt but that Irish immigration into England depressed the high standards of practice of the small English Catholic community, and attempts to restore these standards among a predominantly Irish community had to make do with a lower level of attainment.

If, then, it can be accepted that Catholic practice in England held fast at between 50% and 60% of the total baptized population by the latter decades of the nineteenth century, applying a mean of 55% to the more reliable estimates of baptized Catholics in England and Wales at that time, around 1,500,000, the body of practising Catholics works out, in real terms, at slightly in excess of 800,000.[78] Of these, a substantial majority would have been of Irish birth or descent; though just what this might mean, again in real terms, is difficult to quantify. Irrespective of the obvious pitfalls, a provisional figure can be attained by subtracting a projection of practising English Catholics, 200,000, suggesting an Irish contingent of 600,000.[79] By placing alongside a conjectural Irish presence in England and Wales during the final quarter of the last century, something like 1,500,000, less a speculative reckoning for Irish Protestants, 300,000, the possible size of an Irish Catholic baptized but non-practising population on the English Mission[80] emerges at about 600,00, or 50%.[81] Putting this another way, there seems to have been an evens chance that as many as half the Irish Catholic baptized population failed to persevere with the practice of their inherited religion in England and Wales,[82] continuing, with some, a pattern begun in Ireland.

All this is very tentative, and none of the figures included here ought to be taken too literally. On the other hand, they are respectable estimates, with much to commend them, and all suggested proportions are consonant with what is known of Irish immigrant studies.[83] Taken together, they might be said to translate into a reasonably accurate impression of Irish religious habits on the English Mission in the later decades of the nineteenth century.

But this poses a crucial question. If there is a serious possibility that a half of the Irish immigrants in the towns of England and Wales did not practise their religion to any marked extent, where does this leave the hallowed notion of 'Irish and Catholic', presumed by so many commentators to have been a relationship inseparable from the immigrant experience?[84] The answer might be that if there is a proper Protestant claim to a share in an Irish expatriate identity, with the experience of the non-practising Catholic, then *perhaps* the high profile maintained by Catholicism among immigrants may seem much less impressive after all.[85]

The *perhaps* here is suggested by another dimension beyond that of primitive arithmetic which also demands attention. It has to do with the nature of Catholicism itself, which cannot be stripped to the lowest common denominator of ritual fulfilment. Though, indubitably, positive disassociation from religion does have a place among all immigrants, a succession of recent historians of Irish religious behaviour has been at pains to underline the fallacy of identifying non-practice with indifference to Catholicism, or worse, with irreligion,[86] as did, for perfectly sound motives, many clergy of the English Mission.[87] Counter-Reformation idealism, with its emphasis on observable sacramental habit, was designed in part to put the damper on rowdy expressions of popular culture which threatened to bypass the ministrations of an official clergy and thereby get out of control, and for a variety of reasons it seems not to have caught hold in Ireland.[88] Had the missioners of The Society, who were busy in Munster in 1617, and who recorded, one senses with some Latin indignation, extensive acceptance in sections of Irish society of, at most, annual Communion and the fabled 'lifetime Confession', been permitted to return to their charge in the years before the Irish Famine, they would no doubt have recognised their task unfinished.[89] Catholicism in Ireland retained certain features of what has been vaguely called a 'folk religion' long after Catholics elsewhere had conformed to modernity.[90] The latter term may be taken to include consistent attendance at Sunday Mass in the parish church and a basic grasp of the catechetical mechanics of Christian spiritual welfare.[91]

If words are chosen carefully, this claim need cause no disagreement. For a significant sector of the population of Ireland in the second half of the nineteenth century, religious intuition involved attitudes qualitatively different from the discipline of Tridentine Catholicism.[92] Again, that is not to say better or worse: simply different. Numbers of Catholics in Ireland may have remained, and assuredly did remain, personally devout without frequent recourse to the Sacraments, and maybe even with only minimal contact with the official Church.[93] To talk of neglect of practice in such circumstances is, perhaps, to saddle one body of people with the value judgements of another. The very fact that Irish immigrants on the British mainland boasted of their loyalty to Catholicism while absolving themselves of key aspects of Catholic duty, as in the case of Henry Mayhew's Irish Crossing Sweep, reinforces the point:

> I go to Somers Town chapel being a Catholic for I'm not ashamed to own my religion before any man. When I go it is at siven in the morning. Sometimes I go to St. Patrick's Chapel, Soho Square. I have not been to Confission for two or three years.[94]

An illustration of just how far it is possible to take this general understanding of widespread Irish non-practice is offered by John ó Ríordáin's *Irish Catholics*.[95] Ireland's devotion to Catholicism was by tradition inseparable from Celtic culture, at its most intense as an expression of that culture, and suffered the same disorientation when, in the nineteenth century, Celtic society finally gave way to a more thrusting Anglo-Saxon modernism[96]. In other words the much trumpeted revolution in churchgoing habits brought about among the post-Famine Irish was a development out of step with the Irish heritage, having more in common with fundamentally English sentiments, a sign of the latter's imperialism.[97] From here it is but a short step to imagine the alienation of the loyal Irish Catholic, marooned in a foreign religious environment.[98]

Sub-titled *Tradition and Transition*, ó Ríordáin's work is manifestly, and by his own admission, *not* that of the dispassionate historian, and it is very often difficult to decipher what, if any, criterion of judgement is being exercised beyond a highly emotional nostalgia for something the author is keen on calling 'the ancient faith of the Irish', (a term used so frequently puts the reader in mind of Flan O'Brien's 'plain people of Ireland').[99] But the notion that what is depicted here with unseemly relish as Anglo-Saxon imposition on native Irish spirituality is one that has found a ready audience, notably in the United States, whence comes ó Ríordáin's encouragement.[100] Given this kind of rehabilitation, it may be possible to envisage non-practising Catholics at some future date credited with the maintenance of the authentic tradition of orthodox Irish Christianity.[101]

Ignoring the eccentric slant of ó Ríodáin's proposition, and the extravagant, sometimes preposterous language employed in its service, the gist of what he is saying is far from flippant.[102] The traditionalism of Irish men and women that had amounted to an unwillingness to separate too rigidly the sacred and profane, in consequence convinced them to look upon holiness as *objective*, and therefore, to an extent, *tangible*, and therefore *negotiable*.[103] This was not at all the same as moral obligation.[104] Those interested to explore further in this direction may care to look also at the peculiarly Irish concept of *pobal Dé*.[105] In as much as such traits can be thought to apply to the Irish of the British mainland, however, this point of view has been made to carry greater credibility as well as being couched in rather more subtle fashion by Sheridan Gilley, who prefers to emphasise a perceptible level of general faithfulness among Irish immigrants, irrespective of their compliance with religious stipulations.[106] The description given, again by Henry Mayhew, of an Irish lodging–house keeper in nineteenth–century London, though never actually used by Gilley, would probably count as a fair indication of the sort of impression he seeks to create.[107] And this emphatically so, as the character concerned here is female and such evidence as exists relative to this subject would appear to favour the idea that Catholicism drew the major part of its vitality from the loyalty of women:[108]

> The old woman who kept this lodging house had endeavoured to give it a homely look of comfort by hanging little black frames and pictures scarcely bigger than pocket books on the walls. Most of these were sacred subjects with large yellow glories around their heads; though between the drawing representing the bleeding heart of Christ and the Saviour bearing the Cross was an illustration of a red coated sailor smoking a pipe. The adoration of the shepherds again was matched on the other side of the fireplace by a portrait of Daniel O'Connell.[109]

A readily recognizable vignette: and one, moreover, which may prove more persuasive than any bevy of statistics. On the other hand, Gilley is the first to admit that a generalisation based around this sort of evocation can and does include a substantial number of those for whom Catholicism was in many respects incidental.[110] Were they Catholics in any meaningful sense of the word? Under the circumstances it may be unwise to attempt too confident a response. Nonetheless any useful definition of a Catholic, even in the notoriously ambiguous zone of popular religious mentalities, must stand for something more affirmative than a back–projection of residual willingness of good intent.[111] The reason, one feels simply therefore, is that despite the high profile and unmistakable identity adopted by the Catholic Church in England and Wales during the second half of the nineteenth century, and the clear link of that identity with its role as a major – to some observers *the* major – agency of Irish cultural life in mainland Britain, still a huge proportion of

Irish, most of them baptized Catholics, chose either to reject or ignore the Church's publicised standards for membership criteria.[112] And while this may not be the same as saying that such Irish remained uninfluenced by Catholicism, it does suggest that as an advertisement for the quintessence of Irishness abroad it is not difficult to picture the institutional Catholic Church as having left a significant section of the immigrant population conspicuously unmoved. Even those who insist that the priest's word must have carried weight beyond the ranks of churchgoers, will need to explain why these Irish who ignored the stern dictates of organised Catholicism should have heeded its secular authority.[113]

The following conclusions may be drawn. First, there is a need for a more rigorous quantitative analysis to corroborate the outline here presented, particularly in relation to the non–practising baptized Catholics among the immigrant Irish of England and Wales. This I hope to provide in the not too far distant future.[114] Second, it would appear safe to say that non–practising baptized Catholics formed a substantial and perhaps distinct contingent of the Irish immigrant population, and historians may find it profitable to look beyond a crude distinction between Catholics and Protestants, one the throng and the other from beyond the fringe, towards the possibility of a third category of Irish. And while it would be naive to predict that this category could emerge with the unequivocal characteristics of the former two (it would, for example have to accommodate both Catholics and Protestants similarly distanced from the constraints of public religion), this need not dissuade anyone from taking its existence seriously,[115] as seriously as did the clergy of the English Mission.

There can be no doubt but that baptized Catholic non–practice among the Irish was *the* central issue for the clergy of the English Mission during the nineteenth century.[116] However fascinating such phenomena as the Oxford Movement, or the Modernist Crisis, for the institutional Catholic Church in England these are sideshows by comparison with this, the darker side to the providence of immigration from Ireland.[117] Moreover, having identified the problem first in private and then more openly, the missioners seem to have recognised this fully, through a century of effort to contain a haemorrhage to the Catholic body in England.[118] Such disquiet, the cause of some uncharacteristic plain speaking on the subject by certain clergy, is not difficult to understand.[119] This apart, however, those seeking to put into perspective the emergence of a mightily reinvigorated clerical profession in Victorian England, especially among Catholics, might come to consider Irish non–practice as an intriguing challenge to its omnicompetence, consequently rewarding consideration from this viewpoint alone.[120]

Questions of status and ties of solidarity as between different groups of clergy and society in England have been the subject of recent discussion by historians.[121] The process which restored the prestige to the calling of cleric in Victorian society (due to one belonging to a professional elite) achieved a state of fine tune among the Catholic priesthood by virtue of their claim, via an aggressiv sacerdotalism, to a sacramental monopoly.[122] Thus, having been give something of a hard time by the upper echelons of their native laity the clergy of the English Mission had more cause than most to welcom the arrival of Irish men and women, in theory more dependent and to degree more compliant clients for clerical services.[123] It was amon these immigrants that the Catholic clergy were able to build jurisdictional power–base that was to give them undisputed leadershi of a community over which they had squabbled for power with the lait for nearly three centuries in England, and which, the more forcefull after 1850, they fashioned to resemble a Church, with its accent upo clerical office–holders, their pervading authority, and exclusiv conditions of membership.[124]

There are bound to be those who will find this a rather harsh possibly calculating view of a body of men who rescued the Englis Mission from possible disaster and in many cases paid with their live in doing so.[125] In defence, one must insist on the ofte contradictory promptings of vocation and profession, and a protracte experience of a measure of lay autonomy which had possibly made th clergy of the English Mission zealous for a chance to try out the fu rigour of Tridentine priesthood.[126] Moreover, the clergy displaye even greater anxiety that the laity should be made to try it ou also.[127] When the opportunity came, as it did with the arrival of majority Irish constituency throughout the new urban missions o England, the Catholic clergy, inspired by the spirit of the age seized it with unbecoming alacrity.[128]

It is plain to see where Irish non–practice fits into thi story. The realization that a large number, indeed before 1850 thumping majority, of Irish baptized Catholics were getting by someho with at most the bare essentials of clerical ministration, acted a the keenest rub to an impatient generation of clergy with a collectiv urge for self–improvement.[129] The very existence of many non-practising Irish with a loyalty to Catholicism which involved a sor of 'do–it–yourself religion' must have seemed a challenge to ambitiou clerical Young Turks more fateful tha n apostasy itself.[130] For there is a single notion likely to send the ranks of a profession int a state of near–derangement, it is the prospect of client self-reliance.[131]

At Manchester, Irish non–practice appeared from the earliest a its most provocative, inciting the first organised attempt by th Catholic clergy at self–assertion.[132] Gathering in five or s districts, the two best–known and the more ghetto–like of which, Iris Town and Little Ireland, resembled wholly–owned Irish fiefdoms, th Manchester Irish from the outset led a life removed from th generality of local society, the object of some curiosity and of mor than their fair share of gratuitous hostility.[133] There was much o this last since a mark of the Irish community in Manchester was it less obvious imbalance between immigrant Catholic and Protestant – perhaps about 60% to 40% respectively – during the earlier decades o the nineteenth century than was later the case, as a legacy of tha early heavy immigration from Ireland's northern counties.[134] In 1833, an independent census conducted in Irish Town by the Tipperary–born missioner, Daniel Hearne, enumerated 11,000 baptized Catholics within an immigrant Irish population of 20,000.[135] Moreover, Hearne counted but 'a few hundred' of these regularly at Mass, a problem which had dogged his fellow missioners at the town's three other chapels, and which had prompted the establishment of St. Patrick's, Hearne's chapel, or church as he preferred to call it, as part of a drive against immigrant baptized Catholic non–practice.[136] In 1830 the baptized Catholic population of Manchester probably stood at around 30,000, possibly up to three–quarters of them of Irish birth or descent.[137] By contrast, the effective congregation may have dipped to as low as 7–8,000,[138] including the English Catholics, who had a good record for consistent practice.

Despite religious communal tensions and sporadic violence among the Manchester Irish, especially when the annual July Beargarden got out of control – Manchester has the dubious honour of introducing to the public of the British mainland as early as 1807 the sort of seasonal headbreaking a feature of July in parts of Ireland – relations between local Catholics and Protestants at institutional level had begun in the nineteenth century as moderately good.[139] Though subject to stress during the period of prolonged reaction against liberalism following the outbreak of war with France, local Catholics kept their heads above water largely due to their participation in patriotic jingoism and a fund of goodwill towards them from a more tolerant past.[140] A major reason for this last was the respect accorded to Rowland Broomhead, their senior missioner for over forty years, between 1778 and 1820. Broomhead was an active figure, welcomed at every level of Manchester society, from almsgiving on the streets to chairmanship of many of the town's most prestigious inter–denominational civic agencies, servicing education, poor relief and community health.[141]

But behind the jovial image of the hearty priest at ease with rich and poor, Rowland Broomhead was one of many Catholic clergy to experience for the first time in England since the sixteenth century the full possibilities afforded the Christian missionary in society, and he was daring, perhaps even ruthless, in his determination to exploit them.[142] Chief amongst these possibilities was the prospect that, after 1791, the Catholic priest would be able to perform his missionary duties without obstruction. Second only to this was the chance for a body of men, growing in the confidence of professionalism, to move against their main rivals for the leadership of England's Catholics.[143] Thus, while heading Manchester's powerful Committee for the Relief of the Poor, or personally directing its Quarterly Medical Board, Rowland Broomhead was equally industrious among his own community,[144] yet here his talents seem to have been diverted into the service of something a good deal less magnanimous. Drawing aside funds from lay administration; replacing (or, more accurately, not replacing) lay chapel trustees in favour of sole clerical management; advancing the cause of episcopal monarchy, and abetting every measure which might assist in clipping the heels of lay autonomy, Rowland Broomhead was assiduous in the early service of that clerical expansionism which, by the close of the nineteenth century, had swept the authority of the priest to encompass all, including the most intimate of lay activities.[145]

During Broomhead's lifetime this process of clerical aggrandizement remained relatively low key, and had little effect upon ties with local Protestants.[146] But by 1820 the rising tide of immigration from Ireland, bringing with it the phenomenon of the non-practising baptized Catholic on a scale previously unknown in England, had the missioners distinctly edgy.[147] The progressive sense of professional solidarity which had gripped the Catholic clergy also influenced a Protestant ministry, feeling the pull of an era of aggressive advancement and expressing it through such organs as the Manchester and Salford Auxiliary Bible Society; the Manchester Religious Tract Society; or the much abused local Hibernian Society, all of them constituted specifically to put the cleric in contact with the seemingly new market of mass irreligion.[148] Given the complexion of nineteenth-century religious attitudes in England, the 'ir-religious' now included the huge numbers of non-practising Irish baptized Catholics which the missioners, hampered among other things by want of resources, found it so difficult to reach.[149] Although Protestantism was to prove singularly unappealing to the vast majority of Irish immigrants, Catholic churchgoers or no,[150] many Catholic clergy feared that their clients might be poached from under their noses.[151] And with both Catholic and Protestant ministries charged with the same sense of destiny, the outcome was wholly predictable, starting with a Catholic pre-emptive strike in Manchester.[152]

Perhaps the name most closely associated with this Catholic Jihad against all things Protestant which began with Manchester's notorious – and bitter – 'Bible Controversy' in 1820, is that of Joseph Curr, who arrived there as Broomhead's assistant shortly before the latter's death in the same year.[153] Curr's frontal assault on local Protestantism, his uncompromising belligerence in Liverpool, and his participation in the unpleasantness at Thorpton in Northumberland, and in his native Sheffield, need not be spelt out here,[154] but his activities suggest that Catholic clerical ambition was finding another gear. From roughly 1820 onwards, there began to spread throughout the English Mission a clamour, orchestrated by Catholic clergy, to head off what they perceived as the Protestant menace, usually among the Irish poor, by recourse to affirmative action amounting to an attempt to shut down lay society with non-Catholics outside of their supervision.[155]

Other considerations are involved here, and it might be said that the Catholic clergy simply learnt to live with the inevitable. Despite this, however, there can be no question but that a drive to redefine the Catholic relationship with English society, which was under way with the publication of Joseph Curr's *Familiar Instructions in the Faith and Morality of the Catholic Church* in 1827, and which was the pretext of a backdoor introduction among Catholics in England of measures of a Tridentine character likely to bolster the authority of the priest, took its cue from the exposure of Irish men and women to Protestant blandishments.[156] This state of affairs was at its most acute with those Irish unknowing or unwilling to make the standards of Catholic affirmation acceptable to the clergy.

This onrush of clergy did not score its supreme and ultimate public triumph until the translation of that clerical steamhammer, Herbert Vaughan, to the Archbishopric of Westminster in 1892.[157] Vaughan had the instincts of the English missioner at heart, having served his apprenticeship as Bishop of Salford, and he brought to his office a much greater realization of the preoccupations of the English missionary clergy than either of his predecessors. Under Vaughan the professional and pastoral concerns of Catholic clergymen came to the fore of the Catholic community in England as a matter of agreed policy, a reflection of Vaughan's determination to put to good use lessons on the size of the problem of 'leakage' most of it undoubtedly Irish – learnt from the streets of Manchester and Salford.[158] This culminated in the English clergy taking charge of the direction of Catholicism in England, in the publicised dismissal of Anglican Orders, in the harsh words of the 'Joint Pastoral' of 1900, in *Ne Temere*, and in the Code of Canon Law of 1917–18, a final notice that the Catholic community in England and Wales was under new clerical management.[159]

Long before this, however, the clergy of the Mission had snuffed out the last flickerings of lay independence. Education and the regulation of private sexuality were perhaps the critical conquests from the laity, and provide good illustrations of the effective transfer of power over the Catholic community after 1850.[160] The point is made in Peter Doyle's highly pertinent – not to say highly amusing – suggestion that the clergy of Alexander Goss, the doughty but likeable Bishop of Liverpool between 1856 and 1872, may have found it difficult to take seriously his countless exhortations to win themselves a place among society's learned, since his addresses to the laity treated education as something akin to forbidden fruit.[161] Even for this school builder, no mean scholar in his own right, 'Holy Ignorance' retained a mystical quality strangely relevant to lay men and women. Apropos of the same point, though less amusing, are the twelve or so pages of marital regulations introduced by Joseph Curr into a catechetical manual aimed primarily at children.[162] Predictably, he also seems to have shared Goss's fondness, where the laity were concerned, for keeping things under his own hat, or mitre. Curr was at the forefront of those pressing for a return to Latin to replace English at Catholic services in England, and in his *Familiar Instructions* left no one in any doubt as to the necessity of reinstating his profession's technical vocabulary:

Q. Is this not inconvenient to the faithful?

A. No it is not, for though many of the faithful may not understand Latin, because of the instructions

> which they received from their pastor, they know that the value of the Mass consists not in prayers but in the oblation which the priest as minister of God offers to Him.[163]

The above is the merest sketch of a complex picture embracing issues too far removed from the subject of Irish immigrants to warrant discussion here. It is, however, enough to indicate first, that Irish non–practice has another dimension beyond that of fascination with the fluctuations of immigrant religious behaviour, or the possibilities of secular politics: and second, that the complications of the recent history of the Catholic community of the British mainland and the arrival of the Irish men and women in the new Victorian cities involved more than the happy task of marshalling the forces of overnight Catholic growth.

So then; Irish and Catholic: Myth or Reality? In truth both notions have much to commend them. Nothing has been said of the incontrovertible reality of the thousands of Irish men and women who *did* practise their religion faithfully, swelling the congregations of virtually every Catholic chapel and church of their new home.[164] But on behalf of those less affirmative, however, it must be said that there was a different sort of Irishness from that which Tom Burke found so much to his liking, and there awaits a respectable hearing for the contention that the history and character of Catholicism in England was possibly dictated as much by those Irish men and women who did not practise their religion as by the fabled masses who did. Whether this was an entirely positive development is, of course, another matter. But it is well to conclude with a paradox about a people who have so often overturned assumptions about them.

Notes

1. T.N.A. Burke, 'The Supernatural Life of the Irish People', *Lectures on Faith and the Fatherland* (Cameron and Ferguson, London, 1874), p.117.
2. P.O'Farrell, *England and Ireland Since 1800* (Oxford University Press, Oxford, 1975), p.150.
3. J.R. Hill, 'Nationalism and the Catholic Church in the 1840s: views of Dublin repealers', *Irish Historical Studies*, vol.l9 (1975), pp.371–95.
4. H.O. Evennett, *The Spirit of the Counter Reformation* (Cambridge University Press, Cambridge, 1968), pp.23–43, 89–125; cf. A.D. Wright, *The Counter Reformation* (Weidenfeld and Nicholson, London, 1982), pp.1–83, 186–222.
5. E. Larkin, 'The Devotional Revolution in Ireland, 1850–75', *American Historical Review*, vol.77 (1972), pp.625–52 (henceforth cited as Larkin); D.W. Miller, 'Irish Catholicism and the Great Famine', *Journal of Social History* vol.9 (1975), pp.81–98 (henceforth cited as Miller); Donal Kerr, 'The Early Nineteenth Century: Patterns of

Change', in M. Maher (ed.), *Irish Spirituality* (Veritas, Dublin, 1981), pp.135–44; and D. Kerr, *Peel, Priests and Politics: Sir Robert Peel's Administration and the Roman Catholic Church in Ireland, 1841–1846* (Clarendon Press, Oxford, 1982), pp.47 ff.
6. For a dissenting voice, see D.J. Keenan, *The Catholic Church in Nineteenth–Century Ireland: A Sociological Study* (Gill and Macmillan, Dublin, 1984) (henceforth cited as Keenan).
7. Larkin, pp.635–9.
8. Miller, pp.83–8; S.J. Connolly, *Priests and People in Pre–Famine Ireland, 1780–1845* (Gill and Macmillan, Dublin, 1982), pp.74–134 (henceforth cited as S.J. Connolly).
9. *Royal Commission on the Condition of the Poorer Classes in Ireland: Appendix G, The State of the Irish Poor in Great Britain, 1836* vol.xxiv (40), pp.1–164; G.P. Connolly, *Catholicism in Manchester and Salford, 1770–1850* (unpublished Ph.D. Thesis, 3 vols, University of Manchester, 1980), vol.1, pp.129–56, 414–22; R.E. Kennedy, *The Irish: Emigration, Marriage, Fertility* (University of California Press, Berkeley 1973), p.27; G. O'Brien, *The Economic History of Ireland from the Union to the Famine* (Longmans, London, 1921), pp.222–32; S.H. Cousens, 'The Regional Variation in Emigration from Ireland between 1821 and 1841)', *Transactions and Papers of the Institute of British Geographers*, vol.37 (1965), pp.15–30; *Report from the Select Committee on the Employment of the Poor in Ireland*, 1823, vol.vi (561), pp.3–27; *First Report from the Select Committee on the State of Ireland*, 1825, vol.viii (129), pp.5–172; M.A.G. Ó Tuathaigh, 'The Irish in Nineteenth–Century Britain: Problems of Integration', *Transactions of the Royal Historical Society*, Fifth series, vol. 31 (1981), p.151 (henceforth cited as Ó Tuathaigh).
10. *Report Irish Poor in Great Britain, 1836*, pp.42–85; F.L. Wilson *The Irish Influx into Manchester, 1815–50* (unpublished B.A. Dissertation, University of Manchester, 1940), pp.21–31; G.P. Connolly, 'With more than ordinary devotion to God': The Secular Missioner of the North in the Evangelical Age of the English Mission', *North West Catholic History*, vol.10 (1983), pp.17–20.
11. G.P. Connolly, 'Secular Missioner of the North', p.17; R.J. Cooter, 'On Calculating the Nineteenth–Century Catholic Population of Durham and Newcastle', *Northern Catholic History*, vol.2 (1975), pp.16f.
12. Cousens, 'Regional Variation in Emigration', pp.15–29: L.H. Lees, *Exiles of Erin: Irish Migrants in Victorian London* (Manchester University Press, Manchester, 1979), pp.22–41 (henceforth cited as Lees).
13. Lees, p.44; Ó Tuathaigh, p.152.
14. S.H. Cousens, 'The Regional Pattern of Emigration during the Great Irish Famine, 1846–51', *Transactions of the Institute of British Geographers*, vol.28 (1960), pp.19–34; Lees, pp.38–40.
15. Cousens, 'Regional Variation in Emigration', p.29; *ibid.*, 'Pattern of Emigration during Great Famine', p.133; Lees, pp.39–40. Compare here R. Lawton, 'Irish Immigration to England and Wales in the Mid–Nineteenth Century', *Irish Geography*, vol.4 (1959), (henceforth

cited as Lawton), pp.35–54.
16. Miller, pp.83–7; Lees, pp.38–40; S.J. Connolly, pp.89–90.
17. Larkin, p.651.
18. W. Gillespie, *The Christian Brothers in England* (The Burleigh Press, Bristol, 1975) (henceforth cited as Gillespie), pp.1–9; and contrast G.P. Connolly, 'Shifting Congregations: Catholic rural migration in late eighteenth-century Lancashire', in J. Hilton (ed.), *Catholic Englishmen: Essays presented to Brian Charles Foley* (North West Catholic History Society, Wigan, 1984), pp.13–20; J. Bossy, 'Catholic Lancashire in the Eighteenth Century' in J. Bossy and P. Jupp (eds.), *Essays Presented to Michael Roberts* (Blackstaff, Belfast, 1976), pp.55–69.
19. For some approximation see J.A. Lesourd, *Sociologie du Catholicisme Anglais, 1767–1851* (Publications Université Nancy 11, Nancy, 1981) (henceforth cited as Lesourd), pp.124–53; J. Hickey, *Urban Catholics* (Catholic Book Club, London, 1967), pp.90–4 (henceforth cited as Hickey). Also A.E.C.W. Spencer, 'The Demography and Sociography of the Roman Catholic Community of England and Wales', L. Bright and S. Clements (eds.), *The Committed Church* (Darton, Longman, Todd, London, 1966), pp.60–85; M.P. Hornsby–Smith and R.M. Lee, *Roman Catholic Opinion. A study of Roman Catholics in England and Wales in the 1970s* (University of Surrey, Surrey, 1979), pp.13f, 19–31, and compare 63f. Compare also, P. Hughes, 'The English Catholics in 1850', G.A. Beck (ed.), *The English Catholics, 1850–1950* (Burns Oates, London, 1950), pp.42–58; G.P. Connolly, 'Notes and References of Sources relative to Catholic practice in England, 1750–1918', unpublished paper in the keeping of the author, pp.1–29.
20. Hickey, pp.90–4.
21. G.P. Connolly, 'Secular Missioner of the North', pp.8–27.
22. Lees; J. A. Jackson, *The Irish in Britain* (Routledge and Kegan Paul, London, 1963).
23. Lees, pp.164–212. Although devoting a substantial section of the book to the Catholic mission to the London Irish, the author depicts this as almost purely secular in aim. The role of spirituality is suggested by glimpses into fairyland.
24. *Ibid.*, pp.180–2.
25. *Ibid.*, pp.179–84.
26. *Ibid.*, pp.180–2.
27. *Ibid.*, p.180.
28. *Ibid.*, p.181; K.S. Inglis, *Churches and the Working Classes in Victorian England* (Routledge and Kegan Paul, London, 1964), pp.119–30.
29. Lees, p.179.
30. *Ibid.*, pp.164–212.
31. Lesourd, pp.146–7.
32. *Ibid.*, pp.146–7, 152.
33. *Ibid.*, The crude practice ratio is 28%.
34. It fits in well with what can be gleaned in this respect from other sources. See the comments on Catholicism in London by the (Irish) Christian Brothers at work there between 1826 and 1865 in Gillespie.

35. See G.P. Connolly, 'Notes and References Relative to Catholic Practice', pp.4–17, though most here refer to missions in the north of England. Also G.P. Connolly, 'Secular Missioner of the North', pp.15–21.
36. W. Croft and J. Gillow, *An Historical Acccount of Lisbon College* (St. Andrews Press, Barnet, 1902).
37. Rev. W. Bond to Rev. E. Winstanley, 20 August 1835, Archives of Lisbon College, Ushaw College MSS., Durham (no numeration). I am grateful to the Ushaw College Librarian, the Rev. Michael Sharratt, for permission to publish material from this recently assembled private collection, as from other Ushaw collections.
38. *Ibid.*
39. *Ibid.* Reading between the lines, Bond may have wanted a posting to a fashionable chaplaincy. For the daunting reputations of some urban missions, see D. Milburn, *A History of Ushaw College* (Ushaw College Publications, Durham, 1964), p.129; and G.P. Connolly, 'Secular Missioner of the North ', pp.8, 21–4.
40. S.J. Connolly, pp.87–99; Lees, pp.179–84. Compare here J.P. Dolan, *Catholic Revivalism, The American Experience, 1830–1900* (University of Notre Dame Press, Notre Dame, Indiana, 1978), pp.28, 41–3.
41. J.D. Holmes, *More Roman than Rome: English Catholicism in the Nineteenth Century* (Burns Oates, London, 1978), pp.160–3 (henceforth cited as Holmes), from Hickey, pp.90–4. The proportion of 25% represents my estimated average of the figures supplied by Holmes. A percentage for the effective congregation works out around 37%.
42. Croft and Gillow, Lisbon College, for Rimmer.
43. Rev. T. Rimmer to Rev. E. Winstanley, 1 February 1840, Archives of Lisbon College, Ushaw College MSS., Durham, (no numeration).
44. *Ibid.* Also Hickey, p.148, who alleges that a priest, one 'O'Malley', was elected a Chartist delegate in Nottingham in 1848. Against this, Holmes, p.195 note 6, also pp.182–3. O'Malley may have been a 'stroller', or unofficial Irish cleric wandering between Irish communities on the English Mission. In Edward Bagshawe, Bishop of Nottingham in the later decades of the nineteenth century, Catholics had one of the closest episcopal approximations to the social reformer associated with Anglicanism.
45. Rev. T. Rimmer to E. Winstanley, 1 February 1840, Archives of Lisbon College, Ushaw College MSS., Durham.
46. *Ibid.*
47. G.D. Sweeney, 'History of the Diocese of Nottingham', unpublished material in the keeping of the Archivist of the Diocese of Nottingham; Holmes, p.174.
48. Lesourd, pp.147–8.
49. *Report Irish Poor in Great Britain, 1836*, pp.25, 84.
50. G.P. Connolly, 'Secular Missioner of the North', pp.8–27.
51. *Ibid.*, p.13.
52. *Ibid.*, p.12.
53. *Ibid.*, pp.9–23, 27.
54. *Ibid.*, pp.18–20.

55. *Ibid.*, pp.8–9, 24–7: G.P. Connolly, 'The Transubstantiation of Myth: towards a New Popular History of Nineteenth–Century Catholicism in England', *Journal of Ecclesiastical History*, vol.35, no.1 (1984), pp.78–104, esp. pp.89f, 99–104.
56. For their collected source, G.P. Connolly, 'Notes and References relative to Catholic Practice', pp.4–17.
57. Rev. R. Broomhead to Rev. T. Eyre, 6 November 1806, 26 February 1807, Correspondence A – L, Ushaw College MSS, Durham, documents 47, 49. Broomhead indicates also that three–quarters of those coming to make a General Confession after his periodic Public Instruction were baptized Catholics.
58. 'Draft of Petition from the Manchester Clergy to Bishop Thomas Smith' (no date, probably 1828), Smith Papers, Leeds Diocesan Curial Offices, document 401A.
59. Rev. J. Fisher to Bishop T. Smith, 1 November 1825, *ibid.*, document 201.
60. Bishop J. Briggs to (Rev. James Crook?) 22 August 1835 (fragment of letter), Archives of the Archdiocese of Liverpool, Lancashire County Record Office, RCL v (no numeration). Compare also here, J. Teer, *The Progress of Catholicism* (Liverpool, 1841), p.26.
61. Rev. P. Cullen to Rev. T. Kirby, 25 June 1842, Kirby Correspondence, Irish College, Rome, document 98.
62. *The Catholic Registers of the Secular Mission of Newcastle–on–Tyne*, CRS Monograph Series, vol.35 (Catholic Record Society, London, 1936), p.314.
63. *Manchester Guardian*, 17 June 1846.
64. *Report Irish Poor in Great Britain, 1836*, pp.1–164, esp. pp.1–2, 22–5. Also Larkin, p.638 note 28, for a similar problem among Irish soldiers in England.
65. Gillespie, pp.75–136; M.C. Normoyle, *The Roman Correspondence: Early Years of the Institute of Edmund Rice, 1803–44* (private publication of the Christian Brothers, no place of publication, 1978). The original reports of the Brothers are contained in the Christian Brothers Archive (Fratelli Christiani), Via della Maglionella 375, 0016.6, Rome.
66. Bro. P.J. Murphy to Rev. T. Kirby, 10 March 1843, Kirby Correspondence, Irish College, Rome, document 173. Also M.C. Normoyle, *A Tree is Planted: The Correspondence of Edmund Rice, 1810–42* (private publication for the Christian Brothers, no place of publication, 1977), pp.122–3. It is not clear when presenting totals for converts whether some missioners – notably Irish and Continental missioners – distinguished between converts from another creed and the 'conversion' of non–practising Catholics.
67. Compare here S.W. Gilley, 'The Roman Catholic Mission to the Irish in London', *Recusant History*, vol.10 (1969), pp.124–5.
68. G.P. Connolly,'Secular Missioner of the North', pp.13–14. For an illustration in microcosm, G.P. Connolly, 'Transubstantiation of Myth', pp.91–3. Compare also Lesourd, pp.138–53; and E.R. Norman, *The English Catholic Church in the Nineteenth Century* (Clarendon Press, Oxford, 1984) (henceforth cited as Norman), pp.201–43.

69. W.J. Lowe, 'The Lancashire Irish and the Catholic Church, 1846–71: the social dimension', *Irish Historical Studies*, vol.20 (1976–7), p.147.
70. *Ibid.*, pp.144–7.
71. G.P. Connolly, 'The Rev. Mr. Peter Kaye: Maverick or Englishman?', *North West Catholic History*, vol.11 (1984), pp.8–21, for a Catholic missioner about the kind of business described by Larkin, pp.635–48, albeit in an English setting.
72. Larkin, pp.625f, 630–1, 639f.
73. G.P. Connolly, 'Secular Missioner of the North', pp.10–14; Lesourd, *Sociologie du Catholicisme*, pp.95–102; R. Currie, A. Gilbert, L. Horsley, *Churches and Churchgoers: Patterns of Church Growth in the British Isles since 1700* (Clarendon Press, Oxford, 1977) (henceforth cited as Currie, Gilbert, Horsley), pp.153–5. An informative parallel is Bernard Aspinwall's 'The Formation of the Catholic Community in the West of Scotland: some preliminary outlines', *Innes Review*, vol.33 (1982), pp.44–57.
74. Lesourd, pp.146–7, 152.
75. Lees, pp.179–84; compare Gilley, 'Catholic Mission to Irish in London', pp.124–5.
76. G.P. Connolly, 'Secular Missioner of the North', pp.13–14, 26–7, for observations which underpin this estimate. Compare here, Lesourd, pp.146–53, 163, who attempts a more thorough analysis.
77. Lesourd, pp.146–53, 163. This refers to the late nineteenth century. There is little or nothing with which to explore Catholic practice for the early part of the twentieth century; but see, Hornsby–Smith and Lee, *Roman Catholic Opinion*, pp.19–20. Clearly proportions would not have remained static, and in contrast to Lesourd, pp.147–8, Garret Sweeney supplies a tantalizing clue to volatility well before this, in Nottingham, Holmes, p.174. Though I find Sweeney's suggestion convincing, this need not affect the crude proportion for the community as a credible working average. See Currie, Gilbert, Horsley, pp.21–45, for corroboration of the idea that patterns of religious practice respond to external events. For the now well–known 'leakage debate', 'C.G.', 'The Leakage of the Catholic Church', *The Month*, vol.59 (1887), pp.176–89; and J.G. Snead–Cox, *The Life of Cardinal Vaughan*, 2 vols. (Burns Oates, London, 1910), vol.1, pp.403–29; H. Vaughan, *The Loss of Our Children* (F. Walker, Manchester, 1884); J. Sharpe, 'Juvenile Holiness: Catholic Revivalism among Children in Victorian Britain', *Journal of Ecclesiastical History*, vol.35, no. 2 (1984), pp.222–4, has a different emphasis.
78. All calculations here and at notes 79, 80, 81 and 82 are based upon my interpretation of data in Lesourd, pp.95–153; Spencer, 'Demography and Sociography', pp.61–85, esp. pp.61–2; Currie, Gilbert, Horsley, pp.49–51, 153–5; Hornsby Smith and Lee, *Roman Catholic Opinion*, pp.13f, 19–31; A.D. Gilbert, *Religion and Society in Industrial England* (Longmans, London, 1976), p.46: L.W. Brady, *T.P. O'Connor and the Liverpool Irish* (Royal Historical Society, London, 1983), pp.264–5; W.G. Lumley, 'The Statistics of the Roman Catholic Church in England and Wales', *Journal of the Royal Statistical*

Society, vol.27 (1864), pp.303–23; J. Morris, *Catholic England in Modern Times* (Burns Oates, London, 1892, p.72 (T. Murphy), *The Position of, the Catholic Church in England and Wales during the Last Two Centuries: Retrospect and Forecast* (Burns Oates, London, 1892), pp.63f, 93f. Also Holmes, pp.161–2; J. Bossy, *The English Catholic Community 1570–1850* (Darton, Longman and Todd, London, 1975), p.422. All approximations are rounded tens. For the initial Catholic baptized total, *Missiones ritu Latino cura S. Congregationis de Prop. in 1886* (published by the Office of the Propaganda Fide, Rome, 1886); 'C.G.', 'Leakage of the Catholic Church', pp.176f. My caution about overstating has been allayed by C. Ó Gráda, 'A Note on Nineteenth-Century Emigation Statistics', *Population Studies*, vol.29 (1975), pp.145–8.

79. For the computation of English Catholic numbers see also G.P. Connolly, 'Secular Missioner of the North', pp.10–14. The total for English Catholics around the last quarter of the eighteenth century has been estimated in the region of 80,000. By 1810 the community in England numbered slightly over 200,000, a large percentage of whom were native Catholics. I have made the defensible assumption that by the latter decades of the nineteenth century English Catholics accounted for one fifth of the baptized Catholic population. I have no way of making allowances for continental Catholics save to say that their numbers must have been comparatively small, and probably would not affect my broad conclusions. The possible impact of converts has been ignored in line with the argument presented by Spencer, 'Demography and Sociography', pp.65–6. But compare Currie, Gilbert, Horsley, p.50.

80. By *presence* I refer to those of Irish birth and immediate descent, presupposing Catholic baptism to have become less frequent amongst non-practising Catholics with each further generation, and giving rise to a progressive distancing from the institutional Catholic Church. To obtain the figure for such an Irish presence I have made the conservative presumption that an Irish-born population around 250,000 strong in mainland Britain in 1820, might have grown to represent Irish connections of at least twice the birth figure by 1881 (780,000). See also here, Lees, pp.123–39. There is little or no reliable information on the size of the Protestant Irish population of mainland Britain in the later nineteenth century, but their presence could hardly have accounted for more than a fifth of the total Irish by birth and descent by this date. Se also H. Senior, *Orangeism in Ireland and Britain, 1795–1836* (Routledge and Kegan Paul, London, 1966), pp.230, 270.

81. Brady, *O'Connor*, p.162, for some telling comments on the possible impact of the growth in the 'English-born' Irish.

82. Compare this estimate with the breakdown of practice in percentage terms given by Lesourd, p.165.

83. Lowe, pp.144–6; Ó Tuathaigh, pp.165–7; Lees, pp.172–84.

84. For an interesting exception, a hint at an Irish man of another sort, Brady, *O'Connor*, esp. 9–10, 48–9, 163–4, 177–8, 183, 185.

85. See here the argument developed by O'Farrell, *England and*

Ireland, pp.134–54; and compare G. Simms, 'Irish Spirituality: Some insights from the Churches of the Reformation', in Maher (ed.), *Irish Spirituality*, pp.104–22. Both deal with Ireland itself, though what is said, notably by George Simms, could apply to the British mainland.
86. Lees, pp.183–4; G.P. Connolly, 'Transubstantiation of Myth', p.88.
87. G.P. Connolly, 'Irish Spirituality and the English Christian', paper read to the History Workshop Conference, Religion and Society, London, 1983, and to appear.
88. J. Bossy, 'The Counter Reformation and the People of Catholic Europe', *Past and Present*, no.47 (1970), pp.51–70; *ibid.*, 'The Counter Reformation and the People of Catholic Ireland', in T.D. Willilams (ed.), *Historical Studies*, vol.viii (Gill and Macmillan, Dublin, 1971), pp.155–69. Compare J. Delumeau, *Catholicism between Luther and Voltaire* (Burns Oates, London, 1977), pp.154–201; but see also D. Fenlon, 'Interpretations of Catholic History', *Journal of Ecclesiastical History*, vol.33, no.2 (1982), pp.257–61; and in an Irish setting contrast Keenan.
89. 'Report from East Munster to Muzio Vitillischi, Superior General of the Society of Jesus, 1617', *Journal of the Waterford and South East of Ireland Archaeological Society*, vol.6 (1900), pp.101–22. Compare S.J. Connolly, pp.90–2, 120–2; J. Bossy, 'A Social History of Confession', *Transactions of the Royal Historical Society*, vol.25 (1975), pp.21–38.
90. The complexity behind this sloppy phrase can be glimpsed via P.Ó Fiannachta, 'The Spirituality of the Céili Dé', in Maher (ed.), *Irish Spirituality*, pp.22–32: and P.Ó Héalaí, 'Popular Morality in Irish Religious Tales', *ibid.*, pp.71–87.
91. Bossy, 'Counter Reformation and Catholic Ireland', pp.155–7.
92. G.P. Connolly, 'Irish Spirituality and English Christian'. See Norman, p.21, for an older, yet cannily accurate assessment by the English Catholic, Sir John Throckmorton.
93. Kerr, *Peel, Priests and Politics*, pp.1–67; also Keenan.
94. H. Mayhew, *London Labour and the London Poor*, vol.2 (Reprint, Frank Cass, London, 1967), p.473.
95. J.J. ó Ríordáin, *Irish Catholics. Tradition and Transition* (Veritas, Dublin, 1980), (henceforth cited as ó Ríordáin).
96. *Ibid.*, pp.1–27, 64–75.
97. *Ibid.*, pp.64–75.
98. *Ibid.*
99. The opposite to this 'ancient faith' is an 'Anglo Saxon puritanical culture', a blight ó Ríordáin insists has infected 'not only English society, but that of America and indeed of the entire English-speaking world'! (my exclamation) *ibid.*, p.66.
100. *Ibid.*, pp.xi–xiv. See also here, in a more balanced vein, Ó Tuathaigh, pp.159–61; S.W. Gilley, 'English Attitudes to the Irish in England, 1780–1900', in C. Holmes (ed.), *Immigrants and Minorities in British Society* (Allen Unwin, London, 1977), pp.81–110; Kerr, *Peel, Priests and Politics*, pp.1–67 and also 224–351; and contrast Keenan. Also G.P. Connolly, 'Irish Spirituality and English Christian'.

101. Ó Ríordáin, esp. pp.46–87.
102. *Ibid.*, pp.46–87, a strange compound of real perception and quite stunning gaffes.
103. G.P. Connolly, '"Little Brother be at Peace": The Priest as Holy Man in the Nineteenth-Century Ghetto', W.J. Shiels (ed.), *Studies in Church History: The Churches and Healing*, vol.19 (Blackwell, Oxford, 1982), pp.191–205. Also G.P. Connolly, 'In the footsteps of the Father: Daniel Hearne of Irish Town', unpublished paper in the keeping of the author in preparation with the aid of a Leverhulme Foundation Grant and to appear, for a discussion of some of the prevailing mentalities behind pre-Tridentine Christianity in Ireland.
104. G.P. Connolly, 'In the Footsteps of the Father'. Also S.J. Connolly, pp.74–134, who prefers to view Irish popular religious instincts as conditioned largely by social behaviour. Compare Ó Ríordáin, pp.6–45.
105. J. Macquarrie, *Paths in Spirituality* (SCM Press, London, 1972), pp.53–72, 122–5; and see also here the caveat of Donal Kerr, *Heythrop Journal*, vol.25 (1984), pp.241–2. Again compare C. Mooney, 'The Church in Gaelic Ireland: the thirteenth to fifteenth centuries', P.J. Corish (ed.), *The History of Irish Catholicism*, vol.2, part 5 (Gill and Macmillan, Dublin, 1969).
106. S.W. Gilley, 'Vulgar Piety and the Brompton Oratory 1850–60', *Durham University Journal*, vol.43 (1981), pp.15–25: *ibid.*, 'Roman Catholic Mission to the Irish', pp.123–45; *ibid.*, 'The Catholic Faith of the Irish Slums: London 1840–70', H.J. Dyos and M. Wolff (eds.), *The Victorian City: Images and Realities*, vol.2 (Routledge and Keegan Paul, London, 1973), pp.837–53.
107. As, for example, Gilley, 'The Catholic Faith of the Irish Slums', pp.837–53.
108. Lees, p.184; R. Mudie-Smith, *The Religious Life of London* (Hodder and Stoughton, London, 1904), p.271; A.E.C.W. Spencer, 'The Demography of Catholicism', *The Month*, vol.8 (1975), p.102: Hornsby-Smith and Lee, *Roman Catholic Opinion*, pp.173, 180, 224. See also Currie, Gilbert, Horsley, p.72. B. Heeney, 'The Beginnings of Church Feminism: Women and Councils of the Church of England, 1897–1919', *Journal of Ecclesiastical History*, vol.33, no.1 (1983), pp.83–109, esp. 89–93, 106, though dealing exclusively with Anglicans, supplies the kind of analysis which sooner or later must be applied to Catholicism.
109. Mayhew, *London Labour*, vol.2, p.505.
110. Gilley, 'English Attitudes to Irish', pp.92–3.
111. Compare E.D. Steele, 'The Irish Presence in the North of England, 1850–1914', *Northern History*, vol.12 (1976), p.220.
112. I take it that by the later decades of the nineteenth century, most Irish and their descendants in England would have been aware of such criteria, especially in view of the strong 'advertising campaign' by the Catholic clergy after 1840. See Holmes, pp.55–108. Lesourd, pp.104, 124–53, gives a good statistical account of Catholic attempts to make an impact upon the Irish poor. Also Lees, pp.172–221; and compare Norman, pp.201–43.

113. See Hugh McLeod, in H. McLeod, *Class and Religion in the Late Victorian City* (Croom Helm, London, 1975), pp.34–5. Also 'To the Catholic Clergymen of Manchester' (Petition c. 1833, probably in respect of the Irish Coercion Bill of that year), Archives of the Archdiocese of Liverpool, Lancashire County Record Office (no numeration) RCL v, for an eloquent example of the limits of even faithful Catholic confidence in the clergy's political attitudes. It is perhaps no coincidence that the addressee, an Englishman, John Smith, assistant missioner to Daniel Hearne of St. Patrick's, Manchester, was a reluctant servant of the Irish: for whom see G.P. Connolly, 'Irish Spirituality and the English Christian'.
114. G.P. Connolly, *A Missionary Church in England; Catholics and English Society, 1791–1918* (forthcoming, Croom Helm, London, c.1988).
115. See Hickey, p.94; Hornsby–Smith and Lee, *Roman Catholic Opinion*, p.19.
116. Ó Tuathaigh, p.166–7; also Bossy, *English Catholic Community*, pp.295–316; J. Kent, *Holding the Fort: Studies in Victorian Revivalism* (Epworth Press, London, 1978) (henceforth cited as Kent), pp.94–8.
117. Holmes, pp.160–7. Compare Norman, pp.201–6. Anthony Spencer calculated that around 1850 converts to Catholicism in England and Wales 'were of the order of 1,400–1,450 *per annum* . . . about 83 per annum per million non–Catholics', 'Demography and Sociography', p.65.
118. Holmes, pp.162–7.
119. C. Leetham, *Luigi Gentili: A Sower for the Second Spring* (Burns Oates, London, 1965), p.208 for but one (exaggerated) aspect of this problem. Contrast the argument in G.P. Connolly, 'Irish Spirituality and the English Christian'. For George Brown, in actual fact Vicar Apostolic of the Lancashire District, G.P. Connolly, *Catholicism in Manchester and Salford*, vol.3, pp.437–79. Also here, Snead–Cox, *Vaughan*, vol.1, pp.403–29, who makes it appear as though the problem suddenly dawned on Vaughan, something quite untenable in view of Holmes, pp.162–7.
120. A. Haigh, *The Victorian Clergy* (Croom Helm, London, 1984), pp.1–26, for a summary of the issues here as related to Anglicans. G.P. Connolly, 'Vocation or Profession? English Catholics and the origins of clerical ascendancy, 1791–1840', paper read at the Catholic Record Society Conference, Oxford, 1983, and to appear in *Recusant History*.
121. Again most discussion to date has centred upon Anglicanism. See B. Heeney, *A Different Kind of Gentleman: Parish Clergy as Professional Men in Early and Mid Victorian England* (Shoestring, Connecticut, 1976) (henceforth cited as Heeney). Also A.J. Russell, *The Clerical Profession* (SPCK, London, 1980), pp.9–49, 53–306; A.J. Engel, *From Clergyman to Don: The Rise of the Academic Profession in Nineteenth–Century Oxford* (Clarendon Press, Oxford, 1983), pp.1–13, 14–54; Haigh, *Victorian Clergy*, pp.1–26, 357–61. Compare G. Best, *Temporal Pillars* (Cambridge University Press, Cambridge, 1964), pp.245, 258f, 268; and the fascinating argument developed in Kent, at pp.282–5, 292. A good general background to this question can be had from W.J. Reader, *Professional Men: the rise of the professional*

classes in nineteenth–century England (Weidenfeld and Nicholson, London, 1966), esp. pp.1–24, 55–99. His comments on the Established Church, however, do not apply to Catholic clergymen whose experience may have resembled more that of the secular professions.

122. G.P. Connolly, 'Vocation or Profession?'; Bossy, *Catholic Community*, pp.323–63. I cannot agree with Bossy's remark, p.355, that '. . . . the establishment of a clerical supremacy was a probability so banal as scarcely to need discussion', which seems to contradict his earlier assessment of the problem at p.337.

123. Bossy, *Catholic Community*, pp.323f, esp. 337f.

124. *Ibid.*, pp.295–363, but esp. 302f, 314–6, 347–63. For another view, see G.P. Connolly, 'Cleric: the Re–emergence and Reinvigoration of a Profession amongst Catholics in Nineteenth–Century England', unpublished paper read before the University of Kent Senior Seminar on Religion, 1984.

125. G.P. Connolly, 'Secular Missioner of the North', pp.8–9, 18–24; *ibid.*, 'Transubstantiation of Myth', pp.99–104. Also see Milburn, *Ushaw College*, pp.111–12, 153–4.

126. G.P. Connolly, 'Vocation or Profession?'; P. Doyle, 'The Education and Training of Roman Catholic Priests in Nineteenth–Century England', *Journal of Ecclesiastical History*, vol.35, no.2 (1984), pp.208–19, esp. 216–8; L.E. Halkin, 'Le Formation du clergé Catholique après le Concile de Trent', *Bibliothèque de la Revue d'Histoire Ecclésiastique*, vol.50, *Miscellanea Historiae Ecclesiasticae*, vol.111 (Louvain, 1970), pp.115–24.

127. G.P. Connolly, 'Vocation or Profession?'; Bossy, *Catholic Community*, pp.337–63, esp. 337f, 356–63, and also 364–90.

128. For English missionary clergy appreciative of their opportunities before this, Milburn, *Ushaw*, pp.68–9. Also Bossy, 'Catholic Lancashire', pp.54–69.

129. G.P. Connolly, 'Vocation or Profession?'; *ibid.*, *Catholicism in Manchester and Salford*, vol.2, passim., vol.3, pp.62–147; Bossy, *Catholic Community*, pp.336–7, 349–50.

130. G.P. Connolly, 'Peter Kaye', pp.8–21, outlines more attractive side to this ambition.

131. A crucial factor changing the communal and private piety described by Bossy, *Catholic Community*, pp.364–90. Also G.P. Connolly, 'Transubstantiation of Myth', pp.96–9.

132. G.P. Connolly, *Catholicism in Manchester and Salford*, vol.2, esp. pp.45–100; *ibid.*, 'Vocation or Profession?'. Visitation Returns, Bishop John Briggs, Visitations, 1830–50, Briggs Papers, Leeds Diocesan Curial Offices (no numeration); and Visitations, 1855–71, Archives of the Archdiocese of Liverpool, Lancashire County Records Office (no numeration), RCL v.

133. For the Manchester Irish, see G.P. Connolly, *Catholicism in Manchester and Salford*, vol.3, esp. pp.399–431; *ibid.*, 'Little Brother be of Peace', pp.192–205; *ibid.*, 'In the Footsteps of the Father'; J.M. Werly, 'The Irish in Manchester, 1832–49', *Irish Historical Studies*, vol.18 (1972–3), pp.345–58, esp. 346–7; but compare, R.J. Morris, *Cholera, 1832: Social Responses to an Epidemic* (Holmes and

Meier, London, 1976), pp.110–1. Also here, Wilson, 'Irish Influx', esp. pp.21–31, for Manchester's Irish districts; and *Report Irish Poor in Great Britain, 1836*, pp.42–84.
134. G.P. Connolly, *Catholicism in Manchester and Salford*, vol.3, pp.399–431; and Wilson, 'Irish Influx', pp.21f, the latter of which I now consider to have underestimated the Irish non–Catholic presence in the area. Compare *Report Irish Poor in Great Britain, 1836*, p.62; and see also G.P. Connolly, 'In the Footsteps of the Father'.
135. *Report Irish Poor in Great Britain, 1836*, p.62. The total of 500 Irish Catholics in Irish Town is undoubtedly a misprint or a misunderstanding. Compare Werly, 'Irish in Manchester', p.346, whose figure looks a great deal more credible; and also Wilson, 'Irish Influx', pp.21–31; G.P. Connolly, *Catholicism in Manchester and Salford*, vol.1, pp.445–6, vol.2, pp.284–426, vol.3, p.2–264, 340–502; G.P. Connolly, 'Little Brother be at Peace', pp.192–206 for Hearne. A detailed biography of his early life and work in Manchester is contained in G.P. Connolly, 'In the Footsteps of the Father'. A sketch of this colourful character and his community can be found in the articles by Matthew Butler in *The Waterford News*, 5 September 1941 – 9 January 1942.
136. *The Manchester Guardian*, 17 June 1846. The original choice as Rector of St. Patrick's was Peter Kaye; see G.P. Connolly, 'Peter Kaye', p.12. Also G.P. Connolly, 'Irish Spirituality and the English Christian', for relations between Irish and English clergy on the English Mission.
137. G.P. Connolly, *Catholicism in Manchester and Salford*, vol.1, pp.399–431.
138. *Ibid.*, p.421; G.P. Connolly, 'Transubstantiation of Myth', p.90, where evidence from Catholic Missioners on site in Manchester indicates a practice figure around 2,500, staggering but credible. Compare Lees, p.180.
139. G.P. Connolly, 'Little Brother be at Peace', p.199; *Manchester Mercury*, 14, 22 July, 11 August 1807; Senior, *Orangeism*, pp.151–3, 154–60; *The Manchester Courier*, 20 July 1833, 12, 26 July 1834, 18, 25 July 1835, 19, 26 March 1836, for some of the fiercer exchanges between Orangemen and 'The Boys' in Manchester seen in the *Courier* from a decidedly Protestant viewpoint. A history of local Catholic and Orange communities, notably at street level, is to appear in G.P. Connolly, 'In the Footsteps of the Father'. For general Catholic relations with Protestantism in Manchester, G.P. Connolly, *Catholicism in Manchester and Salford*, esp. vol.1, pp.432–54, vol.2, pp.2–100; and G.P. Connolly, 'Vocation or Profession?'.
140. G.P. Connolly, *Catholicism in Manchester and Salford*, vol.1, esp. pp.432–54; *ibid.*, 'Transubstantiation of Myth', pp.80–7; *ibid.*, 'Vocation or Profession?'
141. Anon, *Brief Memoirs of the Rev. Rowland Broomhead of Manchester* (Manchester, 1820); G.P. Connolly, *Catholicism in Manchester and Salford*, vol. 1, pp.179–454, esp. pp.186–92; G.P. Connolly, 'Vocation or Profession?'
142. G.P. Connolly, 'Vocation or Profession?', provides an attempt

at analysis of this experience and its consequences among the Manchester missioners. But see *ibid.*, 'Secular Missioner of the North', pp.8–27; and compare Bossy, *Catholic Community*, pp.295–390; and E. Duffy, 'Ecclesiastical Democracy Detected', part 1, '1779–87', part 2, '1787–96', *Recusant History*, vol.10 (1970), pp.193–209, 309–31.

143. Bossy, *Catholic Community* pp.355–63; Haigh, *Victorian Clergy*, pp.351–61.

144. G.P. Connolly, 'Vocation or Profession?'

145. *Ibid.*, see also G.P. Connolly, *Catholicism in Manchester and Salford*, vol.1, pp.432–54, also Account Book of John Casey's Charity, Salford Diocesan Archives, Bishop's House, Wardley Hall (no numeration) see handwriten introduction; Milburn, *Ushaw College*. pp.105, 106; Rev. Broomhead to Bishop W. Gibson, 28 October 1803, 31 August 1804, William Gibson Papers, Leeds Diocesan Curial Offices (no numeration).

146. G.P. Connolly, 'Vocation or Profession'?'

147. *Ibid.*, See also *ibid.*, 'Transubstantiation of Myth', p.95,; *ibid.*, *Catholicism in Manchester and Salford*, vol.1, pp.432–54.

148. *Ibid.*, 'Vocation or Profession?'. Compare H.D. Rack, 'Domestic Visitation: a Chapter in Early Nineteenth–Century Evangelism', *Journal of Ecclesiastical History*, vol.24, no.4 (1973), pp.357–76, esp. p.374; W.R. Ward, *Religion and Society in England, 1790–1850* (B.T. Batsford, London, 1972), pp.7–69, 120–1; Gilbert, *Religion and Society*, pp.23–48, esp. 45–8, 125–74.

149. As an illustration of but one aspect of this, G.P. Connolly, 'Institutional Protestantism and the Problem of Catholic Poverty in England, 1839–42', to appear, in W.J. Shiels (ed.), *Studies in Church History: Persecution and Toleration*, vol.21 (Blackwell, Oxford, 1984). Compare here, Spencer, 'Demography and Sociography', p.81, who insists that the problem of 'leakage' was a hidden one until the latter decades of the nineteenth century. While this may be true as a national perspective, at a local level the missions appear well informed: G.P. Connolly, 'Secular Missioner of the North', pp.15–24.

150. Ó Tuathaigh, p.166, and Kent, pp.71–131.

151. See the comments of Sheridan Gilley, 'Roman Catholic Mission to Irish', pp.138–9; and compare G.P. Connolly, 'Catholicism in Manchester and Salford', vol.2, pp.178–274; also G.P. Connolly, 'Institutional Protestantism'. Again here contrast the attitude displayed in the now well-known article, 'The Conversion of England', *The League of the Cross Magazine*, no.20 (1885), pp.117–21. See also Kent, esp. p.71–131.

152. M. Horne, *The Congratulation: An Address to Protestants on the Papal Controversy in Manchester* (Manchester, 1822), p.3–7; G.P. Connolly, 'Vocation or Profession?'

153. G.P. Connolly, 'Transubstantiation of Myth', pp.95–9; *ibid.*, 'Vocation or Profession?'; *ibid.*, *Catholicism in Manchester and Salford*, vol.2, pp.45–100, for the Bible Controversy in Manchester; and see Ward, *Religion and Society*, pp.120–1, for another view. For Curr himself, all these sources and also, C. Hadfield, *A History of*

St. Marie's Mission, Sheffield (Pawson and Brailsworth, Sheffield, 1889), pp.32ff, 58–9. Curr died during a typhus epidemic, having volunteered to take the place of a dead fellow missioner amongst the poor in Leeds.

154. Bishop T. Penswick to Bishop T. Smith, 25 May 1824 (fragment of letter), Smith Papers, Leeds Diocesan Curial Offices, document 167; Papers and Pamphlets relative to the Thorpton Controversy, Printed Matter, Leeds, *ibid.*, packet 96; *The London and Dublin Orthodox Journal*, 27 October 1838, pp.267–70, 16 March 1839, pp.185–7, for these other instances.

155. G.P. Connolly, 'Institutional Protestantism'; *ibid., Catholicism in Manchester and Salford*, vol.2, pp.102–77, 178–247. Compare here R.K. Donovan, 'The Denominational Character of English Catholic Charitable Effort, 1800–65', *Catholic Historical Review*, vol.62 (1976), pp.200–23. For an acute and perhaps uncharitable example of this trend, involving Nicholas Wiseman, Bishop G. Brown to Bishop J. Briggs, 5 November 1840, Briggs Papers, Leeds Diocesan Curial Offices, document 851.

156. J. Curr, *Familiar Instructions in the Faith and Morality of the Catholic Church, adapted to the use of both children and adults compiled from the works of the most approved Christian writers* (Manchester, 1827); and see also the 'much improved' second edition,*ibid.*, 1829, published, so it would seem, due to the 'great popularity' of the first. See G.P. Connolly, 'Vocation or Profession?' for a discussion of this with Curr's other works; also G.P. Connolly, 'Transubstantiation of Myth', pp.96–9. J. Curr, *Catholicism: or the old rule of faith vindicated from the attack of W. Roby* (Manchester, 1821); J. Curr, *Deception Unmasked: Being a review of the statement of facts etc., by the Rev. Robert Green, Vicar of Longhorsely* (Newcastle, 1835); *Orthodox Journal*, 11 June 1819, pp.217–9, provide a useful resumé of Curr's church instincts and their background.

157. Snead–Cox, *Vaughan*, vol.1, pp.154–80, 239–537, 374–453, vol.2, 34–140, 261–76, 277–312, 361–451. See Holmes, pp.199–246, for the only really modern discriminating assessment of Vaughan, a less flattering portrait.

158. Snead–Cox, *Vaughan*, vol.1, pp.270–319, 374–453, vol.2, 1–140, 261–312; Holmes, pp.199–246, esp. 201f, 206–216, 217f, 224, 238–41. Holmes is surely correct to see Vaughan setting the pattern of future English hierarchical preoccupations as a 'devoted and successful, if uncomplicated, pastor of the Irish in Lancashire', p.241. Though the Catholic hierarchy was restored in 1850, it seems fair to argue that Catholic national policymaking did not become effective for some time after this, Norman, pp.69–109.

159. For the 'Joint Pastoral' of 1900, 'The Church and Liberal Catholicism', Holmes pp.238–9. Also Spencer, 'Demography and Sociography', pp.61–2, 72–3, for some insight into the possible workings of the *Ne Temere* canonical legislation invalidating Catholic marriages not performed by a priest. In 1908 the last vestiges of control over the Catholic Church in England by the Propaganda Fide in

Rome were removed, and in 1918 the *Codex Juris Canonici* reintroduced the jurisdiction of the parish priest in ordinary, finally sanctioning an autonomous clergy freed from the constraints of the defunct English Mission.

160. Curr, *Familiar Instructions* (1827), p.125; *ibid.*, (1829), p.85, for what would appear to be straws in the wind.

161. Doyle, 'Education of Priests', p.214. Also *ibid.*, 'Bishop Goss of Liverpool, 1856–72, and the importance of being English', in S. Mews (ed.), *Studies in Church History: Religion and National Identity*, vol.18 (Blackwell, Oxford, 1982), pp.433–47, esp. pp.444–7.

162. Curr, *Familiar Instructions* (1827), pp.i–vii, 118f.

163. *ibid.*, (1829), p.76.

164. For an appreciation of Ireland's worldwide Catholic 'empire' and an analysis decidedly different from the one offered here, S.W. Gilley, 'The Roman Catholic Church and the Nineteenth–Century Irish Diaspora', *Journal of Ecclesiastical History*, vol.35, no.2 (1984), pp.188–207.

VULGAR PIETY AND THE BROMPTON ORATORY, 1850–1860[1]

Sheridan Gilley

The statistics of church–going are one gauge of the secularity of a society; it is more difficult to show the limits set to secularity by the strength and substance of popular religious culture. One obvious measure of both strength and substance is simply vulgarity, for the cultural expression of a really popular religion will be truly of the people. In Ireland, 'religion was a matter of choosing between one appalling vulgarity and another', declares Iris Murdoch of popular Protestantism and Catholicism, while allowing that popular Catholicism was the 'gaudier, more vital and more primitive' of the two.[2] Nineteenth–century Protestantism was vulgar enough wherever it had a working–class following. It is significant of the strength of proletarian Catholicism that its vulgarity was even more pronounced, for this vulgarity was the Catholic shield and buckler against the secularity of that wider working–class indifference to religion especially in evidence in London.

But if vulgarity is to be defined against the standards of upper–crust High Anglican ghastly good taste, one is impressed by the classlessness of Roman Catholic religious culture in Victorian England, in so far as it was transformed by popular continental Ultramontanism between 1840 and 1860. Here was a thoroughly vulgar religious culture accessible and acceptable to many English 'Old Catholics' and ex–Anglicans, as well as to the Irish proletariat – and transcending differences of class. This was of some significance, for it at once defines the difference between the Protestant mission to the nominally Anglican populations of the English towns, and the Roman Catholic endeavour to reclaim the Catholic urban emigrants from Ireland in England who seldom or never went to Mass. Unlike their Protestant neighbours, many of these London Irish were unsecularized to the degree they they still believed in a religion which was vulgar and popular; and if this culture was not simply and solely proletarian, it could be wholeheartedly working class, as it often was, while remaining unselfconsciously classless. There was no obvious social background to the household holy picture of the Sacred Heart with the red lamp before it, or an honest assiduity in lighting candles to bad plaster statues, or in the favourite mid–Victorian Catholic hymns – 'Sweet sacrament divine', 'Faith of our fathers', 'Full in the panting heart of Rome' – which sometime Anglican archdeacons and the 'mere Irishry' sang with equal fervour. There were separate English and Irish versions of 'Faith of our fathers', but the difference was national not social, while the emotion expressed, like lighting candles, could survive the neglect of the more positive precepts of Holy Mother Church. For if these were the old clothes of religion, they fostered a residual piety which an environment indifferent or hostile to Christianity could only with great difficulty wholly overcome; so that in time of need or at the hour of death, a priest might rekindle from the burnt–out embers a final flame of faith.

It may also be argued that this classless religious culture had one support in a distinctly Catholic attitude to poverty itself. For where the Protestant tended to argue that destitution signified moral failure and sought to transform working–class *mores* through religious conversion, the Roman priest accepted poverty as unchanging, unchangeable and god–given, with its own proper ethic and social end. Where the Protestant preached the attractions of wealth in this world and heaven in the next and respectability as the means to both, the priest was less unrealistically dazzled by the golden dream of universal prosperity through self–help, and though prepared to try its methods, was more exclusively concerned with an otherworldly salvation. The Protestant appealed to a minority destined to achieve that modest prosperity which was virtue's reward; the priest did not so much fix his people in their poverty as create an apostolate appropriate to the social pattern and communal solidarity and limited economic opportunity which kept the poor impoverished. The few exceptionally able and ambitious Catholics had their chance of social mobility through the accumulation of small capital to run a lodging house or pub; the rest had to find in their faith consolation for their exclusion from the solid joys of Victorian comfort in an exciting, expanding material world.[3]

Moreover, as the priest's conception of sin was more directly religious than social, less a matter of violation of respectable convention than of injury to Jesus, so he forgave what Protestants damned, with a willingness to forgive if not tolerate even sexual sin which brought down upon him the charge of laxness in his moral theology. So while the Protestant cleric sought to impose on the slums the code of the Protestant State, the priest built up his Church as a kind of state within the State, with other and sometimes opposing aims – the protection of vagrant children from the letter and spirit of Protestant law, even an odd leniency for the person of the prostitute, despite a horror of her prostitution, and the defence of the Irish community from the libels of well–fed heretics who in Catholic eyes, judged the poor from Olympian heights, and had no pity for their suffering.

Again, the Catholic priest came among his poor as a sacred person with a religious authority which blurred his distinct social status as an educated man, or a gentleman like the local Anglican clergyman. The class difference between priest and parishioner was abolished by a more important sort of difference. Thus though Roman Catholic social methods in ragged schools, revivalism and soup and shoe charities resembled their Protestant counterparts, and indeed were often copied from them, the special character of the Roman priest suggests the rather different spirit in which Catholics and Protestants were regarded by their poor, and in which they applied the same social methods among them. The Vicar was respected or reviled in a working-class quarter as a gentleman, but the Catholic priest claimed obedience in virtue of his priesthood alone, for it was in his sacerdotal character that his parishioners received or rejected him.

The mood of this sort of popular Catholicism throughout the English-speaking world was better defined in the 1850s by one man more than any other – Father Frederick William Faber, founder and first superior of the London Oratory, which was established in 1849 as a daughter-house of John Henry Newman's Oratory in Birmingham, and was at first nominally under Newman's authority. 'Mr Faber is teaching the Irish in London to fathom an abyss of blasphemous worship of the Virgin which they did not know before',[4] wrote an Evangelical in 1852; and given Faber's contemporary importance as the guiding spirit of Victorian popular Catholicism, there is a special significance to the local missionary efforts of his Oratory. Not that this personal pupilage was solely Irish[5]; he had a much more socially acceptable following which was far from proletarian. For his personality and ideas found favour with the new Ultramontane generation of English 'Old Catholics' and converts, a wealthy discipleship thirsting for a new wine of the spirit; at their head was Henry Granville Fitzalan Howard, Earl of Arundel and Surrey, who rejoiced in Montalembert's sobriquet of the most pious layman of the century, and who became the fourteenth Duke of Norfolk in 1856. His circle built Faber the Brompton Oratory which was to be the more important for attempting a kind of class co-operation between rich Englishmen and pauper Irishmen, in an uneasy effort to do justice to both. This ideal of class union was conventionally Protestant; rather more unconventional was the boisterous vulgarity with which the Oratorians set out to achieve it, even though as sometime Anglican clergymen they had once been gentlemen themselves.

But even though as priests they had ceased to be mere gentlemen, it was the difficulty of mixing the classes together which brought to an end their first and unhappy encounter with the London Irish, who swamped their chapel off the Strand, and stank it out so effectively that there were complaints from even the Earl of Arundel, who was noted for his tolerance in such things, and a ticket system of admission to the building was introduced, to free it of beggars and fleas and smell. A sense of guilt over this most Protestant proceeding led the Oratorians to attempt a more specialized sort of proletarian mission in 1851, when a member of the institute, Father William Antony Hutchison, organized a ragged school in Rose Street, Covent Garden, transferred in the following year to a former factory in Dunne's

Passage, at the west end of Holborn. This provided accommodation for 400 boys, 150 girls and 150 infants, until with night classes the premises were receiving nearly a thousand children before the schools were moved again in 1858 to still larger premises in Charles Street, Drury Lane. A graduate of Trinity College, Cambridge, Hutchison could feel a hearty contempt for 'dirty Paddies'[6]; unlike his fellow Oratorian Bernard Dalgairns he had little tolerance of Celtic neglect of soap, while unlike another Oratorian, Richard Stanton, he did not think pew-rents so un-Italian that they could not be charged to keep the Irish away.[7] But with the aid of Faber and Dalgairns he brought together fifty Irish artisans in 1852 to form a 'St. Patrick's Society', which with the Brothers of the Little Oratory, formed on the model of the Italian *Oratorium Parvum*, helped him convert and civilize and tame the gutter offspring of the central London rookeries, 'and "affectionately force" the Catholics they found there to come to Mass and the Sacraments'.[8] There were soon 300-400 members of the St. Patrick's Society, which met for concerts and amusements of a popular character in Dunne's Passage, and from there an army of Englishmen and Irishmen sallied forth to gather Catholic children for Hutchison's schools. He had now found his *métier* and life-work in setting up child street-sellers in business with barrows of fruit and fly-paper and home-made coconut-fibre scrubbing brushes, and training them in rope- and mat- and bootmaking, tailoring, book-binding and carpentry, and lodging jobless servants[9] and begging on behalf of old costerwomen.[10] When Newman seemed to demur at all these activities as beyond the community's strength, Hutchison overwhelmed him with a torrent of exposition of his needs and hopes and intentions.[11] A tour of Belgian social welfare institutions furnished him with ideas for his own,[12] most notably a St. Philip's Home staffed by a French religious order, the Sisters of the Compassion, and he founded the first London Catholic reformatory for juvenile delinquents with Henry Edward Manning in 1854,[13] while through his patrons the Howards he organized support for ex-prostitutes and girl-cripples in a St. Martha's refuge and industrial schools,[14] and interested the fashionable Catholic world in his youthful *protégés* just released from prison, or recently seized by the police.[15]

Mingling so much with such everyday sinners, Hutchison fell into a devil-may-care conscience with juvenile crime which put his mission in notable contrast to the greater severity of his Protestant rivals. Equally broad-minded was his attitude to Irish prostitution, which Faber considered almost a 'necessitas peccandi' for the prostitute without other means of livelihood:[16] '. . .our Fathers', wrote Hutchison,

> frequently have cases of poor children under the age of 16 who require a refuge. St Philip's Home cannot receive them because those who have fallen cannot be placed along with those who have not.
>
> Again our Fathers are constantly meeting with cases of penitents who have been in the (convent of the) Good Shepherd & have left it & cannot be received again, because it is against

> the rules. Yet they are exposed to as great danger as they were before. . .The experience of our Fathers makes them somewhat distrust the Good Shepherd as a place of reformation. There is so much woodenness, so little commonsense & above all so little affection displayed compared to what there ought to be in such a place, that very much less good is done than might be. . .[17]

Not that by Hutchison's own lights the unrepentant prostitute could escape hell–fire, but would not God forgive as easily as He showered His grace through the Oratory's indulgenced devotions? This tolerance reflected a real sense of ease with the poor, not least apparent at Hutchison's Whit Monday feasts for his barefoot watercress and orange–girls and crossing–sweepers, who had to be nursed each year through this morally most dangerous holiday. Half the problem was simply solved by feeding them well: 'when they were quite satisfied with meat and cabbage', he wrote, 'we gave them an enormous helping of boiled bolster pudding with raisins. . .there were loud cheers when the pudding entered the room & in a *general* manner presented itself to their consideration, but there was a pause when it was brought home to the notice of each girl in particular, as each in turn saw a vast plateful set before her'. Perhaps more significant of the easy atmosphere was Hutchison's uncomplaining note at the grumbling at the absence of the 'national potatoe'. There were other compensations. The meal was served by Fr. Manning's lady cousins, and was washed down with two barrels of beer. It was followed by a magic–lantern shown, and was eked out with toffee and peppermint rock, and a supper of plum cake and bread and butter.[18]

The Oratorians also flaunted the attractions of the tinsel glory of their bespangled and bedizined church, and of the excitement and even rowdy violence of their mass ragamuffin first communions: 'there will be some little discomfort awaiting you', Hutchison told a visiting bishop, probably Thomas Grant of Southwark, of one such impending service at Dunne's Passage. 'The place is very dirty, the boys will perhaps also be dirty & ragged though that would not so much matter, but I dare say that they will not shew many exterior signs of piety and devotion. Perhaps when they come up to the Communion–rail there may be a scrimmage. . .one will thrust his elbow into another's stomach & so forth. But. . .their hearts will not be so bad – Your Lordship will therefore be prepared not to be scandalized, the ragged First Communion will not be quite so orderly as a 1st Communion of the Orphans [at the convent] at Norwood. . .'[19] Mission services witnessed a similar disorder. One seemed likely to prove the death of a woman 'who in any respectable chapel would be the pew–opener but who in ours is called the Barwoman which has very much of a public–house sound about it. . .she worked indefatigably among the poor & was our Detective policeman when we wanted a suspicious case of distress to be enquired into. . .'[20] The Church was crowded to suffocation for the mission which inaugurated the Oratory's new parish of Brompton in 1856, and which was named in honour of a martyr from the Roman Catacombs, one St. Eutropius whose relics were enshrined in the Oratory church: '. . .the Lady Chapel [was] full to the predella of the altar', the convert Fr. John Bowden told his mother, 'the benches [were] moved together in the middle, the side aisles masses of heads – quite unequalled even in our annals of squash. The Most Eminent [Cardinal] was in the pulpit, just beginning his sermon. . .when there arose a great buzz of talking down the Church, followed by screams, and an alarm of fire was maliciously given by the Protestants . . .Everybody got up, many made for the doors – there was immense confusion and noise – a detachment of reserved ladies, headed by Miss Farrant, charged the sanctuary & got through the sacristy into the house – the leader throwing herself into the Father's arms!'[21] Order was eventually restored, the Cardinal preached for an hour, his sermon was followed by a procession of the Blessed Sacrament, Te Deum and Benediction, and all went as merry as a marriage bell, if in part because the initial excitement had set the tone of the evening and helped it along.

The musical accompaniments of this sort of occasion were of a piece with the agitation of the participants. For the opening of the Charles Street ragged school, Faber had strung together 'an odd doggerell hymn, syllable by syllable, to old Desgenettes, Triomphez, Reine des cieux, & half-clothed urchins sang it with right good will . . .'[22] Hutchison wrote from Rome in similar vein of the Oratorian observance of the Feast of the Assumption in 1856. 'Of course you will have great doings at the Passage of the celebrated Dunne. The procession will go ten times round the room at least, all the Hymns the Father ever wrote to our Lady will be sung twice over – the children will all go to Communion several times, the Rev. Preacher will stamp & shout till he is hoarse, promising all who hear him Eternal Salvation & No Purgatory! if they will only join with him in giving Three Cheers for the Madonna & thus the feast will be kept, as it always is, more solemnly & in a more out & out manner by the Dunne's Passagers than by any other congregation in the Church.'[23] The sort of song they sang may be shown from the martial strains of the rousing chant which Faber wrote for a devotional society in another slum parish, St Anne's, Spitalfields:

> To arms! to arms! for God our King!
> Hark how the sounds of battle ring!
> Unfold the Banner! Raise it high,
> Dear omen of our victory!
> We come, and Sion's songs we sing;
> We come, our hands and hearts we bring
> Unto the Holy Family!
> O Banner bright! How brave the light
> Thy three fair blazoned hearts are showing,
> Where Jesus lovingly imparts
> To Mary's and to Joseph's hearts
> The light with which His Own is glowing!
> Raise, raise the Banner! wave on high
> Its broidered folds against the sky,
> Sons of the Holy Family![24]

This apostrophe to Catholic family virtue was also sung by English noblemen, perhaps to encourage the Irish; Faber wrote as spirited a hymn for the poster advertising the 1852 Advent mission to the Holborn poor, under the headline

> BLESSED BE THE PRECIOUS BLOOD OF JESUS CRUCIFIED!
>
> O come to the merciful Saviour that calls you,
> O come to the Lord who forgives and forgets!
> Tho' dark be the fortune on earth that befalls you,
> There's a bright home above where the sun never sets.
>
> . . .
>
> O Sons of St. Patrick! dear children of Erin!
> 'Tis God that hath kept you his wonderful faith.
> Ah! love Him, then, love Him, for the dark night is nearing,
> And the light of His love shall be with you in death.
>
> . . .
>
> O come, then, to Jesus, and drink of His fountains,
> O come to this mission of mercy and love:
> Believe me, dear children, that Erin's green mountains
> Are dull to the bright land that waits you above.[25]

This invocation of a happy death was anything but accidental: death was a familiar visitant in the insanitary courts, and the subject of grim sacerdotal jesting. 'There are 68 corpses in St Anne's workhouse, & Mr Stanton tells me 43 or 4 in ye dead house of ye Middlesex Hospital', wrote Faber during the cholera epidemic of 1854; '. . .The whole place is enveloped in a canopy of fog, & there is not one breath of air. . . The confessionals are crowded from morning to night. Poor Mr Coates is lying dead, & black as a coal, just outside my window, having made a beautiful death of it. I am investigating ye case of ye four boys at Dunn's passage. . .'[26] The four boys were also apparently dead, an outcome not always regretted for slum children whom it gave a happy exit to heaven, and a deliverance from all their woes. 'He was a good little boy & had been to Confession', wrote Hutchison of one such child, an eight–year old dead of a blow to the heart in a street quarrel, 'so that I doubt not it is a good thing that has happened to him'.[27] There was rather more doubt about the cholera victim who had been in the Norwood Workhouse. 'He had been a good deal damaged there & had a great dislike to making his 1st Confession, running away from School once or twice in order to avoid it. We caught him unawares only a week or two before the holidays & he then made his Confessn. without any difficulty & had behaved very well ever since. One day when he was near Golden Square he saw the cart going round for the dead & this so frightened him that he went home, fell sick & died next morning, having first received the Sacraments. He has had therefore a narrow escape.'[28]

This was a mercilessly technical understanding of the workings of salvation, but its bluntness was easily understood – the more so because the immediacy of death to hard–working casual labourers and the survivors of the Famine was a kind of continuous call to repent. Good religious use was made of the lying-in-state that preceded the funerals of Irish girls of special piety. The poor would bring rosaries and medals to be sanctified by contact with the hands and throat of the corpse, which was placed 'amidst lights and flowers, with a wreath of roses on her brow, and a crucifix on her breast'.[29] It was said of one such lady that six days after her death, 'her body showed no signs of corruption; and many of those who visited her can testify that it had the odour of flowers freshly gathered'.[30] These marvels impressed even the Protestant poor.[31] Among Catholics they were reinforced by a devotional literature which painted in the darkest hues an unsanctified passage to another world: a genre to which Faber contributed himself.[32] Even the worst still hoped for a holy end. Priests were wearily familiar with the agonized reclamation of men forced to remember and regret in an hour the sins of a lifetime,[33] after years of neglect of the rather mechanical Catholic devotional routines – though still placing their hope of salvation in priestly authority alone.

That authority was evident on one level in the crowds whom epidemics brought to confession,[34] through belief in the clergy's miraculous healing powers.[35] Priests were summoned at every hour of the day and night to dispel the cholera – or cure a cold,[36] they could exorcise devils or lay a ghost, kill with a curse from the altar and raise their victims from the dead.[37] The anecdotes of deeds of this sort explain the popular honours which as Mayhew noted, were paid to the priest,[38] and the crowds who thronged to touch Cardinal Wiseman's robes in his tours of the London courts,[39] and who put their trust in the supernatural virtue of holy water, crucifixes and medals, and firmly believed that in a household blessed by the priest, disease could take hold of the pigs alone. This sort of sympathetic magic was meat and drink to the Oratorians, who fostered an underworld of pious legend in the St. Philip's Home conducted by the Sisters of Compassion. St. Joseph himself was said to have called with an order for the artificial lilies made by the children, who when buyers for their wares seemed to fail, unscrewed the wooden Christ-child fastened to their much-revered statue of St. Anthony, and did not return the Christ to the Saint till he had answered their prayers for more customers.[40]

But the upper classes also had souls, and the Oratory succeeded in accommodating the ordinary snobberies of Victorian England while still treating rich and poor as one. Some deference to aristocratic wealth was necessary for money-raising for poor schools and charities. The Earl of Arundel[41] presided over the uppercrust committee – mostly Anglican converts,[42] nominally in charge of the ragged schools, and Hutchison's correspondence with the Countess reflects the whole range of the slum priest's preoccupations, from cooking-manuals for working-class mothers,[43] and the supervision of day-outings to Sydenham,[44] to the marionette shows of Uncle Tom's Cabin and Blue Beard and 'Oratorian Gaffs' intended to keep the Irish free of the 'pernicious "Penny Gaffs"' and other immoral entertainmments of the music hall.[45] These close connections between the Oratory and the Howards continued after the Earl had succeeded to his Dukedom, and Hutchison's Association of Our Lady of Compassion for the care of pauper orphans was patronized and subsidized and personally tended by the Duchess and her daughters.[46] Hutchison's major project for model lodging–houses failed after seven years' labour, several false starts, much money–raising, and innumerable letters,[47] and he died prematurely of overwork in 1863, when the Oratory surrendered his schools to the Archdiocese, after he had run through much of a private fortune in charity.[48] But his success owed much to his fellow–Oratorians, to their aid and counsel – and his endeavour showed what a Catholic religious order might achieve.

Hutchison's affection for his neglected Irish charges is apparent enough; it would be well to know how they regarded him, and whether the priest to them had entirely subsumed the upper–class Englishman. The spirit of his labours is above all interesting because it seems to show a liberation from respectable Victorian convention, as from a puritan piety too narrow for its world. But this freedom was itself a natural growth from a religious culture which was heartily popular because it was so heartily vulgar, and because, being of the people, it was not afraid of theological crudity or illegality or emotional excess to the end of saving pauper souls. The enlightened may consider this folk religion, not of the highest quality; it is not for the historian to judge whether folk faith is better than none at all.

Notes:

Abbreviations: B.O., The Oratory, Birmingham; O.L., Oratory Letters; L.O., The Oratory, Brompton (London). The small Roman numerals refer to the volume numbers in the archives of the Brompton Oratory.

1. I owe debts of gratitude too the late Father Raleigh Addington and to the late Father Charles Stephen Dessain of the Oratories of Brompton and Birmingham for their guidance to their respective archives. The essay reprinted with permission, from the *Durham University Journal*, vol.lxxiv (December, 1981), pp.15–21.
2. Iris Murdoch, *The Red and the Green* (London, 1965), pp.62, 11.
3. On the Catholic attitude to poverty, see my 'Heretic London, Holy Poverty and the Irish Poor, 1830–1870', *Downside Review*, vol.lxxxix (January, 1971), pp.64–89. The Protestant attitude to poverty as a fruit of Popery passed into proverb as 'Popery and wooden shoes'; on the complexities of the Protestant attitude, see K.S. Inglis, *Churches and the Working Classes in Victorian England* (London, 1963), pp.250 *et seq.*
4. Samuel Garratt, 'The Irish in London,' in *Motives for Missions* (London, 1852), p.206.
5. Faber had only one Irish penitent when Garratt made his charge,

and Garratt was thus the object of Mr. Faber's innocent mockery as 'the favourite Spiritual Director of the most devout of the Irish Roman Catholics in London'. Fr. William Antony Hutchison to the Countess of Arundel and Surrey (henceforth called Lady Arundel and, for the period after 1856 the Duchess of Norfolk), 5 January 1853, vol.xxx, 25, L.O.. See also Ronald Chapman, *Father Faber* (London, 1961); and Raleigh Addington (ed.), *Faber Poet and Priest* (London, 1974).

6. '. . .he [Faber] looked to your converting intellectual infidels, lawyers and heretics rather than hearing the general confessions of dirty Paddies': Hutchison to Newman, *c.* 30 March 1849, March–April 1849, O.L., B.O.

7. Hutchison to Newman, 1 January 1851, January–April 1851, O.L., B.O.; Faber to Newman, 22 February 1851, January–April 1851, O.L., B.O.

8. Fr. Ralph Kerr, *The Oratory in London*, L.O., p.161.

9. *Ibid.*; Hutchison to Lady Arundel, 1 July 1852, vol.xxx, 17; Hutchison to Lady Arundel, 12 December 1851, vol.xxx, 13, L.O.

10. Hutchison to Lady Arundel, 27 April 1853, vol.xxx, 26, L.O. on Mrs. Boyle; cf. Fr. Knox or J.B. Rowe to the Earl on Mrs. Donovan, 28 February 1856, Arundel Castle MSS.

11. Hutchison to Newman, 3 May 1851, 6 May 1851, 13 May 1851, May–July 1851, O.L., B.O. See C.S. Dessain and V.F. Blehl (eds.), *The Letters and Diaries of John Henry Newman*, vol.xiv (London ,1963), pp.273–284.

12. Hutchison to Faber, 2 September 1854, vol.xxvi, 135, L.O.

13. Hutchison to Lady Arundel, 30 November 1854, vol.xxx, 53, L.O.

14. Hutchison to the Duchess of Norfolk, 2 January 1857, vol.xxx, 66; Hutchison to the Duke of Norfolk, 15 October 1858, vol.xxx, 75; cf. Fr. Rowe to Lady Arundel, 20 December 1852, vol.xxxi, 77; and for some of their rather gruesome cases, see vol.xxx, 91, L.O.

15. Hutchison to Arundel, 5 November 1851, vol.xxxii, 25, L.O.; 'Some have been in prison, only one since the school has opened. . .'.

16. Faber to Newman, 17 July 1849, July–August 1849, O.L., B.O.: 'We have great numbers of prostitutes to confession, and there is almost a necessitas peccandi on ye poor things if we can't get refuge for them. . .'.

17. Hutchison to the Duchess of Norfolk, 2 January 1857, vol.xxx, 66, L.O.

18. Hutchison to Lady Arundel, 8 June 18(54?), vol.xxx, 48, L.O.

19. Hutchison to (Grant?), 2 December 1851 or 1852, vol.xxviii, 70, L.O.

20. Hutchison to Lady Arundel, 5 January 1853, vol.xxx, 25, L.O.

21. Fr. John Bowden to his mother Elizabeth Bowden, 24 February 1857, vol.xxv, 39–40, L.O.

22. Faber to Lady Arundel, 9 October 1851, vol.xxx, 9, L.O.

23. Hutchison to Fr. J.B. Rowe, August 1856, 'Letters to Father Wilfrid Faber from F.F. Stanton and Hutchison' (Rome), 6 July–25 September 1856, L.O.

24. Faber, *Hymns* (London,1861), p.181.

25. *Oratory Church Notices Book* (1852), L.O.
26. Faber to Lady Arundel, 6 September 1854, vol.xxx, 51, L.O.
27. Hutchison to Lady Arundel, 8 June 18(54?), vol.xxx, 48, L.O.
28. Hutchison to Lady Arundel, September 1854, vol.xxx, 50, L.O.
29. Lady Georgiana Fullerton, *Faithful and True: the Life of Elizabeth Twiddy* (London,1908) [originally published as *Apostleship in Humble Life* (London,1860)], p.9.
30. *Ibid.*, p.42.
31. To the sorrow of the Evangelical City Missionary: *London City Mission Magazine*, vol.xxvi (May 1861), pp.111–12.
32. 'Hell [preached to] The Mission, Dunn's Passage, 1852': *MSS Notes of Sermons, and on Spiritual Subjects*, 124, L.O.; cf. 'Hell', 'Purgatory', 'The death–bed of ye Sinner', 'Eternal Misery', 'The Loss of God', 'The Fewness of the Elect', *ibid.*, 113–14, 120–23. The Dunne's Passage Mission to the Irish appropriately began with an account of 'The miracle of S. Patrick opening hell–ye Irish cry for baptism.'
33. Of the cholera: '. . .the majority of persons who are attacked are neglectful Catholics, some of whom. . .have been hurried into eternity with but little opportunity of preparation. . .', *The Tablet*, vol.xv, p.565, 9 September 1854.
34. *Ibid.*, '. . .it has always been remarked that each visitation of the cholera has produced one gratifying result in sending people to the confessional, and exciting in all Catholics greater earnestness and fervour.'
35. *The Rambler*, vol.iv (November, 1849), p.434: 'the zeal manifested by the Irish for the sight of a priest during illness. . .proceeds from a notion that the priest, *as such*, is endowed with the power of healing diseases. . .'.
36. Frederick Oakeley (an English convert), *The Priest on the Mission: A Course of Lectures on Missionary and Parochial Duties* (London, 1871), p.151: 'The Catholic poor look upon the priest as Protestants do upon the physician. . .'.
37. But see Miss Mason, 'Kate Gearey; or, Irish Life in London', *The Rambler*, vol.ix (June, 1852), p.446, 'A praste ud spile the *charm*'; *The London City Mission Magazine*, vol.xiv (March,1849), p.60.
38. Henry Mayhew, *London Labour and the London Poor* (London,1861), vol.I, p.108.
39. Wiseman to Monsignor George Talbot, 3 August 1851, *The Dublin Review*, vol.164 (January, 1919), p.23; cf. *The London City Mission Magazine*, vol.xii (November 1847), p.242.
40. Kerr, *The Oratory in London*, pp.221–22, L.O.
41. As a member of the Catholic Poor Schools Committee, Arundel had an extensive correspondence with two London slum priests, R.G. Macmullen and Gilbert Talbot, and among laymen with a special social consciousness, Thomas Allies and Charles Langdale. See especially Gilbert Talbot's letter to Arundel as Duke of Norfolk, 22 September 1856, Arundel Castle MSS.
42. See the list of convert names for the first meeting of the ragged school committee in Carlton House Terrace on 17 July 1851: W.G.

Ward, David Lewis, William Monsell (later Baron Emly), Sir John Simeon and William Dodsworth; vol.xxxi, 73, L.O. It is not clear how great their interest was, and the committee was later disbanded (Hutchison to Lord Arundel, 19 January 1854, vol.xxx, 43, L.O.). Monsell seems to have been among the more persevering members (Hutchison to Lady Arundel, 2 February 1854, vol.xxx, 44, L.O.).

43. Hutchison to Lady Arundel, 30 November 1854, vol.xxx, 53, L.O.

44. Hutchison to Lady Arundel, 8 June 18(54?), vol.xxx, 48, L.O.

45. Hutchison to Lady Arundel, 5 January 1853, vol.xxx, 25, L.O.

46. Cecil Kerr, *Memoir of a Sister of Charity (Lady Etheldreda Fitzalan Howard* (London,1928), pp.11–2.

47. See his long account of his failures to create a model lodging-house to the Duchess of Norfolk, 5 May 1859, vol.xxxi, 71, L.O.

48. Hutchison left £5,000 to the Oratory which was unsuccessfully claimed by his sister and her doctor-husband Alfred Smee, on the ground that Hutchison was not of 'sound mind' when he wrote his will. The matter was taken in 1870 by the M.P. Charles Newdegate before a House of Commons Select Committee. See Walter L. Arnstein, *Protestant versus Catholic in Mid-Victorian England: Mr Newdegate and the Nuns* (Columbia and London, 1982), pp.63, 64, 156.

THE ROMAN CATHOLIC CHURCH AND THE IRISH POOR

Raphael Samuel

Father Sheridan, a priest at St. Patrick's, Sutton Street, Soho Square in the 1880s, appears to have shared with the Irishwomen of his congregation – those at any rate gathered together in the meetings of St. Bridget's Confraternity – a familiar relationship which social anthropology may explain – the changing balance of intimacy and unease – but which the historian, for want of supporting evidence, can do little more than record. It seems worth recording at some length, if only because it suggests the peculiar flavour of the subject, and the kind of reality, a context of community, which a merely ecclesiastical history of religion is likely to neglect.

The women of the Confraternity held their meetings on Monday evenings in a room at St. Joseph's, Prince's Row, an infant school maintained by St. Patrick's for the children of the poor Irish in and about Newport Market – 'this miserable outcast locality' as it had been called in 1875, inhabited by 'the poorest of God's poor.'[1] Father Sheridan, who compiled a register of the Confraternity's activities, had come to St. Patrick's in August 1880; he introduced himself to the women for the first time on the 27 September, and thereafter attended their meetings 'as regularly as circumstances allowed'.[2] It was his custom, when he addressed them, to read a selection of anecdotes and stories about Irish life, readings uninhibitedly selected, as the register makes clear, to excite the 'risible qualities' among the listeners, and he seems to have been content when his efforts were rewarded with an appreciative response. More serious questions were mainly reserved for a communal devotion in church, observed by the members on the third Monday of every month, and a directly sacred emphasis appears sometimes to have been confined to the recitation of the Rosary, with which the evening's proceedings were invariably closed. Individual entries in the register begin in January 1881: the following is a selection:

> Monday 31.1.81 – Medals and cards procured of Sisters. Feast of St. Bridget for February 1st to be observed. Read story of the pranks of Irish fairies Carleton's Poor Sch. and other tales com. p.214. Said Rosary; but did not speak on any religious topic. Present about 60.

Monday 7.2.81. – Read . . . the story of Fin Mac Coul, and a giant from Carleton. They were amused, but did not laugh to my satisfaction,for, I fear, their tastes had been vitiated by the excrutiatingly (from Miss Ruffe's collection of words), funny tales read to them at other sittings . . . We said the Rosary & asked the assistance of our dear Saint Bridget. Very good attendance, notwithstanding the heavy downpour. Dispersed at 9.30.

Monday 28.2.81. – . . . read to them a chapter from A. M. Sullivan's 'New Ireland' about F. Mathew which seemingly pleased.[3] *Mem.* Always read beforehand for subject for evening; withdraw the jambreakers & skip French and other quotations. Then said Rosary.

Monday 3.10.81. – This evening fair attendance filling hall. Read for them a few anecdotes concerning Newfoundland dogs taken from Lamp followed by a laughable & entertaining Irish skit entitled Nell Hegarty's visit to Cork from October ('80) no of Lamp. Rosary . . . N.B. the *bete noire* of our meeting Mrs. Mahoney was present with her snuff, coughing & disturbance.

Monday 24.10.81. – This evening we read one of Lover's comic sketches – the Curse of Roshogue. There was a great deal of laughing and would have been much more had I carefully prepared the reading of the piece. The attendance was extremely large and I believe the largest yet. Rosary as usual.

Monday 7.11.81. – . . . This evening having previously read the account of Guy Fawkes Day in the Clifton Tract series I chatted to those present about it. It took, I fancy, pretty well. As large a number as usual were present though I noticed strange faces which were their proprietors to bring them often might add a little respectability to proceedings.

Monday 14.11.81. – . . . This evening very large attendance so much so that the babies gallery was taken possession by benign matres who couldn't sit elsewhere. Reading was choice as the new 'Irish Pleasantry & Fun' furnish some excellent pieces. 'Shemus O'Brien' & 'The Donnybrook Spree' seemed to excite the risible qualities wonderfully.

Monday 12.12.81. – . . . The evening being cold & wet and having been disappointed the two previous evenings the number of people did not exceed forty. Was not up to much myself but as proceeded reading the 'Waiver of Duleck Gate' [?] (Irish Pleasantry and Fun) our spirits rose and we had a few good roaring laughs. Rosary & a few words wishing a happy Xmas.

Monday 2.1.82. – Our first meeting of 1882 was not brilliantly attended. Something like 56 put in an appearance & all of them listened with apparent satisfaction to the veracious narration of 'Puss in Brogues' ('Irish Pleasantry and Fun' p.3). Then Rosary & a few words wishing them a happy New Year.

The last entry is for Monday 5 June 1882.

This evening read the skit by Lover (From Handy Andy) in Father Phil's collection. It took very well, but yet I fancy these

> things can be made to take as well as twenty times better if I were to study them beforehand and read them acting partly the while – giving a romantic recital. Attendance very good something like 70 I fancy.

The meetings evidently prospered under this benign direction – the comic Irish stories, in particular, 'seemed to take them' – and attendance, which had been no more than 'about a dozen' when Father Sheridan began his work, was brought up within a few months to 60. The association had originally been designated and held as a 'Mother's Meeting'; but Father Sheridan objected to the name as too 'Proddy', and in December 1880, at the suggestion of Father Barge, Missionary Rector of the parish, it was raised to the status of a religious fraternity and given a Catholic and Irish dedicatory name. (Father Sheridan wrote to the Archbishop of Dublin 'to know if it were possible to procure a relic of St. Bridget in Ireland'). Rules were drawn up setting out the women's religious obligations ('above all not to neglect their monthly confession and communion'),[4] medals were struck to wear as insignia at Mass ('pleasing to saints P and B to see the green'),[5] and collecting cards distributed. By October 1881 Father Sheridan was hopefully anticipating a banner:

> Monday 3.10.81. – . . . I had a few words with them about our prospects and hopes. First I proposed getting a banner of St. Bridget and expect to make by collecting cards and concerts £15 . . . Secondly I said that we should have our monthly mass on the fourth Sunday and day of general communion, and lastly I informed them that on procession evenings they should take part in our Church procession, wearing their regalia (I can easily fancy how proud they'll be) . . . *an idea* occurring to me is that should I be able to have some money over banners cost could get new medals of St. Bridget with name of conf. attached.

The climax of these activities, as they are recorded in the brief period covered by the register (1880–2), occurs on the Sunday evening when a solemn enrolment of members takes place, and the new members come to the altar rails, 'with candles alight', and form themselves into a procession – 'the first procession in which the women of St. Patrick's ever took part'.

> Sunday evening the 23rd April (1882) was a gala day . . . For on that evening took place our second solemn enrolment of members, the blessing of the Banner & the first procession in which the women of St. Patrick's ever took part. We had first the devotions to Jesus Risen, beautiful . . . prayers which accompanied with the apostles' creed, said by people standing, seemed to take immensely well. Then F. Roche preached an eloquent . . . discourse with which I am sure the people were delighted & tears testified the sincerity of the feelings of many. Text was concerning the brazen serpent put up as a sign. Thence he came to speak of the similarity in many points between the chosen people of ancient days & the chosen ones of today – Jews and Irish. He exhorted all to keep pure and unblemished amongst them their holy religion, many points of which were

> brought to their minds by the emblems on Banner. Then I received the new members who with candles alight came to rails & received their medals. The procession was then formed in this wise: 1st small boys, 2 Brothers, 3 women of the Conf. 4 girls. Incensation of relic followed then procession & afterwards blessing of Relic of St. P & Benediction. The church was indeed full, & many testified as to not having seen such a sight for many years in our church.

It would not be difficult to explain these extracts by reference to the conventional religious practice of the time, and there is no reason to insist upon a peculiarly Catholic inspiration. The Irish of St. Patrick's were not the only congregation to be commended by their pastor as a 'peculiar' people, chosen of God; the interleaving of religious and colloquial effects is often met with in nineteenth-century popular religion – it was a powerful ingredient in Spurgeon's religious oratory, while among the vernacular preachers of the provinces (whose 'vulgarity' fastidious men deplored) it was sometimes rampant; and in the last years of the century, Nonconformist deacons promoted Pleasant Sunday Afternoons.[6] No doubt Father Sheridan's Irish sketches share something of this character, but the 'roaring laughs', whose very decibels he makes the subject of retrospective calculation, do seem at some distance removed from the self-proclaimed 'joyousness'[7] of the revivalist hymn or the religious and moral address. One has only to think of Octavia Hill, little more than a mile away in her Marylebone courts, harassing the lives of her tenantry, or of the Scripture Reader, as he was fondly pictured, at the sinner's bedside, to see that, among the ragged communities of the poor at least, the relationship has a certain individual quality. The priest may be irritated by a particular member of his congregation ('Mrs Mahoney . . . with her snuff, coughing and disturbance') but the hostility seems almost neighbourly in character; he may crave for 'a little respectability' to be added to the proceedings, but it is scarcely an active hope, and he appears well satisfied if attendance has been good, and the membership entertained. The setting is gregarious and familiar, and the moral atmosphere characteristic of the congregations of the Irish poor in England during the second half of the nineteenth century.

The great wave of Irish immigration coincided in years with the Romeward movement among the Tractarians, and the Catholic revival to which Newman gave the name of 'Second Spring'. Indeed it may be said to have engulfed it, and never more obviously so than during the cholera of 1849, when Newman and St. John were sent to adminster the last sacraments to the cholera victims at Walsall and Bilston – 'everyone crying as if we were going to be killed'[8] – while the London house of the Oratory was employed on a similar mission among the poor Irish hop-pickers of Kent.[9] Between, on the one hand, the Catholic yeomen and the farmers of Broughton in the Fylde, whose annual festivities at the Whitsuntide dinner of their Friendly Society in 1843 included the collective rendering of a glee bearing the eloquently hybrid title 'St. Patrick Was a Gentleman',[10] or so distinguished a figure among the Catholic laity of England as Lord Arundel, 'the representative of the Mowbrays and the Howards, whose nobility extends beyond that even of Rodolph of Hapsburgh',[11] who at the Oratorians' first celebration of the Quarant' Ore in 1850 was so alarmed at the number of candles displayed that he brought down a portable fire engine 'which at his request was kept ready charged in the sacristy',[12] and, on the other, the Irish Catholic poor – market people, washerwomen, labourers – congregating together in belligerent fidelity, the contrast in religious sensibility, as in nationality and social station, was not easy to ignore, and Catholicity in England during the second half of the nineteenth century may be said to bear the character, of a plural church. It pursued simultaneously a double mission. It reached out in its proselytising work of conversion to the well–born and the rich – those especially who had come within the Puseyite orbit. At the same time it served as a national church of the Irish poor, planting its chapels and schoolrooms in the close quarters and the narrow streets, seeking out the Irish in the workhouse, the children's orphanage and the reformatory,[13] ministering to the Irish soldier in his barracks[14] and the Irish prisoner in his cell.[15]

The new missions reflected the line and cluster of Irish settlement, following isolated groups of labourers at distant points, like the Franciscan mission in the Monmouthshire hills,[16] or planting themselves in the midst of the densely–crowded pent–up rookeries of the towns, as at Holy Cross, Liverpool, where 'not a house'[17] in the district was more than seven minutes walk from the church. The 'churches', in the newly–founded missions were sometimes no more than temporary chapels, improvised in wood and iron; sometimes merely a hired shop or 'rooms'. The Church of the Sacred Heart, Camberwell, founded as a temporary chapel in 1863, and built upon a site of tumbledown premises – 'comprising a rag–shop with a pig–sty in the rear'[18] – illustrates the characteristically plebeian setting. The mission was deliberately established among the poorest inhabitants, 'so that shabby clothes shall not hinder them from coming to Mass'. It stood on the edge of the Sultan Street area, whose moral and social condition was some years later to invite the anxious investigations of Charles Booth,[19] and it served an Irish colony in densely–crowded conditions – 'seven or eight different surnames and up to twenty inhabitants . . . under one roof'.[20]

The establishment of a new mission was liable to provoke in the local community an outburst of Protestant indignation. Mission rooms were difficult to hire (above all in Wales),[21] obstacles were placed in the way of a purchase of land, and the chapels, as they were building, had sometimes to face a threat of malicious damage: at Carmarthen, 'it was necessary to enlist the help of voluntary watchmen, for otherwise what was being built in the day would have been pulled down in the night by the hands of unfriendly Protestants'.[22] The arrival of a Catholic priest was in some places an historical event. At Pontypool, where a Franciscan mission was established in 1860, the appearance of Father Elzear in their midst ('a real live monk') provoked among the native Welsh inhabitants an animated curiosity which they were not at pains to hide. 'Every time Father Elzear went out . . . he was surrounded by crowds of eager faces, and his progress through the street caused as much excitement as though he had been the Pope in person'.[23] At distant points, where Protestant feeling was strong, the early congregations met under conditions of menace or even siege. At Colne, where a missioner from Burnley attempted to gather a congregation in 1851, the Catholic worshippers, meeting above a stable in the Angel Inn Yard, were surrounded by a No Popery crowd 'sometimes five times as numerous', a factory manager leading his people to demonstrate against the services, and a Protestant agitator haranguing the priest from below.[24] At Wallasey, where a priest from Liverpool crossed the river to celebrate Mass, the congregation had to fill their pockets with stones before setting out for the service, 'it being almost certain that the local Orangemen would assail them either coming or going'.[25] At Cwmbran, in Monmouthshire, where the Irish were employed about the furnaces and iron–works, 'it was for some time no unusual occurrence for stones to be hurled against the windows during Mass or Benediction'; the Catholic chapel, 'an iron building capable of accommodating 250 people', was surrounded by five hostile chapels, in which, 'Sunday after Sunday', Dissenting ministers hurled their anathemas at the stranger in their midst – 'our meek–looking chapel', a Franciscan chronicler wrote, 'standing as a little Goschen amidst the Egyptian darkness'.[26]

The religious orders provoked an especially great reflexive national hostility, and against convents in particular a campaign of virulent insinuation was waged for many years. The appearance of a religious habit in the street, so far from protecting the wearer by the announcement of a religious status, might serve rather as an excitement to insulting personal remarks.[27] Even in the relative seclusion of Woodchester, Father Tom Burke, the Irish Dominican, and his novices, found themselves exposed to the 'unbecoming jibes' of factory girls on the way to work.[28] During the Protestant hysteria of 1850–1, Father Ignatius Spencer, clothed in the coarse black habit of the Passionist Order, was attacked by roughs in Liverpool as he was passing from St. Patrick's chapel, and in a nearby street was 'hustled and . . . thrown down into a cellar full of people';[29] near Charter–house Square, in London, he was mobbed 'and almost killed' by an infuriated crowd.[30] So strong was the popular feeling that, independently of the hostile Parliamentary moves in the same direction, the more timid among the English Catholics were urging the abandonment of religious dress 'on the public road'.[31] An attempt to establish the Sisters of Charity in Salford provoked such violent persecution that they were withdrawn by their Superior to Paris:

> At first . . . the labours of the three sisters whom Father Etienne had sent . . . promised to be conducive to good. They visited the sick unmolested in the daytime, and held classes for factory girls and others in the evening . . . hundreds were prepared for the sacraments . . . (But) the bulk of the people became more and more anti–Catholic. The Sisters were insulted

> wherever they appeared, and one of them was thrown down, and returned home covered with blood; and, on another occasion, while the Sisters were at church, their house was set on fire. The violent treatment frightened Sister de Missy, the Superioress, and led her to relate everything to Father Etienne, who considered it his duty to recall the Sisters.[32]

Some years later, in 1859, when they were installed at York Street, Westminster – 'a very old house . . . in the midst of a swarming population of the poorer people'[33] – the 'cries' and 'shouts of derision' once more sounded on all sides.

> On the evening of the Sisters' arrival a young teacher in the Catholic school, attached to the Church of St. Peter and St. Edward, offered to take them there to Benediction, but no sooner did they appear in the street than they were surrounded by an unfriendly mob. Cries and shouts of derision sounded on all sides; mud and even stones were thrown at the Sisters, and the consequences might have been serious had not some tall Guardsmen from the neighbouring barracks come forward and constituted themselves their protectors, giving them their escort as far as the Church, and even remaining there to see them back to their poor little dwelling in York Street . . . For some time a number of them took it in turn to protect them whenever they went into the streets; but sometimes even their presence was not sufficient to keep the boys, and even men and women, from attacking them, and then the aid of the law had to be evoked, so that it was by no means unusual to see the Sisters walking along with a soldier on one side of them and a policeman on the other.[34]

The native disposition was not kindly, yet these were the streets in which popular Catholicism sought to find a sanctuary and, like the Irish immigrants themselves, to create the familiar surroundings of a home.

The Catholic 'Poor Schools', to which the Church devoted so remarkable an effort in the third quarter of the century, were planted in the very midst of the poor, quite without regard to the reputation of the 'low' Irish neighbourhoods. London Prentice Street, where in 1849 St. Chad's Cathedral set up its poor schools in the seven back rooms of a court,[35] was reputedly the most dangerous street in Birmingham; it carried the stigma of a particularly brutal murder in 1835,[36] and was the centre of a rookery 'notoriously infested with bad characters of every description.'[37] Park Street nearby, where in 1846 the Sisters of Mercy established their Sunday School in a loft,[38] was another very poor street; it had received an early influx of Irish,[39] and in 1867, when 'the ragged Catholic children who squat among the dust–heaps and gutter' were recited as a commonplace feature of the street, they had grown so numerous that it provided a natural focus, as the most Irish street in town, for racial and religious riot. The early schools were in no way cloistered. One at Liverpool was 'a large room or loft above a cow–house, in a dirty, back, ill–ventilated lane';[40] another – rented by Father Parker of St. Patrick's when

Protestant bigotry turned the Catholic children out of the Council schools – was a converted Penny Gaff.[41] At Cardiff, the Catholic school in 1847 was a loft above a cooper's workshop; at Barnsley, 'only a cellar.'[42] In the second half of the century, despite the intense efforts of the Catholic Poor Schools Committee, many of the children continued to be taught in very primitive conditions. The Catholic school in Lincoln, as Joseph O'Connor remembered it in the early 1880s – 'a long walk down the hill . . . through a maze of back streets' – was 'a makeshift of corrugated iron attached to a makeshift chapel of the same depressing material . . . almost hidden on a waste spot in the poorest slum'. . .[43] At Kilburn, in 1871,

> The chief school room where the elder children are taught is the upper room of a shopkeeper's house ill–suited for a school room . . . The infants are taught in a dark kitchen used after the children are dismissed for culinary purposes.[44]

In a crowded part of Westminster, where the Catholic school was housed in a converted theatre, 'formerly . . . very popular among the poor', the children had to make their way at the beginning of the day through a milling crowd of costers:

> there was a very long covered passage leading from the street to the school; to this all the costermongers of the neighbourhood laid claim as having a prescriptive right to deposit there their barrows for the night; so that, what with the children in the morning fighting to get in, and the costers struggling to get out, we may leave the reader to imagine the confusion.[45]

'Child hunting', as Father Vere described it in a memoir of his early days in Soho,[46] was a frequent addition to the ordinary duties of the priest. The children of the Irish poor were apt to be irregular in their attendance at school, more especially in the great cities,[47] and a great deal depended on the pressure which could be brought to bear on 'negligent' parents. Even those – they seem in general to have been a small minority – whom the priest found it otherwise 'difficult to touch', might nevertheless be persuaded on this single point to yield.[48] At Tarry Town, Hackney Wick, 'a poor and woebegone spot at the junction of Hackney Cut and Duckett's Canal', the Servants of the Sacred Heart went out to hunt up the children of a little colony of lapsed Irish Catholics, and bring them to the Catholic school.[49] At a private 'adventure' school in Periwinkle Street, Tower Hamlets, where upwards of one hundred boys and girls, 'the children of very poor parents', were accommodated in the space of a 'wretched hovel', the local Catholic priest was said to treat the children as though they were his own: 'the school being almost wholly composed of the children of Irish Rom. Catholics, the priest periodically, *but unasked*, visits it in order to take the pupils to their religious duties'.[50] At St. Francis Xavier's, Liverpool, the Jesuit Fathers gathered together a host of street urchins on Sunday mornings, provided them with breakfast, and marched them off to Mass, some 'almost "sansculotte"' in appearance, 'most of them shoeless'.[51] Moreover, Protestant aggression – 'the obvious danger of proselytism' – represented in places as potent a danger as apathy or negligence, and the Poor

Schools themselves served in places less as educational establishments than as an improved arm of confessional war. St. Joseph's infant school in Princes Row, Soho, 'that little school with its close atmosphere and dirty children', as Father Vere affectionately recalled it – housed above the parlours of an itinerant Irish shell–fish dealer, who cooked his whelks and winkles in the yard, and sent his own little girls to the school[52] – was set up to counter the rival persuasions of the Puseyite mission which had its headquarters nearby in Crown Street. A scribbled entry in the 'log book' for 1868 (the few tattered pages are all of the school's existence to survive) records an early triumph,

> May 11th until this date 36 children have left the Puseyite schools to come to St. Joseph's only 6 of them have gone back again 3 Griffins Newport Market
> 2 Connolly's Princes Court
> M.A. Morgan Princes Court
> 10 June Anna Griffin again returned having previously been at the Puseyite school[53]

A mile away to the north, at the far end of Charlotte Street, off Fitzroy Square, the Catholic children of another infant school named St. Joseph's – crammed into the space of a single ground floor room – faced the Protestant children of a rival school on opposite sides of the same narrow court. The hectic situation may be imagined. 'Some panes of glass have been removed to ensure ventilation', an Inspector commented, 'but the noise from outside makes satisfactory teaching impossible'.[54]

The priest, in the Irish mission, lived in close vicinity with his flock, having no society other than that of his parishoners: 'no rich to interfere . . . no invitations to ruin the clergy',[55] nor any round save that of the close quarters and the narrow streets. His daily transactions were conducted as those of a familiar, and yet one who at the same time enjoyed a peculiar and esoteric power, a figure at once accessible and remote. His entire life was devoted to his ministry. He might be called out at any hour to visit the sick, to bring the sacraments to the dying or to act as arbiter in a family quarrel. His life was intimately associated with that of the community, even though he was assigned an exalted role in it. As the 'man of God' his blessing was eagerly sought, as the leader of the flock he was looked to for the kindness of a friendly recognition or a brief exchange of words. Mayhew, who accompanied a priest on his round among the street–Irish of London, described how his mere presence brought the people crowding to their doors.

> Everywhere the people ran out to meet him. He had just returned to them I found, and the news spread round, and women crowded to their door–steps, and came creeping up from the cellars through the trap–doors, merely to curtsey to him. One old crone, as he passed, cried 'You're a good father, Heaven comfort you', and the boys playing about stood still to watch him. A lad, in a man's tail coat and a shirt–collar that nearly covered in his head – like the paper round a bouquet – was fortunate enough to

> be noticed, and his eyes sparkled, as he touched his hair at each word he spoke in answer. At a conversation that took place between the priest and a woman who kept a dry fish–stall, the dame excused herself for not having been up to take tea 'with his rivirince's mother lately, for thrade had been so busy, and night was the fullest time.' Even as the priest walked along the street, boys running at full speed would pull up to touch their hair, and the stall–women would rise from their baskets; while all noise – even a quarrel – ceased until he had passed by. Still there was no look of fear in the people. He called them all by their names, and asked after their families, and once or twice the 'father' was taken aside and held by the button while some point that required his advice was whispered in his ear.[56]

The priest's house – no more than a humble workman's cottage in some of the poorest missions[57] – was barely separated from the work of his ministry, but served rather as a second focal point. In earlier years, before the placing of the confessional in church had been made obligatory, it was sometimes used for the reception of penitents: at St. Patrick's, Soho, when the clergy lived in Dean Street, 'a long line of penitents knelt all up the stairs' on confessional nights, 'and took their turns for admission to the priest's room.'[58] It was a recipient for 'American' and 'foreign' letters which arrived for members of the congregation ('for James Hogan . . . from Australia', 'from John Dolan, Royal Marine, for his sister', 'Mr David Magee for Mr P. O'Brien').[59] It was a natural point of call when trouble broke out in any part of the community. Above all the priest was perpetually on call for visits to the sick. Each day there was a lengthy list of the sick to be visited; calls continued to come in through the day ('We generally had to look in at the presbytery about midday, to see if any new . . . calls had been sent in'), and the sick bell might be rung even in the dark hours of night.[60] At St. Peter's, Birmingham, ministering to a very poor community of Irish, the notices suggest that the parishioners were not reticent in calling upon the services of the priest.

> 23 November 1862 – At the approach of winter when sick calls are more numerous, we beg to give notice that such calls must be left at the Chapel house before 10 in the morning.
> January 1863 – *Once more* we beg to remind the congregation that sick calls must be sent to the Chapel house before ten o'clock in the morning, except in very urgent cases which seldom happen as those which are *called* urgent are nearly always nothing of the kind.[61]

Sneyd–Kynnersley's summary of such calls, though highly–coloured, has the authority of one who had many years of professional association, as an Inspector of Schools, with the priests of the Irish mission in the North–west:

> the heavy work undoubtedly comes at night. The door bells seem to get no rest; sometimes it is a drunken woman, who comes to take the pledge, just as a wealthier drunkard might ask for a bottle of seltzer; sometimes, and many times, an urgent demand

> for a speedy visit to Biddy, who is 'dyin' entirely', but turns out to be dismally drunk. The whole force of the mission is sometimes called out . . .
>
> In the small hours of the morning the flock break out afresh. Patsey is brought home helpless at 2 a.m., Michael has his head cut open at 3; Molly upsets the lamp, and sets the baby on fire at 4. In each and every case his reverence is brought down to give the last rites to the afflicted person, and in each and every case he finds he might as well have gone on with his sleep.[62]

The priest's relationship to the individual believer was different in kind from that of the Anglican clergyman or the conscientious 'visitor to the poor'. In Irish missions the period of a ministry often extended to an adult lifetime, and he might know his penitents through two or more generations. He heard the believer's confession from early childhood, preparing him for first communion as for the later crises of life.[63] Preparation for marriage was liable to involve the priest in a far more detailed moral supervision than it did his Protestant counterpart among the poor, and there was nothing of that desultory relationship exemplified, at an opposite extreme, by the notorious 'Red Church' of Bethnal Green.[64]

The priest was the secular as well as the religious leader of his flock, and his authority was recognised not only by the devout, but by some at least who had virtually lapsed from the practice of the Church: 'They rarely deny their own faith . . . and when confronted by it they still accept the authority of the priest.'[65] His personal intervention might bring the most obstinate sinner penitently to his knees, as could 'that champion converter' Father Flynn of St. Vincent's;[66] a single visit could put a stop to Evangelical attack.[67] His jurisdiction extended over the entire range of the community's affairs, and the power which he expressed sacramentally at the altar rail might be no less compelling when exercised in the informal surroundings of the street. Serving a people among whom fighting, as Booth remarked, was 'almost a recreation',[68] and whose drinking was apt to become 'riotous', the pacification of communal disorder was not the least of the extempore duties he was called upon to perform.[69] Family rows, when they exploded into the street, seem to have been an especial care,[70] and the priest was credited with a power of restoring tranquillity in neighbourhoods where the policeman ventured at his peril: 'If in some domestic quarrel the priest interferes, they submit, but let a policeman attempt it, and he may be kicked to death.'[71] In *The Brandons* John Denvir presents the same setting in more sentimental terms, but the role of Father Peter MacMahon – 'as fine a specimen of the good old Irish *soggarth* as you would see in a day's work' – is substantially the same as that described by Booth.

> Often when there was a real row, and No.9, aided by all the constables from the surrounding beats could not cope with the disturbance, as a last resource the cry would be – 'Run for Father MacMahon', and when the well-known face appeared the fiercest storm or strife would be quelled, and peace would again

reign in Homer's Garden.[72]

And yet, if the priest's influence among his people was, in Faucher's phrase, 'absolute',[73] it was also tempered by a realistic appreciation of the nature of the flock, their hereditary weaknesses and strengths. The moral lessons which he taught might be impeccably orthodox, and indistinguishable at times from the conventional homilies of self-help – 'detachment' 'watchfulness' 'peace with our neighbourhood'.[74] But the community context remained obstinately perverse, and offered few points of departure for the improving social career. The administration of the pledge was apt to involve not one but frequent and recurring interventions by the priest. For some, at least, like those who took the pledge from Father Mathew in 1843 'whilst in a state of intoxication',[75] it may have represented less a decision for life – 'to cut off at once and for ever this insidious and devastating temptation',[76] – than an interlude of remorse between compulsive bouts of drink,[77] as in Mayhew's story of old Norah.[78]

One may suggest the same of fighting as of drink. The priest's interventions were frequent, and urgently renewed, but they seem to have carried no expectation of permanent moral reform. Booth describes them as 'lenient judges of the frailties that are not sins, and of the disorder that is not crime,' and suggests a resigned acceptance of the unchangeable necessities of life.

> This kindly gentleness is after the event; at the same time no one could be more uncompromising in denunciation or more prompt in interference. It is said that the voice of the priest or the presence of the Sister will quell any disorder; but the trouble recurs. I do not go so far as to say that the same quarrel breaks out again as soon as the priest or Sister has gone, but it may be so; at any rate the occasions repeat themselves. Savagery is checked, but there is no sign of permanent improvement. Drinking and fighting are the ordinary conditions of life among many of their flock, and the streets in which they dwell show it.[79]

This is a kind of negative capability, extending to every question save those which threatened the fundamentals of the faith.

> As a rule the better Catholic the better Irishman, and the better Irishman the better Catholic: their priests, being often of Irish blood, are at one with the people, and in sentiment are even more Irish than they are Catholic. Amongst the Irish, rebellious blood turns not against both Church and State as in Italy, but against the State alone. With the poor Irish the police are recognised enemies, against whom the whole street is ready to unite . . . Quarrelsome and violent, unrestrained as children, and brutal when their passions are loosed, they are yet full of natural piety, and the priests who live with them and love them 'can find no harm in them'.[80]

The Roman Catholic Church of the second half of the nineteenth century thus occupied a singular position.[81] In districts 'too poor for Dissent', and where the Anglican Church preached its message as to the heathen,[82] amid a people whom rival denominations found it difficult, and even dangerous to touch,[83] Irish congregations flourished. They supported the 'round' of the Church's house–to–house collectors; they crowded the chapels at Sunday Mass; and they gave to the Church, in the neighbourhoods of their settlement, an unmistakeably proletarian complexion: 'A Catholic chapel', complained an estate agent in 1849, 'crowds the streets with the lower classes and deteriorates surrounding property.'[84]

The Irish poor were for half a century the great support of the Church, and it was the increase in their numbers, especially in the decades following the Famine, which was responsible for the multiplication of Catholic missions and schools. So close, indeed, was the association that the Church, which gratefully acknowledged their role as 'eminent propagandists of the faith'[85], sometimes treated 'Catholic' and 'Irish' as interchangeable terms: workhouse registers were diligently scrutinised for children who might be recognised as Catholics 'from their names only';[86] parishes were occasionally credited with 'Catholic' neighbourhoods and 'Catholic' streets;[87] while the appearance of a settled body of Irish in any place was generally a signal for the planting of a Catholic mission. Protestant missionaries, who suffered their persecutions in the street, were accustomed to classify the Irish indiscriminately as 'Romanists', whose 'superstition' and 'ignorance' it was one of their painful duties to meet – one missionary even complained of 'Papist charwomen' at a London hospital, biasing the patients against the influence of 'Bible instructions'.[88] For working people too, like the colliers at Airdrie who struck work in 1854 'until the Catholic miners were dismissed',[89] the religion of the newly–arrived immigrants might appear as distinctive a peculiarity as their race; the Roman Catholic Church, a London street sweeper told Mayhew, was 'a Irish religion' which, as he explained, he 'wasn't to be expected to understand'.[90] The Irish, for their part, rejoiced in the equation and seem to have sought out occasions on which it might be displayed.[91] During the taking of the 1871 Census in Ancoats, a batch of returns was found to have been completed at a local public house – 'the House of Commons for Ireland' – in which religion and social status were interestingly confused: 'Numbers of papers were found filled up in the same handwriting, and the occupation of almost all of them returned as Catholic.'[92]

The Irish stood in a hereditary relationship to their religion. Faith and nationality, hallowed by persecution, reciprocated one another's claims, and in the harsh conditions of their exile, stigmatised alike by religion and by race, the partnership was persistently renewed. Samuel Bamford describes the scene in 1819 when the Rochdale and Middleton people, on their way to Peterloo, stopped their procession at Newtown, just outside Manchester:

> we were welcomed with open arms by the poor Irish weavers, who came out in their best drapery, and uttered blessings and words of endearment, many of which were not understood by our rural patriots. Some of them danced and others stood with clasped hands and tearful eyes, adoring almost, that banner whose

colour was often their national one, and the emblem of their green island home. We thanked them by the band striking up, 'Saint Patrick's day in the morning'. They were electrified; and we passed on , leaving these warm–hearted suburbans capering and whooping like mad.[93]

The nearby community at Wigan displayed an early combativity.[94] Religious spirit among the street folk whom Mayhew wrote about ran high, and they entered keenly into the subject of their faith. 'I don't go much among the English street–dealers', said one, 'They talk like haythens': and he went on to say that he was 'almost glad' to have no 'childer' because of the way that in England they were allowed to run wild: 'They haven't the fear of God or the saints. They'd hang a praste – glory to be to God! they would.'[95] Another, who crossed himself repeatedly as he spoke, claimed to be more tolerant. He had 'nothing to say' against 'Protistints' ('I've heard it said "It's best to pray for them"'), and he observed that the 'Protistint gintlemen and ladies' among his customers 'sometimes . . . talk to me kindly about religion.' But he referred with contempt to the spiritual state of his fellow–costers among the English ('The street–people that call themselves Protistants are no riligion at all'), and as for the Protestant 'gintlemen and ladies', he mused upon the possible fate awaiting them 'in another worruld': 'I can't say what their lot may be . . . for not being of the true faith. No, sir, I'll give no opinions – none.'[96]

The Irish in England defended the Church when under attack with something of that primitive violence which made it dangerous, in the more inflammatory parts of rural Ireland, for a bailiff to serve his writ or for a landlord to reside. The 'rough' elements in the congregation were ready, and indeed eager, to avenge whatever insults were offered to their priests or to the honour of the Church – 'the roughest the readiest', a London priest told Booth.[97] At times like these, the primal solidarities of the community were engaged. The children of the immigrant poor – 'chiefly noisy, unwashed young Hibernians', in the unenthusiastic description of a Schools Inspector,[98] 'very rough and obstreperous', as even their own priests sometimes felt constrained to complain[99] – seem to have shared the combativity of their parents. They might be called upon to defend their very homes against attack, as at Barrack Yard, Wigan, where on the third night of the De Camin rioting in 1859 a mob of English workmen and colliers was 'gallantly resisted by a handful of boys and girls, who showered stones upon the attacking party' and were compelled for a time to retreat:[100] and they seem to have been no less ready to take part in the tumults of the street, as at Failsworth in 1868,[101] and Tredegar in 1882.[102] The turbulent Irishwoman, with her sleeves tucked up, and her apron full of stones,[103] or, flourishing her rolling pin in battle,[104] was as distinguished a presence in the Irish mob as the labourer with his shillelagh. And when the chapel bells pealed their alarms, and the narrow streets echoed to the No Popery cry, the Irishman was ready, with a stone in his hand, an iron stick or cudgel[105] – indeed, as at Ashton–under–Lyne and Stalybridge in 1868, fortified by pistols[106] – to defend his church, as he was wont to do his street, with an impulsive belligerence which the clergy themselves found it impossible to restrain.

However lowly and inferior their position in English society, the Irish maintained an exalted notion of their own religion, and a sovereign contempt for the 'haythen' with whom they were surrounded. Town missionaries, seeking to enlighten their darkness, found them 'warm antagonists of truth' – 'Generally they refuse to take a tract, or to listen to any remarks that may be made for their benefit';[107] the 'pleasing testimonies' which they were able occasionally to record, where an isolated believer had been persuaded to accept a tract or to listen to a reading of the Bible, were apt to collapse under the intervention of a religious member of the family or a visit from the priest.[108] Distrust of Protestantism was, like the faith itself, inveterate, and might survive even a formal separation from the Church. An Irish tinker girl, who admitted to George Borrow that she was 'clane unsettled about religion', and whose family had discarded the Catholic symbols of faith,[109] was nevertheless indignant at the suggestion that she might join the Methodists:

> I have been at their chapels at nights and have listened to their screaming prayers, and have seen what's been going on outside the chapel after their services, as they call them, were over – I never saw the like going on outside Father Toban's chapel, yere hanner![110]

The sorrowing note of a Birmingham town missionary suggests that even among those whom the Evangelical found seemingly complaisant, there remained still a loyalty, furtive but persistent, to the ancient faith:

> In one house that I entered a man & his wife were sitting opposite each other with short pipes in their mouths smoaking & playing at cards, the woman was very much ashamed to see me & shuffled the cards up to hide them. The man seeing he was detected in his hypocrisy for he remembered as well as I did the conversation we had together the week before, and the way in which he had spoken of the religion of the Bible, speaking of it in the highest terms. He said 'I won't deceive you. I am not a Protestant, I am a Roman Catholic and if you should run a spear into me I will not change the religion I believe.' I said I had a good tract which would suit him if he would promise to read it. He said he would and I left with him a tract on the Wrath of the Soul. I asked the woman if she would not be happier reading some good book than playing at cards. She confessed she should, but when I proposed burning the cards she said they were borrowed.[111]

It seems that rush–bearing at Manchester was brought to an end in the 1820s because the Irish, 'taking offence at some orange–coloured lillies adorning a rush–cart', fell upon the hapless dancers accompanying the carts from the outlying townships and dispersed them, a proceeding which was repeated until the visits of the rush–carts ceased.[112] This extreme case illustrates a general truth. For the merest symptom of Protestant activity seems to have been treated by the Irish as a national affront, and to have provoked them, individually or collectively – and often with a reckless disregard of the consequences – to riot. The Anglo–Catholic Father Charles Lowder in St. George's in the East, attempting to open a mission at Lower Wall Walk, where a population of indigenous Irish 'swarmed',[113] was no more immune from their hostile attention, though Catholic in his theology, than was the Hallelujah Band of Accrington, whom a drunken Irishman cursed in the streets,[114] the Temperance Seminary at Oldham, whose Sunday afternoon proceedings were interrupted by a disorderly Irishman calling for 'beer'[115] or Mr. Finnigan, an Irish–speaking Scripture reader, seized by the waistcoat in a Birmingham court.[116] The Irish did not abstain from the early persecutions of the Salvation Army. 'Romanists' ranged themselves with 'infidels' and 'drunkards' at Canning Town, 'set on and backed up by the devil himself', to attempt to drive the Christian Missionary from the field.[117] At Croydon, where the missioner had the misfortune to set up his preaching stand directly opposite an Irish street, the meetings were the subject of their tireless abuse – 'an alley . . . full of Roman Catholics who are bitter opposers to the truth,'[118] while a brother labouring in the vineyard of Stratford Marshes, and asking at each of the houses he canvassed 'if there was anyone there on the way to Heaven', recorded only one, 'a Roman Catholic and a tinker', who was ready to make profession of a faith, 'and when he discovered who I was, he threatened to burn me with his soldering–iron . . .if I did not leave the place.[119] Gipsy Smith, who in his later years as an independent evangelist was to suffer the 'loud and unseemly noises' and 'foul parodies' of the Catholic children of the Liverpool slums,[120] was in his Salvation Army years faced with 'one of those wild Irish Catholic yells', issuing from the throats of the Bolton Irish – an excited, swaying crowd in the Market Square, who took the uttering of Benediction as a signal for attack.[121]

The second and third generations of the immigrants seem to have shared a good deal of the belligerent fidelity of the first. The walls of the Irish home continued to be adorned by a free intermixture of sacred and patriotic subjects, as they had been when Mayhew described them in the middle of the century.[122] 'Often', Joe Toole recalls of the Salford Irish homes of his childhood, 'did I see a picture of the Saviour on one wall and one of J. L. Sullivan, the bare–knuckle fighter, opposite.'[123] For the Home Rule canvasser, indeed, they served indiscriminately as insignia of national support: 'If they see a picture of St. Patrick, or the Pope, or Robert Emmet, they assume they are in an Irish house of the right sort'.[124] On St. Patrick's Day itself, religion and nationality continued to meet in explosive combination with the drink, as a missionary in the East End of London prudently acknowledged:

> Tuesday (St. Patrick's Day). The Irish dock labourer is rampant to–day, and anyone who wishes to be involved in a serious row could not do better than broach the subject of Evangelical religion. I wisely refrain to–day and confine my efforts to

railway men at Millwall.[125]

The spiritual inheritance of the children included a vivid recollection of national wrong. James Sexton, growing up in St. Helens, where his parents kept a stall in the open market, served his political apprenticeship when, as a boy, he accompanied his father and grandfather in their 'missionary' activity among the Irish navvies at work on a nearby railway, to whom they administered the Fenian oath. His mother had been born in Warrington, but her parents had experienced the terrible aftermath of the Irish rebellion of 1798 – 'the days when the pitch–cap and gibbet were the certain fate of any priest caught celebrating Mass, as they were of the peasant who dared to take up arms against injustice': for a young boy of the second generation, to whom the memory was handed down, it still served as a family inheritance:

> The story of those days of terror was handed on to the children of all who endured their agony; it spread all over the world, and engendered in the mind of every Irishman and Irishwoman who heard it hatred – bitter and boundless hatred – of everything connected with the Briton and the British. That, so far as my mind was concerned, was my principal political and spiritual inheritance. Even to–day . . . my mind goes back at times, to the stories of my maternal grandparents – of men being hanged, drawn and quartered . . . of an ancestor, hanged from the shafts of his own cart, and the gruesome story of Donald dun O'Byrne, who, driven mad by the bayoneting of his wife and child, waylaid individual members of the British yeomenry whom he thought responsible for the outrage, and killed them with the primitive flail he used when threshing the wheat, cutting a notch on the hand for every one he slew.[126]

Tom Barclay, recalling a Leicester Irish childhood of the 1860s, describes the militant religion which he took with him to the workshop – 'Protestant hymns disgusted me, and I actually used to spit out to cleanse my mouth if I thoughtlessly had been singing a strain caught from some pious shop–mates.' As a child he had been made familiar with the heritage of national struggle; 'My father was a Limerick man, and we were often hearing of the hero Patrick Sarsfield, and the women of Limerick who fought and repelled the English during the siege of that city'. A quite ordinary scuffle with the children at the other end of the yard took on for him the epic quality of an historical national drama:

> One day the kids from the other end of the court, or 'yard' as we called it, attacked us under Bill, their leader, and broke a pane of glass and thrust a rod through: unable to get out, or fearful of a spanking if we did, we scuttled upstairs and threw cinders from the chamber window on Billy and his pals: they battered the door, and we retaliated as we could. My imagination went to work: Billy was King William and we were the Irish: it was the siege of Limerick being in some mysterious manner enacted over again.[127]

George Lansbury remembered the Irish boys at his school in

Bethnal Green as being 'all "Fenians"':

> consequently, when the wall of Clerkenwell prison was blown down and three Irish martyrs executed in Manchester because a police officer was accidentally killed, very great excitement prevailed in our classes and playground. The teachers tried to make us understand how wicked the Irishmen had been on both occasions, but my Irish friends would have none of it, and when a few months later T.D. Sullivan's song *God Save Ireland* came out, we boys were shouting it at the tops of our voices every playtime.[128]

In Clerkenwell, where the Irish and Italians occupied adjacent quarters, and fought between each other, the name 'Garibaldi' was perpetuated as a ritual challenge in the children's games of the street.[129] 'Faith and fatherland', in short, found their defenders in the tenement streets of East and Central London, and in the back streets of Bradford and the Scholes, as well as in Ireland itself.

Conditions of worship in England were characteristically more retrained than in Ireland, and in the pent-up rookeries where the immigrants made a home, popular Catholicism enjoyed for its arena a less exuberant space. But Father Mathew's reception among the Irish poor of St. Giles, when portraits and medals were on sale in the streets, and the rookery 'poured forth its thousands' ('The windows and even the roofs of many of the surrounding houses . . . crowded with people'),[130] suggests that, however different the material circumstance and setting of life, the new communities shared strong cultural affinities with the old and reproduced some, at least, of their religious and national characteristics.[131]

There is some scattered though strongly suggestive evidence for the survival of folk religious practices among the immigrants. Father Mathew's crusade served as a magnet to the afflicted and diseased, and although it is not possible to pronounce with any confidence upon the motives of those who fell upon their knees before the hustings (many seem to have been anxious to take the pledge not once but repeatedly), it seems clear that the belief in supernatural agency – an important element in his success in Ireland itself[132] – played a part. The pledge was administered to vast assemblies of the Irish poor, and the benediction by which it was accompanied – the sign of the cross which Father Mathew made over the kneeling figure of the postulant, 'descending from the platform and placing his hands upon each person's head',[133] and the temperance medal which he hung with ribbons about the neck – seem to have been credited by some, at least, with a physically healing power. At Glasgow, where 'crowds of diseased persons' were taken to the cattle market, and where the impetuous rush of people was such that 'many who ardently longed for an opportunity of kneeling before the great Apostle of Temperance . . . could not even get a sight of his face', Father Mathew felt obliged specifically to disclaim a supernatural power, 'the power of performing miracles belonging alone to the Supreme Being.'[134] At Kennington Common, where women and children were especially numerous among those who came forward to take the pledge – a feature remarked upon elsewhere

– 'several curious evidences of the spirit of superstition which pervades the lower orders of Irish Roman Catholics' were said to have been exhibited: 'on one occasion a woman having a cancerous deformity in the face and on another a mother with a child afflicted with scrofula, implored the rev. gentleman to place his hand on the part affected.'[135] John Denvir, who took the pledge as a little boy in Liverpool, suggests one explanation for the particular anxiety shown by Irish women to take the pledge:

> My mother took the whole family, and, wherever he was – at St. Patrick's, or in a great field on one side of Crown Street or at St. Anthony's – there she was with her family. She was a woman with the strong Irish faith in the supernatural, and in the power of God and His Church, that can 'move mountains'. A younger brother of mine had a running sore in his foot which the doctors could not cure. She determined to take Bernard to Father Mathew and get him to lay his hands on her boy.
>
> At St. Patrick's with her children kneeling around her, she asked the good Father to touch her son. He, no doubt thinking it would be presumptuous on his part to claim any supernatural gift, passed on without complying with her request.

When Father Mathew came to Crown Street

> my mother was there again with her afflicted boy and the rest of her children, and again she pleaded in vain. She was a courageous woman, with great force of character – and a *third* time she went to Father Mathew's gathering. This was in St. Anthony's chapel yard, and amongst the thousands there to hear him take the pledge she awaited her turn. Again she besought him to touch the boy's foot. He knew her again, and, deeply moved by her importunity and great faith, he, at length to her great joy, put his hand on my brother's foot and gave him his blessing. My mother's faith in the power of God, through his minister, was rewarded for the foot was healed.[136]

The Irish brought with them into the country a complex of popular devotional practices, whose warmth and externality were often contrasted with the more reserved tradition of worship which prevailed among English Catholics. The Irish might carry the signs of religious privilege about their person – the scapular,[137] the crucifix,[138] the picture of Mary,[139] blessed by the priest for members of the congregation and worn close to the heart; they crossed themselves devoutly at the mention of each holy name.[140] The 'rude representation of the Crucifixion'[141] and the show of sacred pictures upon the wall made the mysteries of the faith a commonplace feature of the immigrant family home – 'the adoration of the shepherds', as Mayhew remarked in an Irish lodging house near Drury Lane, 'watched on the other side of the fireplace by a portrait of Daniel O'Connell';[142] 'the very staircase', as he writes of another house he visited, 'having pictures fastened against the wooden partition.'[143] The Rosary served as a focus and discipline of prayer, an instrument of domestic piety by which the spiritual exercises of the Church were reproduced in a kindred ceremonial of the home:

> before going to bed we all knelt down, and after a supper of Indian meal, on the bare uneven brick floor recited the Rosary, father leading off: one Our Father to ten Hail Mary's: one of the prayers spoken fifty times by the help of a string of beads: and we arose feeling good and comforted and strengthened for the morrow's work.[144]

Personal prayer seems to have provided a religious comfort and consolation of the simplest and most elemental kind, as it did for the Irish crossing–sweeper whom Mayhew records, 'a very melancholy–looking man', who could not understand the Mass, but who prayed to the saints every night 'for a blissin', and to rise me out of my misery';[145] or the travelling packman who came to the Franciscans in Wales, an elderly man 'with a sad and weary–looking face' who 'thought he should like to learn a few prayers . . . as he was getting old and did not feel very strong'.[146] Of the strong impression which might be produced upon the mind and imagination of the young, one has a record in Tom Barclay's account of the time when he was 'something like what the Irish call a voteen':

> Just now I am very religious. Every morning on awakening and dressing I make the sign of the Cross from forehead to breast and from shoulder to shoulder, uttering 'In the name of the Father, and the Son, and of the Holy Ghost, Amen.' I say the Our Father, Hail Mary, and Apostle's Creed, and invoke the Holy Family –
>
> Jesus, Mary, Joseph, I offer my heart and life.
> Jesus, Mary, Joseph, assist me in my last agony.
> Jesus, Mary, Joseph, may I die in peace in your blessed company.
>
> . . .I was very devout . . . I chalked an altar on the bare brown wall of the chamber where six of us slept, father, mother, and four children: I sketched candles, three each side of a tabernacle, and a crucifix above it in the centre, all in chalk.[147]

The Irish language, 'the tongue in which they both think and pray',[148] provided one continuing association. Some of the immigrants from the West of Ireland knew no other tongue,[149] and for many, especially among the women, it remained a primary cultural resource.[150] When the new Catholic cemetery was opened at Kensal Town, in 1858,

> A very large number of the poorer class of funerals at the time were those of emigrants from the West of Ireland, all speaking the Irish language . . . . chattering among themselves and collecting the money for the payments of their relations' funerals.[151]

Even those who had ceased to use the Irish in everyday life might revert to it in moments of high feeling. 'When they began to get elevated', a stonemason remarked of the Irish harvesters who spent their Saturday nights at a public house in Mosston, Surrey, 'they always started to talk in their own native tongue, and I noticed it was generally the women who commenced.'[152] Tom Barclay's memoir indicates how it might serve as a common bond of nationality and faith. His mother, whose people were O'Reilly's, and who had been brought up 'in the wilds of County Mayo', could 'sing and recite a goodly number of old Irish songs and poems', a solace amidst the hardship and penury of life in a Leicester back court:

> She was not permitted, even had she the money and leisure, to indulge in beer and dominoes of an evening like my father; her consolation was an old Irish lamentation or love song and the contemplation of the sufferings of 'Our Blessed Lord' and his virgin mother.

She was held to be 'quite exceptional' among her fellow–countrywomen in that she could 'read Dr Gallacher's sermons in Irish', and it was her custom to read them aloud to her neighbours on Good Friday: 'It did them good to hear a . . . sermon . . . in the first language they ever spoke.'

> How she who read English with difficulty could read these sermons, though in Roman characters, with their transliteration nearly as bad as Welsh, is something I do not understand: but . . . often have I seen the tears come into her eyes over the sermon on the Passion of Our Lord.[153]

The Church seems to have followed the practice of sending Irish priests to many of the newly–founded missions, and one reads of Irish–speaking priests ministering in their own native tongue in places as removed from the principal centres of Irish settlement as Bilston, where Father Sherlock, who had been taught Irish in his infancy, 'was able to hear the confessions of his countrymen who could speak in no other tongue,' York, where the Irish Vincentian Fathers from Sheffield were sent to organise the Irish part of the Catholic population into a separate parish, and Merthyr Tydfil, where Father Caroll contracted the Irish fever, and died in 1847.[154]

Sunday Mass provided a natural meeting point in the life of the community. Indeed Mayhew said that it was their 'consistent association' at chapel which kept the street Irish of London so distinct.[155]

For those who during the week suffered the servitude of the workhouse – or of an English lady's household[156] – the privilege of attending Mass offered a solitary occasion of escape; indeed, it was so highly regarded by the inmates of the Birmingham workhouse that Protestant paupers were accused of passing themselves off as Catholic 'in order to get five days' holiday in the month instead of one'.[157] In country missions – remote from the ordinary track of Irish settlement – squads of harvesters, during the season, or contract labourers, when a railway was building or a canal being cut, arrived to swell the numbers attending weekly Mass,[158] as at a Bollington, Cheshire, where the navvies at work on the Macclesfield and Stockport line walked over in a body from Prestbury, 'and as they always knelt on one side of the church this . . . was known . . . as the "Prestbury" side.'[159] At distant points, Sunday brought together isolated groups of labourers to form the nucleus of a congregation, and provided at the same time, as for the street Irish described by

Mayhew, a focal point for social gathering. At Abertillery, where Mass was celebrated in the room of a public house – as in other parts of Wales the only kind of room which could be hired – and where the congregation was recruited from the Irish mine–workers employed about the pits at Coomtillery, higher up the valley, a priest complained that it was 'with the greatest difficulty' that the congregation could be prevented from 'hovering about' though the service had ended, and 'envincing their gratitude to the landlord' when the public–house opened 'by an unlimited consumption of beer'.[160] At Wednesbury in the Black Country, where an Irish community of ironworkers had recently settled, the throng outside Father Montgomery's church – described in a series of articles which appeared in *The Nation* in June 1856 – recalled for A. M. Sullivan the crowded informality of an Irish parish:

> Thronging the gateway, I was glad to perceive that infallible testimony of the presence of a good pastor among his flock – and to be seen at the door of many a soggarth aroon in Ireland, a crowd of poor people who each has need of him in one of the numerous capacities in which the truly good priest is always consulted by his people; arbitrator, magistrate or judge; benefactor, comforter, or friend. A father who had come to complain to him about a rebellious child; a son coming to give the priest some money to send to his poor mother in Ireland; an old man to get a letter which had come from him to the 'care' of the priest; a young girl to seek through him reconciliation with her mother. . .[161]

There is evidence that the new communities retained strong cultural affinities with the old. There were parishes whose congregations were almost exclusively Irish or of Irish extraction, often served by their own fellow countrymen as priests, and where the national influence was so very strong that it was said to produce a linguistic mutation in the rare 'sprinkling' of English priests who found their way among them: 'by dint of living almost wholly with Irish co–religionists they nearly always have a noticeable brogue'.[162] The presence of large and increasing numbers of Irish priests during the second half of the century, 'in sentiment . . . even more Irish than they are Catholic', preserved a line of communication with their native land;[163] so, too, did the continuing arrival of fresh immigrants. The chapel, a 'moral property' in Thomas and Znaniecki's excellent phrase, was a very emblem of the community's collective existence. Its building was in some cases the joint activity of parishioners and priests;[164] its maintenance called forth a loyalty and devotion in singular contrast to the 'eleemosynary' character so often complained of in Evangelical missionary activity among the poor ('some of them would live a week on bread and water rather than be behindhand with their monthly contributions, or their subscription to the Altar Society');[165] its defence, when menaced by No Popery attacks, brought the impetuous violence of the Irish countryside into the heart of the English town. The Church thus served as a nexus of communal solidarity, the very means by which, amidst the deprived conditions of their exile, a national identity among the Irish was preserved.

The Irish congregations of the second half of the nineteenth century may be said to have existed, to some degree, in the original condition of a sect. Their churches were characteristically plain and unadorned, and 'externals', for all the attention they received from Protestant controversialists, counted for very little. St. Patrick's, Liverpool, appears in an early account as 'very large but very ugly, quite methodistick in its architecture' though 'nobly crowded with people';[166] the patronless church in Garstang is described in a Visitation return as 'a very plain square building . . . No tower no bells . . . the sanctuary . . . plain'.[167] The smaller chapels seem to have borne a resemblance to those which George Eliot recorded as being thought characteristic of latter–day Methodism – 'low–pitched gables up dingy streets'.[168] Some in fact were Methodist chapels, or independent meeting–houses converted to Catholic use. St. Mary's, Ashton–under–Lyne, was Joseph Rayner Stephens' old chapel in Charlestown;[169] St. Bridget's, Liverpool, opened 'in a part of town . . . where there was a large Irish Catholic population' was a chapel formerly used by the Methodists;[170] so too was the chapel at Westhoughton, which had also enjoyed a secular period of existence as a weaving shed.[171] Others were commercial buildings, adapted for religious use. At Eldon Street, Liverpool, 'the centre of a most congested district', a warehouse capable of holding one thousand people was opened as a church, 'and in its gloomy and unattractive rooms began the mission of Our Lady of Reconciliation de la Salette'.[172] St. Michael's, Stockport, sacked by the rioters in 1852 ('little else remaining than the four bare walls of the building, and the four bare steps to the altar'), had previously been a theatre, and then a Mechanics' Institute, before it was opened as a Catholic mission in 1851;[173] at Whitworth, near Rochdale, the Catholic mission was opened in a room above the premises of the Co–operative stores;[174] at Kensal New Town in an uninhabited corner building which had been intended for use as a baker's shop ('the inner room served as a sanctuary, the door being removed and the opening widened').[175]

When I was travelling the parishes and record offices of northern England, preparing this paper in the summer of 1966, the old Irish districts had not yet succumbed to the bulldozer and the depradations of comprehensive clearance and re–development. The churches I visited often seemed to stand in half–deserted urban waste–lands, but their original hinterland had not yet been effaced from the map. At St. Patrick's, Wigan, in the heart of the old Irish district of the Schooles, the priest was distinctively an Irishman, deeply 'reactionary' in his views (he was uncomfortable about Vatican II, and hostile to 'progressive' innovations within the Church), utterly devoted to his parishioners, and in his simple manner of life (we shared the dinner–table with his Irish–born housekeeper) – even in his tobacco–stained waistcoat – recalled pictures one might have had of the old–time soggarth, racy of the soil. Next door to the Catholic Church in Bradford, in the old Irish district around Silsbridge Lane, there was a fading notice which read 'J Walsh, undertaker', and a document in the lumber–room of the town hall (they have now been safely deposited in the public library) disclosed that in the late nineteenth century the church was faced by a pub called 'The Harp of Erin': a suggestive cluster for the complex of sociability and communal service which helped to bond together the Irish Catholic communities of later Victorian times. At the time I was looking for continuity, and conceptualising it in terms of a timeless tradition, and the traces of this will be evident in the foregoing pages. Subsequent research is more likely to be interested – quite legitimately – in the mutations which took place, even within an apparently unchanging framework, and more alert than I was to the 'Victorian' transformation of both Irish and English Catholicity. I no longer believe, as I believed in 1966, that the Irish Catholics of the end of the nineteenth century were the same as those of the 1840s and 1850s. But the tenacity of both parish organisation and settlement, not only over the second half of the nineteenth century, but at least in the northern towns, right down to the 1960s (at St. Andrew's, Newcastle, one of the unofficial pastoral duties was still that of giving help to the wandering Irish beggars who came to the door) suggests that there is indeed here a confessional and social reality which historians – locally as well as nationally – should study, a study which could throw new light on one of the more substantial – and one of the more beleaguered – of those minority cultures of which (it could be argued) the 'majority' culture of modern Britain is composed.

Notes

1. 'New Convent and School, Newport Market, Soho' bound with *St. Patrick's, Soho, Reports and Guides, 1870–78.*
2. St. Patrick's, Soho, MSS., 'About St. Bridget's Confraternity'. The register is initialled 'N.T.S.' and the writer identified from the *Catholic Directory*, 1881.
3. A.M. Sullivan was a moderate nationalist and editor of *The Nation*; Father Theobald Mathew was the celebrated Irish temperance advocate.
4. 'About St. Bridget's Confraternity', 20 April 1881.
5. *Ibid.*, 28 February 1881.
6. The title 'pleasant', however, was sometimes looked on with dismay. K.S. Inglis, *Churches and the Working Classes in Victorian England* (London, 1963), pp.79–85.
7. In a report on the Blackburn sewing schools during the cotton famine, there is a striking contrast between the picture given of the factory girls gathered together under the aegis of the Bible women ('hoarse with reading for many hours'), at whose direction they rise from their seats to sing, 'after one or two failures in starting',

> Come let us join our cheerful song
> With angels round the throne

and those in the Roman Catholic sewing school, where the singing under the direction of a priest, was by no means confined to sacred hymns: 'Whenever they sing . . . as they are often asked to do, the mournful song of 'Hard Time', he has it followed by 'There's a Good Time coming, Girls', as a corrective.' Wigan Ref. Lib., 'Y.B.', *The Blackburn Sewing Schools* (1863), bound with Wigan Typographical Pamphlets, vol.vii, pp.344, 346–7.

8. Newman to Bowden, 21 September 1849, in C.S. Dessain (ed.), *The Letters and Diaries of John Henry Newman* (London and Edinburgh, 1963), vol.xiii, pp.260–1.

9. See also R. Chapman, *Father Faber* (London, 1961), p.234, and the printed and MS. volume in the Brompton Oratory archives, *The Oratory in London* , pp.94–5. Forty–six patients were anointed of whom thirty–four died.

10. Other songs included 'The Jolly Miller', the duet, 'All's Well' and a rendering of 'An Old English Gentleman' which followed the address of thanks to the clergy of the district. Dom O. F. Blundell, O.S.B., *Broughton Catholic Charitable Society* (Preston, 1923). The society, 'a native growth of Lancashire piety and good fellowship', had been established in May 1786, 'to assist the living, who were in distress, and to have masses and prayers said for the dead'. *Ibid.*, pp.vii, 1.

11. *British Catholicity, its Position and Wants. Addressed to His Eminence Cardinal Acton* (Edinburgh, 1844), p.16.

12. *The Oratory in London*, pp.109–110.

13. On the agitation to protect the religious status of Catholic pauper children, see P.R.O. H.O. 45/7646, H.O. 45/6840; Ed. 9/31; T. Burke, *Catholic History of Liverpool* (Liverpool, 1910), pp.120–1, 130–34, 141–2. 165; Canon E. St. John, *Manning's Work for Children* (London, 1929).

14. The important question, for this subject, of soldiers is one I have not yet begun to explore. In 1861, out of an army of 205, 829 men, 58,630 were Roman Catholics. W. G. Lumley, 'The Statistics of the Roman Catholics in England and Wales', *Journ. Stat. Soc.*, vol.xxvii (London, 1864), p.322.

15. At Millbank, where the letters 'R.C.' were appended to the name of the Catholic inmate on his cell–door, there was a small room reserved for the Catholic clergyman, 'where the prisoners of that faith confess'. H. Mayhew and J. Binney, *The Criminal Prisons of London and Scenes of Prison Life* (London, 1862), p.257. Cf. also pp.266, 525–7, 530, 564, 568, 569, 617, for the treatment of Catholics in London prisons.

16. *Franciscan Missions among the Colliers and Ironworkers of Monmouthshire* (London, 1876), is an admirable memoir, whose writing takes on something of the dramatic character of the countryside it describes. It is not listed in the recent bibliography of Welsh history.

17. Lancs. C.R.O., Archidocese of Liverpool MSS. (RCLv), Visitation Returns, 1865, Holy Cross.

18. Charles Burke, *History of the Camberwell Catholic Mission, 1860–1910* (London, n.e.), p.7.

19. Booth speaks of a 'citadel of poverty' of which Sultan Street was 'the centre', and described it as 'a strange group of streets, hemmed in on one side by the railway and entered only here and there on the other three sides like a fortress through its gates'. 'Many of the inhabitants', he writes, 'are said to be Cockney Irish, and, whether Irish or not, mostly general labourers'; and he quotes with evident agreement the 'forcible language' used by one of his witnesses,' "a collection of streets where beastly men and women live bestially"'. Charles Booth, *Life and Labour of the People of London* (London, 1902 edn.), 3rd Ser., vol.vi, pp.15–19.
20. H. J. Dyos, *Victorian Suburb, a Study of the Growth of Camberwell* (Leicester, 1961), p.111.
21. D. Attwater, *The Catholic Church in Modern Wales* (London, 1935), pp.72, 137; *Franciscan Missions*, pp.22, 35. On Welsh hostility to Roman Catholics generally see Attwater, pp.33, 38–9, 68–9, 71–2, 91, 101, 115–19, 122, 129–30, 135, 207, 223–4, 275.
22. Attwater, p.91; on the opposition at Wednesbury, where, to undermine the foundations, a Protestant party threatened to purchase the mines and minerals beneath the chapel, see J.F. Ede, *The History of Wednesbury* (Wednesbury, 1950), p.318, and J. F. Bromfield, *St. Mary's Parish Centenary* (Wednesbury, 1950).
23. *Franciscan Missions*, pp.16–17.
24. R. Smith, *Ye Chronicles 306–1910 of Blackburnshire* (Nelson, 1910), p.195. At Burnley itself, the opening of St. Mary's in 1849 provoked an outburst of Protestant hostility, 'the walls of the town were flooded with "no popery" placards, the exterior carvings round the church were gravely damaged and the statue of Our Lady within the church . . . shot at'. Odo Blundell, *Old Catholic Lancashire* (London, 1925), vol.i, p.30.
25. T. Burke, *Catholic History of Liverpool* (Liverpool, 1910), p.45.
26. *Franciscan Missions*, p.38–9.
27. 'Caswall's brother was followed by the rabble the other day in London, having a long cloke, which they took for an Oratorian. He faced round, pulled aside the cloke, and showed his trousers – When they saw him all sound below, they gave him a cheer and left him'. See Newman to Faber, 4 November 1850, in *Letters of Newman*, vol.xiv, pp.117–28.
28. J. F. Cassidy, *The Great Father Tom Burke* (Dublin, 1947), p.31;W. J. Fitzpatrick, *The Life of the Very Rev. T.N. Burke* (London, 1885), vol.1, pp.149–152.
29. Lancs. R.O. DDX.177/5 'Letters and Pictures . . . Liverpool'; U. Young, *Life of . . . Ignatius Spencer* (London, 1933), pp. 137, 141, 143, 175, 178.
30. Young, p.184.
31. *Ibid.*, pp.178, 180, 182, 197, 203; Birm. Dioc. MSS., Shrewsbury to Ullathorne, 29 June 1852.
32. Lady A. Kerr (ed.), *Sister Chatelain: or, Forty Years Work in Westminster* (London, 1900), pp.26–7.
33. Rev. F. J. Kirk, *Reminiscences of an Oblate of St. Charles* (London, 1905), p.99.

34. Kerr, pp.32–3.
35. St. Chad's Cath. MSS., 'Catholic Poor Schools', 21 August, 11 September, 30 November 1849.
36. William Dollman, 'a very powerful, ill–looking man', lodging in London Prentice Street, was alleged to have struck the fatal blow in the Painter murder. Joseph Allday, *Full and Correct Reports of the Trials . . . for the Murder of Mr. Painter, etc.* (Birmingham, 1835), p.30.
37. *Rep . . . St. Peter's District Visiting Society for 1844* (Birmingham, 1845), p.3. Twenty years later the street was described as containing 'a mixture of the worst class of Irish and of regular thieves': 'The Night Side of Birmingham', Osborne Newspaper Cuttings, vol.ii, p.184 (Birm.Ref.Lib.). London Prentice Street was the scene of a famous Protestant scandal in 1848 when Father Molloy, a local Catholic priest, was accused of having seized a New Testament from one of his parishioners, and publicly burnt it in the street. For the indignant sermons see Rev. J. C. Miller, *Bible Burning, the Substance of a Sermon* (Birmingham, 1848); Rev. I. C. Barrett, *The Protestant Bible Burnt, a Sermon . . .* (London, 1848): '. . . My scripture reader was actually kicked by an Irishman, as he went out of the court, who used the strongest language and exclaimed "Break his neck!" "IT WOULD LEAD TO THE BIBLE!"', Miller, pp.7–8.
38. R. H. Kiernan, *The Story of the Archdiocese of Birmingham* (Birmingham,n.d.), p.33.
39. Carr's Lane MSS., 'Mr Clay's Journal', esp. 20 February 1839 on the difficulties among them of a town missionary.
40. Letter signed by 'an English Catholic' in *Birmingham Daily Gazette*, 1 July 1867.
41. James Murphy, *The Religious Problem in English Education: The Crucial Experiment* (Liverpool, 1959), p.17; T. Burke, p.73.
42. *Report . . . Catholic Poor School Committee* (London, 1847), pp.65, 69.
43. Joseph O'Connor, *Host age to Fortune* (Dublin, 1951), p.11.
44. P.R.O. Ed.3/19.
45. Kirk, p.90.
46. L. G. Vere, *Random Recollections of Old Soho* (Barnet, 1912), p.28.
47. Rev. T. Livius, *Father Furniss and his Work for Children* (London and Leamington, 1896), pp.45, 49–50, 143; P.R.O. Ed.3/26 St. Leonard's Bromley, Ed.3/6, St. Francis Xavier's, Seven Dials; St. Peter's Reg., Birmingham 19, 26 July 1863, 27 March, 3 April, 7 August 1864; Lancs. R.O. RCLv Sch. Exam. & Insp.Ret., 1858, St. Pat., Wigan; Visit. Ret., 1858, The Willows; P.R.O. Ed.9/14, Alderson to Sandford, 28 April 1875.
48. Booth, 3rd. Ser., vol.vi, p.105; Vere, p.248.
49. L. G. Vere, *Random Recollections of Homerton Circuit* (Barnet, 1912), p.199. Fr. Vere returned to St. Patrick's, Soho, after a period of service at Homerton.
50. P.R.O. Ed.3/13.
51. S. J. Lond., Foley MSS., vol.iii, Ser.1 & 2, p.728; T. Burke,

p.151.

52. Vere, *Old Soho Days*, pp.31-2.

53. St. Pat., Soho, MSS., 'St. Joseph's School'. In all 71 of the 135 children whose addresses are recorded came from Princes Row itself, and the remainder were drawn almost entirely from the immediately surrounding neighbourhood. In 1875 the Puseyites left, and their school in Princes Row was taken over on behalf of St. Patrick's by the Poor Servants of the Mother of God. Vere, *Old Soho*, pp.21–2, 31.

54. P.R.O. Ed.3/19 St. Joseph's, Fitzroy Court.

55. The words are those of Father Barge, Missionary Rector of St. Patrick's, Soho. Vere, *Old Soho*, p.72.

56. H. Mayhew, *London Labour and the London Poor* (London, 1861), vol.i, p.114.

57. Father Caroll at Merthyr, an Irish priest who covered the district of Merthyr, Dowlais, Rhymney and Tredegar in the 1830s and 1840s (he died of the fever in 1847) lived in a poor workman's cottage in Dowlais, the entrance to which 'was almost blocked up by two or three sacks of meal or potatoes, which he retailed under market price for the benefit of the poor, yet eking out thereby his own maintenance.' Attwater, p.74.

58. Vere, p.87.

59. St. Pet. Reg., Birm., 18 January, 26 April 1863, 31 January 1864. In December 1862 Fr. Patrick McLaughlin, Catholic priest at Eastmuir, a village on the outskirts of Glasgow, was committed to prison for contempt of court. He had addressed an envelope for a member of his flock who was making restitution to a fellow–worker in Ireland, the letter containing money he had embezzled. Fr. McLaughlin refused to disclose the name of the addressee, and served fourteen days of a thirty day sentence to prison. J. E. Handley, *The Irish in Modern Scotland* (Cork, 1947), pp.66–7.

60. Vere, pp.54, 113, Rev. E. Price, *Sick Calls, from the Diary of a Missionary Priest* (London, 1850), pp.423, 318–9. Price was minister at the Sardinian Chapel, Lincoln's Inn Fields.

61. St. Pet. Reg. Birm., 23 November 1862, 11 January 1863. At St. Oswald's Ashton–in–Makerfield, Wigan, it was requested that sick–calls 'Should be sent by some responsible person – not by children', St. Osw.Reg., Ashton–in–M., 25 February 1879.

62. E. M. Sneyd–Kynnersley, *H.M.I. Some Passages in the Life of one of H.M. Inspectorate of Schools* (London, 1908), pp.233–4.

63. Lancs. R.O. RCLv, Bp.Goss Visit, Diary, Great Crosby, 7–8 April 1867; J. R. M. Brennan, *Memories of an old Catholic Doctor* (London, 1937), p.11. On early communion, Livius, p.116–7.

64. Booth, Ser.3, vol.ii, p.79.

65. Booth, Ser.3, vol.vii, p.244. In the doorways of Drury Lane, noted Fr. Edward Price, even the prostitutes – 'groups of girls whose looks and attire betrayed their infamous calling' – curtseyed as he passed. Price, pp.396, 398. 'They are all "convinced at heart"', a priest remarked to Booth of the Catholic London poor, and emphasized his opinion by adding that those accounted lapsed 'were the worst of

all in sending for the priest at "untimely hours"': Booth, Ser.3, vol.vii, p.255.
66. Pat O'Mara, *The Autobiography of a Liverpool Irish Slummy* (London, 1934), p.18. Cf. also the description of one of his successors at St. Vincent's, 'that natural fighter' and 'bitter Fenian', Father Toomer, in *ibid.*, p.69.
67. Carr's Lane MSS, Joseph Frye's Journ. 19 March, 9 May, 4 October 1850.
68. Booth, 3rd. Ser., vol.vii, p.255.
69. Vere, pp.16–17, 43; *St. Mary's Wednesbury*, p.8; Ede, *Wednesbury*, p.318; *P.P.* 1836, *Rept. . . . Irish Poor in Great Britain*, p.18; T. Burke, p.128.
70. O'Mara, p.69.
71. Booth, 3rd. Ser., vol.vii, p.246.
72. J, Denvir, *The Brandons: A story of Irish Life in England* (London, 1903), pp.45–6.
73. L. Faucher, *Manchester in 1844.*
74. St.Pet.Birm., 'Subjects for Sermons', 28 June, 4 October 1857, 15 April 1869.
75. *Times*, 21 August 1843: 'Amongst those who took the pledge was a man in such a drunken state that he could hardly stand, and it having been intimated to Father Mathew that it would be prudent to allow him to take the pledge while under the influence of liquor, he (Father Mathew) said, that he had had many drunken men come to him to take the pledge while under the influence of liquor, and in no one instance did he know of their breaking the promise. The man was therefore allowed to remain': *ibid.*, 10 August 1843.
76. *St. Pat. Soho, Rep . . . 1876.*
77. For a vivid description of this kind of relationship between his mother and Father Ryan, see O'Mara, p.123.
78. Mayhew, vol.i, pp.116–17.
79. Booth, 3rd. Ser., vol.vii, pp.243–4.
80. *Ibid.*, p.246.
81. See also Fr. Daniel Hearne in the *Tablet*, 29 July 1843.
82. At their Mission Room in Haggerston, the Sisters of St. Saviour's held for the children of the neighbourhood what was actually called 'Heathen Teas': Warburton, p.137.
83. *P.P.* 1852–3, *Rept . . . rel. Census*, p.clviii.
84. *The Oratory in London*, vol.i, p.86.
85. Attwater, p.70.
86. P.R.O. H.O.45/6840.
87. St. Pat., Soho, Dioc.Visit., 1869, Q.9/13; Percy Fitzgerald, *Fifty Years of Catholic Life and Social Progress* (London, 1901), vol.ii, p.453.
88. 'A London Rambler', *The Romance of the Streets* (London, 1872), p.298.
89. Handley, p.116.
90. Mayhew, vol.ii, p.251.
91. Even Pagan O'Leary, the Fenian, a 'fiery, truculent man', who 'delighted' in the religious implication of his soubriquet, was ready

to respect the association. Questioned by prison officials after his arrest, and ordered to classify himself under the heading of 'Religion' he attempted at first to claim he was a Pagan. No, they said, they could not accept that – they had headings in their books, 'Roman Catholic ', 'Protestant', and 'Presbyterian', but not 'Pagan '. 'Well', he said, 'You have two kinds, the "Robbers" (meaning Protestants) and the "Beggars" (Catholics), and if I must choose, put me down as a "Beggar"'. Denvir, *Old Rebel*, p.87.

92. Rylands Lib., R.62533, Manch. News. Cutt., 'The Census in the Slums', No.2.

93. S. Bamford, *Passages in the Life of a Radical* (London, 1905), vol.ii, p.153.

94. 'Wigan Examiner', *Local Notes and Queries* (Wigan, 1883), no.xi/198.

95. Mayhew, vol.i, p.110.

96. *Ibid.*, p.111. Some of the English stood in fear of them. A street–patterer who had not hesitated, in quest of newsworthy sensation, to kill off the Duke of Wellington on two separate occasions – 'once by a fall from his horse, and the other time by "a sudden and mysterious death"' – felt it prudent to abstain from exercising his talents upon a comparably prominent Catholic subject: 'He once thought of poisoning the Pope, but was afraid of the street Irish', *ibid.*, vol.i, pp.240, 244.

97. Booth, 3rd. Ser., vol.iv, p.202, vol.vii, p.255; Vere, *Old Soho*, p.27.

98. P.R.O. Ed.9/14, Sandford to Sandford. Matthew Arnold referred to them as 'trying material', *ibid.*, Arnold to Sandford, 29 April 1875.

99. Livius, pp.65, 150; St. Chad's Cath. Reg. Birm., vol.iii, 22 November 1881; St.Pet.Reg., Birm., 29 March 1863, Holy Week 1864.

100. *Wigan Observer*, 1 July 1859.

101. *Preston Guardian*, 30 May 1868.

102. J. Denvir, *The Irish in Britain* (London, 1894), pp.306–7.

103. Cf. e.g. Rev. P. Rogers, *Father Theobald Mathew, Apostle of Temperance* (Dublin, 1943), p.86, for the Irishwomen at Deptford 'with shillelaghs inside their umbrellas' who formed part of a self–appointed bodyguard for Father Mathew; *Aris's Birmingham Gazette*, 28 September 1867, for Mary Ann Gilmour, a rag sorter of 'Little Ireland', Dudley, who disturbed the service at the Wesleyan Free Chapel as the officiating preacher was praying for the conversion of Papists; *Ashton Reporter*, 23 May 1868, for the poor washerwoman of Flag Alley, Bridget Cullen; P.R.O. H.O. 45/36331/2 for the Regent's Park disturbances of 1884, some of the Irishwomen 'having their sleeves tucked up and declaring they were going to "walk in heretic's blood"'.

104. C Aspin, *Haslingden* (Haslingden, 196?), p.133 for an Irishwoman taken in charge with a rolling pin.

105. 'A stick with a cog–wheel at the end', 'short sticks loaded with lead and iron', and 'portions of scythe–blades' were among the weapons recovered from the Ashton–under–Lyne Irish during the Murphy

riots, L.R.O. CPR/1.
106. T. M. Healy, *Letters and Leaders of My Day* (London, 1928), vol.i, pp.24–5. During the Ashton rioting William Ibbetson was shot in the bowels from St. Mary's Roman Catholic church, while at St. Peter's, Stalybridge, the parish priest himself, the Rev. Joseph Daley, was charged with wounding a man with a gun: L.R.O. CPR/1.
107. Carr's Lane MSS., Mr. Jackson's Journ. 20 July 1842, 11 August 1843.
108. *Ibid.*, Joseph Frye's Journ., 19 March, 15 May, 4 October 1850.
109. 'We were once Catholics and carried Saint Colman of Cloyne about wid us in a box; but after hearing a sermon at a church about images, we went home, took the saint out of his box, and cast him into a river'. G. Borrow, *Wild Wales* (World Classics Edn., London, 1927).
110. *Ibid.*, p.610.
111. Carr's Lane MSS., Mr. Sibree's Journal, 28 February 1839.
112. A. Burton, *Rushbearing* (Manchester, 1891), p.64.
113. M. Trench, *Life of Charles Lowder* (London, 1881), p.80.
114. *Preston Guardian*, 27 November 1867.
115. *Oldham Chronicle*, 11 July 1863, in L.R.O. QEV 18/4.
116. Birm. Ref. Lib., Miss Journ. of R. A. Finnigan, pp.44–5, 'abuse from a poor drunken Irishman who laid hold of me, and wanted me to fight him – it was a matter of sport to many persons, and though he tore part of my waistcoat I took it all in good part and quietly got out of his clutches.'
117. *The Christian Mission*, vol.ii/9, September 1870.
118. *Ibid.*, vol.ii/3, March 1870, vol.ii/7, July 1870.
119. *Ibid.*, vol.ii/4, May 1870.
120. O'Mara, p.82.
121. *Gipsy Smith, His Life and Work, by Himself* (London, 1901), pp.102, 105–6. The rioting, which went on for two successive nights, was provoked by the 'several converts' Gipsy Smith had been able to record ('two young women brought their beads and rosary . . . and gave them up.').
122. Mayhew, vol.ii, pp.503–4.
123. J. Toole, *Fighting Through Life* (London, 1935).
124. Denvir, *Old Rebel*, p.244.
125. Booth, 3rd. Ser., vol.iv, p.197.
126. *Sir James Sexton, Agitator. . .An Autobiography* (London, 1936), pp.18–19.
127. T. Barclay, *Memoirs and Medleys, the Autobiography of a Bottle–washer* (Leicester, 1934), pp.5–8, 19.
128. George Lansbury, *My Life* (London, 1928), pp.26–7.
129. T. A. Jackson, *Solo Trumpet* (London, 1953), referring to the time of his father's childhood.
130. *The Times*, 21 August 1843.
131. See also *The Times*, 19 August 1843.
132. J. F. Maguire, *Father Mathew, a Biography* (London, 1863), pp.140–1, 151–2; P. Rogers, *Father Theobald Mathew*,pp.44–5, 56, 60.
133. Birm.Ref.Lib., p.419 (IR 533), 'Father Mathew in Birmingham.'
134. Maguire, p.48. I am very grateful to Mr. Brian Harrison for

this reference.

135. *The Times*, 9 August 1843. During the demonstration at Westminster 'the notorious Captain Acherley, who professes to cure all manner of diseases by the aid of a "wonderful lamp", made his appearance, and for a time divided the attention of those present', *ibid.*, 25 August 1843.

136. Denvir, *Old Rebel*, pp.13–15.

137. Livius, p.90; St. Pet.Reg.Birm., 5 June 1964; O'Mara, pp.143, 153, 218. Sneering at the scapular and *Agnus Dei* which they wore, and in one case destroying them, was one of the humiliations alleged to have been imposed upon the Fenian prisoners in Portland prison: P.R.O. H.O. 45/19461.

138. When the Manchester Martyrs, Larkin, Gould and Allen, were executed, 'each of the men bore a cross upon his breast': *Preston Guardian*, 27 November 1867.

139. Carr's Lane MSS., Mr Jackson's Journ., 11 August 1843.

140. Mayhew, vol.i, p.111.

141. Price, p.82.

142. Mayhew, vol.ii, p.504.

143. *ibid.*, vol.i, p.116. Cf. also *ibid.*, vol.i, pp..111, 114; E. Waugh, *Home–Life of the Lancashire Factory Folk During the Cotton Famine* (London, 1867), pp.76, 77, 85; Denvir, *Irish in Britain*, pp.442–3.

144. Barclay, p.7.

145. Mayhew, vol.i, p.114.

146. *Franciscan Missions*, p.69. 'His parents, who died when he was quite young, were Irish and Catholic, and he had, of course, been baptised . . . but he knew nothing himself'; occasionally he attended Mass on Sundays 'because he saw that other Catholics did so', but 'he had not the faintest notion what it meant.'

147. Barclay, pp.26–7.

148. 'The Irish in England', *Dublin Review*, 1856, p.504.

149. Price, pp.241–5; Denvir, *Old Rebel*, p.15.

150. *The Nation*, 7 June 1856.

151. Kirk.

152. A Working Man, *Reminiscences of a Stonemason* (London, 1908), pp.16–17; cf. also L.R.O. QJD 1/197 for the use of Irish during a riot against the police; *Preston Guardian*, 25 March 1868, for the use of Irish during a neighbourhood row; Borrow, *Wild Wales*, pp.609–11 for the use of Irish in moments of embarrassment; *The Nation*, 7 June 1856, for the prevalence of Irish among the colony at Wednesbury; Birm. Ref.Lib.Journ., of T. A. Finnigan, Birmingham Town Mission, 1837–1838 and F. W. Hackwood, *Religious Wednesbury* (Wednesbury, 190?), p.117 for the use of Irish–speaking Scripture readers.

153. Barclay, pp.3, 10, 23.

154. Denvir, *Irish in Britain*, pp.259–60; St. Vincent's, Sheffield, *Centenary*, p.19; Attwater, pp.70–1. Father Sherlock, 'one of the finest specimens of the good old 'soggarth aroon', presided over the first Home Rule Convention in 1873: Denvir, *Old Rebel*, pp.176–177.

155. Mayhew, vol.i, p.514. Cf. also *ibid.*, vol.i, pp.1123, 151, 515.

156. Sunday evenings appear to have been the only time of the week

when Irish servant girls were allowed by their mistresses to attend their chapels. Vincent Smith MSS., 'Catholic Tyneside', pp.27–8; Price, p.324.

157. *Birmingham Daily Gazette*, 22 May 1879. For a similar situation at the Brownlow Hill workhouse, Liverpool, see Burke, p.133. Cf. also Birm. Dioc.MSS., 'Catholic Chapel in the Birmingham Union Workhouse', 24 February 1858; *Birmingham Daily Post*, 8, 21 May 1879, *Birmingham Daily Gazette*, 18 November 1880. At St. Patrick's, Soho, the fourth confessional in the church, 'a temporary arrangement erected by the side of the Altar of the Seven Dolours', was occasionally used 'for the deaf old people of the Workhouse during Sunday Mass': Vere, *Old Soho*, pp.86–7.

158. Denvir, *Irish in Britain*, pp.408, 410–12; Birm. Dioc. MSS., Lempfried to Ullathorne, 25 December 1848: Foley MSS., vol.iv, p.345.

159. Rev. B. Kelly, 'Bollington Catholicism', MS. hist., 1930–40.

160. *Franciscan Missions*, p.61. For the same complaint about the congregation at Abersychan, *ibid.*, p.26; for a memoir of the congregation at Abertillery, M. F. Ryan, *Fenian Memories* (Dublin, 1945), p.49.

161. *The Nation*, 7 June 1856.

162. Sneyd–Kynnersley, p.231.

163. The Meaneys, 'a family which . . . sent out many priests from Ireland to labour among the Irish poor abroad', provided two missionary priests at Blackburn, and one at St. Mary's Levenshulme. A nephew of the Blackburn Meaneys, Fr. Patrick O'Connor, also worked for a time at Blackburn. Fr. Denis Byrne, the first Rector at St. Patrick's, Bolton, was a brother of Fr. Michael Byrne, of St. Marie's, Bury, and Fr. Thomas Byrne of St. Michael's, Manchester: Bolton, *op.cit.*, pp.80, 107, 109, 120–1, 143, 145, 174, 190, 212. Father Tracy of Heaton Norris, Stockport, who seems himself to have been a Nationalist sympathiser, had a brother Mat, a reporter on the *Cork Examiner*, who was able for carrying a musket during the Fenian rising of 1867, but was able to extract compensation from the British Government for wrongful arrest. 'Friends gathered round him night after night, to enjoy his compensation and hospitality. At the end of his . . . evenings he would raise his glass in pathetic self–pity, crying, "Ah, boys! the British Government has been the ruin of me"': Healey, vol.i, p.25.

164. *Franciscan Missions*, p.27; Bolton, pp.184, 192. When the foundation stone was laid at St. Vincent's, Liverpool, (a ceremony observed on St. Patrick's Day, 1856), 'The Irish ship carpenters of the parish passed in single file, each laying one day's wages on the newly blessed stone. Then followed the dock labourers with their offerings, the total amounting to one hundred pounds, nine shillings': Burke, p.126.

165. *Franciscan Missions*, pp.39–40, 59; Foley MSS.,. vol.iii, Ser.1, 2, p.579; P. Alden, 'The Problem of East London' in R. Mudie–Smith, (ed.), *The Religious Life of London* (London, 1904), p.38; Denvir, p.303; Booth, 3rd. Ser. vol.i, pp.83, 88, 233; vol.ii, pp.38–9; vol.iv, p.127: vol.v, p.68; vol.vii, pp.243, 265.

166. Birm.Dioc.MSS., Phillips to Walsh, 12 September 1836.
167. RCLv, Visit.Rets., 1855–8.
168. George Eliot, *Adam Bede*, vol.i, p.52.
169. W. Bowman, *England in Aston–under–Lyne* (Ashton–under–Lyne, 1963), p.23.
170. RCLv, 'Notes on Diocesan History'.
171. Bolton, p.150.
172. Burke, p.123.
173. Ed. W. Astle, *'Stockport Advertiser' Centenary History of Stockport* (Stockport, 1922), p.141.
174. Bolton, p.177.
175. Kirk, p.32.

SELECT BIBLIOGRAPHY

Contemporary Views:

Anon., 'The London Irish', *Blackwood's Edinburgh Magazine*, vol.170 (July 1901), pp.124–34.

Barclay, T., *Memoirs and Medleys: The Autobiography of a Bottlewasher* (Leicester, 1934).

Booth, C., *Life and Labour of the People of London*, Series I, *Poverty*, 4 vols.: Series 2, *Industry*, 5 vols.; Series 3, *Religious Influences*, 7 vols. (London, 1902–3).

Carlyle, T., *Chartism* (London, 1839).

Denvir, J., *The Irish in Britain* (London, 1892).

Life Story of an Old Rebel (Dublin, 1910).

Engels, F., *The Condition of the Working Classes in England* (1845), in W.O. Henderson and W.H. Chaloner (trans. and ed.) (Oxford, 1958).

Garratt, S., 'The Irish in London', in *Motives for Missions* (London, 1852).

MacGill, P., *Children of the Dead End: The Autobiography of a Navvy* (London, 1914).

Mayhew, H., *London Labour and the London Poor* (4 vols. London, 1861–2, reprinted New York, 1968).

Memoirs of Samuel Tuke (London, 1860).

O'Connor, T.P., *Memoirs of an Old Parliamentarian*, 2 vols. (London, 1929).

O'Neill, J., 'Fifty Years Experience as an Irish Shoemaker in London', *St. Crispin*, nos. 1 and 2 (1869).

Royal Commission on the Conditions of the Poorer Classes in Ireland. Appendix G, The State of the Irish Poor in Great Britain, 1836, *P.P.*, vol.xxxiv (40).

Todd, W.G., 'The Irish in England', *Dublin Review*, vol.41 (September, 1856), pp.470–521.

Historical Perspectives:

Books:

Arnstein, W.L., *Protestant versus Catholic in Mid–Victorian England: Mr. Newdegate and the Nuns* (Columbia & London, 1982).

Bermant, C., *London's East End: Point of Arrival* (New York, 1975).

Belchem J.C., '1848: Feargus O'Connor and the Collapse of the Mass Platform', in J. Epstein and D. Thompson (eds.), *The Chartist Experience* (London, 1982).

Best, G.F.A., 'Popular Protestantism in Victorian Britain', in R. Robson, (ed.), *Ideas and Institutions of Victorian Britain* (London, 1967), pp.115–42.

Bossy, J., *The English Catholic Community, 1570–1850* (London, 1975).

Brady, L.W., *T.P. O'Connor and the Liverpool Irish* (London, 1983).

Clapham, J.H., *An Economic History of Modern Britain*, 3 vols.

(Cambridge, 1926–38).
Coleman, T., *The Railway Navvies* (London, 1965).
Curtis, L.P., *Anglo–Saxons and Celts* (Bridgeport, Connecticut, 1968).
Apes and Angels: The Irishman in Victorian Caricature (Newton Abbot, 1971).
Darragh, J., 'The Catholic Population of Scotland, 1878–1977', in D. McRoberts (ed.), *Modern Scottish Catholicism* (Glasgow, 1979), pp.211–47.
Devoy, J., *Recollections of an Irish Rebel* (New York, 1929).
Epstein, J., *The Lion of Freedom: Feargus O'Connor and the Chartist Movement, 1832–42* (London, 1982).
Edwards, O.D., 'The Irish in Scotland', in D. Daiches, (ed.), *A Companion to Scottish Culture* (London, 1982), pp.182–6.
'The Catholic Press in Scotland since the Restoration of the Hierarchy', in D. McRoberts (ed.), *Modern Scottish Catholicism 1878–1978* (Glasgow, 1979), pp.156–82.
The Mind of an Activist – James Connolly (Dublin, 1971).
(ed., with Bernard Ransom), *James Connolly: Selected Political Writings* (London, 1973).
Burke & Hare (Edinburgh, 1980).
The Quest for Sherlock Holmes (Totowa, New Jersey, 1983).
Finnegan, F., *Poverty and Prejudice: Irish Immigrants in York, 1840–1875* (Cork, 1982).
Gillespie, W., *The Christian Brothers in England* (Bristol, 1975).
Gilley, S.W., 'The Catholic Faith of the Irish Slums: London, 1840–70', in H.J. Dyos and M. Wolff (eds.), *The Victorian City: Images and Reality* 2 vols. (London, 1973), vol. ii, pp.837–53.
'English Attitudes to the Irish in England, 1780–1900', in C. Holmes (ed.), *Immigrants and Minorities in British Society* (London, 1978), pp.81–110.
'Catholics and Socialists in Glasgow, 1906–1912', in K. Lunn (ed.), *Hosts, Immigrants and Minorities: Historical Responses to Newcomers in British Society, 1870–1914* (New York, 1980), pp.160–200.
Gwynn, D., 'The Irish Immigration', in G.A. Beck (ed.), *The English Catholics, 1850–1950* (London, 1950), pp.265–90.
Greaves, C.D., *The Life and Times of James Connolly* (London, 1961).
Handley, J.E. *The Irish in Scotland 1789–1845* (Cork, 1943).
The Irish in Modern Scotland (Cork, 1947).
The Celtic Story: A History of the Celtic Football Club (1960).
The Navvy in Scotland (Cork, 1970).
Hanham, H.J., 'Religion and Nationality in the Mid–Victorian Army', in M.R.D. Foot (ed.), *War and Society: Essays in Honour of J.R. Western* (London, 1973).
Harmon, M. (ed.), *Fenians and Fenianism* (Dublin, 1968).
Hickey, J., *Urban Catholics* (London, 1967).
Holmes, J.D., *More Roman than Rome: English Catholicism in the Nineteenth Century* (London, 1978).
Hunt, E.H., *British Labour History, 1815–1914* (London, 1981).
Inglis, K.S., *Churches and the Working Classes in Victorian England*

(London, 1963).
Jackson, J.A., *The Irish in Britain* (London, 1963).
Kee, R., *The Green Flag* (London, 1972).
Kennedy, R.E., *The Irish: Emigration, Marriage, Fertility* (Berkeley, California, 1973).
Kirby, R.J. and Musson, A.E., *The Voice of the People: A Biography of John Doherty, 1798–1854* (Manchester, 1975).
Kirk, N., 'Ethnicity, Class and Popular Toryism, 1850–1870', in K. Lunn (ed.), *Hosts, Immigrants and Minorities: Historical Responses to Newcomers in British Society, 1870–1914* (Folkestone, 1980), pp.64–106.
Lees, L.H., 'Patterns of Lower–Class Life: Irish Slum Communities in Nineteenth–Century London', in S. Thernstrom and R. Sennett (eds.), *Nineteenth–Century Cities* (New Haven, 1969), pp.359–85.
Exiles of Erin: Irish Migrants in Victorian London (Manchester, 1979).
Leetham, C., *Luigi Gentili: A Sower for the Second Spring* (London, 1965).
Lesourd, J.A., *Sociologie du Catholicisme Anglais, 1767–1851*, 2 vols. (Nancy, 1981).
McCaffrey, J.F., 'Politics and the Catholic Community since 1878', in D. McRoberts (ed.), *Modern Scottish Catholicism* (Glasgow, 1979), pp.140–55.
McClelland, V.A., *Cardinal Manning: His Public Life and Influence 1865–1892* (London, 1962).
MacDermott, T.P., 'Irish Workers on Tyneside in the Nineteenth Century', in N. McCord (ed.), *Essays in Tyneside Labour History* (Newcastle–upon–Tyne, 1977), pp.154–77.
McDonnell, K.G.T., 'Roman Catholics in London, 1850–1865', in A.E.J. Hollaender and William Kellaway (eds.), *Studies in London History presented to Philip Edmund Jones* (London, 1969), pp.429–46.
Machin, G.I.T., *Politics and the Churches in Great Britain, 1832–1868* (Oxford, 1977).
McRoberts, D., (ed.), *Modern Scottish Catholicism* (Glasgow, 1979).
Murray, B., *The Old Firm: Sectarianism, Sport and Society in Scotland* (Edinburgh, 1984).
Norman, E.R., *Anti–Catholicism in Victorian England* (London, 1968).
The English Catholic Church in the Nineteenth Century (Oxford, 1984).
O'Connor, K., *The Irish in Britain* (London, 1972).
O'Day, A., *The English Face of Irish Nationalism: Parnellite Involvement in British Politics, 1880–1886* (Dublin, 1977).
Parnell and the First Home Rule Episode, 1884–87 (Dublin, 1985).
'Irish Home Rule and Liberalism', in A. O'Day (ed.), *The Edwardian Age: Conflict and Stability, 1900–1914* (London and Connecticut, 1979), pp.113–32.
Ó Gráda, C., 'Some Aspects of Nineteenth–Century Irish Emigration', in L.M. Cullen and T.C. Smout (eds.), *Comparative Aspects of*

Scottish and Irish Economic and Social History, 1600–1900 (Edinburgh, 1977), pp.65–73.

Quinlivan, P. and Rose, P., *The Fenians in England, 1865–1872* (London, 1962).

Redford, A., *Labour Migration in England, 1800–1850* (London, 1926, revised ed. Manchester, 1964).

Richter, D.C., *Riotous Victorians* (London, 1970).

Rose, P., *The Manchester Martyrs* (London, 1970).

St. John, E., *Manning's Work for Children: A Second Chapter in Catholic Emancipation*, (London, 1929).

Senior, H., *Orangeism in Ireland and Britain, 1795–1836* (London, 1966).

Short, K.R.M., *The Dynamite War: Irish–American Bombers in Victorian Britain* (Dublin, 1979).

Spencer, A.E.C.W., 'The Demography and Sociography of the Roman Catholic Church of England and Wales',in L. Bright and S. Clements (eds.), *The Committed Church* (London, 1966).

Skinnider, M., 'Catholic Education in Glasgow, 1818–1918', in T.R. Bone (ed.), *Studies in Scottish Education 1872–1939* (London, 1967), pp.13–70.

Stevenson, J., *Popular Disturbances in England, 1700–1870* (London, 1979).

Strauss, E., *Irish Nationalism and British Democracy* (London, 1951).

Thompson, Dorothy, 'Ireland and the Irish in English Radicalism before 1850', in J. Epstein and D. Thompson (eds.), *The Chartist Experience* (London, 1982).

Thompson E.P., *The Making of the English Working Class* (London, 1963).

Treble, J.H., 'The Irish Agitation', in J.T. Ward (ed.), *Popular Movements, c. 1830–1850* (London, 1970).

'Liverpool Working Class Housing, 1800–51', in S. Chapman (ed.), *The History of Working Class Housing: A Symposium* (Newton Abbot, 1971), pp.165–220.

'O'Connor, O'Connell and the Attitudes of Irish Immigrants towards Chartism in the North of England, 1838–48', in J. Butt and I.F. Clarke (eds.), *The Victorians and Social Protest* (Newton Abbot, 1973).

'The Development of Roman Catholic Education in Scotland, 1878–1978', in D. McRoberts (ed.), *Modern Scottish Catholicism 1878–1978* (Glasgow, 1979), pp.111–39.

Waller, P.J., *Democracy and Sectarianism: A Political and Social History of Liverpool, 1868–1939* (Liverpool, 1981).

Walvin, J., *Passage to Britain: Immigration in British History and Politics* (London, 1984).

Waugh, N., *These, My Little Ones* (London, 1911).

Wood, I.S., 'Irish Immigrants and Scottish Radicalism', in I. McDougall (ed.), *Essays in Scottish Labour History* (Edinburgh, 1979), pp.64–89.

Journal Articles:

Arnstein, W.L., 'Victorian Prejudice Re–examined', *Victorian Studies*, vol.xii (1968–9), pp.452–7.

'The Murphy Riots: a Victorian Dilemma', *Victorian Studies*, vol.xix (1975), pp.51–71.

Aspinwall, B., 'The Formation of the Catholic Community in the West of Scotland', *Innes Review*, vol.33 (1982), pp.44–57.

Belchem, J.C., 'English Working–Class Radicalism and the Irish, 1815–50', *North West Labour History Society Bulletin*, no. 8 (1982–3), pp.5–18.

Boyle, J.W., 'Ireland and the First International', *The Journal of British Studies*, vol.xi (May, 1972), pp.44–62.

Brooke, D., 'Railway Navvies on the Pennines, 1841–71', *Journal of Transport History*, New Series, vol.3 (1975–6), pp.41–53.

Cahill, G.A., 'Irish Catholicism and English Toryism', *Review of Politics*, vol.19 (1957), pp.62–76.

Clapham, J.H., 'Irish Immigration into Great Britain in the Nineteenth Century', *Bulletin of the International Committee of Historical Sciences*, vol.v (June, 1933), pp.596–604.

Connolly, G.P., 'The Transubstantiation of Myth: Towards a New Popular History of Nineteenth–Century Catholicism in England', *Journal of Ecclesiastical History*, vol.35 (1984), pp.78–104.

'The Rev. Mr. Peter Kaye: Maverick or Englishman?' *North West Catholic History*, vol.11 (1984), pp.8–21.

'"With more than ordinary devotion to God": The Secular Missioner of the North in the Evangelical Age of the English Mission', *North West Catholic History*, vol.10 (1983), pp.8–31.

'"Little Brother be at Peace": The Priest as Holy Man in the Nineteenth–Century Ghetto', in W.J. Shiels (ed.), *Studies in Church History: The Churches and Healing*, vol.19 (Oxford, 1982), pp.191–205.

Cooter, R.J., 'Lady Londonderry and the Irish Catholics of Seaham Harbour: "No Popery" out of context', *Recusant History*, vol.13 (1975–76), pp.288–98.

'On calculating the Nineteenth–Century Catholic Population of Durham and Newcastle', *Northern Catholic History*, vol.2, (1975).

Cousens, S.H., 'Emigration and Demographic Change in Ireland, 1851–1861', *Economic History Review*, vol.14, 2nd. Series (August 1961–April 1962), pp.275–88.

'The Regional Pattern of Emigration during the Great Irish Famine', *Transactions and Papers of the Institute of British Geographers*, vol.28 (1960), pp.119–34.

'The Regional Variations in Emigration from Ireland between 1821 and 1841', *Transactions and Papers of the Institute of British Geographers*, vol.37 (1965), pp.15–20.

Doyle, P., 'The Education and Training of Roman Catholic Priests in Nineteenth–Century England', *Journal of Ecclesiastical History*, vol.35, no. 2 (1984), pp.208–19.

Gilley, S.W., 'The Roman Catholic Mission to the Irish in London, 1840–1860', *Recusant History*, vol.10 (1969–70), pp.123–145.

'Protestant London, No Popery and the Irish Poor, 1830–60', *Recusant History*, vol.10 (1969–70), pp.210–30; vol. 11 (1971),

pp.21–46.
'Heretic London, Holy Poverty and the Irish Poor, 1830–70', *Downside Review*, vol.89 (1971), pp.64–89.
'The Garibaldi Riots of 1862', *Historical Journal*, vol.16 (1973), pp.697–732.
'The Roman Catholic Church and the Nineteenth-Century Irish Diaspora', *Journal of Ecclesiastical History*, vol.35 (1984), pp.188–207.

Hunter, J., 'The Gaelic Connection: the Highlands, Ireland and Nationalism, 1873–1922', *Scottish Historical Review*, vol.54 (1975), pp.179–204.

Jackson, J.A., 'The Irish', in *London, Aspects of Change* (Centre for Urban Studies, 1964), pp.293–308.

Kemnitz, T.M., 'Approaches to the Chartist Movement: Feargus O'Connor and Chartist Strategy', *Albion*, vol.v (1973), pp.67–73.

Kerr, B.M., 'Irish Seasonal Migration to Great Britain, 1800–1838', *Irish Historical Studies*, vol.ii (1942–3), pp.365–380.

Larkin, E., 'The Devotional Revolution in Ireland, 1850–75', *American Historical Review*, vol.lxxvii (1972), pp.625–52.

Lawton, R., 'Irish Immigration to England and Wales in the Mid-Nineteenth Century', *Irish Geography*, vol.iv (1959–63), pp.35–54.

Lees, L.H., 'Mid-Victorian Migration and the Irish Family Economy', *Victorian Studies*, vol.xx (1976), pp.25–43.

Lobban, R.D., 'The Irish Community in Greenock in the Nineteenth Century', *Irish Geography*, vol.vi (1971), pp.270–81.

Lovell, J., 'The Irish and the London Dockers', *Bulletin of the Society for the Study of Labour History*, vol.ii (1975), pp.63–5.

Lowe, W.J., 'The Irish in Lancashire, 1846–71: A Social History', *Irish Economic and Social History*, vol.ii (975).
'The Lancashire Irish and the Catholic Church, 1846–71', *Irish Historical Studies*, vol.xx (1976), pp.129–55.
'Social Agencies among the Irish in Lancashire during the Mid-Nineteenth Century, *Saothar*, vol.3 (1977), pp.15–20.
'Lancashire Fenianism, 1846–71', *Transactions of the Historic Society of Lancashire and Cheshire*, vol.126 (1977), pp.156–85.

McCaffrey, J.F., 'The Irish Vote in Glasgow in the Later Nineteenth Century', *Innes Review*, vol.21 (1970), pp.30–6.
'Roman Catholics in Scotland in the 19th and 20th centuries', *Records of the Scottish Church Society*, vol.21 (1983).

Miller, D., 'Irish Catholicism and the great Famine', *Journal of Social History*, vol.ix (1975–6), pp.81–98.

Moody, T.W., 'Michael Davitt and the British Labour Movement, 1882–1906, *Transactions of the Royal Historical Society*, 5th. Series vol.3 (1953), pp.53–76.

Neal, F., 'The Birkenhead Garibaldi Riots of 1862', *Transactions of the Historic Society of Lancashire and Cheshire*, vol.131 (1982), pp.87–111.

Ó Gráda, C., 'A Note on Nineteenth-Century Irish Emigration Statistics', *Population Studies*, vol.29 (1975), pp.145–48.

O'Higgins, R., 'The Irish Influence in the Chartist Movement', *Past and Present*, no.2 (1961), pp.83–96.

Ó Tuathaigh, M.A.G., 'The Irish in Nineteenth–Century Britain: Problems of Integration', *Transactions of the Royal Historical Society*, 5th. Series, vol.31 (1981), pp.149–74.

Parry, J., 'The Tredegar Anti–Irish Riots of 1882', *Llafur*, vol.iii (1983), pp.20–3.

Reid, T.D.W., and Reid, N, 'The 1842 "Plug Plot" in Stockport', *International Review of Social History*, vol.xxiv (1979).

Richardson, C., 'Irish Settlement in mid–Nineteenth Century Bradford', *Yorkshire Bulletin of Economic & Social Research*, vol.xx, pp.40–57.

'The Irish in Victorian Bradford', *The Bradford Antiquary*, vol.9 (1976), pp.294–316.

Shallice, A., 'Orange & Green and Militancy: Sectarianism and Working Class politics in Liverpool, 1910–14', *North West Labour History Society*, no.6 (1979–80), pp.15–22.

Smith, A.W., 'Irish Rebels and English Radicals, 1798–1829', *Past and Present*, no.7 (1955), pp.78–85.

Smith, J., 'Labour Tradition in Glasgow and Liverpool', *History Workshop*, vol.17 (Spring, 1974).

Steele, E.D., 'The Irish Presence in the North of England, 1850–1914', *Northern History*, vol.xii (1976), pp.220–41.

Swift, R.E. 'Crime and Ethnicity: The Irish in Early Victorian Wolverhampton', *West Midlands Studies*, vol.13 (1980), pp.1–5.

'Anti–Catholicism and Irish Disturbances: Public Order in Mid–Victorian Wolverhampton', *Midland History*, vol.ix (1984), pp.87–108.

'"Another Stafford Street Row": Law, Order and the Irish Presence in Mid–Victorian Wolverhampton', *Immigrants and Minorities*, vol.3 (1984), pp.5–29.

Treble, J.H., 'The Attitude of the Roman Catholic Church towards Trade Unionism in the North of England, 1833–42', *Northern History*, vol.5 (1970), pp.93–113.

'Irish Navvies in the North of England, 1830–50', *Transport History*, vol.6 (1973), pp.227–47.

Turley, F., 'Centenary of the Fenian Raid', *The Cheshire Sheaf* (October, 1967), pp.45–6.

Walker, W.M., 'Irish Immigrants in Scotland: their Priests, Politics and Parochial Life', *Historical Journal*, vol.15 (1972), pp.649–67.

Werly, J.M., 'The Irish in Manchester, 1832–49', *Irish Historical Studies*, vol.xviii (1973), pp.345–58.

Wood, I.S., 'John Wheatley, the Irish and the Labour Movement in Scotland', *Innes Review*, vol.xxxi (1980), pp.71–85.

Yeo, E., 'Christianity in Chartist Struggle, 1838–42, *Past and Present*, no.91 (1981), pp.83–94.

Unpublished Theses:

Benjamin, H.W., *The London Irish: A Study in Political Activism, 1870–1910* (Ph.D. University of London, 1971).
Cassirer, R., *The Irish Influence on the Liberal Movement in England, 1798–1832* (Ph.D. University of London, 1940).
Collins, B., *Aspects of Irish Immigration into Two Scottish Towns,* [Dundee and Paisley] *in the Mid–Nineteenth Century* (M.Phil. University of Edinburgh, 1978).
Connolly, G.P., *Catholicism in Manchester and Salford* (Ph.D. University of Manchester, 1980).
Cooter, R.J., *The Irish in County Durham and Newcastle, 1840–1880* (M.A. University of Durham, 1973).
Hickey, J.V., *The Origin and Growth of the Irish Community in Cardiff* (M.A. University of Wales, 1959).
Horgan, D.T., *The Irish Catholic Whigs in Parliament 1847–74* (Ph.D. University of Minnesota, 1975).
Hutchinson, I.G.C., *Politics and Society in Mid–Victorian Glasgow, 1846–86* (Ph.D. University of Edinburgh, 1974).
Jackson, J.A., *The Irish in London: a study of migration and settlement in the past hundred years* (M.A. University of London, 1958).
Lees, L. H., *Social Change and Social Stability among the London Irish* (Ph.D. University of Harvard, 1969).
O'Connor, B.J., *The Irish Nationalist Party in Liverpool, 1873–1922* (M.A. University of Liverpool, 1971).
O'Day, A., *The Irish Parliamentary Party in British Politics, 1880–86 (Ph.D. University of London, 1971).*
Papworth, J.D., The Irish in Liverpool, 1835–71: Family Structure and Residential Mobility (Ph.D. University of Liverpool, 1982).
Quirke, J., *The Development of the Roman Catholic Community in Wolverhampton, 1828–67* (M.A. Wolverhampton Polytechnic, 1983).
Reid, C.A.N., *The Chartist Movement in Stockport* (M.A. University of Hull, 1974).
Treble, J.H., *The Place of the Irish Catholics in the Social Life of the North of England, 1829–51* (Ph.D. University of Leeds, 1969).
Savage, D.C., *The General Election of 1886 in Great Britain and Ireland* (Ph.D. King's College, London, 1958).
Wilson, F.L., *The Irish influx into Manchester, 1815–50* (B.A. dissertation, University of Manchester, 1940).
Woolaston, E.P.M., *The Irish Nationalist Movement in Great Britain, 1886–1908* (M.A. University of London, 1958).

SELECT INDEX

Persons and Places only